Rock Music,
Authority and Western Culture,
1964–1980

ALSO BY JAMES A. COSBY

*Devil's Music, Holy Rollers and Hillbillies:
How America Gave Birth to Rock and Roll*
(McFarland, 2016)

Rock Music, Authority and Western Culture, 1964–1980

James A. Cosby

McFarland & Company, Inc., Publishers
Jefferson, North Carolina

LIBRARY OF CONGRESS CATALOGUING-IN-PUBLICATION DATA

Names: Cosby, James A., author.
Title: Rock music, authority and western culture, 1964–1980 / James A. Cosby.
Description: Jefferson, North Carolina : McFarland & Company, Inc., Publishers, 2024. | Includes bibliographical references and index.
Identifiers: LCCN 2023058786 | ISBN 9781476693699 (paperback : acid free paper) ∞
    ISBN 9781476651354 (ebook)
Subjects: LCSH: Rock music—History and criticism. | Rock music—Social aspects—History—20th century. | Counterculture—United States—History—20th century. | Popular culture—United States—History—20th century. | BISAC: MUSIC / Genres & Styles / Rock | SOCIAL SCIENCE / Popular Culture
Classification: LCC ML3534 .C6695 2024 | DDC 781.6609—dc23/eng/20231227
LC record available at https://lccn.loc.gov/2023058786

BRITISH LIBRARY CATALOGUING DATA ARE AVAILABLE

ISBN (print) 978-1-4766-9369-9
ISBN (ebook) 978-1-4766-5135-4

© 2024 James A. Cosby. All rights reserved

No part of this book may be reproduced or transmitted in any form or by any means, electronic or mechanical, including photocopying or recording, or by any information storage and retrieval system, without permission in writing from the publisher.

Front cover images © 2024 Shutterstock

Printed in the United States of America

McFarland & Company, Inc., Publishers
  Box 611, Jefferson, North Carolina 28640
    www.mcfarlandpub.com

To that little rocker in all of us.

"Jesus was all right but his disciples were thick and ordinary. It's them twisting it that ruins it for me."
—John Lennon[1]

"Rock and roll is about a backbeat you can fuck to, but it's also about saying 'fuck you' to people who don't get off on freedom. We're protecting our right to rock."
—Steven Tyler[2]

"We're trying to save the kids … to help them realize a little more what their goals should be. We want them to realize that our music is just as spiritual as going to church. The soul must rule, not money or drugs. You should rule yourself and give God a chance."
—Jimi Hendrix[3]

"James Brown made mainstream cross over to black. He made us acceptable as we were, which was a big deal."
—Al Sharpton[4]

"The worst pain is that of not being wanted, of realizing your parents do not need you in the way you need them."
—John Lennon[5]

Table of Contents

Preface   1

1. Introduction   3

Part One:
A New Day Dawning, 1950s–1967

2. A New Rebel Yell, the First Half of the Twentieth Century   15
3. Cultural Checkpoints: The United States and the United Kingdom Enter the '60s   27
4. Meet the Beatles and the Stones, 1959–1965   33
5. Cultural Checkpoints: The United States, ca. 1965   54
6. The Freaks of Haight-Ashbury, 1965–1966   58
7. The Haight's House Band, Acid Rock, and the Hippies, 1965–1967   65
8. Warhol's House Band, 1962–1967   76
9. The Hippie/Freak Lifestyle, ca. 1966   90
10. Modern Mythic Heroes and the Summer of Love, 1966–1967   96
11. Cultural Checkpoints: Vietnam, Political Divisions, and Race, Late 1966–1967   107

Part Two:
Upheaval, 1966–1980

12. Integration, the Elvis Factor, the New Blues, and Tutwiler, 1954–Present   113
13. James Brown and Soul Brothers and Sisters, 1954–1960s   121

14. Cultural Checkpoints: War, Assassinations, and Chaos, ca. 1968	132
15. The Beatles Come Full Circle, 1968–1970	139
16. "Do What Thou Wilt" (or *Partying with the Stones!*), 1968–Early '70s	145
17. Transitions and Strange Days, End of the '60s	158
18. A Generation Gap, Late '60s–Early '70s	164
19. Cultural Checkpoints: Protests, Imagining a Different World, and a Left-Right Divide Solidifies, Mid-'69–Early '70s	170
20A. Prog and Full Arenas (Also, Jesus Freaks), Early '70s	182
20B. A Very Special '70s Cultural Checkpoint: The Sitcom	187
21. Rock Gods, a Possible Alternate Route to Heaven, and Egos, 1969–1979	191
22. The Big Power Pop Stars, 1972–1977	209
23. Rockers, Dancers, Disco, and Disco's Demolition, 1970s–1980	219
Conclusion	232
Chapter Notes	237
Bibliography	273
Index	281

Preface

Beyond the passions, the hype, the clichés, and a mountain of writings on the subject, I strongly believe that the world has yet to fully grasp the importance of the story of rock and roll. I expect that the perspective afforded by the passage of time and the specific approach taken in this book will allow for a greater and fuller understanding of this topic.

I first had the idea to write a socio-/spiritual history of rock and roll in 2009. What I thought would be one large book morphed into three, this being the second (and the third is already written). Each book stands alone, though they are a de facto trilogy.

The first, *Devil's Music, Holy Rollers, and Hillbillies: How America Gave Birth to Rock and Roll* (McFarland, 2016), is the story of America leading up to rock and roll, from slavery, through a culmination of an array of factors, and ending with the first wave of rock and rollers in about 1959. The book you are reading right now details the "classic" rock era, roughly 1964 to 1980, a rupture of authority in the West at this time, and how all of this ties into a greater historical trajectory. The third book illustrates some crucial social, cultural, and spiritual lessons to be gleaned from the rock phenomenon as it played out from 1980 to 1997.

This second book uses the stories of certain rock artists and social dynamics to reconcile a rock revolution (of sorts) with traditional values and societal stability. The issues discussed here, in fact, also happen to also be relevant today, including disco and the backlash against it (which, for example, provides a vivid illustration of the beginnings of the current "woke"-MAGA divide); sex and morality; ongoing racial dynamics; the liberalization of many drugs, addiction, and recovery; and more.

I was well into writing this book when the idea of rock and an "arc of Western civilization" hit me. Granted, it is a *slightly* ambitious concept, but in retrospect it seems rather obvious. Simply put, there has been a long, ongoing arc in the West in which people strive both to find better ways of getting along with one another *and* to better express their own individuality. The basic human conundrum, really, but seen here through music. Rock and roll is a key event on this arc, and analyzing it is crucial to understanding where we come from, where we really are today, and where we might be headed.

There has been a ton already said and written about rock and roll. With that in mind, my research consisted of scouring that abundant record to find the right dots to start connecting. There is a mountain of endnotes to show for it. I did make two trips each to Memphis, Tennessee, and surrounding environs, as well as to Liverpool and London in the United Kingdom. These trips were part personal pilgrimages of sorts, but they also allowed me to get a much stronger feel for what transpired in those places, as well as specific whys and hows.

I personally interviewed two people: Rock and Roll Hall of Famer Lloyd Price and psychologist and progenitor of primal scream therapy Dr. Arthur Janov. Sadly, both have since passed, but I am profoundly grateful for my time with each. My interactions with both are reflected in relatively small but crucial parts of this story.

In the end, this book seeks to clarify what exactly happened with rock and the West from 1964 to 1980, why it matters today, and how it can help us plan for tomorrow.

Special thanks for the invaluable input and feedback of Fred Aceves and, on all things Warhol, Timothy Churchill. Any errors are mine.

1

Introduction

In 1835, famed French political theorist Alexis de Tocqueville declared that the literary and cultural output of a then-young American democracy would be "strange, incorrect, overburdened, and loose, and almost always strong and bold."[1] In other words, he predicted rock and roll.

The story of rock and roll indeed occupies a special place in the historical trajectory of Western culture. That is, there is a long trend where more dominant, top-down hierarchies—be they religious, governmental, or cultural—have tended to give way to new movements more in touch with the interests and expressions of the individual. That is, Catholicism saw a Protestant Reformation, monarchies gave way to democracies, classicism (i.e., calm, order) was followed by Romanticism (i.e., emotional, individualism), and enslavement of human beings and segregation gave way to freedom and increased equality. These events would all also be crucial in the formation and evolution of the dominant force of the West, the United States of America.

Musically, in twentieth-century America, and precisely as Tocqueville predicted, came the "loose" and "bold" music of itinerant bluesmen, improvisational jazz musicians, spirited practitioners of Black gospel, including the so-called holy roller Pentecostals, and the sometimes plaintive, sometimes raucous, early country of Appalachia and the South. These genres and other factors would all culminate in rock and roll and serve to directly challenge institutional authority in parents, the church, corporations, and the government.[2] Safe to say, and as will be explained, the impact of all of these events are with us today in almost every aspect of our lives, and from the most practical to the even spiritual.

The unique story of rock music can indeed be placed squarely into this still-unfolding great arc of Western civilization and an ongoing quest to reconcile authority with greater individuality. Interestingly, and curiously enough, the advent of rock music would be the most spontaneous of events ... and quite predictable.

Consider that rock was first conceived by America's most marginalized people—that is, poor, rural African Americans who were soon joined by poor, rural white folks. Through the power of music, artists would do no less than transform themselves, the country, and the world. "C'mon Everybody!," "Like a Rolling Stone," "Respect," "Keep on Rockin' in the Free World," and "Bring the Noise" ... rock legacy continues to be a life-affirming, authentic, unifying, and inspirational force across almost all demographics. Like few other times in history, deeply personal change was affected and on a scale of millions. Thus, while rock music may or may not be shown to be *miraculous*, it has been a profound development.

This book discusses rock and roll's inception but mostly focuses on arguably its greatest era of music as well as its greatest social, cultural, and political impact, from 1964 to 1980. Thus, there is a summation of rock's origins in the 1950s, followed by a more in-depth focus on the British invaders, the early soul brothers and sisters of Detroit and Memphis, and on through to the hippies especially, proto-punks, powerhouse blues rockers, power pop acts, and disco artists, along with disco's detractors.

With all of the above in mind, I will further submit that the story of rock and roll may in fact be the ideal vehicle with which to understand Western culture, if not the human condition. Too bold? Consider music in general. Music manages to both deeply inspire and reflect where people are in any given moment of their lives. It is almost a DNA-like record of people's values, hopes, dreams, fears, strengths, weaknesses, and frustrations. Thus, the blues came out of a particular time and place *for a reason*, as did Black gospel music, as did country music, and so on. And for some seven decades, for so much of Western and even world culture, rock and roll music has been precisely that sort of DNA evidence.

To get as full of a picture as possible, this book will unravel rock's story on both the macro and micro levels. The broadest of societal levels includes, for example, the onset of the "generation gap"; moral issues such as the loosening of sexual mores; and issues of race, including how rock went from a "Black" genre to an "integrated" one to a "white" one.[3] Important social, cultural, and political events are woven into these stories, along the way, here in the form of "Cultural Checkpoints" that will provide the proper context for the music discussed.

At the micro level, rock's story will be told at the most personal level. From its start, rock has been embraced by individuals as they felt their way through a rapidly changing, often anxiety-producing, postindustrial, and capitalist, modern world. It is no coincidence that in the twentieth century, this same "greater arc" of Western civilization has also included phenomena like Sigmund Freud and the advent of psychotherapy, modern psychology, and the self-help and recovery movements.

To put this in raw rock-and-roll terms, Mark E. Smith of the punk group The Fall once explained, "Rock 'n' roll isn't even music really. It's a mistreating of instruments to get feelings over."[4] More famously in his iconic 1965 song, "Like a Rolling Stone," Bob Dylan used rock to help connect the blues and America's roots to a youth culture yearning for emotional connection. He asked the simplest but most important question in the history of rock: "How does it *feel*?" And funnily enough, this is also the go-to question of every good psychotherapist: "But how do you *feel* about that?"[5] So this book is not only a history of rock and roll but also what will amount to something of a psychoanalysis of the Western world.

Deeply personal stories will afford the greatest understanding of the rock phenomenon and, ultimately, its relationship with authority. For example, as to family and childhood issues, there is Lennon and McCartney bonding over the early losses of their mothers; James Brown growing up in abject poverty and subject to severe racism; and Ozzy Osbourne growing up in abuse and a postwar, industrial dystopia.

And rock's story does permeate much of society, and to thus include everything from rock's connections to LSD, Andy Warhol, primal scream therapy, the story of tiny Tutwiler, Mississippi, occultist Aleister Crowley, "Jesus freaks," the Brady Bunch, masculinity, and more.

As these stories unfold over these years, rock will be shown not only as great entertainment but as something a '60s youth generation used to recalibrate its relationship with authority. They would adjust to a world undergoing the constant and rapid changes of modern life. In rock's early stages, it would be the fuel for a countercultural movement. The kids would stop seeing a parental generation and its institutions as so trustworthy, given civil rights injustices, a deeply unpopular war corporate greed, and church authorities that seemed out of touch, hypocritical, and domineering. Rock and roll and its attendant ethos would be crucial to those youth and efforts to challenge, undermine, and change both those institutions and their own lives.

At the same time, the establishment provided order and certain fixed points that help to facilitate a working and mostly orderly society. Attempts to throw out *all* that the establishment stood for and those fixed points would lead to its own problems. As an obvious example, look no further than the early rock and rollers' notorious relationship with drugs and alcohol. Certainly, good times were had, but a great many would also suffer from abuse and addiction. In fact, a who's who of early rock icons would die young and, in time, be filing into rehab facilities and embracing sobriety with all they had.

To be sure, rock and roll's story is one of freedom but also a certain recklessness. Legendary owner of Sun Studio in Memphis, Sam Phillips, once called all of the historic blues, R&B, and rock songs recorded at his studio to be "just a big original mistake…. That's what we are." "Perfectly imperfect," he would call it.[6] The era of rock covered in this book would be part of a mass resetting of society, and at the time, no one knew what the results would be. Risks were taken.

Something else will be made quite clear in the process: this ongoing greater arc itself will be seen as evidence of a clear pattern of sorts. That is, something in humanity drives an individual's need to *feel*, to seek clarity and truth, and to understand who we are and our place in the world. Call this ongoing, collective arc a special direction, or *order*, if you will— or, dare I even say it, evidence of some form of *higher intelligence*. Wait, rock and roll and a *higher intelligence*? Rock and roll … like, *Whop bop b-luma blop bam bom* rock and roll? Ozzy Osbourne and higher intelligence? What about a band like GWAR, the whacko, self-proclaimed, heavy metal "scumdogs of the universe"?[7] *GWAR?* Well, not GWAR but rock in general.

Rock and, Yes, Morality

Before proceeding any further, the notion of rock as *inherently* immoral should be debunked. Take the famous rallying cry of so many rock and rollers since the 1960s in which the keys to life were reduced to "sex, drugs, and rock and roll."[8] Conversely, this phrase has also been exhibit A in claims to dismiss rock as simple and immoral. Clearly, permissive views of sex and drugs have been a part of rock and roll's ethos and its very DNA. However, this is not the same as saying that rock has ever been entirely defined by this slogan either. The spirit of rock and roll is much more despite the clichés that have often dominated perceptions of it.

It helps to recall exactly where rock and roll came from. Rock first arose in the United States of the 1950s in response to and in defiance of a moral code handed down by parents and the establishment. This code, formally and informally, included various restrictions on things such as extramarital sexual activity in any form (and sometimes even disfavored forms of *intra*marital sex, for that matter); racial discrimination; underage drinking and marijuana use; and suppression of any popular music deviating from a staid, safe, and frankly, soul-numbing status quo. For much of a country's youth, such restrictions were largely repressive and untenable.

By the end of the upheaval of the 1960s, these particular moral restrictions were already seen by many as antiquated and no longer taboo. Of course, although some rock and rollers pushed matters to questionable hedonistic extremes, such excesses have never been actual requirements in the world of rock and roll either. For example, some of the most successful and beloved rock artists would simply sing of freedom, love, heartbreak, redemption, introspection, and so on. Precisely because of rock and roll's most-anything-goes attitude and spirit, it has always accommodated and reflected a fairly diverse array of mindsets, beliefs, and lifestyles. As will be shown, the '60s and '70s could be wild, but the biggest fears for rock would also be off the mark. To illustrate, just look ahead for a moment at three of the biggest modern rock and roll acts that would come out of that classic rock era: Bruce Springsteen, R.E.M., and U2.

For decades, Bruce Springsteen, often with the E Street Band, has packed arenas with tens of thousands of fans who sing along to songs in concerts long noted for their religious fervor.[9] Springsteen, of course, came from humble blue-collar origins and started out singing in a bar band in the New Jersey shore town of Asbury Park toward the end of the '60s. His heart-on-his-sleeve style, a sort of "heartland" rock meets what Springsteen has called "a Jersey stew of almost punk soul," quickly attracted a cult following.[10] By the mid-'70s, a mass audience flocked to him and he began filling ever-larger venues. Springsteen, however, told soulful tales of regular people dealing with life with some integrity, some courage, and a certain everyman decency that fans responded to—it is almost the antithesis of hedonism or wild excesses. Yet Springsteen is one of the most definitive of rock and roll superstars.

Forming in the early '80s in Athens, Georgia, R.E.M was a jangly, post-punk, country-rock-infused rock band. They were an ambitious and unique force in a then-burgeoning new college music scene. Their story is that through a decade of relentless touring—and with relatively little controversy or excesses—a larger commercial audience caught up to them as well. By the start of the '90s, R.E.M. had become the model for an alternative rock music scene, revered by peers, and earning platinum-album sales and Grammy awards.[11]

Singer Michael Stipe conveyed an array of deep and murky feelings in songs that were never about the virtues of sexual promiscuity or the joys of drug use or abuse. As an example, their song "Everybody Hurts" heals and unifies, not unlike a hymn. Yet R.E.M., too, is a quintessential rock band.

Taking this a step further, what about rock and religion and especially concerning the Western establishment and Christianity? Is rock music even non- or anti–Christian? Over the years, many have certainly seen it that way. Yet all four members of another renowned, anthemic, and moody, modern rock band, Dublin's U2, identify as Christian. One of the group's biggest hits, "I Still Haven't Found What I'm Looking For," for example, is solidly gospel in style, with lead singer Bono expressing his yearning to more fully understand his place in life and better know God.

His biblical references and reference to a person breaking out of bondage and carrying a cross for the song's protagonist are clear enough.[12]

Bono has not been especially explicit in expressing his faith in U2 lyrics, but it is no secret either. With some trepidation—to some rock fans, rock and religion are all but inapposite—he gradually became more public about his Christian faith.[13] Still, those Christian values have always been embedded in the group's songs, and one would certainly be hard-pressed to find any of the group's lyrics that directly contradict the teachings of Christ. And U2 is also a definitive, superstar rock band.

Many other rock icons have openly embraced Christianity, from Jerry Lee Lewis to Bob Dylan to Alice Cooper and too many more to list.

Indeed, and as will be shown throughout this book, for all of rock's "bad boy" reputation, its ethos has always allowed virtually any belief, including religious, as well as the complete *disregard* of religion. Thus, rock's special capacity to be both highly subversive, even profane, *and* moral and spiritual will be a theme throughout.

Layout

Admittedly, this is all fairly ambitious. How to tackle such a subject? Instead of attempting an exhaustive recap of every significant band, song, and album in the history of rock, certain stories will be presented in a framework designed to be as illustrative, orderly, and cohesive as possible.

First, these stories will be presented chronologically, starting with a relatively brief summation of how rock and roll came to be in the 1950s, followed by the upheaval of the '60s, and into the '70s, both its brilliance and its excesses and how it challenged authority, for better and for worse. Because this is the story of rock music, there is an immense diversity of subject matter, from gospel stars to hippies to southern rockers to art rockers. Thus, to maintain the clearest and deepest analysis possible over each chapter, three main tracks, or threads, will illuminate and illustrate trends that evolve over the years. The first two tracks focus on rock's extremes of dark and light—yin ("dark") and yang ("light")—with the "light" being rock's more upbeat and melodic side and the "dark" representing rock's grittier, heavier, and sometimes angrier side. This will simply provide focus on some more extreme ends of the genre. In fact, rock's inherently "strong and bold" extremes are precisely what makes it so helpful in such a broad analysis.

No groups better exemplify this dynamic than the Beatles and the Rolling Stones, very possibly the two best and most influential rock groups of all time. A fresh and concise analysis of each group will form the foundation for much of the analysis that follows.

While sharing similar musical roots and basic styles, the groups' differences are well established. The Beatles were melodic optimists, more pop-oriented, and generally had a thematic focus on peace and love and a more life-affirming, often transcendent approach (e.g., "All You Need Is Love" and "Across the Universe"). In contrast, the Stones have a more down-and-dirty feel, more synonymous with the blues and R&B, as well as edgier themes and hedonistic pursuits in the face of an establishment often seen as oppressive and self-serving (e.g., "[I Can't Get No] Satisfaction"). While the universe may not always seem so benevolent, why not freely embrace those very basic drives such as for sex, drugs, and rock and roll while we can (e.g., "Let's Spend the Night Together" and "Let It Bleed")?

Although not everything in this book will fall perfectly in line with this yin-yang framework, the trend is remarkably consistent and helpful throughout. In the '60s, there was a focus on peace and love, epitomized by the hippie house band of San Francisco and the Summer of Love, the Grateful Dead, in contrast with the simultaneous rise in Manhattan of the dark, proto-punk house band of Andy Warhol's "factory," the Velvet Underground. Into the '70s were the cult heroes of power pop, Big Star, along with bands like Cheap Trick, as opposed to the heavy power of Led Zeppelin and Black Sabbath.

To fully capture the rock story, a third thread is the story of rock and race, which will be understood as the James Brown thread. Brown, the "Godfather of Soul," had a remarkable career, musically and otherwise. Brown started in rock's earliest days, was part of the inception of both soul and funk, and was a key figure during the civil rights era.

Even though the initial rock and roll explosion of the '50s did help wipe out many social restraints and divisions with regard to race, it did not entirely do away with the vestiges of centuries of racial wounds or end all ongoing racial divisions and strife. This examination starts with the legacy of Elvis Presley, before illustrating the sort of racial restratification of rock music during the '60s and showing how blues-based rock would come to be considered a "white" genre. And there was a Black- as well as Hispanic-, female-, and gay-dominated disco era and the subsequent rocker-fueled backlash against it, which may encapsulate the roots of a current left-right political divide as much as anything. (Note: this is not a political book, but the story of rock touches on such issues. The intention is to show how artists were impacted by political issues and how their perspectives were changed.)

The Beatles/Stones/Brown dynamic can easily be followed through the rock and soul of the late '70s and even through the '80s and '90s. But rock's foundational era from 1964 to 1980 encapsulates crucial shifts not only in rock music but also some seismic changes in Western civilization with regard to authority, freedom, and individual expression. That is, many stopped trusting authority, be that parental, governmental, "the experts," and so on. Hence this book's specific focus.

In the end, what will be shown is that rock and roll is simply a deeply personal and liberating form of musical expression. Crazy sometimes? Absolutely, like any true freedom. In the end, though, the freedoms embodied by rock and roll will be seen as vital in the face of any repression.

For those born before maybe about 1980 or so, it can be difficult to even imagine life before rock and roll. Yet make no mistake, when rock music blew up in the mainstream in the mid–1950s, parents, the church, and government officials all truly wished they could erase it from the face of the earth.[14] Teens were blasting this loud music, letting loose, gyrating lasciviously on dance floors, and otherwise trashing some long-standing rules of decency, decorum, and conformity. Authenticity and raw energy prevailed over maintaining facades and emotional repression. In dealing with early rock and roll, the establishment had come to a harrowing realization: it couldn't control or subdue the minds and souls of its youth. The establishment was, literally and figuratively, rocked to its core. Some actually called rock the "devil's music," while a columnist for the *New York Times* had simply asked, "Is this generation going to hell?"[15]

Coming into the '60s, the challenge for rebellious rock performers, fans, and the counterculture at large would be that rejecting the establishment would mean lives with fewer fixed moral principles and less established direction going forward. It is the classic conundrum of maintaining valued traditional institutions while also changing with the times and evolving as a people. In many ways, this rock revolution would work incredibly well, though at times young people would lose their way. To many of the parental generation, it was all a whole lot of disorder and decadence. To many on the religious right, it was even worse: souls were being damned.

Rock music, of course, not only survived but thrived, coming to dominate popular culture into the 1990s, while it continues and its early impact reverberates strongly still today. Billions of rock records, downloads, and streams have been enjoyed, and billions of concertgoers have enthusiastically attended rock shows. Even the Western establishment largely came to embrace rock. An article in the Vatican's official newspaper, *L'osservatore romano*, even made positive references to Elvis Presley and the Beatles in 2008.[16] The heavy riffs of Led Zeppelin were once used to sell Cadillacs.[17]

Rock has come to empower people, to give a voice, and provide a release of anger and outrage on the biggest of world stages, during civil and political upheavals, playing a profound role in democratic reforms in the 1980s such as glasnost in the Soviet Union and Czechoslovakia's Velvet Revolution. Rock even showed up to play a large, symbolic role during the Tiananmen Square protest.[18]

So how exactly did rock music go from being seen as the "devil's music" in the '50s to mass acceptance a decade later? How could something so bad be so *good*? Did rock and roll even become a religion or a quasi-religion, and if so, was that for good or ill? Has the rock and roll ethos been a better alternative than the morality that the so-called establishment had to offer? And how exactly can rock and roll be reconciled with religious belief?

By the end of this book, there will be clear answers to all the above. Ultimately, the rebellious nature of rock and roll will be reconciled with various forms of authority as well as a sense of morality, "family values," and even religious faith. Further, this book will establish when raucous rebellion, even within traditional family structures, is *entirely* appropriate.

This history of rock will demonstrate that there is indeed common ground, whether one is a fan of the Beatles or the pope, or both, or the blues, country, folk, punk, metal, rap, or whatever, and whether one is a politically staunch left-winger (say, David Crosby) or right-winger (say, Ted Nugent). We all seem to want much the same things: as much freedom and fulfillment as possible without unfairly disrupting others and while hopefully contributing to a reasonably well-functioning society. By obtaining some insights and clarity about where we, as a society, have been and exactly what changed, especially from about 1964 to 1980, we may better understand how exactly we got to where we are today. We may even discover some more truths about the human condition—and even possibly find some keys to the universe. Hey, aim high. Rock and roll is not timid.

Part One

A New Day Dawning, 1950s–1967

2

A New Rebel Yell, the First Half of the Twentieth Century

Entering the 1950s, America was still living in the victorious glow of a just war and the triumph of Western democracies over the very worst of human nature: fascism and genocide. American governance, its booming economy, and its social and cultural values were all casting a vast influence over much of what was going on across the globe. America was the envy of the world and even a beacon of hope for the future of humankind.

At home, it was becoming more and more expected that one would conform to such a successful society. At the same time, however, things were changing fast. This was a more complex, fast-paced, postindustrial, nuclear age. Among the many achievements in America and elsewhere, it seemed that the human intellect had brought an economic system that some called a "rat race" and a peace that came only with the threat of mushroom clouds.

Before rock and roll's arrival onto the scene in mainstream America in 1956, it was already abundantly clear that many were feeling emotionally and psychologically overwhelmed and spiritually confused. W.H. Auden had touched on the realities of the times in his Pulitzer Prize–winning poem, aptly titled "The Age of Anxiety" (1947). Then–U.S. president Dwight D. Eisenhower had lamented in his 1953 State of the Union address, "How far the advances of science have outraced our social consciousness, how much more we have developed scientifically than we are capable of handling emotionally and intellectually."[1] In 1951, a similarly themed op-ed piece from *Cleveland Plain Dealer* editor Louis B. Seltzer had been widely syndicated, including its appearance in *Time* magazine. The piece began:

> There are those who think science and the assembly line started it as we turn into the Twentieth Century.... We have everything. We abound with all the

things that make us comfortable. We are, on the average, rich beyond the dreams of the kinds of old. Yet something is not there that should be—something we once had.[2]

This was the context for a coming dissent and "counterculture." The United States had indeed made historic financial and material gains for a great many since the stock market crash and the Great Depression (1929–1939), although there were also still marked disparities between the haves and have-nots. And as Seltzer had described, even the economic successes did not necessarily translate into the bliss one might have expected. White-collar workers were part of a new corporate culture where corporate life could take precedence over all else, as reflected in Sloan Wilson's popular novel *The Man in the Gray Flannel Suit* (1955). For blue- and white-collar workers alike, the workday could resemble the classic factory scene from the Charlie Chaplin comedy *Modern Times*. There, despite the worker's best efforts, the forces of commerce literally suck him into and through the gears of the machine that used the human, instead of the other way around.

Morally, the so-called establishment (used throughout this book to refer to the government, corporate interests, church leaders, and a parental generation) was generally understood to be deeply informed by and devoted to Christianity. Yet this generation was also having to reconcile free-flowing capitalism, racism, gender discrimination, a war of choice (in Korea), and the stockpiling of nuclear weapons, with those religious principles that included shunning materialism and embracing equality, faith, peace, love, and nonviolence.[3]

Further, society had yet to wrap its collective mind around the ongoing existential threat of nuclear annihilation and the unsettling reality that humankind's worst enemy was indeed humankind. Mind-boggling amounts of wealth were being spent to prepare for a war no one even wanted to win. As Albert Einstein had said, "I do not know how the Third World War will be fought, but I can tell you what they will use in the Fourth—rocks!"[4] Few would forget the 1950s training film images of air raid drills and little American schoolchildren scurrying under their tiny wooden desks for "cover" from potential nuclear devastation.[5]

America of the 1950s simply had yet to process and work these issues out, many of which were unlike anything humanity had ever faced. To be entirely fair, many wanted some peace and calm after a depression and a world war. But complacency would not sit well with many, especially a younger generation.

Sexuality was largely being ignored. Sex lives were all but nonexistent on television shows, and top pop music hits of the time were incredibly innocuous and lacking substance, such as Perry Como's nice-enough but snooze-inducing "'A,' You're Adorable."[6]

As to drugs, the establishment wholeheartedly embraced things like "three-martini lunches" and "pep" pills, while the popularity of prescription drugs soared, including psychotropic drugs and tranquilizers like the newly invented Valium (often for what was deemed the "anxious housewife").[7] This happened as underage alcohol consumption, marijuana, and other drugs were criminalized.[8]

As to that pre–rock and roll pop music, the country's postwar and early '50s music was indeed remarkably tepid and shallow. Further consider the unspeakably saccharine number one hit "How Much Is That Doggie in the Window?"

For all of America's successes by important, traditional measures, many were also losing faith in the nation's institutions. Church and synagogue attendance, after rising in the early '50s, would begin to slide by the end of the decade.[9] America was in the midst of an unsettling emotional and psychological transition, and in short, America badly *needed* emotional and psychological outlets. Thankfully, it turned out that there were groups of Americans who had already been dealing with their own existential crises and severe life challenges, and they had managed to produce a remarkable body of music in the process that would be precisely on point.

The First Rock Era

The story of the early Black experience in America and how the sound of African American blues, Black gospel music, and white country music, all from America's southern and rural regions, would impact the white mainstream is an epic story unto itself and well beyond the scope of this book. (Luckily, everything in this chapter and much more is addressed in the book titled *Devil's Music, Holy Rollers, and Hillbillies: How America Gave Birth to Rock and Roll*.) Very briefly, the blues and Black gospel arose directly out of the secular work songs, field hollers, and "Negro spirituals" of the era of slavery. These genres were the distillations of the Black experience through centuries of repression and voiceless-ness, from West Africa to the Middle Passage to the centuries-long tragedy of enslavement to another century of Jim Crow.

But moving into the first half of the twentieth century, mainstream America largely repressed and was otherwise largely oblivious to the lives of African Americans, including their traditional music of blues and Black gospel. Jazz, mostly of Black origins, would have an enormous impact in the 1920s, '30s, and '40s, though it would not reach the cultural tipping point in upending societal norms in the way that rock and roll would.

Certainly by the '40s and '50s, jazz would be a part from the mainstream, often the niche domain of intellectual types.[10]

To summarize, during the first half of the twentieth century, the music of certain racial and socioeconomic fringe classes would continue to morph and evolve outside the mainstream, all seemingly on an inevitable collision course. Specifically, this was the blues, particularly those from the especially harsh, isolated, and racist world of the Mississippi Delta (e.g., Robert Johnson, Muddy Waters, B.B. King), and transcendent southern Black gospel singers (e.g., Mahalia Jackson), including an influence of high-spirited Pentecostalism (especially Sister Rosetta Tharpe). Pentecostals were sometimes derisively referred to as "holy rollers" due to members being "slain" by the Holy Spirit and "rolling" in the church aisles. Along with all of this was a parallel track of country music from rural, white, more aggressive old-time country bands (e.g., the Skillet Lickers), and a stirring and more plaintive, traditional country (e.g., the Carter family), and blues- and jazz-infused western music (e.g., Jimmie Rodgers).[11]

These genres coalesced with one another. By the end of the '40s and into the early 50s, the blues would fuse with boogie piano (e.g., Fats Domino) and gospel to make rhythm and blues (R&B) (e.g., Amos Milburn, Big Joe Turner) and the swing of jazz to make jump blues (e.g., Louis Jordan).

By the late '40s, *Billboard* magazine was acknowledging the "umpteenth" exciting song by Black artists with a strong beat and the word "rock" in their titles, such as "Good Rocking Tonight," "All She Wants to Do Is Rock," and "Rock Awhile." As such, this could be called the first "rock" era. In the commercially segregated terms of the time, however, it was all still being called "race" music, which would soon be changed to the more mainstream-friendly R&B.[12]

There are a dozen or more legitimate contenders for the title of the First Rock Record, depending on one's precise definition of "rock and roll" (which is not nearly as simple as it might sound). The consensus pick for most historians came from what was really African American Ike Turner's band, though marketed as Jackie Brenston & His Delta Kings, in 1951. The record "Rocket 88" was recorded and produced by Sam Phillips at Sun Studio in Memphis. It was boisterous, cutting-edge R&B, with some distorted guitar, and lyrics about a hot rod and girls.[13] Only the song's shuffling drumbeat, as opposed to having more of a swing, leaves any room for debate as to "first."[14]

As performed by African Americans, this R&B/proto-rock/earliest rock and roll was groundbreaking, exciting, and filled with emotion, as well as often also having sexually suggestive lyrics, such as in "60-Minute Man" or "Work with Me, Annie." For all of these reasons, the music was shunned by a staid and conformant white mainstream.

2. *A New Rebel Yell*   19

Sister Rosetta Tharpe, promotional photograph, ca. 1940s.

Also in the late-'40s and early '50s, country music absorbed both the influence of jazz—that is, western swing (e.g., Bob Wills and His Texas Playboys), and the blues—that is, honky-tonk (e.g., Hank Williams), while old-time string bands took on blues *and* jazz influences, resulting in bluegrass (e.g., Flatt and Scruggs).[15] This also led to the fusion of R&B and country or "hillbilly," and key white performers in an early form of rock and roll—that is, "rockabilly." This included Bill Haley and the Comets from Chester, Pennsylvania, and soon Memphis's Elvis Presley. Also, Black St. Louis blues/R&B singer-guitarist Chuck Berry would draw from the "hillbilly" sound as well, which would allow him to perfect his own style.

Dewey Phillips, in the wake of the success of the Black-run, Black music-playing WDIA radio in Memphis, began his own genre- and race-busting radio show in Memphis in 1949. Phillips worked closely with his best friend, Sam Phillips (no relation). At the time, Sam was recording some of the greatest Black Delta bluesmen, including Howlin' Wolf, B.B. King, and Turner.

The term "rock and roll" is an old African American slang term for sex and also used as an adjective to describe R&B. Alan Freed witnessed white teens going crazy over R&B and then began to refer to the music itself as "rock 'n' roll" to distinguish it from being identified solely as Black music and to make it more palatable to the commercial mainstream.[16]

But to truly launch rock and roll to the stratosphere took something more.

Elvis

Elvis Presley (1935–1977) would be the focal point of the rock and roll phenomenon, and his legacy would touch on a remarkable array of other topics crucial to American history as well, including sex, class, and especially race. Better understanding rock, America, and race going forward, in fact, requires a better understanding of Elvis's story.

Elvis grew up a poor white kid in rural Tupelo, Mississippi, with his parents, living in a shotgun shack and alongside poor African Americans, though in a segregated South. Elvis would be one of a handful of white kids in America exposed not only to Black people in this way but also to the Delta blues and Black gospel. Along with his family's own Pentecostal services and his favorite country and pop singers, Elvis's childhood was an utterly unique melting pot of rock's origins from the start.[17]

Presley's persona was then further shaped by pre-rock, mainstream pop superstars, especially Dean Martin, Bing Crosby, and Frank Sinatra. Those three, in fact, crossed over to become mainstream movie stars when such crossover success was the pinnacle of pop stardom.[18]

When the Presleys moved to Memphis in 1948, a middle school–aged Elvis was further exposed to a phenomenal amount of historically great Black music. There was the groundbreaking radio of WDIA and WHBQ and the blues clubs on Beale Street, aka the "Home of the Blues." Elvis and friends even attended all–Black church services at East Trigg Baptist Church, though due to segregation, they sat either in the back or in the balcony and listened to the music of legendary gospel composer Reverend W. Herbert Brewster.[19]

2. A New Rebel Yell

Elvis Presley (right), performing with Scotty Moore in 1956. *Look* magazine photograph collection (Library of Congress).

Crucially, from the world of film came two of the biggest and *coolest* movie stars of the time: the iconic young rebels Marlon Brando and James Dean. In a time of social transition and an age of anxiety, Brando and Dean, both white, boldly challenged establishment figures on-screen, including parents, merchants, and the police. Both actors had hit films, starting with Brando's breakout biker film *Wild One* (1953), and Dean's *Rebel without a Cause* (1955) about a troubled teen fighting with his father. The two actors would be widely accepted in the mainstream, earning box office receipts, accolades, and Academy Awards.[20] Thus, in the mid–'50s, certain kinds of rebels were being completely embraced by the Western mainstream.

Elvis was so enamored with both actors that he grew his sideburns out like Brando and memorized all of Dean's film lines. He learned that this new cool meant that pop stars no longer needed to be smiling *do-gooders*. Instead, he developed a trademark lip-curl sneer, which was visually evident as well as reflected in his basic attitude and singing style.[21]

Musically, by the time the 19-year-old Presley first walked into Sun Studio in 1954, everything was in place as well: Memphis already had radio stations and a record label bridging the Black-white divide and rock and roll records had already been recorded in Memphis and elsewhere by both Black and white artists.

Presley's debut single in June 1954 was a timeless, hillbilly-infused cover of his Delta blues idol Arthur Crudup and his proto-rock song "That's

All Right (1946). Presley had unintentionally stumbled onto his own "blacker" singing style late at night at his first recording session at Sun Studio.[22] It was an exciting, often sexually charged style still foreign to the vast majority of the mainstream at the time; even the term "rock and roll" had yet to catch on.[23]

When Dewey Phillips put Elvis's single on Memphis radio, it became an instant smash among both white and Black kids.[24] Sam Phillips would immediately go on to record other white, rock and roll/rockabilly performers like Jerry Lee Lewis, Carl Perkins, and others, and they, too, became massive stars.

Elvis was a truly transcendent talent. He fully and credibly incorporated the best of all of the relevant musical genres—pop, country, blues, R&B, and gospel—into a single sound. He had an electrifying and sexual style, great emotional depth, and a unique voice with great range.

Presley cut loose on television with wild, hip-swiveling, and overtly sexual moves, largely inspired by Black R&B artists on Beale Street. Audiences responded, especially teen girls, many of whom would go into full hysterics, screaming wildly.[25] Elvis had a culture-changing, live TV performance on the immensely popular *Ed Sullivan Show* in September 1956. There were only three U.S. television networks at the time, and his performance drew an astonishing 82.6 percent of the U.S. television audience.[26] He stunned America with another of his breakout hits, the explosive rock and roll version of "Hound Dog," first popularized by African American shout-blues singer Big Mama Thornton in 1953.

As mainstream America didn't yet even have a frame of reference for rock and roll, it is hard to convey just how shocking and scandalous it all was at that time. In trying to grasp the sway rock music suddenly had over America's youth, a 1956 *Time* magazine article opined that rock music bore "a passing resemblance to Hitler's mass meetings."[27] The *New York Times* quoted a psychiatrist who referred to rock as "cannibalistic and tribalistic."[28]

For a time, white artists would release watered-down cover versions of the most exciting of Black artists' tracks, which did allow rock to gain greater mainstream acceptance. Pat Boone, for example, had huge hits with covers of Fats Domino's "Ain't That a Shame" (1955) and Little Richard's "Tutti Frutti" (1956).[29] White deejays on mainstream radio would play the white artists' versions, which then garnered far superior sales; Little Richard's "Long Tall Sally" (1955) would be the first to outsell the cover version and reverse that trend.[30]

The mainstream opened up for the most crucial rock pioneers. Particularly thrilling were those artists raised in Southern Pentecostal churches that brought some of that Holy Spirit: Presley, Little Richard ("Tutti

Frutti," "Lucille"), and Jerry Lee Lewis ("Whole Lotta Shakin' Goin' On," "Great Balls of Fire"). Those three brought a special energy, both sexual and spiritual, and an almost unhinged excitement that would help define the genre.

Guitar legends Bo Diddley ("Bo Diddley," "Who Do You Love"), Carl Perkins ("Blue Suede Shoes," "Matchbox"), and especially, Chuck Berry ("Maybellene," "School Daze") helped establish the blueprint for guitar-based rock for the rest of the century. Texan Buddy Holly brought a new level of pop songcraft to rock without losing any of its heart. Southern stars Ray Charles and James Brown were creating new offshoots with soul. Harmonizing vocal groups brought R&B and gospel to the street corner and the development of doo-wop, with groups like the Penguins and the Platters. All of the above were the foundations for rock music and a whole new world of popular music.

For rock and roll to first kick the door in on the American mainstream, however, it was always going to be a white guy and for many reasons. For all of Presley's significant talents, he was also in precisely the right place at the right time.

Elvis's very approach to rock and roll music and his confidence as a rebel was rooted in his race. Writer James Baldwin once said that being white is not a color; "it's an attitude."[31] Elvis had every reason to believe that even as the most brazen of rebels, he would be accepted into the mainstream, precisely as Brando and Dean had been. Further, he already knew full well that white kids loved "Black" music or did when exposed to it. As a result, Elvis transformed from a shy, poor white kid singing country and pop ballads but with a genuine feel for "Black" music to an explosive crossover performer in just a few months. He also knew he had no real limits in the music world and he sang like it. As Sam Phillips had famously noted shortly before finding Elvis, "If I could find a white man who had the Negro sound and the Negro feel, I could make a billion dollars."[32]

Conversely, of course, there were no Black equivalents of Brando and Dean on the big screen, sticking it to white authority figures. And as Sam Phillips had also said, the Black artists at Sun "unfortunately did not *have* an ego" in that these were people "that had dreamed, and dreamed, and dreamed ... and were afraid of being denied again."[33] This was, of course, a time of events such as the 1955 murder of 14-year-old Emmett Till for an offhand comment in Money, Mississippi, and the blatantly racist acquittal of his murderers, as well as federal troops being needed to integrate Little Rock High School in Arkansas in 1957.[34]

Ultimately, it was the fully integrated racial crossover of rock and roll that made it feel and sound so epic. Rock drew on the entire American experience, with the best aspects of the so-called Black (blues, Black gospel, jazz) and white (country, pop) musical genres. The deeply felt blues were about making a life in an alienating and hostile world. Gospel brought exuberance and transcendence and engaged the audience. Pop was accessible and catchy. Country music kept it simple, it was rooted in deep traditions, and it told great stories. To draw from only the best parts of even one or two of these styles was inherently limiting. But Elvis was in an utterly unique position to confidently and competently draw from all of it. He had no limits. Thus, as one (this) writer put it, while Elvis was not the first to play rock and roll, he was in a perfect position to be "the first to knock it out of the park."[35]

Rock and roll further helped crack the foundations of the establishment's institutions regarding music, race, sex, and class, as well as repressed emotions. To the young and future rock hero in the United Kingdom, Keith Richards, hearing rock and roll for the first time was everything: "It was like the world went from black & white to Technicolor."[36]

Once rock music broke, it quickly became the world's dominant popular music. Rock and roll would drive the record industry to nearly triple its sales in just five years, from $213 million in 1954 to $613 million in 1959.[37] The previous reigning pop superstar, Sinatra, went from calling Presley's music a "rancid smelling aphrodisiac" to even covering a couple of rock songs himself.[38] Ed Sullivan went from hating rock to praising Presley on-air as "a real decent, fine boy."[39]

By 1958, the most important rock pioneers would be sidelined for a variety of reasons. Presley was drafted into the army for two years. Chuck Berry and Jerry Lee Lewis became embroiled in sex scandals involving underage women. Little Richard chose to go back to gospel music.[40]

By the end of the '50s and into the early '60s, rock and roll was also being co-opted by mainstream and corporate interests (and not for the last time). The direction of rock and roll in the mainstream was controlled by people like television personality and producer Dick Clark and singer-actor Pat Boone. Both Clark and Boone were white, had matinee-star good looks, and conveyed safe personas acceptable to mainstream America. Clark had rather luckily escaped the Payola scandal with his career intact. He continued to host the smash, live teen dance-and-music showcase *American Bandstand* as well as running his own highly successful TV production company.[41] Boone scored 38 top-40 hits through the decade and hosted his own popular TV show from 1957 to 1960.[42]

Both Boone and Clark somehow managed to both embrace rock and roll *and* be proud conformists. Clark once jokingly referred to himself as a "fluffmeister."[43] As Boone, a devout Christian, had explained to his teen fans in one interview, resistance against parental authority was like a "large dog" pulling on a choke chain: "the more he struggles and pulls, the tighter the collar gets."[44]

Further, even once rock broke, for the next several years artists who wanted to compete on the pop charts, especially Black artists, had to water down their playing style. There was a shift to romantic ballads if an artist wanted to be heard on the radio, though even that music could also be quite inspired, such as doo-wop artists the Penguins' "Earth Angel" and the Crests' "Sixteen Candles."[45] Still, Boone's and Clark's success further opened the door for and normalized commercial success for rockers, both Black and white.

By 1960, several of the remaining original rock pioneers met tragedy in two separate accidents. In 1958, Buddy Holly, 22, Richie Valens, 17, and the deejay-performer the Big Bopper, 28, all died in a tragic plane crash in Wisconsin. Then, in 1960, a car accident in London badly injured Gene Vincent and took the life of Eddie Cochran, who was just 21.[46]

In the first few years of the 1960s, there would be successful, more pop-oriented girl groups, such as the Crystals, the Shirelles, the Ronettes, and the Shangri-Las, and exciting new studio sounds like Phil Spector's "Wall of Sound." There would be something of a lull on the rock and roll timeline before the next major phenomenon, but the shock waves of those first pioneers were still reverberating in places like Liverpool, London, Memphis (again), and Detroit. Rock and roll was being reconfigured in exciting new ways.[47]

In the '60s, rock music would come to reflect and inspire a larger generational shift not only in music but also in social, cultural, and even political matters. From the establishment's perspective, however, the American democracy, capitalism, and the church were all still better than any alternatives. As such, the more people could accept these institutions and fall in line, the better off everyone would be.

Author and non-rock fan Robert Pattison would later describe rock as "pantheist" in that it usually rejected the traditional Christian monotheism of one all-powerful God. Instead, the seeming chaos of the genre seemed to want to replace that with an anything-goes morality. *Any* conceptions of God, or even just nature itself, could be considered divine. To many, it would look like anarchy devoid of even basic decency. According to Pattison, the rock and rollers' perspective would lack "any transcendent vantage from which to promulgate artistic standards." Thus, it was all an excuse to be "tasteless and uncritical" and unapologetically embrace "immorality."[48]

But the establishment would face stark challenges to both its hegemony and its credibility, and a rock and roll–fueled countercultural movement was just getting started. A rising counterculture was no longer unquestioningly accepting whatever doctrines were being handed down. New directions in life were being sought.

Certainly, rock and roll could be a lot of things, including hedonistic, self-indulgent, self-destructive, and sometimes just ridiculous. But the sum of rock music would also be far more than any of that. It would connect with millions worldwide in deep and meaningful ways and inspire new directions. Rock would have some incredible highs and it would continue to transform the world in profound ways.

3

Cultural Checkpoints: The United States and the United Kingdom Enter the '60s

The 1960s were a time of immense social and political unrest and change as well as being the most crucial era of rock and roll music. It is thus equally crucial to properly establish its social, political, and cultural landscape.

First, this chapter will recap key social and cultural points in the United States. This will be followed by a brief introduction to the late '50s and early '60s in the United Kingdom, which would become the new de facto capital of rock and roll.

The United States

Culture

Censorship lessens: Films challenged social norms, such as director Billy Wilder's risqué comedy *Some Like It Hot* (1959) and *The Apartment* (1960) which depicted corporate executives and their sexual trysts, and director Alfred Hitchcock's *Psycho* (1960) with jarring scenes of violence, including shots from a killer's perspective.

The Beat poets and controversial New York comedian Lenny Bruce would push notions of art and decency in their fields.[1]

On American television, Americans continued to find comfort in the depictions of the cowboy and law and order prevailing in uncertain times.[2] A peak came when the top-three-rated shows in both 1960 and '61 were westerns.[3]

POLITICS/WAR

Eisenhower and McCarthyism: General-turned-president Dwight D. Eisenhower (1953–1961) was business-friendly, though he did not reduce New Deal and Fair Deal spending policies.[4]

Eisenhower also battled Senator Joe McCarthy (R–Wisconsin) and McCarthyism, a reckless persecution of communists in the U.S., while his vice president, Richard Nixon, had made his name teaming with McCarthy.[5]

Through the 1950s, McCarthy largely relied on lies and innuendos in attacking and smearing many Americans, though some Soviet spies were found out. Before the decade ended, his political career would crash in ignominy. Still, the Soviets and their nuclear arsenal were also real, and Republicans as well as New Deal liberal Democrats all remained stridently anti-communist.[6]

President Kennedy: Democrat John F. Kennedy narrowly defeated Nixon in the 1960 presidential race. Kennedy was only 43 when he first took office, the youngest president ever; he was also charismatic and handsome. For much of America's youth especially, he represented a wanted change from corporate dominance, an over reliance on a massive military-industrial complex, and deeply ingrained discrimination.

During his election campaign, Kennedy had first suggested that the United States lagged behind the USSR in nuclear weaponry, a "missile gap," which he knew to be false.[7]

Under Kennedy, the CIA failed in a clandestine overthrow of Fidel Castro's communist Cuba in 1961 by CIA-trained, anti–Castro operatives, in what became known as the Bay of Pigs debacle.[8]

Subsequently, in 1962, Soviet premier Nikita Khrushchev sent nuclear missiles to Cuba, 90 miles from Florida, and in part to counter the United States deploying similar short-range missiles in Turkey. In October 1962, U.S. Air Force U2 spy planes photographed the Cuban facilities, and the United States blockaded Cuba to prevent the delivery of further missiles. Kennedy demanded the missiles be removed.[9]

For 13 grueling days in November 1963, the world could do nothing but watch and wait, fully knowing that one rash decision or technical mistake could trigger nuclear Armageddon. The Cuban Missile Crisis was an age of anxiety personified. Some of Kennedy's advisers, including all the Joint Chiefs of Staff, called for an airstrike on the missile sites followed by a land invasion.[10] Instead, Kennedy and Khrushchev finally reached an agreement in which the Soviets would dismantle and remove their offensive weapons from Cuba, while the United States publicly agreed to not invade Cuba again unless directly provoked. Secretly, the United States also agreed it would dismantle its missiles deployed in Turkey and Italy. The entire future of humanity was exposed as precarious, and even

The Economy

Europe and Japan continued to dig out of rubble and buried millions of war dead, while economic production soared in the United States, where factory jobs were plentiful, unions obtained good wages and benefits for their members, and corporations thrived.[11] The U.S. standard of living went up 50 percent from 1947 to 1960.[12] World War II and Korean War (1950–1953) G.I.s returned home to prosperity and gave birth to the baby boomer generation, the most populous generation in U.S. history.[13]

In housing, white flight had also kicked in, as did de facto segregation in cities across the United States, with various illegal real estate tactics exacerbating the phenomenon. Also, blue-collar workers often received overtime but worked long hours to get it, and white-collar workers saw an increasingly competitive and stressful lifestyle.[14] If the promise of technological miracles was a direct increase in leisure time, it had not yet seemed to have arrived.

By the early '60s, the postwar economic boom was ending. Manufacturing employment declined as automation increased in factories, and the rest of the world got back on its feet and offered competition.[15] For the African Americans who had fled from the white supremacist South for the North, good jobs became harder to find.[16]

America's corporate mentality impacted all aspects of life. American schools of the 1950s became more and more about "bottom lines" and were marked by "bubble filling tests, military-style exercise, and standard corporal punishment."[17] In fact, it could be said that even the human mind had become a commodity to exploit. In a 1963 lecture, the president of the University of California, Berkley, Clark Kerr, had stated,

> The production, distribution, and consumption of knowledge is said to account for 29 percent of gross national product, and knowledge production is growing at about twice the rate of the rest of the economy. What the railroads did for the second half of the last century, and the automobile for the first half of this century, may be done for the second half of this century by the knowledge industry; and that is, to serve as the focal point for national growth.[18]

Civil Rights

The Warren Court: In 1953, Chief Justice Earl Warren was appointed to the U.S. Supreme Court by Eisenhower, although he unexpectedly headed up a more liberal court that would desegregate schools, end racial gerrymandering, advance Miranda rights for the criminally accused, and recognize a woman's right to privacy in obtaining birth control, even if unmarried, which was said to be a constitutional "zone of privacy."[19]

Martin Luther King, Jr.: Rev. Martin Luther King, Jr., from Atlanta, would be the focal point of the civil rights movement.[20] In December 1955, local civil rights advocates in Montgomery, Alabama, where King lived with his family, organized a protest against the city's segregated public transit system, starting with African American Rosa Parks refusing to give up her seat to a white person. Despite threats and the King family home being dynamited, the boycott was successful. From there, King organized the Southern Christian Leadership Conference (SCLC) and would continue the cause while following the doctrine of nonviolence modeled by Jesus in the Bible.[21]

In 1963, King helped organize the March on Washington to advance the legal and economic interests of African Americans and delivered his famous "I Have a Dream" speech. In that, King brought forth his vision of a racially just America that would indeed "rise up and live out the true meaning of its creed: 'We hold these truths to be self-evident, that all men are created equal.'"[22]

College students followed up on the *Brown v. Board of Education* decisions and adopted King's plan of nonviolence to integrate public spaces throughout the South. This often led to violent reprisals and often with the unofficial acquiescence of local police until federal troops were called in.[23]

As a more radical counterpoint to King, African American activist Malcolm X of the Nation of Islam connected with those African Americans who had lost patience with a country that had seemingly been asking for their patience forever.[24] After splitting with the Nation of Islam, Malcolm X was assassinated by members of the church in February 1965.

Sex, Gender, and Morals

Marriage and Sex: At the dawn of the '60s, the average age of marriage was rising and premarital sex was becoming more common.[25] Before 1960, unmarried young men were expected to seek sex with women, while single young women were expected to avoid permanently tarnishing their reputations before marrying.[26] Married couples stopped staying together no matter what. Divorce and out-of-wedlock birth rates increased.[27]

The censorship of books, plays, poetry readings, and films effectively ended.[28]

The curing of syphilis, followed by the invention of the birth control pill in 1960 and its widespread use shortly thereafter, removed some of the biggest roadblocks to increased sexual relations.[29]

Gender and Sexual Orientation: Married women could only get credit cards with their husband's permission, and jobs were listed in newspaper classified ads as "Jobs for Men" versus "Jobs for Women." Homosexuals generally had to hide their sexuality at all times or otherwise endure ostracism from family and church and face criminal penalties and/or severe violence.

In 1962, Grace Metalious's 1956 novel *Peyton Place* was adapted for the small screen, exposing suburban dramas behind familial facades of normalcy, if not perfection. The same year, Helen Gurley Brown's *Sex and the Single Girl* told one of the first stories of financially independent and sexually liberated young women, while Betty Friedan's bestselling *The Feminine Mystique* (1963) related the dilemma of many women feeling stuck in a narrow and artificially constructed role as subservient, never-complaining homemakers.

Religion/Spirituality: Aside from the "moral fervor" engendered by Martin Luther King, Jr., by the end of the '50s, attendance at religious services in the United States had begun to decline. The Baptist preacher Billy Graham, however, was packing stadiums worldwide on his ongoing "crusade."[30]

The Brits

Youth Culture and the Beginnings of an Invasion

Postwar England: Virtually all of the major musical players of the British Invasion were born during World War II. Over 3 million fathers and brothers were off at war, nearly 400,000 never came back, and thousands more came back deeply impacted emotionally and psychologically.[31] British life in the '50s was further marked by a deep economic recession, worse even than Germany or Japan, due to the war, inflation, and dreadful labor relations.[32]

The Teds: The "Teddy Boy" teen subculture phenomenon took hold in the late '40s. It began as the "new Edwardian look," named for the British fashion styles during the reign of King Edward VII, from 1901 to 1910, and *Edwardian* being shortened to *Ted*. It was an aristocratic and dandyish look of upper- and middle-class style with long jackets and tight trousers, all adopted by the working class when wartime austerity came to an end.[33] Around 1951, working-class teenagers defied the class structure and began adapting their own sharp and bold variations of the look as "Teds."[34]

In the mid–'50s, the U.S. actors Marlon Brando and James Dean spoke to a disaffected youth culture in the United Kingdom as well. Musically, the Teds were embracing jazz and then skiffle—a genre based on jazz and American folk music.

Rock and Roll Arrives: Bill Haley's smash hit "Rock around the Clock" first appeared in the 1955 film *The Blackboard Jungle*, which arrived in the

United Kingdom in 1956. At a screening of the film in London that year, Teds started dancing in the aisles and slashed some of the seats, while some shop windows were smashed outside.[35] There was panic over the "teen menace."[36]

The working-class Teds then adopted more Western, rock-inspired touches, à la Elvis Presley and Gene Vincent, resulting in "a quiff with greased back DA [duck's arse] hairstyle, drape coat with velvet collar, bootlace tie, drainpipe trousers, and brothel-creeper shoes."[37]

Playwright John Osborne was the first under the label of the "Angry Young Men" movement with his play *Look Back in Anger* (1956), later adapted into a 1959 film.[38]

Public Morals

Censorship and Class: In August 1960, Penguin Books was prosecuted for publishing D.H. Lawrence's *Lady Chatterley's Lover*, which, as one newspaper summarized, was "notable only for its use of the f-word and some sublimely silly sex scenes."[39] The British upper class's institutionalized arrogance and paternalism were exposed as well. At one point in the trial, one of the prosecuting attorneys had famously asked jurors if the book was one "you would wish your wife or servants to read?"[40]

In 1962, the satirical late-night TV show *That Was the Week That Was* first aired, spoofing religion, politics, royalty, and sex and turned host David Frost into a national celebrity.[41]

The Profumo Affair: Prominent politician John Profumo was caught in lies regarding his 19-year-old mistress, Christine Keeler. A series of newspaper articles further alleged Keeler to have slept with a Soviet spy, raising the possibility of nuclear secrets having been passed on.[42] The British establishment was quickly losing prestige and its moral legitimacy.[43]

The Church of England: It was no secret that the Church of England had been seeing dwindling attendance since World War I.[44] Legendary Rolling Stones guitarist Keith Richards reflected on his and his family's experience with religion growing up, with his views echoing many of his generation:

> And the church, organized religion, was something to be avoided. Nobody minded what Christ said, nobody said there wasn't a God or anything like that, but stay away from organizations. Priests would be considered with much suspicion.[45]

Much change was on the horizon.

4

Meet the Beatles and the Stones, 1959–1965

The Early Beatles

> In the evening, especially when the sailors are gathered in great numbers, these streets present a most singular spectacle, the entire population of the vicinity seemingly turned into them. Hand-organs, fiddles and cymbals, plied by strolling musicians, mix with the songs of the seamen, the babble of women and children and the whining of beggars. From the various boarding houses ... proceeds the noise of revelry and dancing.[1]
> —HERMAN MELVILLE, upon visiting Liverpool in 1839

The Beatles are very possibly the most revered and most talked about music act in history, and probably none of it is too much. Still, as much has been written about them, their story, as told here, will be told in a fresh and concise manner, focusing on the most salient of biographical points as they relate to this book and how they place the group in the larger arc of Western civilization.

The impact of Beatlemania in 1964 would be so outrageous that most believed that it couldn't possibly be sustainable; it *had* to be a fad. Ed Sullivan's musical director declared, "I give them a year," or something along the lines of the Hula-Hoop fad of the '50s.[2] For younger readers, the initial frenzy around the Beatles was something akin to the primal impact of Beiberfever, One Direction, and BTS combined, but instead of a segment of the world's preteen and teenage girls flipping out, it was a significant portion of the world.

Most highbrow critics of the time still scarcely considered rock and roll as *music*, let alone art. The *New York Times* decided that the mop-tops were "a fine mass placebo." *Newsweek* described the monster hit "I Want to Hold Your Hand" as "stupefyingly repetitive."[3]

Yet every release by the Beatles would be a major, worldwide event, speculated on and discussed in the weeks leading up. Once released, the Beatles would reclaim the top spot in the charts; every lyric would be scoured for meaning, real or imagined, by fans as well as academics. All 13 of their U.S.-released studio albums would go to number one.[4]

To begin with, the band, as a whole, was special, but the group's primary creative engine would be the songwriting team of John Lennon and Paul McCartney, arguably the greatest of the twentieth century. How did this duo come to be? That these two historic talents grew up in the same area at the same time in Liverpool, England, is either an outrageous statistical coincidence or other factors helped to create their seemingly almost-otherworldly chemistry, along with George Harrison and Ringo Starr.

The band would end rather abruptly, after producing 13 legendary albums in the U.S., and more, over just seven years. Various reasons have been cited for their breakup, and for a long time it had been popular to blame Lennon's girlfriend and then wife, Yoko Ono, or for others, it was simply the ugly side of the music business poisoning the members' personal and creative relationships. This, especially after the passing of the band's trusted manager, Brian Epstein. To others, it was because McCartney became too overbearing, or maybe because Lennon was too prickly.

One fresh way of understanding the Beatles phenomenon is to see their run as a remarkable band but also something that ran along a relatively simple and natural life cycle. Writer Dirk Dunbar provides a helpful thematic framework for understanding the Beatles from start to finish by highlighting lyrical themes throughout their career in five distinct stages: (1) a burst of youthful joy, (2) dealing with the real world, (3) visualizing a surrealistic, psychedelic, new future, (4) "acceptance of life in the mainstream," and (5) "a cosmic return" home.[5] Thus, the band exploded into the world's consciousness and completed a mission of sorts before disbanding. In the end, they were infinitely better for the experience, as were their fans who shared in that process.

So how did it all happen?

The background. All four of the Beatles were born in the United Kingdom in the early 1940s, far from London, in the northwestern city of Liverpool. Liverpool is a major port sitting on the eastern side of the Mersey estuary, a few kilometers in from the Irish Sea. Historically, the city had been the "Gateway to the British Empire" as well as a major port in the slave trade until 1807, though it later saw economic decline after World War I.[6] The city would long be partly defined by the open seas and the sailor's life as well as immigration from Ireland and elsewhere.[7]

Liverpudlians were colloquially known as "Scousers," a name derived from a local stew for sailors once common on sailing ships, and generally were seen as humble, blue collar, and proud.[8] A seafaring life was tough but also made for a uniquely adventurous way of life. It was also understood that in part because life wasn't easy in Liverpool, one needed a sense of humor.[9] In the 1800s, antsy Liverpudlian sailors out at sea had a tradition of forming impromptu "Foo Foo" bands, playing noisy songs with kazoos while dressed in drag.[10]

Cosmopolitan London, on the other hand, had long mostly ignored what happened in Liverpool, lumping the city in with Manchester and other similarly situated, blue-collar cities to the north as culturally irrelevant. Liverpudlians, on the other hand, didn't tolerate pretentious elitists, a common view of Londoners.[11] Liverpool's suburban neighborhoods, which would house the young Beatles, were modest.

Due to its importance as a port, from August 1940 until January 1942, Liverpool was hit hard by some 80 air raids by the Luftwaffe. The city's casualties by air were second only to London's. McCartney's parents even met during one such raid.[12]

Postwar Liverpool was diverse, with Chinese and African settlements, and it teemed with merchant and military seamen, including American sailors. Those Americans brought the latest musical releases of American country and western, R&B, and then rock and roll. This further created a market for live music and performers in a city already known for being musical.[13]

Julia Stanley and Freddie Lennon were married after a brief courtship and soon gave birth to John Lennon in 1940. Julia was a lovely but terribly impulsive woman who liked to get out on the town and went from one relationship to the next. Freddie was a merchant seaman and no more responsible and would disappear for long stretches.[14]

When the pair split, neither was in a position to adequately care for their child. John would later recall, "The worst pain is that of not being wanted, of realizing your parents do not need you in the way you need them."[15]

In 1944, Julia moved in with Bobby Dykins, a sometimes violent drunk.[16] John's aunt Mimi Smith later recalled John at four years old showing up at her door crying, having run away from loud arguments and physical violence.[17] Freddie would then disappear altogether for the next 20 years of John's life, and John would "write him off as dead."[18]

Julia eventually turned over the complete care of John to Mimi and John's uncle George, themselves childless. They would provide John with a stable home life, along with help from John's other three aunts.[19] Lennon thus experienced the trauma of total parental rejection and abandonment, trauma that would stay with him. Yet, in another sense, he was liberated as well, gaining some clarity in the process. As he later put it, "The fact that I wasn't with my parents made me see that parents are not gods."[20] He would certainly be an independent and bold spirit.

John and Julia did maintain contact in an odd relationship, described by those close as buddy-buddy or almost even a platonic boyfriend-girlfriend-type relationship, rather than mother-son. Julia always supported John in his passion for music and was the one to introduce him to the likes of Jerry Lee Lewis, Elvis Presley, and Fats Domino as well as the banjo and bought John his first guitar.[21]

Despite his aunt's care and his loving and funny Uncle George, Lennon recalled being angry and envious of other children with regular parents. Lennon was a bright and brash kid. He was also a class clown and a troublemaker who would lose interest in school. Along with being charismatic, he had a bit of a mean streak and could be difficult, sarcastic, and abrasive. In his teens, Lennon adopted the rebellious Teddy Boy look of the times.[22]

All of the future Beatles in a pre-rock England embraced skiffle. The skiffle craze was led by another major Beatles' influence, the Scotsman Lonnie Donegan.[23]

In 1957, at age 16, Lennon and some schoolmates formed the Quarrymen, named for their high school and a nearby quarry. As the story goes, Lennon soon joined up with then-15-year-old guitarist Paul McCartney and McCartney's 14-year-old guitarist friend George Harrison. All three were becoming less enamored with traditional school and more fixated on music. Lennon moved on to art school in Liverpool. Lennon's best friend, Stu Sutcliffe, a talented artist but just passable bass player, joined the group as well. Despite Lennon entering university, he knew he had something with his young schoolboy friends and they stuck together.

Paul McCartney was born in 1942, with a younger brother, Michael. McCartney's home was blue collar, contrasting with Lennon's more comfortable middle-class upbringing, but his earliest home life was as stable as Lennon's was unstable.[24] McCartney's father, Jim, worked at the Liverpool Cotton Exchange and was a semiprofessional musician, and his mother, Mary, a devoted midwife. Much time was spent around the family piano, which Paul learned to play, as well as the trumpet, a gift from his father. Jim would take his kids to see performances of traditional brass bands and music hall (akin to vaudeville in the United States), sounds that Paul would draw from throughout his career.[25]

Young Paul was described as bright, charming, and a bit mischievous. Like many British kids of the time, McCartney listened to Radio Luxembourg on Saturday and Sunday evenings, which played American R&B and early rock.[26]

When Paul was 14, Mary's cancer from previous years came back and suddenly took her life in late 1956, devastating the family. At one point, Jim considered suicide, while Paul was inconsolable and lost himself in his guitar.[27]

4. Meet the Beatles and the Stones, 1959–1965 37

Still 14, McCartney wrote his first song, "I Lost My Little Girl," which he later acknowledged was "subconsciously" written about his mother.[28] Over a decade later, a dream of McCartney's resulted in another homage to his mother in the Aretha Franklin and gospel-inspired classic "Let It Be." That song was written in 1969 when the Beatles were in tumult and on the verge of breaking up, though McCartney also said that it was directed toward all of "the broken-hearted people living in the world" looking to make sense of their lives. In McCartney's dream, Mary had told him, "It will be all right, just let it be."[29]

As McCartney would also say later, the Radio Luxembourg broadcasts gave kids "plenty to dream about."[30] All of the band members would be blown away by the American rock and roll, including Presley's "Heartbreak Hotel" in 1956. McCartney began devoting all of his free time to playing the guitar. Because the older Lennon was such a strong and formidable personality, McCartney had to elevate in stature to keep up.[31]

The future Beatles would be influenced by the entire Sun Records lineup, Chuck Berry and Chess, and they would cover both of Motown's Smokey Robinson and Berry Gordy on their early records. The ecstatic style of Little Richard was especially key; McCartney's cover of Richard's "Long Tall Sally" had been his audition for the Quarrymen.[32]

The group also collectively fell for the harmonies of the Everly Brothers and girl groups like the Shirelles and the Ronettes. Finally, the classic song craft of Buddy Holly and the late '50s and early '60s Brill Building songwriters helped give the Lennon and McCartney team a structure to bring it all together.[33]

Lennon and McCartney shared songwriting duties and credits and collaborated with each other on songs the other had started. They also shared lead vocal duties depending on the primary songwriter of the song.

The group would further bond through what would become their trademark and irreverent sense of humor. Each had been a huge fan of the popular 1950s British comedy TV show *The Goon Show*, featuring Spike Milligan and Peter Sellers, among others.

In June 1958, and just as McCartney's life had been altered forever a year and a half earlier, when Lennon was 17, Julia was struck down and killed by a drunk driver while crossing a street leaving Mimi and George's home. Now it was Lennon's turn to be inconsolable as he retreated into solitude, grief, and bitterness. Lennon wouldn't talk about his loss with anyone and indulged in the British, male tradition of keeping a "stiff upper lip" as well as heavy drinking. As Lennon would say later, "I lost [my mother] twice. Once as a five-year-old when I moved in with my auntie. And once again at fifteen when she actually, physically died."[34]

The adult Lennon would write two songs that directly addressed his relationship with his mother. The first, "Julia," appeared on the band's self-titled album, better known as the "White Album," in 1968. "Julia," an affecting song, is regarded by many fans as one of the Beatles' most underrated. It is slow and acoustic with no drums. Lennon's vocals are almost delicate as well as dreamy and touching, but he also seems to more express a longing for that connection with his mother that he never fully had; it is more of a what-could-have-been song.

Lennon's second "mom" record was the post–Beatles solo song, simply titled "Mother." That song was directly fueled by Lennon's doing primal scream therapy work with Dr. Arthur Janov in 1970 (more on that later). Lennon emotes deep anguish over his lack of relationships with Julia as well as Freddie. It starts off as a fairly simple ballad with Lennon directly addressing each parent and seeking closure. He acknowledges his sadness from his parents first not being there emotionally and then being physically absent from his life. He finishes the song off by giving voice to deeply felt anguish and rage, wringing and screaming the emotion out of the final notes.

The young Lennon slowly came around. He and McCartney already had a bond—they may have been the youngest songwriting duo ever (e.g., the brothers George and Ira Gershwin did not start writing until they were 20 and 21, respectively), but now they found a greater understanding and deeper trust in each other. McCartney later explained how the shared tragedies shaped their relationship: "Now we were both in this, both losing our mothers. This was a bond for guys, something of ours, a special thing."[35] Further, "We both knew the pain of it and we both knew that we had to put on a brave face because we were kind of teenage guys and you didn't talk about that sort of thing where we came from."[36] Although McCartney noted that such conversations were not the norm for young men, in Key West, Florida, in 1964, when a hurricane diverted their flight and the two spent free time together, they stayed up all night drinking and "talking, talking, talking like it was going out of style." They bonded even further over their shared loss and cried.[37]

Seemingly easygoing on the surface, McCartney could be caustic and tough. Lennon, on the other hand, had his hard, sharp-witted exterior as protection but a soft interior once you got to know him. Each recognized as much in the other.[38] Lennon told of moments when he and McCartney found themselves arguing early on, and Lennon would drop his glasses, look at McCartney, smile, and remind him, "It's only me."[39]

In 1960, the group continued to play gigs around Liverpool as the Quarrymen, including the all-ages Casbah coffee shop in the basement of the Bests' house, run by future–Beatle drummer Pete Best's mother, Mona. They then got their first gigs downtown at the Cavern Club, then a jazz club but tolerant of skiffle. They settled on the name the Beatles, a reference to Buddy Holly and the Crickets, as well as the signature backbeat of rock music.[40]

Also in 1960, the group's then-unofficial manager in Liverpool, Allan Williams, obtained a booking for the group as a resident band at a club in, oddly enough, Hamburg, Germany. Hamburg had an age-old tradition of being an "anything goes" town, complete with a thriving red-light district, where Germans came to blow off steam and indulge in any number of adult activities.[41] Like Liverpool, Hamburg was also an important port city on the Elbe River, about 70 miles from the North Sea—and far removed from the traditional pop culture centers of Los Angeles, New York, and London. The city had also been devastated by British and U.S. air forces during the war, but it had bounced back.

Hamburg boasted of its "mile of sin" centered on an infamous stretch of the Reperbahn: a haven of neon lights, saloons, gangster-owned nightclubs, brothels, live sex shows, lots of U.S. and British sailors and soldiers, and fights. The only thing lacking in Hamburg in the early 1960s was quality rock bands to get crowds into the clubs and excited enough to stay and spend money.

By a quirk of fate, a Hamburg club owner had asked Williams to supply bands, assuming the promoter would tap London for talent. The Beatles were becoming the leaders of a "Mersey Beat" sound, with a strong backbeat and harmonies, and catchy hooks, along with the likes of Gerry & The Pacemakers, the Searchers, and Cilla Black. With Williams's hometown music scene thriving, he had plenty of top-notch bands to draw from. Tony Sheridan helped set the tone with wild shows, covering early rock and roll favorites in drunken performances including sometimes mooning the audience.[42]

Only 15 years since the end of World War II, the Beatles landed in former enemy territory possibly partying with and being employed by former members of the Wehrmacht or their children. George, Paul, and John started their first Hamburg residency at 17, 18, and 20 years of age, respectively. The group had needed a drummer and tapped Liverpool's Pete Best. Sutcliffe filled in on bass in August 1960, and left the band to go back to school in 1961, only to suffer a sudden and tragic death due to a ruptured aneurysm in 1962.[43] McCartney took over on bass. They would have a three-and-a-half-month run in Hamburg at the end of 1960, another three-month stay in the middle of 1961, and a final two-week stretch in 1962.

In Hamburg, the band had been obligated to play for six- to eight-hour blocks of time per night, seven days a week. The Beatles quickly found "diet pills"—that is, speed. Biographer Mark Lewisohn estimated that on their longest stint in Germany, the band played some 415 hours in 14 weeks at the Kaiserkeller and the Star-Club.[44]

Those demands also forced the group to dig deep into their oeuvre. This included learning seemingly every rock and roll and R&B song that had been recorded to that point, as well as pop, country, even show tunes, and turning a song like Ray Charles's "What'd I Say" into an extended workout, *and* coming up with original jams.[45]

In Germany, the Beatles had the kind of fun many young men away from home for the first time tend to have, including indulging in free-flowing booze and running around with the women of Hamburg. Still, the demands of their gig actually spurred the Beatles to practice harder on their limited downtime so that they could provide as solid and as long of performances as possible. Their chemistry developed even further.[46]

The Beatles gained a reputation for not only playing great music but also for being raucous and unpredictable: Lennon would take advantage of the language barrier, at times swearing at and insulting the audience for the band's amusement or greeting the audience with "Heil, Hitler" and a Nazi salute. One friend recalled, "He'd pull out a black comb and pretend it was a moustache.... People laughed."[47]

In sum, in Lennon's words, "I was born in Liverpool, but I grew up in Hamburg."[48]

The Lennon and McCartney songwriting tandem continued to create original compositions, improving rapidly, and would become wildly prolific for the next seven years, virtually nonstop.

Brian Epstein of Liverpool signed on to manage the group, yet they were rejected by multiple record labels before Parlophone gave them a shot. There, producer George Martin's background was more in classical music and recording comedy albums, including those of band favorites, the Goon Squad, which gave Martin and the young rock and rollers an instant connection.

Martin had also then told John, Paul, and George that Best was not a good enough drummer for the recordings. Because of this and also feeling an apparent lack of chemistry with Best, the three decided to let him go. The group had already performed with top Liverpool drummer Ringo Starr (Richard Starkey) of Rory Storm and the Hurricane on a record backing Tony Sheridan, and he was asked to join, cementing the lineup.[49] The four quickly established a relationship akin to brothers. As McCartney put it, "We weren't the Beatles until we had all four Beatles." With Starr, Martin noted, their sound "really took off."[50]

Each Beatle also now sported the same iconic long, "bowl-cut" hairstyle, picked up at the suggestion of Hamburg photographer-artist friend Astrid Kirchherr. Something far out of line with societal norms of the time, the hairstyle broke out of rigid views of masculinity and conformity. While in Hamburg, the group members sported black leather jackets, but as their star rose, they took to matching suits on stage, an uncomfortable acquiescence to their label.

The Beatles—Stage One (Youthful Joy)

The American model of rock and roll to that point had been either a lone rebel or otherwise a vocal front for a star producer or songwriter. In the Beatles, Lennon and McCartney began writing original songs themselves, a first for a British rock band. They alternated on lead vocals on most songs, with Harrison singing on some and Starr usually one per album; the four would also harmonize to perfection. The Beatles were, as one writer put it, "a vision of self-sufficiency, interdependence, and shared ambition."[51] In their early interviews, in fact, the British press often simply attributed quotes to a collective "the Beatles."[52]

Their early recordings, coinciding with Dunbar's first stage, described as a burst of youthful joy, created enormous excitement in the United Kingdom. Lennon and McCartney's first compositions throughout 1963 and 1964 would be entirely focused on boy-girl love themes, including "Love Me Do," "Please Please Me," "She Loves You," "I Saw Her Standing There," and "I Want to Hold Your Hand." All were more expansive translations of their core American influences and especially the energy of the blues and R&B, turned into something else entirely; it was still strong and raucous but melodic and sensitive.[53]

The lyrics, too, were fairly simple though they avoided clichés. Some saw songs like "I Want to Hold Your Hand" as fluff, but fans were moved by their descriptions of, as one writer put it, "both the awkwardness and exhilaration of the first moments of physical intimacy."[54] Further, while the Beatles were able to sing *lyrics* of fairly innocent love, the music and the performances also boldly spoke to the physical and sexual tensions that helped define rock music. It was unabashed romanticism, yet raw and real and neither too soft nor too precious. Even the sweetest of pop choruses, such as McCartney's on "Please Please Me," could be emboldened by the subtly gritty, sexual undercurrent of Lennon's backup vocals urging on the girl and driving the song forward.

By November 4, 1963, the Beatles were the hottest group in England and they were tapped to play at the annual Royal Command Variety Performance charity gala in front of the royal family. How could the rising young representatives of the ongoing rock and roll rebellion, all still under 24 but otherwise proud Brits, handle an invitation into the heart of the upper-class establishment?[55] Could they avoid being co-opted by the older generation, without being nasty or unnecessarily disrespectful? Prior to closing out their set with an inspired cover of the Isley Brothers' blowout "Twist and Shout," Lennon took a moment to address the queen and the royal audience: "For our last number, I'd like to ask your help. Would the people in the cheaper seats clap your hands, and the rest of you, if you'll just rattle your jewelry."[56] It was pitch-perfect.

Less than three weeks later, on November 22, 1963, not yet two years into his term and, shockingly, President Kennedy was assassinated in Dallas, Texas, by what was determined to be lone gunman Lee Harvey Oswald. A nation and the entire world's presents and futures were turned upside-down. The United States came to a stop to mourn when Kennedy's services were broadcast on Monday, November 25. The only comparable events in modern U.S. history are the attack on Pearl Harbor in 1941, and the events of September 11, 2001. Suddenly, nothing seemed so sure in the world, not even an ability to protect the life of the leader of the free world. Conspiracy theories abounded. Kennedy's assassination was also a massive blow to the hopes of the ongoing civil rights causes that he and his supporters were advancing.

Ten weeks later, the Beatles flew to America to try to accomplish what British musical acts of the time did not even dream of, let alone four Scousers: to conquer America. On February 9, 1964, with a record-setting TV audience of 73 million people, the Beatles performed on the *Ed Sullivan Show*, driving the audience to hysterics with five songs, starting with "All My Lovin'" and closing with the hits "I Saw Her Standing There" and "I Want to Hold Your Hand."[57]

The Beatles represented a freedom and an excitement that millions of kids in America, and more than a few adults, were longing for. Squarely in the face of so much change, uncertainty, and dread, here was a focused, successful group of mates, clearly tight but maintaining their individuality, bold but not a gang of hoodlums, and clearly having the time of their lives. Where Elvis was already sinking under the weight of his intense fame and an entourage with many hangers-on and sycophants, the four Beatles were able to support and thrive off one another.

Despite having no road map for their career path and none being older than 23, each seemed to have an innate understanding of how to pull the rug out from under the expectations of pop culture fame and the media. They eschewed canned, mechanical responses as well as the traps that they had seen Presley fall into. In short, all four avoided false modesty, exaggerated sincerity, and platitudes and they undercut their own "importance."

McCartney closed the first U.S. press conference after being asked seemingly every inane biographical question possible: "We have a message.

4. Meet the Beatles and the Stones, 1959–1965

The Beatles on the *Ed Sullivan Show*, from left, Ringo Starr, Paul McCartney, John Lennon, and George Harrison. [New York] 1964. Bernard Gotfryd photograph collection (Library of Congress).

Our message is: buy more Beatles records!"[58] Although their humor was fairly typical of many of the lads of Liverpool at the time, they were nearly as funny as the top comedians of the day:

> **Press:** Will you sing something for us?
> **All four in unison:** *No!*
> **Lennon:** We need money first.
>
> * * *
>
> **Press:** In Detroit Michigan, they're handing out car stickers saying, "Stamp Out the Beatles."
> **McCartney:** Yeah well ... first of all, we're bringing out a 'Stamp Out Detroit' campaign.

While the Beatles didn't take themselves too seriously, they did take their art seriously, even beginning to incorporate avant-garde influences. The cover of their second album, *With the Beatles*, for example, was a black-and-white photo of four reserved, quite serious faces. As Lennon biographer Philip Norman wrote, "the demeaning" and limited view of rock and rollers being simply "proletarian vulgarity" suddenly "vanished forever."[59]

The Beatles live performances had an impact on teenage girls that surpassed even what Elvis Presley had wrought. Hysterical girls screamed through performances to the point that no one could even hear the music on the primitive sound systems of the '60s.

Certainly, coming out of a more conformist world of the 1950s, and under stricter controls and standards than boys as far as sexuality, young women were rebelling and claiming their sexual feelings. They knew that no one could stop what they thought or felt. Female fans could listen to Beatles records on their home phonographs in their bedrooms, with magazine photos and album covers. They could also completely throw themselves into the Fab Four emotionally and never have to fear the pains of actual breakups. Of course, the impact of the Beatles themselves and their music on male fans was over the top in its own way as well. In short, the Beatles expressed an emotional freedom and joy that they modeled for fans, giving them permission to do the same.

By 1964, the Beatles had taken over the pop charts in the United States and at home. Such was their enormity that when their tour finally found its way to Australia in June of that year, some 300,000 fans greeted them at the city center in Adelaide.[60]

The Beatles—Stage Two (Overcoming Societal Obstacles)

The Fab Four were quickly maturing young men in a world grappling with some epic struggles. As Lennon put it, "We have been Beatles as best we ever will be—those four jolly lads. But we're not those people anymore."[61] Partly inspired by folk rocker Bob Dylan, the group's second stage covered the albums *A Hard Day's Night* (1964), *Help!*, and *Rubber Soul* (both 1965). As Dunbar wrote, now their work "assail[ed] society's obstacles to spiritual development such as money in 'Can't Buy Me Love,' conformity in 'Nowhere Man,' and 'Think for Yourself'; prayerful call for 'Help,' while remaining inescapably hopeful that 'We Can Work it Out.'"[62]

By 1965, the Beatles were the focal point of a slew of British bands that had absorbed '50s American rock and roll and R&B influences, were taking it in unexpected and exciting directions, and were now returning it back to the States. Along with the Beatles and Stones, this so-called British Invasion included the Who, the Kinks, the Animals, the Hollies, Dusty Springfield, Herman's Hermits, the Zombies, and the Dave Clark Five, among others.[63]

Culturally, London had become "Swinging London" and the center of popular music and youth culture while pushing society in new directions. The music was the best and most popular pop music in the world. Men were sporting long hair and women miniskirts, and the shopping district on Carnaby Street had the hippest fashions. Young people attended new dance clubs and attended and watched live-music TV shows like *Ready Steady Go!*[64]

Another major force in rock at that time, and socially and culturally in the same stratosphere as the Beatles, was Bob Dylan. Dylan (b. 1941, Robert Zimmerman) was an American folk musician from Minnesota via Greenwich Village who learned to embrace rock and roll.

Bob Dylan

Bob Dylan would have a significant impact on the social movements of the time, and his music would become a guiding force, and even a conscience, for a burgeoning counterculture.

Dylan was born into a tight-knit Jewish community and family, with his parents and a live-in, wizened maternal grandmother, in Duluth, Minnesota. Dylan thus grew up in small-town America, but as Dylan recalled, it was also an era of constant fear and kids being told tales not just of imminent Russian bombs but imminent Russian paratroopers coming "to slit our throats and incinerate us." As he later explained, it was life under "a cloud of fear" that "robs a child of his spirit." His father did not understand his son or his artistic restlessness. The young Dylan ran away numerous times.[65]

As a teen, Dylan largely saw rock and roll as lightweight, while folk music resonated with him as the real stories of humankind. He started his folk career and soon moved to a thriving folk scene in New York City in 1961. Infatuated with folk–protest performer Woody Guthrie, Dylan even went to visit the elderly Guthrie that year in a psychiatric ward before the legend passed months later.[66]

In 1963, Dylan released two major folk-protest songs: "Masters of War" and "Blowin' in the Wind." The former was directly inspired by President Eisenhower's warning against the detrimental impact of the military-industrial complex's profit motives on American foreign policy.[67] Dylan turned folk music into something more biting, as he said of that song, "I don't sing songs which hope people will die, but I couldn't help it in this one. The song is a sort of striking out, a reaction to the last straw, a feeling of what can you do?"[68]

The melody for "Blowin' in the Wind" is rooted in an old slave spiritual, "No More Auction Block," which Dylan was playing in his live sets at the time.[69] The song would be adopted by both the civil rights movement and the anti-war movement.[70]

"Blowin' in the Wind" offered an answer to the question of how to end a seemingly unending cycle of war, poverty, and injustice and reflected both Eastern and Taoist philosophy as well as drawing inspiration from the Bible. The Taoist part was that the answer seemed amorphous but spiritual in nature.[71] That was also evident in the lyrics that echoed the biblical verse "They have eyes to see but see not; ears to hear, but hear not."[72] As Dylan had explained when the song first came out, "There ain't much I can say about this song, except the answer is blowin' in the wind. It ain't no book or movie or TV show or discussion group, man. It's in the wind."[73] That song was, in fact, one of three Dylan would perform at a 1997 Catholic Church congress in front of Pope John Paul II. Afterward, the pontiff told a crowd of some 300,000 that the answer to lead them to Christ was indeed "in the wind of the spirit."[74]

Dylan had a profound impact on the Beatles and seemingly every other songwriter of the time. Not only did Dylan help make folk and roots music integral to rock, but he inspired the Beatles to shift their focus from straight love songs and boy-girl relationships to serious introspection and weightier topics, helping to spur the Beatles' second thematic stage.

Lennon described Dylan's impact on him: "I'd started thinking about my own emotions.... Instead of projecting myself into a situation, I would try to express what I felt about myself."[75] Deeper introspection not only allowed for a greater understanding of one's self, but it helped keep the rock movement more grounded and more clear-eyed. It is a wisdom found throughout history. From the Bible: "Examine yourselves, whether ye be in the faith; prove your own selves. Know ye not your own selves, how that Jesus Christ is in you, except ye be reprobates?" And Aristotle: "Knowing yourself is the beginning of all wisdom." In psychotherapy, Carl Jung stated: "Your visions will become clear only when you can look into your own heart. Who looks outside, dreams; who looks inside, awakes."[76]

The Beatles' own albums released in 1965, *Help!* and *Rubber Soul*, had moved them forward from the *yeah-yeah-yeahs* and wanting to hold hands, to address topics of materialism ("Can't Buy Me Love"), conformity ("Nowhere Man"), and more complicated aspects of relationships (e.g., "You Won't See Me"). Lennon's very personal cry on "Help!" reflects his dealing with the exciting but intense fishbowl life at the center of Beatlemania and also representing a universal need for emotional support.[77] It wasn't widely known at the time, but Bob Dylan had introduced the Beatles to pot in a hotel room in August 1964, and the Brits had been regular users since. Pot would then have a significant influence on the making of the Beatles' next record, *Rubber Soul*.[78]

Once Dylan understood the power of rock music, he had a conversion of sorts and made a controversial decision to "go electric" in 1965. On "Maggie's Farm," he declared himself free of the confines and expectations

4. Meet the Beatles and the Stones, 1959–1965

of the folk community.[79] Dylan released his first electric rock record with side one of *Bringing It All Back Home* in March 1965, and all of *Highway 61 Revisited* that August.

Bringing It All Back Home burst with originality, especially in opening the door for more poetic themes and lyrics in rock.[80] Prime examples included the stream-of-consciousness, spoken-word romp "Subterranean Homesick Blues," the surreal humor of "Bob Dylan's 115th Dream," and the paranoid lament "It's Alright, Ma (I'm Only Bleeding)." On "It's Alright, Ma," Dylan sings of feeling trapped in a thoroughly commercialized world, though he also manages to find some peace of mind for himself. As author Paul Williams described it, Dylan saw the worst issue of the times as being beyond politics because "we are all being fed a false picture of reality, and it's coming at us from every direction."[81] People related.

Dylan would describe the societal shift he saw in the '60s in his 2004 memoir:

> The dominant myth of the day seemed to be that anybody could do anything, even go to the moon. You could do whatever you wanted—in the ads and in the articles, ignore your limitations, defy them. If you were an indecisive person, you could become leader and wear lederhosen. If you were a housewife, you could become a glamour girl with rhinestone sunglasses. Are you slow-witted? No worries—you can be an intellectual genius. If you're old, you can be young. Anything was possible. It was almost like a war against the self.[82]

On *Highway 61 Revisited*, Dylan toured the heart of America, using imagery alternately vivid, murky, and surreal. America's Highway 61 actually starts in Dylan's hometown of Duluth, and moving southward it connects with cities key to the history of the blues, including St. Louis, Memphis, and New Orleans, as well as Clarksdale and the rest of the Mississippi Delta. Dylan recruited guitarist Michael Bloomfield of the Paul Butterfield Blues Band for an album with fresh takes on traditional blues and the new blues rock (e.g., "It Takes a Lot to Laugh, It Takes a Train to Cry," "Tombstone Blues," "From a Buick 6") as well as folk rock ("Queen Jane Approximately") and garage rock ("Like a Rolling Stone," "Highway 61 Revisited"). Lyrically, Dylan uses borrowed blues lyrics throughout, along with making numerous literary, historical, and biblical references.

Starting sometime in the 1890s, the itinerant, Black, Delta bluesman had been newly emancipated yet not actually welcome anywhere, save the hardscrabble, futureless life of a sharecropper or places like the brutal levee and lumber camps. Hence, themes of dislocation and struggle to find one's self and one's place in the world were common in songs like Muddy Waters' "Rollin' Stone" or Robert Johnson's "Walkin' Blues" (later covered by both Son House and Waters).[83] These blues expressed a depth of humanity and emotion that in 1965, Dylan and so much of America's youth were yearning for.

The title of the album's most famous track and a regular candidate for the greatest rock song ever, "Like a Rolling Stone," echoes Clarksdale-native Waters' song, though Dylan got the title from a line in Hank Williams's "Lost Highway."[84] Here, Dylan sings of a woman born of privilege but whom he sees as inauthentic and having lost her way. The song is rumored to have been inspired by the ill-fated Edie Sedgwick, a friend of Dylan's and a star of Andy Warhol's experimental films. Sedgwick would die of a heroin overdose in 1971 at age 28.[85] The song is also a commentary on America at large and possibly on Dylan himself. One observer of *Highway 61* noted that the record was "the first inclination that the Age of Aquarius was not all peace and love."[86] Dylan also, again, asked the most pressing question with regard to the greater arc of Western civilization: (paraphrasing) How are you *feeling*?

Dylan became a countercultural figurehead, essentially on the level of Lennon and McCartney, and many wanted to bestow on him the unofficial title of "Spokesperson of His Generation." Dylan well understood, however, and as the Beatles had, that as soon as someone gave another that much power in their own lives, the whole enterprise was doomed. As late as 1969, even *Rolling Stone* founder and editor Jann Wenner would be having a hard time letting go of Dylan as the man with "The Answer." From a November 1969 interview:

> **WENNER:** Many people—writers, college students, college writers, all felt tremendously affected by your music and what you're saying in the lyrics.
> **DYLAN:** Did they?
> **WENNER:** Sure. They felt it had a particular relevance to their lives.... I mean you must be aware of the way that people come on to you.
> **DYLAN:** Not entirely. Why don't you explain it to me.
> **WENNER:** I guess if you reduce it to its simplest terms the expectation of your audience—the portion of your audience that I'm familiar with—feels that you have the answer.
> **DYLAN:** What answer?[87]

The Early Stones

Mick Jagger and Keith Richards were both born in 1943, just outside London, in Dartford, England. It was another area hit especially hard in the war, as it sat right in the flight line of the Luftwaffe's attacks on London. The town had even garnered the nickname "The Graveyard." Richards later recalled, "After the war was over—my first memory actually is looking up in the sky and sort of pointing up and my mom saying, 'It's

4. Meet the Beatles and the Stones, 1959–1965

a Spitfire.'"[88] Jagger would later reference those chaotic conditions in the opening line of "Jumping Jack Flash."[89]

Jagger, "Mike" to his family, was four years older than his only sibling, his brother Chris, in a solidly middle-class family. The boys' mother, Eva, was a hairdresser and their father, Joe, was a physical education teacher and an expert of note; he was even a key figure in bringing basketball to England, having written a book on the subject.[90]

Joe had come from a strict, nondrinking Baptist family and instilled the same strict and regimented values in his own family. One of Mick's early friends characterized Joe as a "very demanding, unyielding person."[91] Young Mick could expect a spank or a slap if he left the house before performing his daily exercise regimen, something enforced into his teens.

Moving into young adulthood, Mick had a strained relationship with his parents. Paul McCartney once recalled with surprise the deep anger and disgust Mick seemed to have toward the older generation and especially toward his parents.[92] Still, Mick would later comment that he had come to appreciate that his father had taught him "how to apply myself and how to distribute myself."[93]

Mick and Keith were schoolmates at Wentworth Primary School from 1950 to 1954, until Mick passed the eleven-plus and transferred to Dartford Grammar School and the friends fell out of touch.[94]

Keith Richards was the only child of Bert and Doris Richards and grew up in a working-class home in Dartford. It was a decidedly tough neighborhood, with much of it still rubble from the war. Richards himself later once described it simply as "shit."[95]

Bert had been injured in Normandy and worked as a supervisor in a factory, getting up at 5:00 a.m. and returning, always exhausted, at 6:00 p.m. Doris was 33 when she had Keith, her only child, doing so for the explicit, stated purpose of avoiding wartime work. As a child, Richards was, in his words, "fearful and timid" and the family home an "emotional cold war."[96] The Richards parents would separate and divorce when Keith was 18.[97]

Richards's mother had, however, introduced him to the sounds of great American jazz performers such as Billie Holiday, Louis Armstrong, and Duke Ellington. He learned guitar from his maternal grandfather, Theodore Augustus "Gus" Dupree, who had been a sax player until his lungs were burned by chlorine gas in World War I.[98]

The story goes that since Keith had been about six, he would visit his grandfather, and there would always be a guitar sitting on his piano, though he'd never even mention it to Keith. Keith didn't know it at the time, but Dupree only brought the guitar out for Keith's visits. After about six years of this, Keith finally did ask about the guitar, and Dupree gladly let him check it out. "Never tried to force it on me at all," Richards recalled.[99]

Dupree gave his grandson a few pointers and encouraged him as well: "I mean, it must have been *appalling*. And every time, he would pretend he liked the way I played it, and so, wow, I'm turnin' my granddad on—which is an amazing way of teaching things."[100]

Richards was never a motivated student at school, and when he heard "Heartbreak Hotel" in 1956, that was it. His first guitar idol was Elvis Presley's guitarist Scott "Scotty" Moore, soon to be followed by the man who would be his be-all and end-all in rock guitar, Chuck Berry.[101]

One day in 1961, 18-year-olds Jagger and Richards ran into each other again on a train. The pair quickly discovered that along with being huge rock fans, both were also more specifically devout fans of the blues and R&B and especially the artists at Chess Records. Jagger, in fact, was already a part of the label's tiny fan base in England and was receiving mail-order records from Chicago.[102]

Both had been enamored with Berry, Presley, and Little Richard and then searched to see where those guys had found their sound. The pair would then be turned on to the Delta blues of Jimmy Reed, Elmore James, Bo Diddley, Muddy Waters, and Little Walter.[103]

This was at a time when England was rife with its own second-rate rockers and the overall state of American rock had become bland; Richards recalled the top ten hits of the time as "intensely boring."[104]

By the end of sixth form (akin to precollege in U.S. terms), Mick had become bored with school. Even though admitted to the prestigious London School of Economics, Jagger dropped out to pursue music full time. Richards also committed full time, and partially as a result, he fell out of touch with his father; Keith would not see him for another twenty years.[105]

The founder of the Rolling Stones, Brian Jones, born in 1942, was a troubled kid from Cheltenham. Jones was a talented guitarist/multi-instrumentalist and would be the group's lead guitarist until his drug-related drowning in 1969.[106]

Jones also came from a well-to-do, middle-class family and had a musical background. At 16, Jones impregnated his 13-year-old girlfriend and ran away from home, guitar in hand. By the time he was 24, he would have four children with four different women.[107]

Jones first met Richards and Jagger at the Ealing Club in West London, where a small group of blues fanatics from the area congregated. The three moved into a cheap flat together in 1962.[108] The young British bluesmen were glad to have a place to play, while the notion of ever making a living with traditional blues music was scarcely imaginable. That all changed when the Beatles hit the U.K. charts in 1963. Like the Cavern Club to the north, more London clubs opened up to the new rock and R&B sound.

Jagger, Richards, and Jones had already played their first show together at the Marquee Club in June 1962 and, in April 1963, started a residency at the Crawdaddy Club. There, they met their rhythm section of bassist Bill Wyman and drummer Charlie Watts, who were also steeped in jazz; it was also where future members of the group the Yardbirds were hanging out and playing as well, including future guitar luminary Eric Clapton.[109]

The Stones and the Beatles started with the same basic musical template, but although the Beatles could rock out, they had more of a focus on melodies and vocal harmonies and, later, the psychedelic movement. Meanwhile, the Stones focused more on the heavier and harder electric blues and R&B of Chicago. The young Beatles would be thought more of as relative innocents and hopeless romantics, while the Stones were the "bad boys."

In truth, the Beatles' members' lifestyles were not *completely* different from the Stones' as far as indulging in eager sex partners/groupies and significant drug and alcohol use. Ultimately, though, the Beatles were embraced as utterly culture changing but still lovable, while the Stones actively cultivated and played up their not-undeserved reputation as rather dangerous and more than a little debauched.

In the '60s and later, the press would play up the bands as rivals, but despite some minor slights toward one another that ended up in the headlines, the bands were always friendly and would remain so. As the Beatles' star first began to rise, they announced the Stones to the press as the new, heavier sound coming out of London. They even gave the Stones one of their Lennon and McCartney compositions to record for themselves, "I Wanna Be Your Man," the Stones' first hit.[110]

As for their sound, Jones and Richards strayed from the standard lead guitar flash, overlaying a staid rhythm guitar. Instead, the pair wove their two guitars together, recalling the dense, driving sound of Muddy Waters' band, while also drawing heavily from Chuck Berry and Robert Johnson. Charlie Watts was originally a jazz drummer, and he and Wyman idealized Count Basie's rhythm section. Thus, the Stones, as Richards would later say, were able "to fly, to move and to swing" and not just "hit you on the head."[111] Ian Stewart's boogie piano helped shape the sound initially, although he was dropped as a regular member of the band early on, becoming the band's road manager while supplying some keyboards over the years.[112]

Fronting the band, Jagger had a deep appreciation for African American R&B singers. Although not possessing a classically great voice, he could deftly change his approach from song to song.[113] Jagger also quickly became a sex symbol, pushing limits by simultaneously drawing from both James Brown's bold sexuality as well as Little Richard's more flamboyant and androgynous style. Such unapologetic, sexual swagger completely undermined the then–British establishment's moral code.

The Stones' first albums, from 1963 to 1965, were heavy on cover songs, including multiple Chuck Berry covers, a bold interpretation of the Willie Dixon–written "I Just Want to Make Love to You" that Howlin' Wolf had made famous, and a New Orleans soul song, "Time Is on My Side." They also pulled from American soul of the mid-1960s, covering songs by Solomon Burke and Marvin Gaye. Like Lennon and McCartney, Richards' and Jagger's songwriting abilities would evolve rapidly.

The Stones' early self-composed singles included stirring melodic work in songs like "As Tears Go By" (1965), an affecting goodbye to youthful innocence, the dark exoticism of "Paint It Black" (1966), highlighted by Jones's sitar, and being sexually forward on songs like "Get Off My Cloud" (1965) and "Let's Spend the Night Together" (1967).

The Stones' live shows had an "aura of frenzied excitement," replete with fainting girls and brawling and rioting boys.[114] The group simply conveyed a genuine sense of danger. Their first manager, Andrew Oldham, played up the image even more for marketing purposes, famously asking the press, "Would you let your daughter marry a Rolling Stone?"[115]

In 1965, Jagger and Richards' original compositions had begun to hit home. "Play with Fire" was stirring and smoldering. Their biggest hit, "(I Can't Get No) Satisfaction," was driven by Richards' brilliant opening riff. It was the power of the Delta through a chiming British Invasion sound and distorted by a Gibson fuzzbox, making it all sound fresh and electrifying. While Richards got the listener's attention, Jagger's vocals connected with dissatisfied and anxious youth around the world. "Satisfaction" struck a nerve socially for its commentary on the increasing emptiness of a consumer culture. Even more so, as author Steven Appleford put it, it was the "sound of testosterone boiling over, Jagger demanding sexual healing, Richards' fuzzy guitar a fucking ball of nerves."[116]

The next biggest act on the London scene at the time was the Who, who also brought a harder take on American R&B. By 1965, guitarist Pete Townshend would strike power chords with a trademark, hard, windmill motion of his arm, and the group would regularly smash their gear at the end of shows.[117] A live–British TV performance of "I Can't Explain" and their end-of-song destruction helped put them in the spotlight.[118]

Later that year, "My Generation" made the Who stars. At the time, a British youth subculture called "mods" (from *jazz modernists*) had taken shape as a contrast to the leather-jacketed rocker style derived from the '50s. Mods valued a new look, which included fashionable suits despite not being upper-class kids, and new sounds, more based on soul and R&B.

4. Meet the Beatles and the Stones, 1959–1965

The Rolling Stones performing in West Berlin, front to back, Brian Jones, Mick Jagger, and Keith Richards (not visible: Charlie Watts) [West Germany], 1965 (dpa picture alliance/Alamy Stock Photo).

On "My Generation," Pete Townshend's driving guitar and Keith Moon's crashing drums are interrupted only by John Entwistle's wild bass flourishes and a solo. Singer Roger Daltrey saw an older generation that judged them as immoral, on drugs, and even dumb as out of touch and jealous. More famously, Daltrey sang that dying young might be preferable to the lives being lived by the older Brits.[119] Although, the Who themselves weren't mods, the mods adopted "My Generation" as their anthem.

The year 1965 was the height of the Swinging London era, with the Beatles at the center. It scarcely seemed that the Beatles could get any bigger, but they would. It was unprecedented that four young men from modest backgrounds could have such a powerful impact on such a mass scale, musically and beyond.

For many of the West and the world's youth, however, the peace-and-love optimism of the Beatles could give way to something darker and more aligned with the Stones' outlook. There had, of course, just been the near-miss of the Cuban Missile Crisis and thermonuclear war seemed only one human mistake away and very possibly, it seemed, inevitable. If there was a Christian God, He did not seem to be making Himself very evident. Seemingly, the world's greatest hope for peace and a new and better future, John F. Kennedy, was gone, while the United States (and a few allies) was already well into another war of choice in Vietnam.

5

Cultural Checkpoints: The United States, ca. 1965

Politics/War

The Vietnam War: Along with the civil rights movement, the Vietnam War would most define America's changing relationship with authority in the '60s.

The Southeast Asian nation of Vietnam had endured a century of French colonization, Japanese occupation during World War II, and then going back to French control after that. In 1954, Marxist-Leninist revolutionary Ho Chi Minh, operating from the north of the country, led forces that expelled the French. At the Geneva Conference that year, Vietnam was arbitrarily divided by the world powers into a communist North and noncommunist South, at the 17th Parallel, a compromise expected to be temporary.[1]

With Cold War tensions high, the United States feared the Chinese and Soviets would force communism into South Vietnam. A few years earlier, President Eisenhower had famously set out the "domino theory" in which communism could gain momentum and spread from country to country, gathering power and resources along the way.[2] The longer countries fell, the harder it would all be to stop, not unlike it had been with the Nazis.[3]

In 1955, Eisenhower sent aid via military advisers and machinery to the southern Vietnamese, and Kennedy would continue the same as well as send special forces.[4] During the 1964 presidential campaign, incumbent Democrat Lyndon Johnson of Texas (who had been Kennedy's vice president) established himself as the deescalation candidate, along with a plan for a "Great Society" that would end poverty and racial injustice.[5] Johnson won in a landslide.[6]

In August 1964, the destroyers U.S.S. *Maddox* and U.S.S. *Turnery Joy* were allegedly fired on by three North Vietnamese patrol torpedo boats in two hazy incidents in the Tonkin Gulf, international waters just off the coast of North Vietnam. It was later determined that the incidents may have been mischaracterized, though there was no evidence that Johnson had done so intentionally.[7]

Johnson went to Congress for approval of military action, again claiming he sought "no wider war," although that was patently untrue. With no formal declaration of war, the U.S. Congress authorized Johnson to "take all necessary measures to repel any armed attack against forces of the United States and to prevent further aggression."[8]

In February 1965, the United States launched full-scale combat and a "police action," with those in power believing Vietnam would be quick work.[9] Despite the nation's massive technological and financial advantages, several factors would stymie if not doom the effort. The United States limited its tactics to avoid an escalation of events that would draw the Soviets and China into combat and it badly underestimated both the Vietcong's well-honed guerrilla tactics in the jungles and its willingness to absorb astonishing casualty rates in defending themselves from outsiders.[10] The war would last a decade.

By January 1966, the United States would have 181,000 troops in the theater of operations.[11] In March 1966, 56 percent of Americans supported Johnson's policies on the war and only 26 percent opposed.[12]

The Draft: The military draft existed in different forms throughout the war, while draft exemptions were obtained based on college enrollment, marital status, being married with children, and preexisting medical conditions. Money and both political and personal connections could further increase a person's ability to, for example, find a friendly doctor who could sign off on medical exemptions or, if not avoid serving at all, at least avoid dangerous combat assignments. Reporter and historian David Halberstam noted that as many Harvard graduates won Pulitzer Prizes for journalism covering Vietnam as died there.[13]

It was understood that both African Americans and poorer people in general were drafted and killed in combat at higher rates than whites. That was partly addressed by the Pentagon with a draft lottery in 1969.[14]

In 1968, Creedence Clearwater Revival, a San Francisco–area roots-rock band, released "Fortunate Son," a hit record that has been synonymous with the Vietnam War and the draft ever since.[15] John Fogerty wrote and sang the song. Fogerty himself had been drafted in 1965, though he was able to get into the reserves and he served six months of active duty stateside.[16]

The song is swamp rock in overdrive, with a fiery Fogerty calling out the hypocrisy of a privileged political class and wealthy elite. Fogerty derides those calling themselves patriots yet making no sacrifice themselves and profiting off the backs and the blood of the underclass.[17] Fogerty later explained that by 1968, he had believed few soldiers knew why they were even going to the war zone, beyond some vague concept of "dominoes." Most, Fogerty thought, believed that it was about politics and money.[18]

The name of the song refers to the son of a senator who stands in for all of the privileged families that did not have to play by the same rules as everyone else. Fogerty had David Eisenhower specifically in mind, who was the son of a former president and whose father-in-law was President Nixon. Fogerty knew the younger Eisenhower had zero chance of ever serving in combat, and he did not.[19] Fogerty's voice sears when he mocks the personal anthem for the president of the United States, "Hail to the Chief."

And Fogerty wasn't wrong. College and medical deferments were common for certain parts of society. Notably, future presidents Bill Clinton, George W. Bush, Donald Trump, and Joe Biden, as well as Bush's co-architect of the oft-maligned Iraq War (2003–2011), former vice president Dick Cheney, all used various manipulations, special connections, and numerous and suspect deferments to avoid serving in Vietnam.[20]

Clinton, who protested the war as a student, managed to work the draft system by submitting a letter of intent to join the Army Reserve Officers' Training Corps (ROTC), keeping him safe, only to later withdraw his letter so that he could instead take his much better chances with the coming draft lottery system. His number was not called.[21] Bush, the son of then-serving Texas congressman and later senator and president George H.W. Bush, ended up flying part time for the National Guard out of his hometown of Houston for the duration of the war.[22] Biden, Cheney, and Trump each obtained five or six medical and student deferments and never served. Biden and Trump, in fact, obtained medical deferments while both had been active athletes in high school.[23]

Meanwhile, others who avoided the draft—some leaving for Canada—were derisively labeled "draft dodgers."[24]

Civil Rights

Church Bombing: In September 1963, the predominantly African American 16th Street Baptist Church in Birmingham, Alabama, a rallying place for organizing civil rights activities, was bombed by the Ku Klux Klan, killing four young, Black girls.[25]

Freedom Summer: The following summer, college students from the North worked with southern Black activists to educate and increase voter participation of southern Blacks to combat baseless and discriminatory voting rules. In June, three activists—two white men from the North, Michael Schwerner and Andrew Goodman, and a Black man from Mississippi, James Chaney—were kidnapped and murdered.[26]

Selma: In March 1965, Martin Luther King, Jr., helped to organize 600 freedom marchers to walk from Selma to Montgomery, Alabama, to highlight civil rights and voting issues. At the Edmund Pettus Bridge, Alabama, state troopers attacked marchers with whips, nightsticks, tear gas, and dogs, which was televised and shown around the world.[27] Ultimately, Congress would pass the Voting Rights Act of 1965.

Free Speech

Berkeley Protests: In September 1964, the school administration at the University of California in Berkeley banned student groups from disseminating information on a small piece of campus property.[28] Students moved to other campus locations and began protests.[29]

A change in the law had meant that college students previously treated by school administrators under in loco parentis now enjoyed First Amendment rights to speech and assembly. (An aside, the voting age would later similarly be dropped from 21 to 18 with the 26th Amendment in 1971, mainly due to the seemingly inherent absurdity of persons being old enough to be drafted to sacrifice their lives in combat but not have a voice in elections.[30]) Students found a voice to speak on civil rights, opposition to the war, and the increasing corporate control over society.[31] Student leader Mario Savio gave a fiery and memorable speech, including the line, "And you've got to put your bodies upon the gears and upon the wheels, upon the levers, upon all the apparatus, and you've got to make it stop!"[32]

Students took over Sproul Hall until President Kerr called in police to have them forcibly removed. Ultimately, though, the university recognized the students' rights to free speech on campus.[33]

In the rest of the state, older and more conservative Californians generally saw the movement as representing a basic lack of respect for authority. Former successful B-movie actor and former president of the Screen Actors Guild Ronald Reagan was elected governor of California in 1966. Reagan promised to restore capital punishment, crack down on obscenity, and punish Berkeley's rebel students.[34] Reagan would go on to become the face of modern conservatism and a two-term president in the 1980s.

Still, the Bay Area was becoming the scene of a new movement, not only socially but also where rock music would have its next major transformation.

6

The Freaks of Haight-Ashbury, 1965–1966

By the mid-'60s, the Fab Four and the rest of the British Invasion had reconfigured possibly America's greatest cultural export, rock and roll, and brought it back as something even more powerful and dynamic. The Beatles were the biggest pop stars on the planet, as well as a focal point for the youth of the West and beyond, socially and culturally, and even inspiring activism and political involvement.

Rock music was central to a new, youth-driven subculture taking shape around the world and a new approach to life that either boldly or recklessly, depending on one's view, challenged the reigning status quo. This mass movement would become most embodied by a group that would be known as "the hippies."

The physical roots of the hippies began with a group of American poets turned conscientious objectors who were interned in Oregon during World War II. After the war, many first migrated to the North Beach neighborhood of San Francisco.

Around the same time, a so-called Beat generation was taking shape in New York in the 1940s. Beat originally meant "weary," though to Beat writer Jack Kerouac, Beats were also "beautiful in an ugly graceful new way."[1] Artistic, bohemian-type Beats first formed a scene of a few thousand in New York's postwar Greenwich Village.

The Beats congregated in bars, coffee shops, and jazz clubs. As a group, they were disaffected and opposed industrial capitalism's consumer culture, government bureaucracies, and establishment attitudes toward sex and drugs.[2] As a result, detractors sometimes mockingly referred to the group as the pseudo-Russian-sounding "beatniks."[3]

The Beats further prized authenticity and individualism and saw jazz, sex, drugs, and Buddhist practices as forms of purification.[4] Beat philosophies were represented by three prominent Beat poets and writers in particular.

William S. Burroughs (1914–1997) was a Harvard-educated poet whose first novel, *Junkie* (1953), was a semiautobiographical and raw account of the life of a heroin addict.[5]

Allen Ginsberg (1926–1997) came of age in the 1940s as a gay man at a time when Sigmund Freud had already declared such an orientation to be a sickness and where society simply referred to them as "perverts."[6] His public reading of the scandalous and part-peyote (a hallucinogen)-influenced poem "Howl" in 1955 in San Francisco first garnered the Beats wider attention.[7]

Jack Kerouac (1922–1969) dropped out of Columbia University to be a novelist. He used a spontaneous and methamphetamine-fueled writing style to recount his open-road adventures across the United States in the '40s, resulting in the hugely influential novel *On the Road* (1957).[8] One of the key characters in the book was based on Kerouac's real-life friend Neal Cassady. Cassady embodied Beat cool: rugged but literate, a free spirit and rebel, and traveling around and experiencing America with open eyes and a fresh perspective.

As to drug use, the Beats had come on the heels of the drug culture of the 1940s Harlem jazz scene of primarily pot and heroin.[9] All of the primary Beat writers drank and many were heavily into marijuana and other drugs, including heroin and methamphetamines. The Beats were thus part of a drug culture before such a thing had entered a broader national consciousness.[10]

In the mid-'50s, Beats migrated to western locales, and Kerouac and Ginsberg settled temporarily in North Beach.[11] Others of the movement moved to Los Angeles, New Orleans, and various other college towns.[12]

Those Beat writers would provide some of the philosophical underpinnings for the future hippies and rock musicians. Lennon and McCartney, members of the Velvet Underground, the Grateful Dead, David Bowie, and others all acknowledged a major Beat influence and *On the Road* in particular. Bob Dylan said of the book, "It changed my life like it changed everyone else's."[13] Jerry Garcia of the Grateful Dead talked about the spirit of Kerouac as being a part of the "Dead" experience: "That's what motivates the audience. The spirit of being able to go out and have an adventure in America at large."[14] A teenage blues-rock singer, Janis Joplin, was not fitting in as a conventional person or as a traditionally "pretty" girl in her East Texas hometown of Port Arthur. *On the Road* inspired Joplin to leave Texas for San Francisco in 1963.[15] In her biography about Joplin, Alice Echola noted a similar Beat influence across the country:

Mass-circulation magazine stories about beatniks invariably vilified or ridiculed them, often calling into question the masculinity of the men. These articles may have scared off most Americans, but they also alerted all those kids who felt like mutants in fifties America to an alternative existence.[16]

San Francisco seemed to be a community where "mutants" and other fringe types were not only being accepted but were thriving.

California had been the farthest destination of the original western pioneers as well as the most socially open and progressive state, not to mention the home of Hollywood and much of the music business. In less urbanized Northern California, the culture was more in tune with a back-to-nature lifestyle, and San Francisco and Berkeley already had strong folk music scenes.

In the 1950s, to cut commute times, the city of San Francisco had proposed that a freeway be built that would cut through the neighborhood known as Haight-Ashbury, named for the intersection of Haight and Ashbury Streets, and only a few miles from North Beach. In opposition, locals in "the Haight" formed the Haight-Ashbury Neighborhood Council in 1959 and eventually fought off the development for good.[17]

In the early '60s, the Haight was a relatively low-income, cheap-rent neighborhood comprised of old Victorian homes, which drew the Oregon transplants, college students from nearby San Francisco State University, college dropouts, and other countercultural types. A massive Victorian or Edwardian house built after the earthquake of 1906 could be rented for $120 and split among numerous housemates.[18]

The precise origins of the "hippie" moniker are not entirely clear. "Hip," "hipster," and then "hippie" had been referenced in various places, with "hip" being "cool" or "aware," though African American musicians in jazz circles of the '30s and '40s also used "hipster" to humorously describe white jazz wannabees.[19] According to author Charles Perry, the Beat poets used the term to describe Bay Area bohemians they saw as "junior grade hipsters."[20]

The manager of the Rolling Stones, Andrew Loog Oldham, also used the term "hippies" in text on the cover of the Stones' 1965 U.S. release of *The Rolling Stones, Now!* The Oldham reference would be more in line with the young people that would oppose the mainstream, including opposing the Vietnam War and runaway capitalism, and supporting more open attitudes socially, including toward sex and drugs.[21] Ultimately, the media popularized the term "hippie" in describing the countercultural movement centered on San Francisco and specifically in Haight-Ashbury.[22]

The early hippies did not necessarily appreciate the term, as it was a media label and often used dismissively or derisively such as to mean someone out of touch with the realities of life. Many hippies preferred their own term, "freaks," meaning people proudly living far outside of and in opposition to a status quo seen as broken and repressed but that passed for normalcy.[23] The hippie/freak cohort generally also adopted the monikers of "love generation" or "flower children" to highlight their focus on peace and beauty.[24] With regard to love, though, distinctions between love and sex could be murky or even nonexistent; both often fell under the phrase "free love."[25]

Hippies were young, middle class, and 97 percent white, and though never a majority, as a part of the baby boomer generation, they existed in large numbers.[26] In short, hippies saw Western society as emotionally stunted and overintellectualized. Where Western, Judeo-Christian traditions emphasized the uniqueness of the individual—that is, individualism/the Bill of Rights—in practice, it was seen as too often being twisted around to justify domination and greed. This included a Manifest Destiny, colonialism, slavery, segregation, and a capitalist economic system run amok.

Many hippies developed philosophical underpinnings borrowed from the Beats and others, such as the French existentialists Albert Camus and Jean-Paul Sartre and Eastern religious philosophies.[27] Ultimately, though, hippies were more about promoting an authentic, truer individual spirit that could still unite communities than it was about a particular philosophical bent.[28]

The Haight community largely removed itself from the straight world, and residents often declined to pursue careers and income in traditional ways. Those with full-time jobs and occasional part-time work or who came from money tended to sustain things, but money was only needed to support a minimalist lifestyle. This maximized time for art, literature, music, activism, hanging out in coffee shops, as well as doing drugs and being much more sexually active than their parents. Thrift stores sold secondhand and cheaper clothes instead of mass-consumer brands and represented various classic styles, including nostalgic Edwardian and Victorian.[29]

Alcohol was used more liberally by the younger generation (though with less media attention than other drugs[30]), but the hippie lifestyle really became near synonymous with smoking marijuana.[31] Illegally selling pot brought up from Mexico was a significant, informal economic engine for Haight-Ashbury hippies. There was plenty of additional demand from the local college kids at San Francisco State, but since the middle-class pot smokers had no reason to risk criminal penalties, hippies filled the void.[32]

Early on, hippies also embraced the hallucinogen peyote, long a crucial sacrament among Native Americans, and ordered from cactus farms in Texas.[33] The new hallucinogen LSD was about to become popular as well, which would strongly influence hippie philosophies as well as the rock music being made at the time. That is to say, things were about to get weird.

In 1943, the Swiss researcher Albert Hofmann accidentally ingested a tiny amount of a respiratory and circulatory stimulant, lysergic acid diethylamide, later to be called LSD or just acid.[34] Hofmann quickly discovered the hallucinogenic qualities of the drug and experienced the first acid "trip." As he would go on to write,

> In a dreamlike state, with eyes closed (I found the daylight to be unpleasantly glaring), I perceived an uninterrupted stream of fantastic pictures, extraordinary shapes with intense, kaleidoscopic play of colors. After some two hours this condition faded away.[35]

Three days later, Hofmann isolated LSD as the likely cause for his experience and he continued to self-experiment with higher doses to similar and greater results.[36]

In the mid- and late '40s, psychiatrists used LSD in an attempt to treat psychosis, something no drug had ever seemed to help. In the late '40s and the '50s, the U.S. Army and the CIA conducted experiments with the drug and other hallucinogens in part to find a truth serum and to otherwise counter the rumored use of LSD in interrogations of U.S. soldiers captured in Korea.[37] Further, the bizarre MK-ULTRA program (1953–1964) saw the CIA dose civilians and military people without their knowledge to see how they reacted.[38]

Many initial LSD researchers saw a virtual miracle drug with transcendent emotional and psychological qualities. Between 1943 and 1970, LSD became, according to one scholar, "the most intensively researched pharmacological substance ever."[39]

As Hofmann had attested, the LSD experience was a consuming and transformative one for the user, with visual distortions and even hallucinations. The drug also seemed to offer a glimpse into the depths of one's being, almost as if poking a hole through all of one's accumulated neuroses, anxieties, and illusions to see a world beyond those entanglements. Charles Perry called it "recovering childhood's lost 'tense of presence.'"[40] And whatever it was underneath all of that, it seemed to connect with *everything* else, including other people, nature, and even the universe itself. Many users most certainly believed they had profound experiences that increased their ability to see the world's truer nature, though the drug generally wore off some 6–15 hours later.[41]

The LSD experience was entirely different than the effects of alcohol, pot, cocaine, or heroin. Acid can potentially cause emotional and psychological harms and it can be abused, but it is not physically addictive. The other four mentioned drugs can also be abused and cause adverse psychological effects, but all but marijuana are also very much physically addictive.

Pot was relaxing, could leave one in a bit of a haze, and could also leave users feeling lethargic. Alcohol lowered social inhibitions as well as clouding judgment and stunting impulse control. Cocaine was euphoric but would also result in a crash. Heroin initially brought on an intense, "warm, glowing sensation," though it would also lead to a crash and devastating withdrawals.[42]

Also, from the perspective of the drug's proponents, LSD's altered state of consciousness was in line with other traditional psychological, religious, and spiritual practices as well. Carl Jung, the renowned twentieth-century psychoanalyst, for example, had written of a necessity to "surrender consciously to the power of the unconscious" so as to drop a "mask" used to deal with childhood and adolescence and then engage in a slow process of "creative self-realization."[43] LSD, to many, seemed to allow for some level of unmasking and immediately, albeit temporarily.

In the early '60s, the major LSD advocates included Harvard-trained psychologist Timothy Leary, acclaimed author and intellectual Aldous Huxley (*A Brave New World*, 1932), and another early proponent, Al Hubbard. They were soon joined by others, such as Ginsberg and author Ken Kesey (*One Flew over the Cuckoo's Nest*, 1962), who had both volunteered for government LSD testing.[44]

Leary quit Harvard and became the most visible and outspoken advocate and, to the dismay of many of his fellow LSD advocates, espoused a goal to get the drug out to as many people and as quickly as possible. An opposing camp, which included Huxley, believed that because the drug was so powerful, its spread among a larger populace needed to be controlled and slow in part so as not to alarm or scare the establishment into counteraction and repression.[45] One way to be much more cautious would be to carefully distribute the drug through highly respected doctors and to select patients.[46]

All agreed that administration of the drug was best done with a strong focus on "set and setting," meaning administering the drug in a mellow, controlled, and comfortable setting such as with no bright lights or anything that would agitate. Leary saw sex as another key component to getting the full LSD experience.[47]

There was also a perceived connection between the LSD experience and the spiritual experiences described in both Buddhist and Hindu texts.[48] Leary even cowrote *The Psychedelic Experience: A Manual Based on the Tibetan Book of the Dead*, a psychedelic interpretation of the *Tibetan Book of the Dead*, which dealt with literal death but also very much with the death and rebirth of the ego.[49] This further dovetailed with the counterculture's disillusionment with Western religion and top-down patriarchy. Buddhism and Hinduism instead saw the individual as akin to a single particle flowing down the great river of life that contained all and, in the bigger picture, with everything in harmony. In this view, God was everywhere.

Still, Ginsberg had a non-drug-related spiritual experience while in India that led him to conclude, as others would, that lasting enlightenment could only come from great personal effort unaided by chemicals. The idea was that one would be better off working through the blocked neuroses and emotions.[50] Ginsberg came to believe that, if necessary, all healthy persons in the United States over the age of 14 should "have a mass emotional nervous breakdown in these States once and for all."[51]

Once Kesey's *Cuckoo's Nest* became a bestseller (and was later adapted into the Academy Award–winning film of the same name), he began to use his earnings and his celebrity to promote the LSD revolution. In Haight-Ashbury, Kesey met Owsley "Bear" Stanley, a chemistry dropout from Berkeley who became the Haight's key LSD manufacturer.[52] The pair then also began to collaborate on a new conception of LSD-inspired events. Stanley would further create state-of-the-art sound systems for the local band the Grateful Dead and others.[53]

In 1964, Bob Dylan took LSD for the first time, though he downplayed the drug's impact on his songwriting. By 1966, all four members of the Beatles would ingest LSD, which would play a key role in their songwriting development as they continued to pursue ever-greater artistic heights.

7

The Haight's House Band, Acid Rock, and the Hippies, 1965–1967

> "To *be*, that is, to really be—to sprout naturally from the ground of Being and assume the form you were meant to have."
> —Haight chronicler CHARLES PERRY[1]

> "Spontaneity was proof of authenticity."
> —Hippie chronicler W.J. RORABAUGH[2]

The story of the San Francisco music scene and the rock subgenre called psychedelic rock, psych rock, or acid rock starts in Virginia City, Nevada, in 1965, and a group called the Charlatans. The Charlatans had formed in San Francisco but then took up a residency in an odd western-themed community in the desert, playing music and soon incorporating the influence of LSD. The Charlatans then returned to San Francisco and didn't so much spur any major musical innovations, but their offbeat live shows sparked a nascent San Francisco music scene to cut loose and have fun.[3]

Around the same time, Kesey had decided to stock up on LSD, grab a group of friends known as the Merry Pranksters, paint a school bus wild, psychedelic colors, and drive cross-country to the 1964 World's Fair in New York. The excursion was immortalized in Tom Wolfe's book *The Electric Kool-Aid Acid Test* (1968). The bus driver, an extremely high Neal Cassady, was driving so fast and out of control that it had been too much for one San Francisco musician who got off the bus after a short time, Jerry Garcia.[4] The bus trip also captured the mindset and wide-open communal dreams of the era and would inspire the Beatles' 1967 album and film *Magical Mystery Tour* and the Who hit "Magic Bus" (1968).

Kesey came to realize that under the influence of LSD, things like color and sound intermingled. Thus, he developed concert/multimedia events that would best enhance LSD's ability to wildly distort, yet heighten, all senses simultaneously.[5] Kesey wanted music, incense, flavorful foods, and a light show, including the newly invented strobe light, and began to develop what would soon become the "Electric Kool-Aid Acid Tests." The actual Kool-Aid would be laced with acid in a tub in the middle of the venue, and there was no actual "test," but the name sounded mysterious and it was thought that it would intrigue local college students.[6] For the denizens of the Haight, LSD provided a dynamic and direct spiritual experience, right now, as opposed to what many saw as irrational interpretations of dated scriptures pushed on them by a parental generation.

Kesey also came to believe that music was the key to maximizing the LSD experience and funded Stanley's work on the ultimate psychedelic sound system.[7] Jazz, classical, and folk, however, did not appear to have any special impact with LSD users, while rock and roll was making stronger, direct connections.[8] As such, he turned to Garcia and the band that would come to be the Grateful Dead.

Jerome "Jerry" Garcia was born in 1942, the child of a Spanish immigrant bandleader father and a nurse mother living in the Bay Area. In 1946, Garcia lost part of his middle finger in a woodcutting accident with his brother, Tiff. Worse tragedy followed the next year when Garcia witnessed his father drown in a fishing accident.[9]

Jerry was a reader and a music fan, primarily jazz, folk, and country, and he started playing the guitar at 15. At 19, he experienced another tragedy and had a wake-up call in his life when he survived a car accident that took the life of a friend. Garcia refocused himself on music and became a bluegrass banjoist with one of his first bands, the Sleepy Hollow Hog Stompers.[10] Garcia would maintain those musical roots, but in 1964, he experienced the Beatles, who instantly turned him onto the power of rock and roll. Garcia next started a group in the Haight called the Warlocks that became the Grateful Dead, two words randomly pulled out of the dictionary.[11] Rounding out the classic Dead lineup would be jazz- and classically trained and electronic music composer Phil Lesh, the folk-influenced guitarist Bob Weir, blues- and gospel-rooted keyboardist Ron "Pigpen" McKernan, and the "Rhythm Devil" drummers Bill Kreutzmann and Mickey Hart.[12]

The band pulled from their respective influences along with rock and roll and, while under the daily influence of LSD, synthesized it all to become an utterly spontaneous, free-flowing jam band. One key to the Dead's sound was that where in early rock music the guitar lines echoed the main melody, Garcia used variants of guitar melodies and contrasted them with the vocals. As Charles Perry described it, to a listener on LSD, "the surprising interplay of the two lines built tension, teased out meaning

7. The Haight's House Band, Acid Rock, and Hippies, 1965–1967 67

in the contrasts, and eased tension in grand resolutions." These moments of tension and release could be repeated multiple times in a single song.[13] Further, at times, two, three, or four different instruments might all be soloing at the same time, yet remain entirely cohesive.[14] The group's deep roots in traditional musical stylings managed to keep them feeling grounded even when being wildly adventurous. Live crowds would stay in sync with the band's ebbs and flows throughout long, extended jams. Their improvisations meant that live, songs never sounded the same twice. Even without drugs, the band could put a listener into a certain state, but with the crowd on LSD along with the band, a concert could alter an entire crowd's consciousness. As Garcia described the band, "I think of the Grateful Dead as being a crossroads or a pointer sign, and what we're pointing to is that there's a lot of universe available, that there's a whole lot of experience available over here."[15]

Lyrically, the Dead had come out of the rock of the '50s and early '60s, which had been marked by relatively simple lyrics most relevant to teens—for example, boy-girl relations. But by 1965, the Beatles' and Bob Dylan's new lyrical themes, especially, had already shifted to being deeply introspective and personal. Rock fans and rock artists were growing up, broadening their views, and wanting more. The youth culture trusted such rock poets in helping to guide things in new directions. Rock lyrics helped to fill a void where traditional institutions were failing to connect. Along with the fact that rock had always ultimately been more about feelings than just words, anyway (e.g., Little Richard: "Whop bop b-luma b-lop bam bom"), and the LSD influence was right on time.

Early Dead themes reflected their folk and blues roots in cover songs as well as cosmic ("Cosmic Charlie") and mystical themes ("New Potato Caboose"), love ("Turn on Your Love Light"), the death of their friend Neal Cassady ("That's It for the Other One"), and surrealism ("China Cat Sunflower"). One of the group's key lyricists, in fact, the nonperforming Robert Hunter, had participated in government psychedelic experiments along with Kesey and Ginsberg.[16]

At the same time, to the counterculture, an older generation twisted words anyway. Many hippies saw Christians as selectively quoting the Bible or otherwise twisting meanings to justify their own wants. Countercultural writer Paul Krassner had said at the time in an interview regarding the notion of a collective truth, "I don't believe in the biblical concept, 'Ye shall know the truth and the truth shall make ye free.'… The truth can always be rationalized."[17] As writer W.J. Rorabaugh had put it, "Spontaneity was proof of authenticity."[18] A new era of music and even a new consciousness took shape.

Along with being anti-war and pro–civil rights, there were

Part One—A New Day Dawning, 1950s–1967

Grateful Dead in Haight Ashbury, ca. 1965 (Pictorial Press Ltd/Alamy Stock Photo).

amorphous, cosmic elements to the hippie philosophy, evidenced by the use of positive adjectives such as "groovy" and "far out."[19] And where the Beats had been heavy and often quite dark in their societal outlook, the hippies were mostly bright and optimistic.

As to the Dead, toward the end of the '60s, the band would shift from harder blues rock to more use of harmonies, largely due to the influence of Crosby, Stills, and Nash from Los Angeles.[20] The Dead's allure was so strong that they would become rock's first "lifestyle" band. That is, thousands of self-described "Deadheads" would drop out of their day-to-day lives, at least for a spell or longer, following the Dead from city to city on tour on a three-decade run. Across well over 2,000 live shows, they became one of rock's most revered live acts. This despite having exactly zero hits for the first twenty-two years of the group's existence.[21] Only Garcia's passing at a drug treatment center in 1995 ended the run of the group's classic lineup.

The hippies did not trust or even fully understand establishment authority figures or the police (and vice versa), and there was a fascination with outlaw culture.[22] In San Francisco, this led to an odd and often uneasy union between the freaks and the local outlaw biker gang the Hell's Angels. Kesey welcomed the Angels and they guarded equipment at concerts.[23] Kesey also thought that LSD might mellow out the oft-violent bikers, but even though they had liked acid, they mostly stayed violent.[24] Some Angel's members were soon thought to be involved in some drug-related murders in the area as well.[25]

The first of Kesey's so-called acid tests occurred in November '65. Members of the Dead attended but did not play the first night. Attendance immediately exceeded all expectations, and with only two days of advance notice, 2,400 people filled the Fillmore.[26] Attendees took acid together via LSD-laced Kool-Aid from a baby's bathtub placed in the middle of the floor.[27] Acid was so new and so beyond the pale that outside observers were clueless as to what exactly was going on with the first events.[28]

The test venues would otherwise be filled with crates of speakers and amps, portable video systems displaying closed-circuit images around the auditorium, odd sculptures like vultures or an oversized clamshell that one could get "lost in," random microphones placed around the venue that picked up and broadcast scraps of sound and conversation, sometimes with a time delay, and so on.[29] Attendees ate, drank, and embraced avant-garde art, psychedelic rock music, and light shows synched up with the music.[30] Kesey would have one group of musicians on one end of the auditorium and usually the Dead on the other.[31] In short, danced, contemplated life, weirded out, and just plain tripped.[32]

Several more shows would follow. As the tests gained popularity and word got around about the truth of the Kool-Aid, the authorities caught on and attendees had to start supplying their own LSD.[33]

At the same time in New York, renowned pop artist Andy Warhol and his "Factory" crew were putting together their own multimedia rock show called the "Exploding Plastic Inevitable" (EPI), featuring the rock group the Velvet Underground (more on them and Warhol shortly). In May '65, the EPI was presented at the Fillmore in San Francisco. Warhol and his people brought their own light show, utilizing stroboscopes, slides and film projections onstage, and decadent dancers, and produced a very different and decidedly heavier vibe.

In March 1966, *Science* magazine falsely suggested that because LSD damaged the chromosomes in lab rats, it would do the same to humans. This came at a time when the public was still reeling from the horrific case of the drug thalidomide being given to pregnant women in Europe from 1958 to 1961, causing thousands of babies to be born without limbs. Many, correctly, believed that the LSD article was an oddly and conveniently timed scare tactic.[34]

Also in March 1966, *Life* magazine ran the story, "LSD: The Exploding Threat of the Mind Drug That Got Out of Control." The article supported only limited use of LSD in controlled, scientific environments. There were still no studies to indicate the danger of LSD itself, not even in comparison to other legal drugs such as alcohol, tobacco, or psychotropic drugs. Still, California legislators began putting a bill together to designate LSD (as well as another strong psychedelic, DMT) as a danger.[35]

In early 1966, a medical school dropout who had admittedly been "flying on acid for three days" committed murder in what became a highly publicized case. In the aftermath, the major LSD manufacturer Sandoz Pharmaceuticals announced that it would no longer sell the drug, pushing the drug further into the black markets.[36]

By the summer of '66, the rock music being made in the Haight was also shifting with the social changes and the influence of acid, and a public rock concert first replaced the usual formal benefit or protest event. The neighborhood also gained its own countercultural newspaper, the *City of San Francisco Oracle*, aka "the Oracle." A self-proclaimed "community anarchist" group called the Diggers (taking their name from a similarly minded English group of the 1700s) began to shape the scene also, with their more radical broadsides and an anti-money, anti-capitalist message.[37]

Musically, rock continued to be even more assertive. In August 1965, Barry McGuire's stirring folk-rock protest song "Eve of Destruction," written by P.F. Sloan, became a hit in the United States and the United Kingdom. McGuire's ballad was angry and voiced a deep frustration, with no illusions as to where the world seemed to be at.[38] It was extremely heavy for a pop hit.

In America at large, by September '66, while many did not fully understand the purpose of the Vietnam War, it raged on. The nightly news broadcast the war into America's living rooms, unlike any war ever. The military reported daily enemy death counts with the intent of reassuring Americans with a measure of progress in a guerrilla-style war. Those numbers lost all meaning, however, as the war continued with no end in sight. More and more of America's youth, especially, were already losing confidence in the ability of America's traditional institutions to solve the world's ills, and to now include the U.S. military.[39]

In October '66, California made it a misdemeanor to possess LSD and a felony to sell it. It was a blow to the freak lifestyle and, in the freaks' view, a blow to the very notion of free minds. Still, LSD remained easy enough to obtain through illicit channels.[40]

In the Haight, there was a continuous stream of young and hopeful newcomers from all around the country wanting to experience a new way of living. Many were idealists and activists, some were looking to have some fun, and others were disenfranchised and directionless including runaways. A lot of kids would not find an easy go of it. Some would sleep in parks and eat for free at Digger Feeds, while others panhandled just enough to stay above water.[41] Teenagers were also vulnerable to the abundance of drugs and "free love" leading to an underbelly of exploitation.[42]

As to free love, the notion that the West was too repressed sexually, leading to all kinds of social ills, including violence and wars, was not new. Some hippies read up on radical psychology experts like Wilhelm Reich, who believed that the sexual repression of youth and lack of healthy orgasms was a major social problem.[43] Casual sex was now being seen as personal liberation to the dismay (and sometimes jealousy) of an older generation.[44]

The rock scene continued to develop rapidly. In December '65, and shortly after Dylan switched to rock, a San Francisco mime troupe manager, Bill Graham, started renting the Fillmore for the growing "acid" rock music scene. Crowds went from a dozen to several hundred in a few weeks.[45] Other local promoters started up regular rock shows and the San Francisco folk scene was effectively over. Although the acid tests were done by early '66, the music and the music scene it helped inspire was taking off.[46]

The Beatles—Stage Two (Maturing) (Continued)

In England at the time, the Beatles and Beatlemania were not only not burning out, but the entire enterprise was growing and evolving by leaps and bounds. In 1965, *Rubber Soul* marked a new artistic high-water mark. Each of the 14 songs on the record sounded decidedly more developed and more mature than the group's previous efforts. It was impeccably produced and remarkably cohesive yet with diverse stylings. The Beatles established themselves as being more committed to their artistic standards than their commercial success. Shortly after the album's release, *Newsweek* declared that with the album, "the Beatles had a foothold in the world of art; in the months that followed, their efforts would lead to the full acceptance and legitimization of rock and roll as an art form."[47] It was pop/rock music that even an older generation had to acknowledge was pretty great.

There was the usual slew of standout love ballads ("Michelle," "Girl"), though, and per Dunbar's second thematic stage of confronting the real world, there were now love songs with more grown-up doubts and problems ("You Won't See Me," "I'm Looking through You"). Lennon's more inward approach also resulted in non–love songs. This included the empathetic but stark self-assessment of Lennon himself as well as modern man in "Nowhere Man" and the remarkably way-beyond-his-years self-reflection of "In My Life."

Dylan and the folk rock of the Byrds also had clear influences on the Beatles, leading to their forays into folk rock and lots of acoustic guitar by Lennon. The Beatles were not the first rock and rollers to touch on certain new styles, but here they further opened the door for baroque rock, the use of the harpsichord and the sitar, and also helping to set the stage for an entire psychedelic genre.[48]

Among the first LSD-inspired psychedelic bands were Austin, Texas's 13th Floor Elevators, who formed in 1965 and debuted with *The Psychedelic Sounds of the 13th Floor Elevators* the following year. San Jose, California's, the Count Five's "Psychotic Reaction" cracked the top ten in June 1966, first marking the commercial promise of the genre. From the East Coast, New York City vocal group the Mamas & the Papas would have a hit in '66 as well with the landmark and more pop-friendly "California Dreamin'."

In early February 1966, Bill Graham obtained a long-term lease for the Fillmore and it became the Haight's main venue for weekly shows.[49] Graham and others used intricate psychedelic posters with cosmic- and surreal-themed art for promoting shows that reflected the LSD experience and the new vision of the times.[50]

The Grateful Dead were such a constant from the beginning that they quickly became known by the slogan "The Good Ol' Grateful Dead," which was printed on buttons.[51] Other local San Francisco bands on the scene included Moby Grape, Jefferson Airplane, and the transplanted Joplin, now fronting Big Brother and the Holding Company. Graham also made a concerted effort to bring African American roots music acts to the Fillmore, particularly those that were the inspirations of the local musicians, such as blues legends John Lee Hooker and B.B. King. Other out-of-town bands on the scene included New York City's Lovin' Spoonful, Chicago's Paul Butterfield Blues Band, and Southern California's Frank Zappa and his Mothers of Invention.

Many of the members of these psych bands were immersed in the drug culture, which was evident in their music, their band names (e.g., a "holding company" was a fully-stocked drug dealer), and in the lyrics (e.g., the Airplane's 1967 drug-trip song "White Rabbit," one of the era's defining hits).

Fashion-wise, men tended toward secondhand Edwardian and Victorian clothes and favored rustic and Native American styles of buckskin, fringe, beads, and Indian headbands, representing a back-to-nature lifestyle and renewed spiritual views.[52] Typical for female freaks was Janis Joplin, who wore plain hair, sack dresses, ponchos, and self-made jewelry.[53]

Musically, the psychedelic rock era would have at least three masterpiece albums: the Beach Boys' *Pet Sounds* (May 1966) and then the Beatles' *Revolver* (August 1966) and *Sgt. Pepper's Lonely Heart's Club Band* (1967).

The Beatles—Stage Three (Psychedelia)

In 1965, John Lennon and George Harrison first stumbled onto LSD at a dinner party in London. As Harrison told *Rolling Stone*, "I had such an overwhelming feeling of well-being, that there was a God, and I could see him in every blade of grass. It was like gaining hundreds of years of experience in 12 hours." Harrison added, "It was like opening the door, really, and before, you didn't even know there was a door there." Lennon was equally floored. He became so immersed in LSD that by the next year, then-wife Cynthia had called it "his religion."[54]

Lennon and Harrison felt that Starr and McCartney had to be initiated as well so that the whole band would be on the same page. Starr obliged, but McCartney declined at first.[55]

The Beatles' third thematic stage would be their psychedelic stage, touched on in *Rubber Soul* (1965) but fully realized with the albums *Revolver* (1966), *Sgt. Pepper's Lonely Hearts Club Band* (1967), *Magical Mystery Tour* (1967), and the White Album (1968). As Dirk Dunbar described it, in this phase the Beatles attempted to "mythologize a new world-view that they believed would help direct the counterculture."[56]

With three-quarters of the band members' minds newly expanded, on *Revolver*, they continued to master the making of pop hits in varying styles to include "Taxman," "Good Day, Sunshine," and "Got to Get You into My Life." But they would also open up to a whole other, more transcendent level of music making (although they did not play while under the influence of LSD).[57] Like *Pet Sounds*, *Revolver* would further blow up the very notion of what rock songs even were.

In the studio, the group made more quantum leaps forward in creating an array of new sounds and effects. The group came to have complete confidence that they could throw any idea at Martin and new engineer Geoff Emerick and they would make it happen. From rock, classical, avant-garde experiments in musique concrète (the electronic sampling of sounds), and electro-acoustic sound manipulation, the Beatles' musical palette became seemingly unlimited.[58] In making the record, Martin firmly established himself as one of the most important producers of the century and earned the unofficial title of the "Fifth Beatle." As always, underlying the whole affair seemed to be the band's collective chemistry and shared joy for making music.

Revolver's opening track (on the running order of the British release), Lennon's "I'm Only Sleeping," was music from a half-waking state, conjuring Jungian dreams, and the LSD influence. The song was also strongly influenced by the Leary cowritten *The Psychedelic Experience: A Manual Based on the Tibetan Book of the Dead*. Lennon quoted the book in "Tomorrow Never Knows," in turning one's mind off and simply going with the flow of life and the universe. The song included various effects that seemed to allude to other dimensions.[59] The non-album psych single "Rain," recorded during the same sessions, also included backward vocals, as if reconfiguring time.[60]

"Eleanor Rigby" was another entirely unexpected turn and scarcely even a rock song. At the time, McCartney had been discovering new classical and other contemporary music. McCartney then wrote "Rigby" singing and playing the piano with no other Beatles accompanying. The song would be driven by a remarkable string section provided by Martin. McCartney sang a deeply affecting and empathetic tale of a lonely woman's life and her passing, as well as a priest's apparent inability to reach his congregation.[61] It was about as far from typical pop or rock music themes as one could get.

Another song, "Yellow Submarine," captured the band's unifying dreamy vision. It is actually a children's singalong, but childlike wonder is the point. Even the Bible recognized "Except ye be converted, and become as little children, ye shall not enter into the kingdom of heaven."[62]

McCartney specifically wrote the song to be sung by the guileless Starr to narrate a fantastical, underwater world. The song would also inspire a very well-received Beatle-authorized and animated feature film, with the band's music but voice-over actors for the band members themselves.[63]

Starr sang of coming across an old sailor telling tales from the sea, and a story unfolds as a big submarine party, with all of their friends on board joining in a singalong. There is even a brass band, as if right out of an alternate-world Liverpool. Additional submarine sound effects and Lennon sounding like a seasoned sailor bring the song even more to life.[64]

"Yellow Submarine" was adopted by protesters in San Francisco and striking workers around the world.[65] The Fab Four were fully realizing their musical dreams and reaching millions in myriad ways.

More standout psych rock tracks of the era included the free jazz and Indian-inflected Byrds' hit "Eight Miles High" (March 1966) and Country Joe McDonald's "Colors for Susan" (1967), while in England, Donovan (Leitch) released the infinitely groovy "Mellow Yellow" (1968). The first songs to address the threat of nuclear Armageddon came in 1967 with the Dead's "Morning Dew" and Quicksilver Messenger Service's "Pride of Man."

Jefferson Airplane's "White Rabbit" (1967) introduced a dramatic and quasi-flamenco intro that sounded much like Ravel's *Bolero*.

The first anti–Vietnam War rock song of the era was the L.A. band the Doors' hit single "Unknown Soldier" in 1968. The Doors had taken their name from Aldous Huxley's book about his experiences with the hallucinogenic drug mescaline, *The Doors of Perception* (1954). In turn, that book title was a reference to a William Blake quote: "If the doors of perception were cleansed, everything would appear to man as it is, infinite."[66]

Where the San Francisco music scene was "improvisations, feedback, and weird distortions" to trip on, the Doors were poetic, overtly pro-drug, and more sexual.[67] Instead of a bass guitar, Ray Manzarek played an electric organ, which made the group sound both more traditionally commercial but often also gave them a more mysterious and sometimes seedier vibe. Magnetic and poetic lead singer Jim Morrison used his literate and murky lyrics, charisma, and sexuality to push himself and his audience to their limits; he was even arrested for exposing himself at a show in Miami.

The sprawling nature of psychedelic rock and extended jams and excursions did not fit the mold of mid–'60s radio stations at the time and their preference for three-minute pop songs. Gradually, however, album rock stations saw where the market was moving and the restrictions were changed.[68]

The media continued to run stories about the Haight as well as of other smaller hippie enclaves elsewhere, bringing such places more attention, more people, and, often, more trouble.[69] By 1966, the Haight was starting to get overwhelmed due to housing problems as well as drug abuse and addiction, and related crime.[70]

Philosophically, at this point, the counterculture could be summed up by three ideals: a search for authenticity, an insistence on individualism, and a desire for community.[71] Where it was all heading was still up in the air. Clearer was that the music of the era was often exceptional and arguably as good and as influential as the popular music of any era of the twentieth century.

8

Warhol's House Band, 1962–1967

As the Dead became the house band for the acid tests and for Haight-Ashbury, across the United States in New York City, at the same time, the group Velvet Underground was becoming a house band as well. That band would be linked with artist Andy Warhol's EPI shows and his famed New York studio space, the Factory. The Factory was an artistic, social, and sometimes decadent focal point of 1960s New York City. Instead of peace, love, optimism, back to nature, and mind-expanding hallucinogens, however, the Factory was marked by bold artistic ambition, gritty urban realism, compassion for the outsider, more sex than love, and sometimes a certain nihilism that often went along with being cast aside by society, as well as heroin and methamphetamine use.[1]

Formed in New York in 1964, the Velvets would be another of rock's most legendary and most influential bands. In 2003, *Rolling Stone* would declare their debut to be the "most prophetic rock album ever made."[2] Another writer noted that just with that debut alone, "the Velvets invented—or at the very least inspired—art-rock, punk, garage, grunge, shoegaze, goth, indie and any other alternative music you care to mention."[3]

The band members' musical lives would be shaped by '50s rock and rollers and the British Invasion, the Beats and other literary influences, and then very much by their surroundings in the fringes and underground environs of New York City. To fully understand where the Velvets come from and some of the deeper roots of their musical styles, it helps to understand one of the twentieth century's most celebrated artists, Andy Warhol.

Warhol would help launch the Velvets as their initial benefactor, promoter, and producer. He would also provide a platform and credibility that was a godsend for a controversial and ahead-of-their-time rock band. Ultimately, Warhol's legacy in rock would include his influence on Reed and the Velvets and many others, including David Bowie and Bob Dylan, among countless others. These three in particular would even write some important songs about Warhol himself and/or the lives of the Factory regulars.

Andy Warhol (1928–1987) was born Andrew Warhola, the child of Czech immigrants, raised in an ethnic slum in Pittsburgh. Warhol grew up during the Depression. As a kid, Warhol was at Byzantine Catholic services every Sunday; he would soak in the religious imagery and file it away. He was already a nervous and sickly child and then, at eight, he contracted a condition of the central nervous system called St. Vitus' dance, which left him bedridden for a month.[4] His father, a coal miner, died when Andy was 13.[5]

Warhol would lose himself in glossy movie magazines, collected photos of Hollywood stars, and then became a photographer himself. He was a pale, painfully shy kid and would soon identify as gay. Thus, Warhol was already a quintessential outsider and observer, traits that would help to define his artistry.[6]

After graduating from Carnegie Mellon University in Pittsburgh in 1949, Warhol moved to New York City where he found success drawing commercial fashion ads.[7] This led to his famously spearheading what became known as the pop art movement at the start of the '60s, along with the likes of Roy Lichtenstein, Robert Rauschenberg, and Claes Oldenburg.

In the '40s, the abstract expressionists like Jackson Pollock and others rejected representationism or even any external reference points at all. The movement was personified by Pollock's emotionally direct, "drip and slash" style of painting.[8]

Pop art, on the other hand, was all representation. Warhol and company utilized the very iconography of the mass media that the public was familiar with, such as advertising, comic books, television, and film. Warhol believed that pop culture could be high art but also something that the public could recognize and enjoy at the same time.[9]

In 1962, Warhol showed his famous *Campbell's Soup Cans* exhibit in New York, which was simply repeated silkscreens of the different types of the iconic soup cans (though each with slight and unique imperfections). The show was both sensational and controversial. Observers could see cans, art, an economy, a food distribution system, the power of commercial imagery, or just comfort food, and many saw an entirely new form of art.

Warhol would blur the lines between "high" culture, "mass" culture, and commercialism, as well as explore the connection between celebrity and religious imagery. He would further challenge the art world hierarchy as far as who determined what art was. Pop art would assert that anyone could make and appreciate art, thus demystifying and democratizing the whole concept. For many, Warhol would both mirror and expose late–twentieth-century American culture more than any other artist.

On one early Warhol silk screen piece, *Triple Elvis (Ferus Type)*, he took a single movie still of the rock icon dressed up as a cowboy and pointing a gun toward the camera (from the film *Flaming Star*, 1960), arguably the most all-American image one could imagine, and reproduced it three times. Warhol's otherwise very simple and mechanical technology was illuminating. In this case, it captured something of the post-'50s legacy of rock's once-brightest star. As one critic explained, "Toe to toe, repeated atop one another, poor Elvis becomes as thin and hazy as the idyllic illusion he publicly symbolizes; the assembly line produces the emptiness and sterility of soulless, over-managed puppetry."[10] Pop art could thus seem utterly *in*artistic or even be purely commercial—that is, the mechanized silk screen process, yet still be highly artistic.

Of course, rock and roll itself was already blurring those lines between "mass"/popular culture and high art. From its beginning, rock was rooted in romanticist idealism, celebrating the power and spirit of regular people, as well as of society's fringes. Thus, Chuck Berry's "Roll Over, Beethoven" (1956) definitively marked rock's overthrow of "high" art. The Beatles would then expand on the original rock template as they aspired to a "higher," more complex art, while still maintaining their authenticity. This all culminated with *Revolver* and soon *Sgt. Pepper's Lonely Hearts Club Band* (1967), *Magical Mystery Tour* (1967), and into the White Album (1968).

In his song "Visions of Johanna" (1966), Bob Dylan also skewered the notion that those in power in the art world should have the sole voice in determining what constituted timeless beauty and what ended up in elite museums.[11] He had further commented, "Museums are cemeteries. Paintings should be on the walls of restaurants, in dime stores, in gas stations, in men's rooms.... Music is the only thing that's in tune with what's happening."[12]

As to consumer culture, Warhol's take was very different than the hippie counterculture's minimalism and "dropping out," though it was still remarkable in its own way. Both viewpoints challenged the role of commercial and corporate forces in society. Warhol, however, more embraced the system from within, whether re-contextualizing Campbell's soup cans or having his workers mass-produce his pieces, he used the system for his own needs. He even made a fortune for himself in the process.[13]

At the Factory, Warhol's people steadily executed his visions, often fueled by amphetamines, producing silk screens, making experimental films, and putting on exhibits, along with socializing and having long parties. There was also a lot of heroin and other drugs being consumed and free-spirited views on sex.[14]

The Factory people were New York's artistic types as well as transvestites, homosexuals, drug abusers, and what an observer otherwise described as a collection of "outcast/loose-cannon/mad-genius freaks," of which Warhol "fed off their crazy, literally crazy, energy."[15] Of Warhol's hundreds of experimental films, most featured untrained actors and those people at the Factory that Warhol found to be most interesting, talented, beautiful, bizarre, or tragic, or all of the above. Warhol later admitted that he was afraid that "without the crazy, druggy people around jabbering away and doing their insane things, I would lose my creativity."[16] These became known as the "Warhol superstars."[17]

As Warhol's reputation continued to grow, other major figures of the time would stop in as well, from rockers Dylan and Jagger to acting-singing legend Judy Garland and ballet icon Rudolf Nureyev.[18] Warhol adopted a trademark white suit and a silver wig and was always in the middle of it all, quietly directing things and observing, using everything he saw as creative fodder and inspiration.

Warhol understood fame in America like few others. He would perhaps become most well known for his famed and spot-on prediction that "in the future, everyone will be world-famous for 15 minutes," which had appeared in a program for a 1968 exhibition of his work.[19]

Other prominent, early Warhol works explored his views of the media, fame, and tragedy. Some of his most noted pieces included his use of images of Marilyn Monroe, produced shortly after her suicide, and there was an infamous "death and disaster" series with silk screen images of tragic news photos of subjects including a grieving Jacqueline Kennedy Onassis, an electric chair, and car crashes.[20]

Also of note, Warhol made hundreds of what he called "screen tests" in which he turned his video camera on a seated subject and simply let the camera run for several minutes. Sometimes he walked away while the camera ran. The results were sometimes uncomfortable, three-minute, living-and-breathing portraits, yet where the "artist" had little to no active participation.[21]

In a "test" of famed surrealist artist Salvador Dalí, for example, Dalí is at first seen seeming to put on airs worthy of his legend. Dalí did, after all, consciously maintain a larger-than-life persona and was probably the most visibly recognizable artist of his time, especially due to his famous waxed mustache. Yet, under the unyielding gaze of the camera lens, Dalí's outward persona fades, leaving a rather normal underlying man.[22] In short, Warhol was using his almost anti-art as a mirror to our culture and ourselves, often with stunning results.

Still today, Warhol remains enigmatic and polarizing. Many of those closest to him liked and admired him greatly for his vision and his inspiration. Reed once remarked that Warhol "was an *astonishing* person in every way."²³ On the other hand, he often quite literally used people for his art, and even people he knew were emotionally unstable. He would also often fall behind on payments for work despite his immense wealth. Warhol still got his way by often fostering conflict among others and stringing along those starved for the fame they knew he could provide. Warhol's Factory people even gave Warhol a nickname he hated: Drella, a hybrid of "Dracula" and "Cinderella." One of Warhol's closest associates, Bob Colacello, explained, "It almost developed into a love-hate thing. Because, you know, you, started off feeling inspired by Andy and then feeling used. He really sucked you dry. Drella."²⁴ Thus, while many thrived in the Factory, as one art critic observed, "a lot of people had their hearts broken."²⁵

With so many talented people but also many who came to the Factory already deeply wounded, there were breakdowns, overdoses, and even suicides among the superstar crew. Warhol's one-time brightest star actor, the beautiful but heroin-addicted Edie Sedgwick, took her own life in 1974, at just 28 years old. Warhol's response to Sedgwick's struggles and ultimate passing was seen as cold and indifferent, the same way he had dealt with some other Factory tragedies.²⁶ Bob Dylan was close with Sedgwick, and she had dated Dylan's close friend Bobby Neuwirth. Her story and her seeming manipulation by Warhol are said to be the inspiration for Dylan's classic 1966 songs "Leopard-Skin Pill-Box Hat" and "Just Like a Woman."²⁷

Warhol's personal dealings would also play a part in his being shot and nearly dying at the Factory in 1968 at the hands of a mentally unstable activist and screenwriter, Valerie Solanas. Solanas had given Warhol a script to read, but when she came to believe that Warhol was stringing her along, she finally snapped.²⁸

In Warhol's defense, in his eyes, he was not indifferent but simply aware that no one was so powerful as to be able to change the life trajectory of others:

> When people are ready to, they change. They never do it before then, and sometimes they die before they get around to it. You can't make them change if they don't want to, just like when they do want to, you can't stop them.²⁹

To Warhol, the car crashes and human tragedies of life were simply the natural output of the same society that produced two of its greatest icons, the self-destructive Monroe and Elvis. Life in the Factory was a life in the extremes and on the fringes, which could afford certain personal freedom not found anywhere else. Yet it was also a very raw and very *real* place to be, too, fascinating but with no safety nets. Said, Warhol,

> The Factory was a place where you could let your "problems" show and nobody would hate you for it. And if you worked your problems up into entertaining

routines, people would like you even more for being strong enough to say you were different and actually have fun with it. What I mean is there was no hypocrisy at the Factory.[30]

In many ways, Lou Reed and the Velvets would do what Warhol had been doing. The Velvets would produce raw, proto-punk songs presenting their and others' unvarnished selves and exposing life beyond modern society's facades and more superficial constructs. With some influence and help from Warhol, the Velvets would bring an entirely original voice to rock. No other band would blur and even erase any dividing line between the primal power of rock and roll and "high" art and literature in the same way. The Velvets would help give fringe people and societal castoffs the space to be seen and heard and support them in being what social scientists call "socially productive" when no one else would.[31] In short, this time and place in New York was in fact an ideal breeding ground for punk rock and more ambitious art punk.

Lou Reed was born in 1942, in Brooklyn, to a middle-class Jewish family and grew up in Freeport, Long Island.[32] Lou's mother, Toby, was a stenographer and a housewife; his father, Sidney, an accountant. Lou was troubled at an early age. His only sibling, his sister Merrill, recalled Lou "harboring incredible rage, particularly towards our father," "a controlling man," and Lou making accusations of abuse and "a lack of love."[33]

Reed's grade school years were marked by panic attacks and a lot of social awkwardness. His junior high had a gang problem, and Reed was victimized, though he himself provoked and challenged as well. At 15, Lou first picked up the guitar and began to focus his energies into rock music.[34] Reed later explained, "If I hadn't heard rock and roll on the radio, I would have had no idea there was life on this planet."[35]

By Reed's late teens, he had effectively stopped communicating with his parents at all except for occasional shouting matches. He also discovered drugs. According to Merrill, their mother could do nothing with Lou, while their father resorted to more "rules and yelling," but "nothing worked."[36]

Prior to starting his freshman year at New York University, Reed had been exhibiting more mood swings and exhibiting homosexual inclinations. This, again, at a time when homosexuality was considered a mental disorder as well as a crime, Reed's parents would later send him to the notorious Creedmore State Psychiatric Hospital for electroshock therapy three times a week for eight weeks, genuinely believing that they were helping him.[37] The treatment was long a tightly kept family secret.[38] Reed later recalled the experience in an interview:

> They put the thing down your throat so you don't swallow your tongue, and they put electrodes on your head. That's what was recommended in Rockland

County then to discourage homosexual feelings. The effect is that you lose your memory and become a vegetable. You can't read a book because you get to page 17 and have to go right back to page one again.[39]

Merrill recalled Lou coming back home after the first treatment "limp and unresponsive."[40]

One effect of the treatment was that Reed became more fully committed to life as a social outsider and living in the underground.[41] Lou also wrote about the events in his 1974 solo song, "Kill Your Sons," singing of bad psychiatrists and an entirely out-of-touch family. Thus, it was a system that destroyed society's kids and caused them to run far away.[42]

Lou and his parents decided that he would be better off away from New York City at Syracuse University, four hours north. There, Lou first met future Velvets bandmate Sterling Morrison, while he focused on journalism, film directing, and creative writing. He also studied under poet Delmore Schwartz, a major influence.[43] Despite the remoteness, he also discovered heroin there.

In 1964, Reed graduated from Syracuse with honors, moved to New York's Lower East Side, and began working as an in-house songwriter for a small record label.[44] He then met the classically trained bassist and violist John Cale from Wales and recruited Morrison for a new band. The band's first drummer, Angus Maclise, did not believe in accepting money for art, nor did he want to participate in a structured gig. He was replaced by Maureen Tucker, and the Velvets' classic lineup was set.[45]

Reed wrote songs, often drawing on his poetic influences, and the group embraced rock and roll, R&B, classic and avant-garde influences, and the various influences of life in underground New York.

The novel *A Walk on the Wild Side* (1956) by Nelson Algren, and later supplying the title of Reed's classic solo hit, would capture some of Reed's perspective going forward. The book jacket described a tale of "a bard of the down-and-outer."[46] The band's first name was—ironically, the same as the Grateful Dead's—Warlocks, then the Falling Spikes, before they settled on the Velvet Underground. That name came from another sensationalistic paperback, which on its cover promised to expose "the sexual corruption of our age."

Cale had previously been involved in a group that collectively sustained notes for up to two hours at a time and with an intonation system similar to Indian drone music. Cale would string his viola with guitar strings, resulting in what he called "a drone that sounded like a jet-engine!"[47] It could also be trance inducing and cut to the listener's bone.

On the first Velvets album, the guitars were set up to produce a "lower, fuller" sound that Cale considered "sexy."[48] In the midst of a loud and sometimes chaotic sound, Tucker kept the pulsing, exotic rhythms with her bass drum turned upright and often using tom-tom mallets instead of drumsticks.[49] Morrison essentially shared lead and rhythm guitar with Reed, with Morrison the stabilizing force to Reed's more adventurous style.

The band members were immersed in New York's fringe communities at bars, cafés, clubs, and parties with a variety of societal outcasts, including hard drug users and abusers, homosexuals, cross-dressers, transsexuals, and anyone else who had found the small corner of acceptance in 1960s America. Reed would incorporate all of this into his Velvet songs and later into his solo career.

Reed's singing voice has been called "outrageously unmusical."[50] Reed certainly didn't oversing, and he would instead let the emotion come out of the song. As he explained it, he wanted his voice to be intimate, like he was "sitting right next to you."[51] Yet his voice also possessed an authenticity that could carry some beautiful and melodic songs, while being powerful and defiant enough to inspire punk rock.

By the winter of 1965, Andy Warhol was a star in the art world and beyond, with his work even adorning the cover of *Time* magazine.[52] A Broadway producer was looking to publicize his new discotheque in Queens and asked Warhol to lend his name and put on some of his multifaceted productions.[53] Warhol's films were not very profitable and he saw the request as a chance at something he did not have: a rock band that would draw a paying crowd and make money.[54] Warhol had high hopes for a Brian Epstein/Beatles-type management situation. Factory dancer Gerard Malanga found the Velvets playing a club one night and brought them to Warhol's attention. Warhol quickly understood the band to be precisely what he was looking for and became their manager.[55]

Some of the group's first shows were playing at Warhol's art exhibitions. Visually, the foursome sounded and presented as a bit menacing. They usually wore all black, often with black sunglasses, initially for the practical reality of having to face Warhol's intense light shows.[56] According to Warhol business manager Paul Morrissey, the group needed "something beautiful to counteract" the harshness of the band, "and the combination of a really beautiful girl standing in front of all of this decadence was what was needed."[57]

The German-born Nico (born Christa Päffgen) was a stunning model and singer; she also had a bit part in Federico Fellini's *La Dolce Vida*. Nico was already known to the Factory people and happened to be present the night the Velvets were first scouted.[58]

Nico was tall, blonde, and blue eyed and had a mesmerizing, symmetrical beauty, along with an icy coolness. Reed would write three songs specifically for her on her debut. Nico sang standing in front of the band in a chic, all-white pantsuit with her own spotlight, giving the music some relief. She did not have a classic voice either—it was almost monotone even—but it was ethereal and haunting. She would later be called "the original goth rocker."[59]

Nico had been romantically involved with both Bob Dylan and Lou Reed by the time of the Velvet's debut, but according to Sterling Morrison, her almost emotionless delivery was not about breakups with either man; she was "just really depressed."[60] Although not a full-fledged member of the band, Nico was a revelation singing "Femme Fatale," "All Tomorrow's Parties," and "I'll Be Your Mirror," as well as backing Reed on "Sunday Morning."

Warhol asked Reed to write a song about Edie Sedgwick, which became the song about a wounded, beautiful, and tragic "Femme Fatale."[61] "All Tomorrow's Parties" showcased Nico's vocals, singing about one party at the Factory blurring into the next and was, as Reed biographer Anthony DeCurtis put it, "a pre-emptive eulogy" for Warhol's crowd. Reed's song sympathetically memorialized this edgy, hip crowd with their oft-shattered identities and all.[62]

Reed later described the Nico-sung "I'll Be Your Mirror" as Warholian in that it was about reflecting back to people "more than just what they want to see, and sometimes reflecting back to people what they should see and don't know."[63] Indeed, Reed further developed an eye for observation with Warhol and his experience at the Factory.[64]

These were some incredibly well-crafted and melodic songs, yet entirely atypical for pop and rock music. "Sunday Morning," which opens the album, is a surprisingly lovely song about waking up on a Sunday morning. It is not, however, a song about waking up with optimism toward a leisurely day of rest. This is Reed singing about being glad he has survived the weekend and dealing with a lingering paranoia. Yet, like the entire album, the song has its own sort of beauty.

"I'm Waiting for the Man," "Run, Run, Run," and "There She Goes Again" are all gritty and inventive blues-guitar rock. They are catchy but also hard and unforgiving, something like the city streets themselves. "I'm Waiting for the Man" is a prime example of Reed's storytelling ability, with a frank and yet darkly funny telling of a trip to Harlem to score heroin (more on this song shortly).

"Venus in Furs" is droning, Eastern-tinged rock and, lyrically, an interpretation of a nineteenth-century novel of the same name, involving sadomasochism and other themes. This at a time when such topics as well as other album topics like drug abuse and prostitution were nonexistent in popular music.

8. Warhol's House Band, 1962–1967   85

Listening to the song "Heroin" may be as close as one might want to get to experiencing the drug without actually using it. It is a seductive song, yet not exactly glamorous. The band slowly builds tension, especially Cale's droning viola, and then the music begins to surge forward. Reed's rising excitement is scary but, again, a bit alluring, even while he sings that he is aware that heroin could be his demise. As the narrator, he makes vague references to God, sounding as if at that moment he either doesn't care about God or that heroin is simply filling that role in his life.

On the final two songs of the record, the Velvets push things even further. "The Black Angel's Death Song" and "European Son" are utterly engrossing, and hearing them, even 50 years later, is still bracing and a bit unnerving. These two songs in particular helped spawn a wealth of avant-garde experimentation and art punk ambitions. The former encapsulates what sounds like a world going haywire via discordant noises and feedback. It then becomes the sound akin to a machine seizing up, immediately followed by something shattering—actually Cale pushing a chair into some metal plates.[65]

"European Son" is nearly eight minutes of searing blues-rock guitar and wild excursions and experimentations. It is something of an annihilation of any pretensions and preconceptions in rock and roll.

The Velvets played those first songs at preliminary EPI shows in January 1966, followed by full shows starting in April 1966 at the Dom in New York. Those events were billed as "The Silver Dream Factory Presents the Exploding Plastic Inevitable with Andy Warhol/The Velvet Underground/and Nico."[66] More shows were put on at other venues in New York and then in cities around the country, including San Francisco that May. The shows would be over by early 1967.[67]

The EPI shows featured dancers Malanga and Mary Woronov prowling around the stage, she in shiny, black, spike-heeled boots, with whips, and with both dancers gyrating. Malanga acted out the lyrics to "Venus in Furs," played at top volume, and would kiss Woronov's boots. Warhol added a battery of strobe lights and two projectors showing two parts of clips from his films on a wide screen behind the band and even projected onto the band.[68] Sometimes it was images of Malanga dancing and also being beaten and stripped to the waist.[69] The effect was to blur the line between what was the film, what was the screen, what was live performers, and what was the audience.

When the band performed "Heroin," Malanga would light a candle in the middle of the dance floor, pull out a spoon, and pretend to cook up a dose of heroin. He would then use what looked like a hypodermic needle, really a pencil, and simulate injecting himself. At that moment, Malanga would stand up and whirl around the stage while the band hit its frenzied

The Velvet Underground and Nico, ca. 1968 (Pictorial Press Ltd/Alamy Stock Photo).

crescendo.[70] Sometimes audience members did the real thing on the venue floors.[71]

As to their counterparts in San Francisco, the two camps didn't exactly mesh. On the one hand, the freaks didn't care for the New Yorkers' squalling feedback or their "posturing." On the other hand, the New Yorkers saw themselves as realists with a toughness that they thought the hippies lacked. John Cale said of the San Franciscans, "The hippie scene was not for us. They were scruffy, dirty people."[72] Filmmaker Paul Morrisey once told Warhol, "You have to be alone to develop all your idiosyncrasies that make a person interesting. In San Francisco, instead of becoming outcasts like you're *supposed* to when you take drugs, the organize communities around it!"[73]

On a personal level, Lou Reed was a lot of things. Sterling Morrison had said of Reed, "I love Lou, but he has what must be a fragmented personality, so you're never too sure under any conditions what you're going to have to deal with."[74] Reed did not necessarily disagree: "I think everybody has any number of personalities, just in themselves.... That's why if there's no one left to talk to you can listen to a couple of them talking in your head."[75] It was a true yin and yang situation.

Reed could also be incredibly difficult and arrogant to say the least. This was something particularly evident with interviewers. He once threw a question back at one reporter: "Are you happy being a schmuck?"[76] In Rome in 1975, he intentionally shocked reporters by telling them in vulgar terms that he was there to have sex with the pope.[77]

But Reed also had, as Sterling Morrison put it, a special "love" and "compassion" for outsiders in particular.[78] Of the song "Heroin," Morrison noted, "Some people say, 'Well, it's just about a junkie.' But why is he a junkie? What are the alternatives? What would make someone want to nullify his life, as the song says, rather than participate in society?"[79] At times, Reed's viewpoint could in fact seem nihilistic, but it was also an unvarnished acknowledgment of the very real, harsh, and darker aspects of the world. He very much found beauty and value in that darkness and in the most marginalized of people. Famed music writer and Reed acquaintance Lester Bangs once poetically captured Reed's dualities: "Lou Reed is a prick and a jerkoff who frequently commits the ultimate sin of treating his audience with contempt. He's also a person with deep compassion for a great many other people about whom almost nobody else gives a shit."[80]

Warhol financed the Velvet's recording sessions and was formally credited as album producer despite knowing nothing about actual record production.[81] However, along with discovering the group, Warhol also inspired them and gave them immense freedom to fully develop their highly noncommercial sound.[82] In Reed's words, "[Warhol] just made it possible for us to be ourselves and go right ahead with it because he was Andy Warhol. In a sense, he really did produce it, because he was this umbrella that absorbed all the attacks when we weren't large enough to be attacked."[83] Thus, a fringe band like the Velvets could not only get their album made but, miraculously enough, retain total artistic control and freedom as well.

Upon submission of the record, Atlantic rejected it due to its drug references, while Elektra disliked Cale's viola. Eventually, the MGM Records–owned Verve Records accepted the recordings.[84] The album title, *The Velvet Underground & Nico*, gave Nico billing while clarifying that the band did not see her as a permanent member. The album cover is memorable for featuring a Warhol print of a banana. Early copies of the album invited the owner to "peel slowly and see," and peeling back the banana skin to reveal a flesh-colored banana underneath. (Warhol would also design the iconic cover for the Rolling Stones' *Sticky Fingers* [1971] with its close-up of Mick Jagger's crotch area in jeans, with a conspicuous bulge, and a functioning zipper.[85])

The Velvet's debut was released in March 1967, but it was initially a commercial failure. First, the album had been hindered by a yearlong distribution delay. Next, in 1967, for fear of industry and legal repercussions, commercial radio refused to play even Dylan's humorous reference to getting stoned in "Rainy Day Women #12 & 35" and the Byrd's otherwise vague reference to being "Eight Miles High," let alone the Velvet's far more explicit themes. For the same reasons, record stores didn't want it either, and there was no real underground rock radio at that point. As a result, the album peaked at a disappointing number 103 on the Cashbox charts and barely cracked the *Billboard* 200, peaking at number 171.[86]

Of course, none of the Velvets cared much for commercial success anyway. As Morrison put it,

> We never did anything to ingratiate ourselves with the media, through lack of interest more than arrogance. I was convinced that if it was going to happen it would happen anyway. We were all really contemptuous of hype. Crusading is the word I always used. It took absolute conviction that we were doing the right thing—that was the only thing that could sustain us.[87]

For many critics, the debut was simply obscene and noisy. Lou Reed later stated that the band's favorite line from a critic was that "the flowers of evil are in bloom. Someone has to stamp them out before they spread."[88]

Due to the release delays, poor sales, and Warhol's attention going to other projects, Reed fired Warhol as manager and replaced him with Steve Sesnick.[89] Nico was forced out, too, though Velvet members contributed five songs to Nico's acclaimed solo debut in October '67, *Chelsea Girl*.[90]

The record's impact would continue to reverberate across a couple of generations of rock artists. The Velvets produced a second classic album, taking things to even greater artistic extremes, on the 1968 record *White Light/White Heat* (the title being a methamphetamine reference).

Cale and Reed, both with notably strong egos, butted heads regularly. In September 1968, Reed told Morrison and Tucker that either he or Cale had to go. Morrison and Tucker reluctantly sided with Reed, and Reed replaced Cale with Doug Yule.[91] The new lineup put out two more classic albums before Reed embarked on a solo career in 1972.

Morrison would step back from music, becoming a teacher and then a licensed tugboat captain. Tucker and Cale continued on long, critically well-received solo careers, with Cale also producing.

Reed continued his success solo over the ensuing decades and became one of rock's most respected figures. He had some commercial highs, especially with the classic glam rock album *Transformer* (1972) and its single, and his only hit, the ode to the Factory crowd, "Walk on the Wild Side." His many other offerings included the bold but arguably unlistenable *Metal Machine Music* (1975) and an Edgar Allan Poe concept album. His last studio album was an angry and unexpected effort backed by thrash metal superstars Metallica for the album *Lulu* (2011). Most fans and critics were not quite sure what to make of *Lulu*. One who was sure was David Bowie, who was quoted as saying that *Lulu* was a master work that people will be catching up to in the years to come.[92] As Laurie Anderson described it, "It's written by a man who understood fear and rage and venom and terror and revenge and love."[93]

And Reed did grow and change. Reed and Cale reconnected after Warhol's death to collaborate on *Songs for Drella* (1990). Reed also eventually got clean and sober for an extended period and was with his third wife, avant-garde performance artist Laurie Anderson, for the last 21 years of his life before passing in 2013.[94]

Reed had once said, "My God is rock 'n' roll. It's an obscure power that can change your life. The most important part of my religion is to play guitar."[95] Reed's spiritual life will be revisited later, but one of his most intriguing songs, from a personal perspective, is "Jesus" from the Velvet's third album, *Velvet Underground* (1969). It is a *very* different sort of "gospel" song. Reed, accompanied just by two acoustic guitars, poignantly sings of having fallen and pleads for help from what seems to be the only thing left. The song is the first of a three-part story on the album, the other two being "Beginning to See the Light" and "I'm Set Free." Even if not literally autobiographical—or all explicitly Christian—they are all three certainly honest and vulnerable efforts.

9

The Hippie/Freak Lifestyle, ca. 1966

In 1965 and '66, the hippie scene in Haight-Ashbury was becoming a bona fide social phenomenon. The Mamas & the Papas' lush, longing, and endlessly optimistic 1966 hit "California Dreamin'" captured the feel of the time and place.

Yet it still was not clear how this spontaneous movement was going to move forward. Politically-minded hippies had begun to take direct action in a variety of ways. This could mean being "leftist," defined as anything from pushing for an expanded welfare state or self-identifying as Marxist or as a pro–Castro revolutionary.[1] For others, being in the Haight entailed grassroots activism or something akin to the Peace Corps. Others still were simply trying to "be" the lifestyle they were espousing and thus be a model for a new society that others would gravitate toward. And, again, some were letting loose and having fun, including getting high and enjoying the "free love" ethos. The mainstream media struggled with defining the scene in simple terms.[2]

Along with a pro–civil rights stance, the other most well-defined hippie position was opposition to the Vietnam War. By 1965, the war that was supposedly in hand and not likely to last long was still going on, with body counts escalating fast. While some 400 U.S. servicemen had been killed in Vietnam in the years through 1964, 1965 saw 1,928 killed in action and 6,350 were killed in 1966 alone.[3]

A group called the Vietnam Day Committee organized what they called the Greatest Anti-war Protest Ever, in Berkeley. Thousands came by bus from LA, Portland, and other western cities. Folk bands performed, including Country Joe and the Fish, a "good-timey jug band" with washboard and kazoo, who did a famous rendition of "I Feel-like-I'm-Fixin'-to-Die Rag." Some 14,000 protesters eventually marched from Berkeley to Oakland.[4]

In one of the early signs of fractures in the Haight scene, the Hell's

Angels decided to oppose the march and blocked the route. Ken Kesey's bus could not get close enough to talk to them.[5] Later, Angels' leader Sonny Barger announced at a press conference that the Hell's Angels were available to act as a "crack troop of trained guerillas" in Vietnam on behalf of the United States.[6]

San Francisco had become a new epicenter of a social revolution, trying to fill a perceived massive void left by an establishment's ineffective and outdated institutions. There were a great many problems being exposed in the American dream; Berkeley activist Michael Grossman said at the time, "We have no precedent for the depth of the cultural transformation we are entering."[7]

In basic terms, hippies believed that life in straight culture was unjust, mentally debilitating, soul crushing, depressing, bad for their mental and spiritual health, and unsustainable.[8] Charles B. Reich captured as much in his 1970 book *The Greening of America*: "Older people are inclined to think of work, injustice and war, and the bitter frustrations of life, as the human condition…. But to those who have glimpsed the real possibilities of life … the prospect of a dreary corporate job, a ranch-house life, or a miserable death in a war is utterly intolerable."[9]

With the San Francisco music scene making a national impact and free love, pot, and LSD capturing imaginations, young people around the country were inspired to seek new directions and a new purpose, or otherwise at least be wild and free.

Further, and again, many of those kids who landed in the Haight were fleeing from the nation's broken and abusive homes. As Joan Didion wrote in her essay "Slouching toward Bethlehem" (1967), despite a steady stock market and a high GNP, "San Francisco was where the social hemorrhaging was showing up. San Francisco was where the missing children were gathering and calling themselves 'hippies.'"[10] Didion further described,

> These were children who grew up cut loose from the web of cousins and great-aunts and family doctors and lifelong neighbors who had traditionally suggested and enforced the society's values. They are children who have moved around a lot, San Jose, Chula Vista, here. They are less in rebellion against the society than ignorant of it, able only to feed back certain of its most publicized self-doubts, Vietnam, Saran-Wrap, diet pills, the Bomb.

The Haight was becoming overwhelmed by these newcomers, and the hippies were being further challenged to maintain a sustainable community with the various problems brought on by transients and wayward youth, including panhandling, crime, and drug abuse. One *Oracle* columnist asked, "Will success spoil the Haight-Ashbury?"[11] Another *Oracle* columnist suggested that people try to start their own Haight-Ashbury-type neighborhood in their own communities.[12] To accommodate the migrants, the Diggers appealed to the freak and straight crowds to "help the Diggers do what Jesus told us all to do," to help house and feed people.[13]

A Coalescing Freak Ideology

Where a parental generation had abandoned city life for the suburbs in droves, many of their children now saw life in the burbs as stifling, with homogenous populations, malls, and cul-de-sacs and thus limited social circles. Cities, however, although perhaps less "safe" in many ways, were being seen as vibrant and more alive. Hippies, college students, and young single people continued to gravitate toward lower-income urban areas and often shared the rent on large houses and apartments in communal-style living in San Francisco and elsewhere.[14]

On the plus side, for many, communal living became an ideal and even a sort of prototype for a new societal direction, with cooperation trumping competition.[15] On the other hand, less formal rules could lead to strong personalities dominating matters as well as a new form of paternalism.[16]

Hippie lifestyles evolved as well. As one example, the youth generation had also grown up under the incessant sway of Madison Avenue and corporate messaging. One of the largest advertising industries, in fact, was the soap and personal hygiene industry (e.g., "soap operas"), which many came to see as a manipulation that amounted to "buy our products … or be shunned by society." According to one freak, this new generation equated "cleanliness with unreality." One perspective was that being more natural meant less hung-up about dirt or natural body aromas. Men growing long hair also shocked the mainstream, but it was a calculated decision to reject both military-like discipline and symbolic crew cuts popular in the '50s, as well as rigid gender norms and behaviors.[17] However, to many outside observers, they were simply "dirty hippies."[18]

Hippie women saw brassieres as an unnatural and outdated method of restriction along the lines of a corset; bras were burned in literal and symbolic protest.[19] At the same time, women took to short "mini" skirts and hip-hugging jeans, and men had long hair and were wearing tight-legged pants.[20]

In sum, dropping out of organized society and its customs become a statement unto itself, meaning one would no longer expend the energy or sell oneself out to keep the gears of a corrupt machine turning.[21] The movement was instead finding new ways to deal with life through rock music and the rock ethos including the realms of sex and drugs as well as morality.

Sex

In the mid- and late '60s, nudity and faux nudity were showing up in avant-garde plays, foreign films, and in art house theaters.[22] Poets were reading controversial works in public in San Francisco and elsewhere.[23] Haight resident R. Crumb, as another example, became a major underground cartoonist with his *Zap Comix* (1968), which were so edgy and sexual in nature that they were sold as pornographic material. Also, while in the '60s the federal workforce had been purged of homosexuals as "security risks," the hippies questioned and sometimes denounced the vilification and criminalization of homosexuality.[24]

Most hippies had come to see the sexual mores they were raised on as either prudish, shaming, unrealistic, or hypocritical. Author and publisher Helen Gurley Brown, for example, voicing one view of countercultural sexuality, wrote, "Being sexy means that you accept all the parts of your body as worthy and loveable."[25] The *Oracle* called for "the freedom of the body and the 'pursuit of joy.'"[26] Sexuality was experienced without external judgment and shame. On the other hand, young people found their way with little in external guidance or limits. One person living in a commune noted, "It was pretty interesting to wake up in the night and find someone in your sleeping bag with you. It was just kind of an assumed thing that everybody wanted to have sex with everybody else."[27]

For people like countercultural poet and cofounder of the outrageous Bohemian band the Fugs Tuli Kupferberg, the older generation only hated the youth because they "love more, fuck more, take more drugs."[28] No doubt there was *some* sort of truth in such a statement but there was another view, too. To some, without a more substantive conception of love, or presumably without strong emotional, psychological, or even spiritual components, sex could become a soulless, mechanical act, a possibly unhealthy exercise in power, or the subjugation of one's self. These scenarios had their own serious repercussions. Journalist Margot Adler opined that "many of us were simply too young to love well."[29]

In the establishment's eyes, as expressed by nationally syndicated advice columnist Ann Landers, for example, "What they call love is often a temporary feeling of euphoria produced by drugs."[30] Another national columnist, Jeff Berner, wrote, "The four-letter word LOVE is just what kids around the country haven't been brought up with."[31] As another indicator of hippies' lifestyles, sexually transmitted diseases rose; gonorrhea, for example, nearly doubled nationally from 1965 to 1970.[32]

Men were generally the more enthusiastic gender regarding the sexual liberation movement.[33] Women who did not sleep around risked being labeled "uptight" and "not with it."[34] This led some women to reconsider what the counterculture meant to them. As W.J. Rorabaugh observed, "Down that road was feminism, either with or without the counterculture."[35]

Drugs

For many hippies, marijuana had become almost as common as cigarettes or alcohol. Pot produced a mellowing effect, it was rarely directly associated with violence or other criminal acts, and it was cheap. Many people could even function in day-to-day life while under its influence. Nonetheless, marijuana was treated with stiff, mandatory criminal sentences. Ken Kesey, for example, was busted for pot in La Honda in '65 and served five months on a work farm.[36] He could have faced up to five years with no parole for a second offense.[37]

As to LSD, the biggest era of its use was 1965–1975, which also, interestingly, happened to largely correspond with the Vietnam War years. One rough estimate was that 10–30 million people took LSD an average of six times each.[38]

A great many attested to the psychological benefits of LSD, and others had life-altering, transcendent experiences.

However, not all even in the counterculture were approving of how the freaks used LSD. Esteemed *Rolling Stone* social and political writer and unapologetically massive drug user Hunter S. Thompson described it as "pathetically eager acid Freaks who thought they could buy peace and understanding for three bucks a hit."[39] Furthermore, Charles Perry observed, "The one thing nearly everybody experienced from acid was the disappointment of realizing there was a point of diminishing returns, after which it was just a hall of mirrors."[40]

Certainly, LSD could bring emotional and psychological harm and, on occasion, lead to psychotic breaks and even suicide. More and more news stories of the time, though often inaccurately and sensationally, focused on the very worst LSD episodes and where people may well have already had severe mental health problems to begin with.[41] Still, poet Allen Cohen observed, "But given the amount of its use, I would say it was one of our least destructive national obsessions."[42]

Noteworthy, after a long period of the drug's criminalization, by the 2010s, LSD was being studied again and proving to be very promising in the treatment of mental health problems such as alcoholism, PTSD, and depression.[43]

Problems with hard drugs like heroin and methamphetamines worsened in the Haight, and by 1966, felony drug arrests were up to 100 a month.[44] Even most hippies acknowledged these were not the "good" drugs and that often led to intense addiction and dramatic harms in physical and mental well-being (though so could alcohol and prescription drugs).[45]

Religious Concerns

Cohen, also one of the founders of the *Oracle*, gave his summary of the Haight scene:

> Gandhi and Martin Luther King were our heroes and we had turned to the rich heritage of Asian mysticism and metaphysics for our inspiration and our practice. We leaped across oceans and through time to pre–Christian mythologies like the American Indian, the Egyptian and the occult and pagan philosophies of Europe. We studied with Buddhists and Indian gurus, native shamans, witches and yogis.[46]

Some hippies also became followers of Hare Krishna, which meant being opposed to drugs, eating vegetarian, shaving their heads, wearing robes, performing chants regularly, and selling literature and soliciting donations on local sidewalks.[47]

Christian evangelicals came to the Haight and converted some kids into what became known as the large Jesus People movement in '67, which had more than 100 programs in Southern California by the end of the decade.[48] Even Billy Graham endorsed the movement.[49]

Some other hippies had no problem embracing Jesus, who was indeed anti-violence, favored helping the poor over seeking material comforts, and even had long hair. It was not uncommon to hear hippies state, or see on signs and T-shirts, that "Jesus was a hippy."[50] Of course, Jesus wasn't sleeping around and high all the time, either.

10

Modern Mythic Heroes and the Summer of Love, 1966–1967

The trend of declining church attendance that had taken root earlier in the United Kingdom since World War I followed much the same path in the United States.[1] The trend kept up virtually every year into the next century. The number of priests being ordained was in steady decline as well.[2]

The Catholic Church also looked to adjust to modern times. In 1870, the Church had formally declared the pope "infallible" and asserted itself as "the one Church of Christ which in the Creed is professed one, holy, catholic and apostolic."[3] To more conservative Catholics, this was the end of any discussion of need for reform, which would indeed be the case for nearly a century.

By 1959, however, Pope John XXIII and the Catholic leadership saw the Church as becoming too detached from the rest of society and its institutions. Thus, it was decided that the Church would undergo significant reformation with the Second Vatican Council (1962–1965), or "Vatican II," to provide both spiritual renewal and a reconsideration of the Church's position in the modern world.[4]

Illustrative was that representatives of Protestant and Orthodox Eastern Churches were invited to the council as nonvoting attendees, and Latin was dropped as a requirement for mass.[5] To Catholic traditionalists, such changes undermined the real authority of the Church and its "objective and rigorous demands."[6]

Most organized religions in the United States were dealing with similar struggles and the decline in attendance at religious services due in large part to attrition and a younger generation not filling the pews back up at the same rate.[7] According to Gallup, church attendance among U.S. Catholics dropped from 75 percent in 1955 to 54 percent by 1975. The importance of religion in people's lives decreased as well. Harris polls indicated

10. Modern Mythic Heroes and the Summer of Love, 1966–1967

that of the 97 percent of Americans who said they believed in God, only 27 percent identified as "deeply religious."[8] Theologian John Country Murray remarked, "The great American proposition is 'religion is good for the kids, though I'm not religious myself.'"[9] In April 1966, a *Time* magazine cover article provocatively asked (though the article was really a philosophical discussion), "Is God Dead?"[10]

At this same time, the Beatles had exceeded all previous forms of pop culture idolatry. Their fans were so rabid that comparisons to religious fervor were not uncommon. In 1964, a writer for the *Partisan Review* noted that Beatle fans clung to "icons, devotional photos, and illuminated missals which keep the tiny earthbound fans in touch with the provocatively absconded deities" and going on as far as to state that the Beatles had "become religion in fact."[11]

The group had certainly taken on an outsized role in the world, in ways that were once the sole domain of establishment institutions. The lovable mop tops scared and unsettled many with the incredible levels of admiration and attention they received.

It was a strange time in this new era of rock and roll versus the establishment's status quo. Instead of being reserved, placid, or obedient, many were instead choosing more joy and excitement in their lives, something along the lines of "Twist and Shout." Be dutiful workers and consumers? Well, "Money Can't Buy Me Love." Follow someone else's interpretation of a book written by someone else a couple of thousand years ago, rigidly and literally? Maybe "All You Need Is Love."

In early 1966, *London Evening Standard* reporter Maureen Cleave, a longtime friend of the then 25-year-old John Lennon, hung out for three days as she interviewed him. Cleave captured the Beatles' status at the time, writing,

> They are famous in the way the Queen is famous. When John Lennon's Rolls-Royce, with its black wheels and its black windows, goes past, people say: "It's the Queen," or "It's the Beatles." With her they share the security of a stable life at the top.

At one point during the three days, Cleave also recorded Lennon's comment about Jesus, as follows:

> Experience has sown few seeds of doubt in him: not that his mind is closed, but it's closed round whatever he believes at the time. "Christianity will go," he said. "It will vanish and shrink. I needn't argue about that; I'm right and I will be proved right. We're more popular than Jesus now; I don't know which will go first—rock 'n' roll or Christianity. Jesus was all right but his disciples were thick and ordinary. It's them twisting it that ruins it for me." He is reading extensively about religion.[12]

Cleave's interview ran in the *Standard* on March 4, 1966, and the quote drew no attention in England. To British readers, "Christianity" simply meant the Church of England and its flagging support, something that had begun well before the explosion of Beatlemania.[13]

However, in the United States, the partial "more famous than Jesus" quote appeared on the front cover of a U.S. teen magazine, *Datebook*, on July 29, 1966 (as did McCartney's apparently noncontroversial quote decrying racism in the United States: "[America's] a lousy country where anyone black is a dirty nigger!").[14]

In context, Lennon's statement does not seem particularly well thought out; it was insensitive and more than a bit brash. Yet the comment explicitly does not demean *Jesus* in any way either. Lennon's entire point was to distinguish Jesus from church leaders and followers and noting an otherwise already well-documented trend. Even the Jesuit journal *America* wrote at the time that "Lennon was simply stating what many a Christian educator would readily admit."[15]

Nonetheless, by August, Lennon's remark became a lightning rod for various religious camps and especially America's southern Christian fundamentalists. On August 5, *Revolver* was released and the Beatles' U.S. tour was approaching, making them the highest profile group of human beings on the planet. The Beatles had also hardly ingratiated themselves with the southern establishment on a previous tour when they had integrated the Gator Bowl in Jacksonville, Florida, by refusing to perform in front of segregated fans.[16]

The Lennon quote became a chance for their detractors to challenge the group's almost golden aura and immense influence and maybe at least knock them down a peg. The backlash grew quickly and even included death threats. Fundamentalist Christians staged protests and Beatles record burnings all over the South. The KKK came out in Memphis, while the Memphis City Council canceled the Beatles' show, declaring that no "municipal facilities be used as a forum to ridicule anyone's religion."[17] Others rallied in support of the Beatles.

Lennon was shaken by the surprising intensity of the situation and finally relented enough to give something of an apology/clarification at a press conference on August 11. Said Lennon, "If I had said television was more popular than Jesus, I might have gotten away with it. I used the word Beatles as a remote thing."[18] He added, "You can't keep quiet about everything that is going on in the world, unless you're a monk. Sorry monks, I didn't mean it."[19] A couple of years later, Lennon would tell a CBC interviewer, "I'm one of Christ's biggest fans."[20]

In a Beatles' divine karma victory, one of the stations that organized the public bonfires of their records on August 13, KLUE in Longview,

Texas, was struck by lightning the next day, causing extensive damage to their radio equipment and knocking their news director unconscious.[21]

In a horrific twist, 14 years later, in December 1980, Lennon would be murdered outside his home at the Dakota apartment building in New York City by the deranged gunman Mark David Chapman. Chapman identified as a born-again Christian and years earlier had shared with his prayer group how especially upset he was by Lennon's quote regarding Jesus. Chapman would say that he was in part provoked to kill Lennon because of it, although he also had a long random list of other celebrities he had considered killing as well.[22]

Despite the turmoil, the Beatles finished an otherwise successful tour. The commotion initially overshadowed the Beatles quantum leap forward in music with the release of *Revolver*, for many, their greatest work.

The Summer of Love

At the beginning of 1967, *Time* magazine named the entire baby boomer generation, "Twenty-Five and Under," as its Man of the Year, describing them as "well educated, affluent, rebellious, responsible, pragmatic, idealistic, brave, 'alienated' and hopeful."[23] Also in 1967, a formal "hippie" subculture movement was being recognized in the mainstream media, and a "Summer of Love" in Haight-Ashbury would embody all of the freak ideals.[24]

There was still not a clear platform for all hippies to agree on what would move their collective interests forward. The main ideas seemed to be a return to a simpler life, less materialism, living off and with the land, promoting meditation, exploring one's consciousness, being less greedy, having more peace and less war, less reliance on modern technology, and more personal freedom.[25]

Media attention on the Haight, including features in *Time* and *Newsweek*, ensured a continued influx of youth.[26]

In psych rock, a new British, proto-prog/space rock group, Pink Floyd, released their eponymous debut, *The Piper at the Gates of Dawn* (1967). The album was a mix of British Invasion and spacey sound experiments. Primary songwriter Syd Barrett took the album title from a favorite children's book, and the songs were playful and colorful. Lyrically, Barrett further equated hallucinogenic trips with interstellar trips, and the record became a landmark of the psych genre. The record also had a dark undercurrent, however, which would become even more evident when Barrett's severe mental health problems surfaced. Apparent underlying issues combined with too much LSD led Barrett to a severe mental breakdown, ending his time with the band.[27] Barrett would release two solo albums in 1970, but that would be it. The band would continue on without him and have great success over the decades that followed.[28]

Again, in October 1966, the state of California had outlawed LSD. In response, the editors of the *Oracle* and LSD researcher Richard Alpert organized what they called a "Human Be-In" of some 20,000–30,000 people in January '67 at a park in the Haight.[29] The name was a play on the words "human being" and a reference to the political "sit-ins" and "teach-ins" of the civil rights movement.[30] Beat poet Gary Snyder opened the event by blowing in a conch shell, and Ginsberg chanted the Hindi mantra, "om." Leary made his famous pronouncement to the youth to "tune in, turn on, and drop out."[31]

The Be-In, followed by several others in other cities, confused the establishment. The hippies didn't set out a clear purpose or goals for the event, yet people did seem in on a "shared secret" of some sort.[32] As one writer later put it, "For a brief period, 'peace and love' was an un-ironic shorthand for a belief system vividly distinct from mainstream Western values."[33]

Back in New York, the Be-Ins, the growing popularity of astrology, and a deep desire for profound change all inspired the Broadway smash *Hair*, featuring the 5th Dimension's rock-inspired hit "Age of Aquarius/Let the Sunshine In." Some astrologers declared that the age had either already started or was an inevitable pathway in the future.[34]

The Beatles and rock music had seemingly all but conquered the world or at least much of the world's youth, giving the countercultural movement immense confidence. Popular buttons in Haight-Ashbury at the time read, "We Are Everywhere."[35] Scott McKenzie, though not from the area, had a hit single in May 1967, "San Francisco (Be Sure to Wear Flowers in Your Hair)," romanticizing the Haight scene even more, though with an idealized view that did not necessarily exist.[36]

All of the events in the Haight and the psych rock of the mid-'60s culminated in the Summer of 1967, which came to be known as the Summer of Love. This was the high point of the hippie era, though it also coincided with the beginning of the scene's decline. The same year, the Gray Line bus company began tourist trips on its "Hippie-Hop" tour of the Haight, which included a "Glossary of Hippie Terms."[37] Hollywood produced the first hippie-exploitation film, *The Love-Ins*, in July 1967.[38]

Another key hit came with English rock band Procol Harum's marriage of psychedelic rock to a Johann Sebastian Bach melody, the timeless "A Whiter Shade of Pale." Other top ten hit songs on the 1967 charts included the relentlessly upbeat psych-pop of "Happy Together" by the Turtles, the "Groovin'" of the Young Rascals, Bobbie Gentry's murky

10. Modern Mythic Heroes and the Summer of Love, 1966–1967

country-folk ballad, in part exploring a familial disconnect, "Ode to Billie Joe," Memphis's Box Tops with the blue-eyed soul of "The Letter," and the hard psychedelia and overt sexuality of the Doors' "Light My Fire."[39]

In early 1967, Buffalo Springfield, whose members included future Crosby, Stills, Nash & Young members, Stephen Stills and Neil Young, released the remarkable and beautifully eerie wake-up call and call for peace, "For What It's Worth."

For the Summer of Love, an estimated 75,000 additional young people came through the Haight.[40] In 1967, the FBI recorded a record 90,000 runaways nationally, and in the first three months of the year, the police in Haight-Ashbury's district picked up 114 underage runaways and arrested 87 minors and 184 adults.[41]

The Dead and Jefferson Airplane played free concerts at Golden Gate Park, though financial pressures on the Dead led Jerry Garcia to drop the idea that every show had to be free.[42] Jefferson Airplane released the hit single "White Rabbit" in June 1967, leading up to their highly regarded psych-album *Surreal Pillow*. Grace Slick had been on an acid trip and listening to Miles Davis's *Sketches of Spain* for 24 hours straight when she wrote the song.[43] Slick delivered powerful and surreal references to drugs, to Lewis Carroll's *Alice in Wonderland*, and a withdrawal from society. The song ends abruptly and on a dramatic, emotionally unresolved peak, seeming to reflect the import of the times but also the vast uncertainty of the future.

The highlight of the summer was the Monterey Pop Festival, June 16–18, a couple of hours south of San Francisco, featuring the established entities the Mamas & the Papas and Jefferson Airplane, along with breakout performances from Janis Joplin and Jimi Hendrix.[44] The Beatles and the Stones were touring at the time and were no-shows.[45] Souvenir programs included a personal greeting from the Beatles, and acid point man Owsley Stanley had a special batch of Monterey Purple, or Purple Haze, tabs of LSD.[46]

Jimi Hendrix was born in Seattle in 1942, coming from a badly broken home. Hendrix had a brief stint in the army before being discharged because, as his commanding officer wrote, the guitar-obsessed Hendrix apparently could not "function while performing duties and thinking about his guitar."[47] Hendrix, who was African American, took to the Black southern "chitlin circuit" where he spent time with the Isley Brothers and then hooked up with Little Richard's band. He went solo when he was 23, but he and a new manager decided he had a better chance of catching on in Swinging London, where he would be less confined by race.[48]

Hendrix was a virtuoso and utterly original. He was left-handed but learned to play a right-handed guitar upside down, making his style even more unique. His sound and look conveyed a mix of blues mastery, a psych-gypsy look, and Black pride all at once.[49] Hendrix's first shows in London brought out the top guitar legends of the time. Such was Hendrix's talent that he didn't merely impress, but he even shook their confidence as musicians.[50]

The Jim Hendrix Experience's appearance at Monterey, their first U.S. show, saw Hendrix put on one of the most renowned performances in rock history. His reinvention of the Troggs' hit "Wild Thing" was stunning, oozed sexuality, and transfixed the crowd. Seemingly the only way to end such a show, he destroyed his guitar in a voodoo-esque ceremony by setting it alight. Hendrix would go on to be widely accepted as the greatest instrumentalist in rock history and one of the great musicians of the twentieth century.

Joplin, backed by Big Brother and the Holding Company, brought the combined influences of the Black church and honky-tonks and a remarkable blues feel.[51]

Stax Records' soul luminaries out of Memphis, including Otis Redding and Booker T and the mixed-race MGs, were a revelation for the mostly white crowd. Redding turned in a rousing set, including a soul version of the Stones' "Satisfaction."

Somewhere between 55,000 and 90,000 people attended over the weekend. The Monterey police chief, Frank Marinello, remarked how smoothly and crime-free it had all gone.[52]

The Beatles—Stage Three (Psychedelia) (Continued)

Sgt. Pepper's

Firmly into their third, psychedelic, stage, the Beatles would continue to make their most ambitious and greatest artistic efforts, while setting out a worldview for the counterculture.

The scope of the Beatles' fame, impact, and fan reverence were indeed all quasi-religious. The crowds and the constant expectations and demands being placed on them and their time were becoming overwhelming as well. By necessity, band members were living more and more insular lives. Observers noted that the four were becoming more "hard-shelled" and developing an "Us and Them" perspective.[53] For all of the perks, it was becoming hard to be the Beatles. McCartney had the idea that instead of trying to meet the expectations being placed on the Beatles, the group could simply become a new identity entirely distinct from the Fab Four. The result was the psychedelic music hall band Sgt. Pepper's Lonely Hearts Club Band and the album of the same name.

10. Modern Mythic Heroes and the Summer of Love, 1966–1967

With some inspiration from Brian Wilson, the main creative force behind the Beach Boys, and that group's album *Pet Sounds* and building both on *Revolver* and their experiences with LSD, the Beatles found a new creative freedom. The album, released in May 1967, was a jolt not just to screaming teens but to Western culture. The Fab Four produced classics in the styles of acid rock (the lead-off title track), one of the most vivid, pure psychedelic tracks ("Lucy in the Sky with Diamonds"), and brilliant pop ("A Little Help from My Friends," "Getting Better"). They also pulled from the traditional pop songwriting of Tin Pan Alley and vaudeville and their British equivalents of "Denmark Street" and music hall (e.g., "When I'm Sixty-Four," the piano in "Lovely Rita," the brass and strings throughout). Added to that was a touch of sitar and Indian music ("Within You without You") and a just plain strange, avant-garde excursion ("Being for the Benefit of Mr. Kite!").

Martin and Emerick again fully realized and enhanced every one of the group's creative ideas. As Martin put it, "every trick" was "brought out of the bag," including tape loops and found sounds such as alarm clocks and rooster crows. The group's ambitions were so ahead of their time that studio techniques were invented as they went.[54]

Generally considered the greatest track on the album is the closer that somehow tied together not only everything on the album but the Beatles' entire career to that point: "A Day in the Life." The song opens with Lennon's stark, surreal storytelling, building dramatic tension. McCartney then takes over and sings his more straight-pop part about real life starting with waking up and combing his hair, until that narrative fades into a dream. Soon, a furious, swirling orchestral crescendo, as the dynamic, psychedelic vision literally crashes into present-day reality. The ending is the most dramatic of final chords consisting of multiple pianos simultaneously hammering an E major, which rings out for 40 seconds, and then silence. It was an awe-inspiring moment for millions. The record was one of those rare works of art that seemed to have no preexisting frame of reference for even understanding it.

In less than five years since the Beatles' debut album, the world of high culture had gone from deeming the Fab Four a silly curiosity to a sensation/curiosity, to an okay-that's-not-bad-for-a-rock-band, to finally something else altogether. With *Sgt. Pepper's*, *Time* magazine announced "a historic departure in the progress of music—any music."[55] Writing for the *Times* (London), prominent critic Kenneth Tynan went so far as to describe *Sgt. Pepper's* as "a decisive moment in the history of Western civilisation."[56] Literary critic Richard Poirier observed that "listening to the *Sgt. Pepper* album one thinks not simply of the history of popular music but the history of this century."[57] The album went on to win five Grammys, including Album of the Year, the first rock album to ever receive that award.[58]

Sgt. Pepper's is a concept album with a remarkable cohesiveness, even while its lyrical themes and musical styles are wildly disparate. It is an alternate universe of rock and post–rock and roll and seemingly most every other style of music under the sun.

As to the apparent LSD influence on the album, Timothy Leary declared upon hearing the record, "My work is finished. Now, it's out."[59]

Sgt. Pepper's has long been a consensus pick for the greatest pop-rock album of all time.[60] It is one of a handful of such albums that is so fantastic and so immersive that a listener can get entirely lost in it for its 40-minute running time. The album cover alone was iconic art, featuring the band as their alter egos in the middle of a psychedelic landscape, with over 60 photos and waxworks representing a collage of historical figures, many famous, some not.[61]

There has also been reassessment of *Sgt. Pepper's* over the years, often in the form of bringing it down a notch, a perhaps inevitable correction given such an overwhelming initial response. Some of the sheer shock and awe present with the album's first plays have naturally worn off. It is also true that *Sgt. Pepper's* may not necessarily be the single greatest collection of pop or rock and roll songs ever put together. "She's Leaving Home" features a most nonrocking *harp* and can be heard as rather maudlin. "When I'm Sixty-Four" has been accused of being overly cute if not simply being from the wrong era. "Fixing a Hole" is interesting but perhaps just meandering. Arguably, "Being for the Benefit of Mr. Kite!" is simply too weird, period.

In any event, the album is a crucial artifact of twentieth-century music and history and for many reasons. The Beatles created an album perhaps as timeless and all-encompassing as could be. A young *Washington Post* reporter, Carl Bernstein (soon to be known for his Watergate reportage), wrote in his review upon the album's release,

> In their latest album, the Beatles have managed to create a musical infinity through a miraculous metamorphosis of dozens of Eastern and Western musical ideas, some centuries old, others from our own era and more than a few from the future.[62]

Even further, considering that at the time rock and roll itself was seen as in direct opposition to, and in deep contempt of, an entire older generation, *Sgt. Pepper's* cannot be so simply contained. For starters, "When I'm Sixty-Four" and other references to more traditional British music can be seen as tame but also as boldly inclusive choices. On that track in particular, McCartney specifically romanticizes music of the older generation

10. Modern Mythic Heroes and the Summer of Love, 1966–1967

and even of himself getting old (while in love). This, in contrast with the Who's war cry on "My Generation" that they would prefer to be *dead* than to grow old.

Sgt. Pepper's also possessed a fairly remarkable empathy for that parental generation, even if the band obviously wasn't seeing eye to eye on all accounts. "She's Leaving Home," based on a real news story, is McCartney's tale of parents realizing that their daughter, likely a late–teen/young adult, has run away, presumably off to some countercultural-type destination. The then-25-year-old McCartney's vocals and the backup vocals are from the perspective of the parents and capture wrenching parental heartbreak and the shattering of familial denial. Not only has the child in question grown up and suddenly left, but it is painfully clear that she had never really bought into the family system as the parents had believed. McCartney acknowledges the parents' pain and sacrifice and that they provided for their daughter, or at least materially so. Yet, even while being empathetic, the Beatles also well understood why a younger person would want to break away from a family situation that may clearly have been emotionally, psychologically, or spiritually untenable.

The song is reminiscent of "Eleanor Rigby" in the sense that it acknowledges the perspective of the older generation and does so with sincerity and stark honesty. Both songs similarly incorporate the instrumentation of the older generation with classical string instruments.

Also of note, during those same *Sgt. Pepper's* recording sessions, the Beatles recorded two other of their most highly regarded songs, "Penny Lane" and "Strawberry Fields." Both songs were released three months prior to *Sgt Pepper's* as a double-A-side single and were then included on the following Beatle album later that year, *Magical Mystery Tour*. Each surreal-pop song is rooted in McCartney's and Lennon's childhood memories, respectively, from their beloved Liverpool. The group was rebelling and shaking things up, but they still had a fond appreciation of where they came from.

On *Sgt Pepper's*, the Beatles and studio friends created a stunningly original work without catering or adapting to the establishment or anyone else's concept of what greatness, art, or rock even were. Once dismissed as the disgraceful sound of primitives, rock and roll was now shown to have seemingly limitless possibilities. And no one needed to be excluded from this new vision for the world, whether parents of runaways, people over 64, or those raised on music hall. It was an epic achievement and perhaps as ambitious as anything one could expect from some pop stars. What else could unify so many people in a meaningful way?

A month after *Sgt. Pepper's* release, the Beatles were showcased on a live TV special and the first global satellite hookup to an audience of

500 million people in 31 countries. Sitting among a crowd of their Love Generation fans, friends, and musician friends, they performed a rousing, singalong of Lennon's "All You Need Is Love." That song features a repetitive use of a background harmony that consists solely of the word love. In the hands of a lesser group, that could have been painfully sappy. Here, though, the sheer simplicity and the integrity of the performance make for a captivating performance.[63]

By the end of the Summer of Love, the Haight-Ashbury scene was continuing to unravel due to the impact of misplaced youth and drug abuse as well as police harassment.[64] In August 1967, two prominent acid dealers were murdered.[65] Methamphetamine and heroin became more prevalent and brought all of the ills that come with those drugs.

The members of the Dead and Jefferson Airplane had already moved out of the neighborhood.[66] Many of the remaining Haight freak community began to look for living spaces away from the city, some establishing rural communes.[67] From 1967 on, the remaining Diggers sensed the end and the co-opting of the movement from the outside. The group held a public "Death of Hippie" ceremony on October 6, 1967, marking the one-year anniversary of California outlawing LSD.[68] Years later, the Dead's Bob Weir gave his take on the Diggers era:

> They were trying to impose their rules and order on a totally, and necessarily, fluid and amorphous situation. I didn't see the point—nor the future—in that. Not much of the ideology survived, but the music, the art, and the feeling behind it flourished.[69]

Rock and roll would move forward in a new era of cultural dominance, but the transition would not be easy.

11

Cultural Checkpoints: Vietnam, Political Divisions, and Race, Late 1966–1967

Politics/War: Vietnam

Martin Luther King Speaks Out against the Vietnam War. In April 1967, King calls the United States "the greatest purveyor of violence in the world," encouraged draft evasion, and suggested a merger between the anti-war and civil rights movements.[1]

Muhammad Ali Refuses Draft. Also in April 1967, and despite an assured position boxing in exhibitions or on goodwill tours with the USO, 25-year-old African American world champion boxer Muhammad Ali (formerly Cassius Clay) refused to avail himself to the draft.[2] As a result, Ali was convicted of draft evasion, sentenced to five years in prison, and banned from boxing for three of his most prime fighting years. As Ali had previously stated about the war,

> And shoot them for what? They never called me nigger, they never lynched me, they didn't put no dogs on me, they didn't rob me of my nationality, rape and kill my mother and father.... Shoot them for what? How can I shoot them poor people? Just take me to jail.[3]

Ali stayed out of prison while his case was appealed, and the U.S. Supreme Court eventually overturned his conviction in 1971, granting his status as a conscientious objector. Ali was vilified by much of mainstream America, both on the right and some on the left.[4]

Johnson's Popularity Peaks. In June 1967, President Johnson's popularity had risen from 42 percent to what would be his peak of 58 percent.[5] By the end of July '67, however, Gallup showed that less than a majority of Americans still thought getting involved in Vietnam was a good idea.[6] The war was costing the United States billions of dollars a month.[7]

Bombing Ineffective: Bombing Laos. In August '67, the U.S. military also admitted to having bombed Laos daily over the preceding three years without the public's knowledge.⁸

Romney Ignored. In September 1967, Michigan governor George Romney told the press that during his recent trip to Vietnam, military higher-ups had intentionally given him a distorted and positive view of the situation. As he put it bluntly, "I was brainwashed." The public, however, largely, did not appreciate his less-than-rosy view of the war effort and Romney's presidential aspirations were dashed.⁹

Call for Escalation. Also in September 1967, California governor Ronald Reagan called for a sharp escalation of the nation's war commitment.¹⁰

Operation CHAOS Begins. President Johnson greenlighted the CIA's Operation CHAOS in 1967 to infiltrate groups in the student and civil rights movements, including the Students for a Democratic Society, the Southern Christian Leadership Conference, and the Black Panther Party.¹¹ The programs were later exposed for using illegal surveillance, which had been expanded under President Nixon.¹²

Social Issues

Preservation of the Grand Canyon. In September 1967, the U.S. Bureau of Reclamation devised a plan to turn the Grand Canyon into a reservoir.¹³ The Sierra Club worked to oppose it, including a national ad campaign raising awareness that ultimately ended the effort.¹⁴

Pot Petition. The Beatles were among 55 signers of a petition to legalize marijuana presented in a full-page ad in the London *Times* in July '67.¹⁵

Urban Riots. Also in July '67, the ghetto in Newark erupted in rioting, as did Spanish Harlem in New York. U.S. Army tanks were deployed in Detroit, and there was firebombing in Detroit and Oakland.¹⁶

NOW Becomes More Overtly Political. In November '67, partly inspired by the effectiveness of the civil rights movement, the National Organization of Women (NOW) became overtly political, including advancing a Bill of Rights for Women and calling for a constitutional amendment to include the Equal Rights Amendment (ERA). The ERA sought to effectively end the legal distinctions between men and women in terms of divorce, property, employment, and other matters.

NOW also adopted strong language favoring abortion rights, leading to a splintering of the group.¹⁷ NOW members protested the 1968 Miss America pageant in Atlantic City and attracted national TV exposure by protesting, including crowning a sheep Miss America.¹⁸

Radical/Hippie Politics. In an attempt to politically mobilize the freaks, social activist Jerry Rubin teamed up with college dropout Abbie

Hoffman to form the Youth International Party, the "Yippies," to target the media with theatrical protests.[19] At their radical best, Rubin and Hoffman infiltrated the NYSE, and standing at a balcony overlooking the trading floor, they hurled handfuls of dollar bills onto the floor. As expected, the brokers scurried after the money, thus providing a literal demonstration of the phrase "money grubbing capitalists."[20]

Senator Robert Kennedy Rises as Voice of the Left/The Rights Seeks Calm. In March 1968, Robert Kennedy, the Democratic Party's leading candidate for the presidency, spelled out his political views:

> Our Gross National Product, now, is over $800 billion dollars a year, but that Gross National Product ... does not allow for the health of our children, the quality of their education or the joy of their play. It does not include the beauty of our poetry or the strength of our marriages, the intelligence of our public debate or the integrity of our public officials.[21]

On the other hand, among the chaos, the violence, and the uprisings in Watts and Detroit, many blue-collar and middle-class white Americans, in particular, had had enough. The Republicans were positioned as the party of law and order and consistency. Barry Goldwater and others saw it as a moral/religious issue:

> The laws of God, and of nature, have no dateline.... To suggest that the Conservative philosophy is out of date is akin to saying that the Golden Rule, or the Ten Commandments or Aristotle's Politics are out of date.[22]

Opposing positions continued to take shape.

Black Pride/Black Power. In the late '60s and early '70s, African American civil rights efforts included embracing a concept of "Black Pride," as they bolstered self-pride and self-worth and to counter pressures rejecting African and African American history and cultures. Instead of Jim Crow–era hair straightening and skin lightening, for example, natural afros, natural looks, and a "Black is beautiful" attitude were embraced.[23]

The Black Panther Party. The Black Panthers were founded by Huey Newton and Bobby Seale in Oakland, California, in 1966. Even with the end of formal segregation and the passage of crucial civil rights litigation, many African Americans, in urban centers especially, were in dire straits. Neighborhoods were deeply entrenched in poverty, high crime, and a lack of jobs and social services and with no private investment coming in. Primary governmental responses were seen solely as stricter, and sometimes abusive, policing. The Panthers were originally formed to counter police brutality and broadened to include "community survival programs."[24]

In late 1967, Newton was arrested after a shootout with police in which an officer was killed. Newton was convicted of manslaughter, but the conviction was overturned two years later due to improper deliberation procedures and he was released.[25]

The Panthers then morphed into a Marxist revolutionary group that called for arming all African Americans, exempting African Americans from the draft, releasing all African Americans from jail, and a payment of compensation to African Americans.[26] The group also launched a Ten-Point Program for community projects and alliances with progressive white radicals and others.[27]

Part One Summary: Rock Rises ... and the Arc Continues

The American mainstream of the 1950s had found itself in an otherwise materially plentiful time but also with a vast emotional disconnect in a rapidly changing and unsettled world. Starting with a nation's fringes, and precisely when it was needed, rock music not only entertained but inspired millions to simply feel, to let loose, strive to get more out of life, and break societal restrictions. The story of early rock and roll was a huge success by most measures, and it fit squarely into the ongoing arc of Western civilization and individual expressions of freedom.

A generation gap took root and rock music became synonymous with a youth counterculture and change. The heroes of the rock and roll phenomenon took positions not unlike "high priests" or mythological heroes of societies' past and further challenged the establishment and authority in myriad ways, socially, culturally, politically, and spiritually. For all of the attention and hype, the biggest of those rock and roll heroes could not rule over or save an entire generation, but they did speak out. It wasn't always pretty, but a vast amount of inspired music was made, and things and people were certainly changing.

Part Two

Upheaval, 1966–1980

12

Integration, the Elvis Factor, the New Blues, and Tutwiler, 1954–Present

The first wave of '50s rock and roll certainly played an enormous role in helping the United States in breaking out of some of its major racial divisions, musically, socially, politically, and psychologically. Nothing would be the same. Still, there was a very long way to go to resolve and heal a nation's deep and complex racial issues.

Despite progress, in the early '60s many African Americans still experienced America in very different ways than white Americans. This was reflected in, and illuminated by, the story of the blues and rock and roll during this era and how an essentially Black-invented genre could come to be understood as a "white" one.

Rock and Roll Hall of Famer Lloyd Price's story is a remarkable microcosm of the tragedy of racism in America but also of the transformative power of rock and roll. Price, who was African American, was born during the Great Depression in 1933, deep in the Jim Crow South in the small rural town of Kenner, Louisiana. Price has since written of the realities of growing up as a Black kid in that time and place, including how he and his friends were terrorized by local police, many of whom were Ku Klux Klan members.[1] It was a racism so deeply ingrained and inextricably linked with religion that Price observed that the most racist people often seemed to be the most devoutly religious. As he explained,

> He couldn't understand, because he believed "God created man in his own image" and he wasn't no nigger. That was something he believed strongly. Every time he looked at that picture, at that white painting of The Last Supper by Michelangelo [sic], he believed it.[2]

And that hold over the Black community in Kenner was total. Price further wrote, "Two friends of mine, A-Jones and E-Saw, were so afraid of white men they truly thought they walked on water, just like Jesus did."[3]

In 1951, the then-18-year-old singer and songwriter was discovered by the legendary New Orleans musician and producer Dave Bartholomew of Specialty Records. Along with Bartholomew's colleague, the incomparable Fats Domino, on the piano, Price recorded the smash hit "Lawdy Miss Clawdy," which was released in 1952. The song is an all-time, soul-infused, early rock and roll track. It crossed racial lines perhaps in a way that no song had before it.[4] Both Elvis and the Beatles would cover it, and it would long be a staple of Presley's live shows.[5]

In New Orleans, the song dominated jukeboxes in both white and Black bars and restaurants. Back in Kenner, Price noticed something else: "My mother's and father's house was right across the street from the Kenner High School. I'd known these kids all my life. They'd never cross the street to come to my house until 'Lawdy Miss Clawdy,'" but cross over they did.[6]

At that point in his life, Price had only known the extreme world of segregation in which Black artists played for all-white crowds before performing an entirely separate "colored" set.[7] Through rock music, however, Price soon saw integrated shows. From Price's view:

> There was nothing more personal to one's heart and ears than a love of music. When the white man finally started talking to us, it was because his sons and daughters had a love for our music. It was not Rosa Parks, or Martin Luther King, even though those were great people who did great things. The significant events they started means a lot in Black history, but none of it could have happened if it wasn't already happening with our music.[8]

Truly nothing would be the same again.

Still, white and Black musical stylings and fandoms would again stratify along racial lines in the '60s. Moving forward, one big question would be whether African Americans could avoid what had happened years before with jazz and what had just happened with R&B and rock and roll in the '50s. Doors opened for Black artists, but white figures like Boone and Clark and the corporate record labels and radio stations ran the show. Could Black artists continue to succeed and be part of the mainstream in a genre they largely created, while maintaining their identity, their creative control, and their share of the profits?

Put another way, how to deal with what could be understood as the *Elvis factor*?

The Elvis Factor

Again, an even further understanding of Elvis Presley's legacy is critical to understanding America, race, and music moving forward. In one

12. Integration, Elvis, the Blues and Tutwiler, 1954–Present   115

sense, Presley was simply a talented individual who, as all artists, took in the musical influences he loved and, in his case, many of whom were Black. In this way, Presley became one of the true pop culture giants of the twentieth century. Even though this narrative tells much of the story, there is a lot more.

Presley's legacy has tended to eclipse the Black pioneers that came before him as well as the attention paid to both his Black and white contemporaries. The mainstream media did, after all, crown him the "king of rock and roll."[9] What happened, though, was that once Elvis became embraced and then engulfed by the American mainstream, his legacy became badly distorted in both positive and negative ways.

The problem, as explained in chapter 2, is that the social and historical factors that shaped Elvis at every step run so deep and are so murky. Without a full reconciliation as to how it is that Elvis could simultaneously be a positive, white civil rights figure *and* be profoundly shaped by, and benefit from, being white, the gray areas of his story have been filled in with misinformation and projections.

For Elvis's most devout fans, largely white folks, not appreciating this context meant Elvis was seen almost literally as a god that had dropped out of the sky. Over a decade after Presley's drug-related death in 1977, his legacy could still be summed up as being no less than a "religion in embryo."[10] Country music legend Dolly Parton, for example, once stated that where she is from in rural Tennessee, "I don't think he will ever die down. He's considered by many to be like a religious figure, like Jesus…. I don't know how to explain it, but it's there, and it's real, and people love it."[11] Into the '90s, there were tabloid rumors of Presley still being alive at a Burger King or a mall or somewhere, long after his death, making for one of the more bizarre of modern myths.[12]

On the other hand, many long had a feeling that race played some larger role in the story of Elvis but could not put their finger on exactly how that was. One result was that Elvis was sometimes unfairly disparaged as a cultural thief and even labeled a racist.

To begin with, Elvis was immensely talented. Also crucial to clarify is that nothing in the Presley story indicates that he consciously set out to exploit or *steal* from Black culture and Black people. It is well established that from an early age, Presley had a deep appreciation and understanding of the blues and Black gospel, and he had strong personal relationships with African Americans throughout his life.

Still, at its core, this is also the story of a white guy who saw his entire attitude and performance style greatly shaped and defined by outside social and racial factors, as well as the needs and allowances of the mainstream. With that, he took something of immense value out of Black America and then reaped all of the rewards and credit in the world.

Something akin to the Elvis factor would continue to play out in the music business going forward.

The New Blues

As to the blues, in the early '60s, the British Invasion bands had fully embraced it and they were now conquering the United States with a new version of it that reflected their lives and influences. Blues guitar legends such as Robert Johnson, B.B. King, John Lee Hooker, and Muddy Waters—artists who were still unknown to the U.S. mainstream at the time—were worshipped. The young Brits, unfettered by the baggage and history around race in the same way as their white American counterparts, did not hesitate to more directly embrace them. When the Beatles first came to the United States and told reporters they wanted to meet "Muddy Waters," a reporter had asked, "Where is that?"[13]

The Brits built on this musical foundation and soon came white British rock guitar heroes like Keith Richards, Eric Clapton, Jimmy Page, and Jeff Beck and in a style far more accessible to a Western, white mainstream.

Ironically, this was at about the same time that many African American artists were distancing themselves from the blues. The first Black-conceived "rock era" of the jump blues and R&B in the late '40s had ultimately become rock and roll, but by the '60s, that rock and roll was becoming known as just *rock*—actually a *sub*genre of rock and roll and parallel to funk, soul, R&B, Motown, and country music—and it was being performed by long-haired white guys.

While the blues convey a people's historic spirit, creativity, and immense capacity to feel and emote despite tragic conditions, it is also synonymous with a dated, rural past marked by decades of severe social and political oppression. The blues represented the long post-slavery era. This was a life where efforts simply to raise issues of racial equality were regularly met with brutal and even violent reprisal.[14] Even the integration of the U.S. military and of baseball, both in 1947, did not immediately transform day-to-day life for most Black Americans.

So pronounced were the racial divisions of the South that for generations, African Americans had developed "two minds," one to safely interact with white authority and the other being their truer selves. Following World War I, when millions of African Americans embarked on the Great Migration out of the Jim Crow South, southern whites were caught almost entirely by surprise by the sheer volume of the exodus.[15]

With few exceptions, in the first half of the twentieth century, southern

12. Integration, Elvis, the Blues and Tutwiler, 1954–Present 117

African Americans' only viable options for making a living was often work like sharecropping or other jobs paying scarcely subsistence-level wages. White families owned all of the largest farms, and soon it would be "industrial crop factories."[16] African Americans had little capital, and when they did obtain land, they were denied crucial loans that traditionally kept smaller farms afloat as a matter of course.[17]

Still, and while a new Black middle class would take hold in America, the Great Migration itself was an immense challenge. This was a wholesale relocation of an agrarian culture made by people regularly denied education, still reeling from life under segregation, and relocated to an urban, industrialized, and also white-controlled world. A great many transplanted African Americans struggled in the unfamiliar North without social connections or inroads. Some African Americans took on side hustles, and others resorted to informal and black market economies to survive.[18]

This drastic and sudden dislocation had other effects. In the '70s, Black civil rights leader Jesse Jackson decried the loss of social order and religious communities. This was said to be the cause of various social ills, including "materialism and rootlessness," and further coincided with the other socially liberal aspects of the counterculture of the times.[19]

The 1950s and '60s were a time of enormous change and dislocation across the nation but no doubt especially for African Americans. During this transition, the trajectory of the blues was altered as well. On the one hand, the blues were rooted in an agrarian lifestyle and simple living in the harshest of times. "The King of the Blues," B.B. King, for example, rose from the humblest of origins as an orphaned, Delta sharecropper. But he would shape the rock guitar style as much as any guitarist in history, eventually being hosted by presidents and a pope.[20] King stressed the importance of the blues: "To be a black person and sing the blues, you are Black twice. I've heard it said, 'If we don't know whence we came, we don't know how to go where we are trying to go.'"[21]

In the 1960s, the bluesmen retained some level of popularity with an older generation of Black Americans, but they played shows at mostly white-attended rock venues, while a younger Black generation was moving on altogether, embracing soul music and "dashikis, Afro Picks, and bell bottoms."[22] Those blues roots were also forever intertwined with a world perceived as outdated backwoods and a painful past, one too close to the dated stereotypes of Jim Crow and pop culture characters like Stepin Fetchit and Amos 'n' Andy that many only wanted to distance themselves from.

To a large degree, making a break from the blues became synonymous with Black progress. *Chicago Times* writer Clarence Page once explained, "In the early 1960s, amid the rise of Motown and soul music [there was] widespread mockery of the blues in black communities as 'gold tooth' or 'handkerchief-head music.'"[23] B.B. King recalled a show in Baltimore with Sam Cooke. The mostly Black crowd warmly embraced Cooke's smooth soul pop—while King was booed. In Chicago, a Black nightclub announcer mocked King with references to chitterlings, collard greens, pig's feet, and watermelons.[24]

Currently, Gary Clark, Jr., a relative rarity as an African American guitar player rooted in the traditional blues (though with contemporary soul and hip-hop influences as well), explains, "For a black male, the sound of the blues is pre–Civil Rights. It's oppression. In high school I had a friend who asked me why I played the blues, that black people don't play blues."[25] Writer Kerry Melonson further notes, "Black folks have seemingly abandoned the blues at the street level and even in a commercial sense."[26] Finally, based on author B. Brian Foster's recent interviews with African Americans in historic blues city Clarksdale, Mississippi, in *I Don't Like the Blues: Race, Place, and the Backbeat of Black Life*, the blues were "something they [southern Black people] lived, something that belonged to them, something they took pride in [and] a part of who they were [but] We ain't that no mo."[27] Besides, as local Black people had explained to Foster, the feeling is that the Clarksdale blues clubs cashing in on the white tourists are white-owned anyway.[28]

Tutwiler

A short history and geography lesson from tiny Tutwiler, Mississippi, helps sum up the legacy of the blues. In 1903, the famed W.C. Handy, a cornet-playing Memphis bandleader, was waiting for a train in Tutwiler, which sits in the rural heart of the Delta, 90 miles south of Memphis. There, Handy had the pleasure of hearing a most interesting local musician busking. Handy told the famous story of "[a] lean loose-jointed Negro ... accompanying himself on the guitar with the weirdest music I had ever heard."[29] What had been a unique strain of folk music—at the time mostly only known to those African Americans deep in the Delta—was now being heard by an "outsider." That outsider also happened to be in a unique position to bring the music to a broader audience.

Handy quickly understood the commercial potential of the music and composed his own blues pieces, including "Memphis Blues" (1912) and "The St. Louis Blues" (1914). He had great success with the genre, or a vaudevillian-flavored version of it, and became known as the "Father of the Blues." Beale Street—where Handy's Memphis office was located—would

12. Integration, Elvis, the Blues and Tutwiler, 1954–Present   119

Tutwiler, Mississippi, and Tallahatchie Correctional Facility (Lesley Young, 2018).

flourish with blues clubs and become known as the "Home of the Blues."[30] From there, the blues became the foundation of the world's popular music.

One might think that Tutwiler would be a celebrated historic landmark. After all, jazz has the celebrated French Quarter and rock has focal points in the immensely popular Rock & Roll Hall of Fame in Cleveland and in Memphis at both Graceland and Sun Studio, where Elvis lived and where the first rock record was recorded, respectively. Tutwiler is different.

Today, Tutwiler is barely a town, really, and extremely economically depressed. A brief excursion there, however, is illuminating. About 75 miles south of Memphis on U.S. 61 is Clarksdale, Mississippi, the birthplace of Son House, Muddy Waters, and Ike Turner and home to the Delta Blues Museum. Another 15 miles down U.S. 49 is Tutwiler. That route from Clarksdale to Tutwiler remains a quiet, expansive stretch of highway with all farmland on either side and the occasional old farmhouse. Just outside Clarksdale, one is greeted by two massive, very modern brick homes of several thousand square feet. They look like they belong in some lavish, suburban neighborhood but were incongruously airdropped into this stretch of the Delta—presumably the landowners.[31]

The first sign of Tutwiler is its water tower, which bears the greeting, "Welcome to Tutwiler, MS, Where the Blues Was Born." Just before the water tower, almost at its base, is the only sign of modernity around, found in a bright, gleaming, oddly metallic compound: the Tallahatchie County Correctional Facility. This not only houses locals, but in need of revenue and jobs, the county contracts with California to house their incarcerated there as well.[32]

Tutwiler is a small grouping of homes, many dilapidated, and about 3,000 residents.[33] One of the only commercial spaces is a gas station with a small convenience store for people passing through. A group of African American men hang out by a coin-operated laundry. The only mention of Handy's history-altering discovery is a small marker and a faded mural commemorating the same.[34] It seems to reflect an enormous hole in the region's history.

The blues continued to shape Black music, but Tutwiler today is a reflection of not only Jim Crow but of a distancing from the blues. Into the '70s, many Black musicians would come to more embrace other distinctly African American musical characteristics, including syncopated rhythms, the swagger of urban R&B, and the soulfulness of the Black church. It would be white rockers, many from the United Kingdom especially, who would pick up the blues legacy and run with it.

Because of the original rock and roll explosion, African American artists were now accepted by the mainstream, but going forward, Black music would less cater to, and be less homogenized by, that mainstream world. Popular music from Black artists would be secular but retain the soulfulness of gospel, be exciting but rooted in real life, and be distinctly African American yet still more widely accessible.

These new strains would come in the form of soul and funk, epitomized by the legendary James Brown, the polished Motown brand of pop/soul and the Memphis soul of Stax Records.

13

James Brown and Soul Brothers and Sisters, 1954–1960s

What would become soul music had first begun to take shape with the gospel music stars of the '40s and '50s such as Mahalia Jackson (e.g., "Move on up a Little Higher") and Sister Rosetta Tharpe ("Up above My Head") and former Soul Stirrers, gospel-star-turned-R&B-star Sam Cooke ("You Send Me"). On the secular side was the electrifying Jackie Wilson ("Lonely Teardrops") and early rock and rollers like Lloyd Price ("Lawdy Miss Clawdy"). This all led to Ray Charles. As Charles would famously explain, converting gospel to secular music wasn't that hard; "you just change Jesus to baby, and you got the blues."[1]

Charles (1930–2004) was born in Georgia and grew up in Greenville, Florida. Charles suffered from glaucoma and was fully blind by seven. His musical life started with his playing with a local boogie-woogie-blues pianist and in the Baptist Church.[2]

Charles toured the so-called southern chitlin' circuit in the late '40s. His early sound was heavily influenced by jazz-pop star Nat King Cole, and he found some success between 1949 and 1952. At that point, however, he started to find his own unique sound. In 1954, as music writer Lindsay Planer explained, "As legend has it, [Charles and co-songwriter Renald Richard] were listening to a gospel number on the radio when Richard began to improvise scat vocals atop the soulful groove."[3] That led to Charles's seminal and thrilling "I Got a Woman," which went to number two on the R&B chart, and started a long run of success. In 1959, Charles recorded another signature song, the extended call-and-response romp "What'd I Say."

Charles continued to score major pop hits throughout the '60s (e.g., "Unchain My Heart" and "Hit the Road Jack") and even released a classic country music album (*Modern Sounds in Country and Western Music*,

1962). His recordings of "Georgia on My Mind" and "America the Beautiful" became staples of Americana.

Singer James Brown was making his mark by the mid-'50s as well. Brown was born in Barnwell, South Carolina, in 1933, also in the middle of severe poverty, the Great Depression, Jim Crow, and a broken home. From the age of four, Brown lived in Augusta, Georgia, where he was raised by his aunt Honey, a brothel madam. As a young child, Brown scrapped for money by picking cotton, shining shoes, and dancing for soldiers from nearby Fort Gordon. At age 12, Brown was dismissed from school for "insufficient clothing."[4]

A young Brown attended Pentecostal church services but especially took to the church music and the choir. At the same time, he also started to get into trouble, and at 15, he was incarcerated for three years for car theft. Brown formed a gospel group, which became the R&B group the Famous Flames, with his future longtime music partner and singer Bobby Byrd.[5]

The Famous Flames caught the attention of Brown's idol, Little Richard, and the group relocated to Richard's hometown of Macon, Georgia, where Richard set the Flames up with his management. At one point, Richard gave Brown a napkin that consisted of nothing more than the words "please, please, please." That later led to Brown's breakthrough hit "Please, Please, Please" in 1956.[6]

Brown was a consummate bandleader and maximized and controlled every aspect of his shows. He was notoriously strict with band members, even fining them for miscues. The result was impeccably polished sets that provided the perfect framework for Brown's otherwise wildly explosive and dramatic performances. Brown's energy was immense, and his impassioned vocals, sometimes a pure stream of consciousness, were accentuated by wordless noises and shrieks. Into the '60s, Brown's sound got harder and he added Latin- and jazz-influenced rhythms to go along with heart-wrenching ballads.

Brown's approach showcased the best of African and African American stylings, including the soulfulness and exuberance of the Black church, but then turned it into something entirely new. One writer described Brown's music of the time as "the most Africanized, built on dynamic, highly syncopated polyrhythms" over a deep bass and "an interlocking web of short, scratchy guitar chords and blaring horns over the top."[7] Brown also changed up the accents on beats, often cueing his band to hit the accents "on the one!"[8] His dancing was a revelation of power, intensity, and dazzling footwork all light years from the twist and the other dance crazes of the early '60s. As exciting as Brown was and as much sex appeal as he had, there was no overt sexuality or cursing.[9]

Brown is arguably the most dynamic performer of the rock era. His singing and performing style would make him a primary influence on everyone from Mick Jagger to Michael Jackson. Brown's powerhouse 1963 album *Live at the Apollo* brought his live act to white America and reached number two on the pop charts.[10] His explosive performance of "Night Train" was a highlight of the star-studded, one-off 1964 television showcase the *T.A.M.I. Show*. The proto-funk of "Out of Sight" was followed in 1965 by two top-ten songs, "Papa's Got a Brand New Bag" and "I Got You (I Feel Good)," which began a run of enormous crossover commercial success.[11]

While soul music was taking root in American urban centers like Detroit, New York, Chicago, and Philadelphia, Brown and his band were further in the process of developing what would be called funk music. Funk was soul and R&B but with unexpected, off-kilter beats, both making the music come alive and be inherently danceable. It practically forced people out of their seats. In 1967, Brown released the consensus first funk song, "Cold Sweat," which was number one on the R&B chart and top-ten pop.[12]

The word "funk" had come out of jazz circles in the '50s signifying "an association with harsh realities" and, according to *Encyclopædia Britannica*, referring to an "unpleasant odor" but also the overcoming of racial strife, violence, and crushed aspirations.[13]

Indeed, as energizing and as ecstatic as Brown's music was, it was also clearly born out of real wounds and anguish. Brown's music turned anger and frustrations with being Black in America into elation and entertainment. Brown thus had a universal cultural appeal, but he would develop a special bond with African Americans. Brown would not only come to define funk's early years, but he would be central in defining the Black Pride movement in the '60s and '70s.[14] Brown would further work directly with local Black-owned theaters, retail music outlets, and radio stations in each town on tour, and he promoted his ownership of radio stations and real estate as a model of "black capitalism" for Black Americans.[15]

Soul and funk, in part, marked a commitment to core African American ideals, both musically and thematically, during some challenging times in Black history. A great many Black people were still not fully engaged with mainstream social and economic systems and faced imminent challenges in day-to-day life, physically, economically, and psychologically. To meet such immediate real-world needs, secular Black music needed to be deeply soulful.

Again, in the early and mid-'60s, rock and popular music were still largely integrated in many ways. In 1961, for example, three of the five nominees for the first rock and roll Grammy had been Black, and integrated rock and roll had become the new norm. As to Black performers, Brown, a slew of acts from Motown, and Ray Charles in particular were all continuing to cross over and become mainstream cultural icons.

The *T.A.M.I. Show* had combined top American acts with top British Invasion groups for an incredibly diverse mix of ethnicities, nationalities, and musical styles to include Brown, Motown's top acts, the Beach Boys, Chuck Berry, the Stones, and Gerry and the Pacemakers. By the end of 1963, R&B music and blues and gospel-influenced records were such a part of white mainstream radio that Billboard stopped publishing a separate R&B chart.[16] The times were exemplified by a young Daryl Hall, soon of the "blue-eyed soul" duo Hall & Oates and who started as a backup singer at Black-owned Philadelphia International Records in the mid-'60s. At that time, Hall only knew integrated sounds in his native Philadelphia: "We were not influenced that much, believe it or not, by black music per se. We were influenced by early rock & roll and soul music, which was not black. It was *INTEGRATED* music. There was no difference between black and white."[17]

By the mid-'60s, however, a shift in rock's racial dynamics, reflecting America's dynamics at large, was underway. In 1966, for example, there were four Grammy performance categories under "contemporary (rock & roll)," and white artists won each of them. Of the 20 nominees for those four awards, only three were African American and all were women. For the Rhythm & Blues Recording Grammy, all five nominees were Black male artists.[18] By 1967, it could be said that the racially mixed, soul-rock group Sly and the Family Stone was the only major act with strong followings in both the white and Black markets.[19]

There were many reasons for this racial separation. At that time, in both northern and southern states of the United States, "white flight" out of the cities and to the suburbs continued, not to mention the ongoing challenges that two cultures that had often experienced life in America in very different ways had in trying to relate to each other.[20]

Shifting gears for a moment, the classic comedy film *National Lampoon's Animal House* (1978), surprisingly enough, helps to illustrate how these dynamics unfolded. The film is fictitious, although drawn from and inspired by the multiple screenwriters' actual college experiences.[21] It is set at an all-white, wild, and unruly fraternity, Delta House, on a fictitious American college campus in 1962.

The party band for the fun-loving Delta crew is Otis Day and the Knights, an also fictitious, all–Black R&B/rock ensemble (although future real-life blues star Robert Cray played the bass and Lloyd Williams's vocals are overdubbed).[22] Day is a charismatic, high-energy singer in a James Brown/Little Richard/Sam Cooke mold, backed by drums, sax, guitar, bass, and piano.

In the film's famous toga party scene, the band delivers a performance that would become virtually synonymous with the word "party," with their version of the Isley Brothers' "Shout." "Shout" had been a big hit in the early '60s and then covered by many while again bringing the ecstatic energy of early R&B and the Black church to the mainstream.[23] The song itself and the live performance, with its call-and-response and the dancing it inspires, is effectively the heart and soul of the entire film. One of the frat members lip-synchs and mimics every moment of Day's performance off to the side of the stage. The song's usage in the film was so powerful that it has remained a staple at parties and wedding receptions ever since.

Sometime after the toga party, a group of the fraternity brothers and their white dates come across the band's name on the marquee at a roadside club, the Dexter Lake Club, and decide to stop in. After all, as one frat brother says of Day, "He *loves* us!" The frat boys and their dates enter and it turns out that the club clientele is otherwise 100-percent African American. Upon seeing the white visitors enter, the club comes to a dead stop. One frat brother says in an aside to another, "We are gonna die." When one of the white guys yells out a greeting to Day on stage, Day embarrassedly tries to ignore him.[24] The whole group is terrified. When the Black patrons begin to mess with them, they leave quickly, scared to death.

It is a comedic scene, but it is an unintentionally sad one, too. It is an approximation of what was going on not only with rock music at the time but the country at large. In many ways, the worlds of Black and white America (the specific location of the fictitious college is never identified, although it is not the South) were so far apart that here, it was laughable that these white people would even enter this Black world. Further, that life should be so differently experienced by Black people is an utter revelation to the white folks.

Otis Day may very well have loved the white frat brothers, but the roadside club was a respite from a white-dominated world that sometimes seemed only interested enough to stop in when it wanted to be entertained. The rock and roll phenomenon, the Great Migration, and the civil rights movement all represented massive strides toward a more integrated and just country, but they were all still pieces of a much bigger picture.

The two racial demographics continued to shift into the more racially defined musical tracks of rock versus R&B and soul. Some of this was perception and marketing. For example, top soul music performers included African Americans, such as Otis Redding and Sam & Dave, recording at Stax in Memphis, and Aretha Franklin, Wilson Pickett, and the Staple Singers, recorded at FAME Studio and the offshoot Muscle Shoals Sound Studio in Muscle Shoals, Alabama. But the crucial house bands backing all of the above were mixed-race at Stax and all white at Fame.

Conversely, R&B and blues-based performers like the Rolling Stones and Janis Joplin would always be considered *white* and *rockers* first.[25]

Motown

In Detroit in the late '50s, former auto worker Barry Gordy was envisioning a Black-owned label with a new, modern sound less connected to a southern, rural past, thus allowing it to more easily cross over into the mainstream.

While musical interests of white and Black listeners were still more closely aligned, the music business was controlled by a white majority. As James Brown had put it, for too long, Black artists had been "in the show, but not in show business."[26] Further, as author Elijah Wald noted, most African American musicians of the time were not "convinced by the Beatles' assurances that all they needed was love and everything would be all right if they could free their minds."[27] African Americans were, as one unnamed member of soul group the 5th Dimension had put it, "trying to grab onto exactly the things that the white kids are trying to give up," such as "fancy houses" and "good jobs."[28]

Gordy became a songwriter for Jackie Wilson and then the Miracles, featuring singer and songwriter Smokey Robinson.[29] Wanting to take total control of his own compositions, Gordy borrowed $800 from his family and started his own record label, Tamla, followed by the Motown Record Corporation, which absorbed Tamla in 1961.[30]

Gordy's vision for his label was something of a musical assembly line inspired by his time in the auto plants, starting with how composers put songs together, to recording, the polishing of artists' media skills, and their immaculate stage performances. Gordy sought to move his artists past negative racial stereotypes and classifications. He branded Motown "the Sound of Young America."[31] The formula would produce a slew of the very best songs of the era, and the best and most iconic pop singers, both male and female, and ultimately, one of the most successful record labels ever.[32]

Musically, Gordy combined the sound and feel of the Black church with the most current pop trends and production. By 1965, as writer Charles Gillette noted, Motown was incorporating the "tambourines ... clapping ... moralizing songs," as well as the "call-and-response harmony structure" from the church and thus producing a "fully conceived" modern pop sound.[33]

The Miracles' "Shop Around" (1961), written by Robinson, reached number one on the R&B national chart and number two on *Billboard*'s pop chart.[34] Motown's girl groups included the Marvelettes, with timeless hits like "Please, Mr. Postman" (1961), Martha and the Vandellas' brilliant "Heat Wave" (1963) and "Dancing in the Street" (1964), the Supremes' (featuring future solo star Diana Ross) "Stop in the Name of Love" (1965) and "You Can't Hurry Love" (1966), and Gladys Knight and the Pips' "I Heard It through the Grapevine" (1967). Motown also developed star male vocal groups, with the Temptations (e.g., "Ain't Too Proud to Beg" [1966]) and the Four Tops (e.g., "Reach Out I'll Be There" [1966]) and individuals like superstar Marvin Gaye (e.g., "Heard It through the Grapevine" [1966]).

The label had not, however, been the sound of Black youth and anger, nor was it trying to be. Gordy avoided controversy, believing that bringing the white and Black teen markets together and becoming the first, true crossover label would be of the greatest benefit for advancing the interests of African Americans.[35] Martha Reeves, for example, had a brother in Vietnam, but she did not connect her music to those outside issues, even when others would. She also, however, summed up how most at Motown saw it: "We were always political. We sold love in front of segregated audiences. That's political."[36]

Gordy was keenly aware of what he was up against as a trailblazer and a role model. He was the grandson of former slaves, and he had risen to be the owner of one of the most important and most prosperous entertainment entities in the world. As writer Mark Kurlansky noted, Gordy was "in fact a black power ideal."[37] As poet and author Amiri Baraka had put it, "Merely by being a Negro in America, one was a nonconformist."[38] In '67 and '68, 23 consecutive Motown singles landed in the pop top ten. Gordy and his Motown roster had reached across the ongoing racial divide and came to positively impact Black, American, and world cultures.

Also, during the mid-'60s, soul music was taking hold in the South, especially in Memphis as well as Muscle Shoals, Alabama.

Stax

Stax Records of Memphis would be the most crucial label for soul music. Its story would also speak uniquely and directly to the intersection of race, rock, and America.

Stax's founder, Jim Stewart, was born in 1930, in Middleton, Tennessee, an hour and a half east of Memphis. Stewart was a white bank teller and half-decent country fiddler. Realizing he was not going to make it as a musician, however, Stewart started Satellite Records with some partners. He first set up at a remote site in Memphis before relocating to a more central location in an old movie theater on College and McLemore Avenues.

Early on, with a shoestring budget and looking for a pop or country hit, Stewart had no success.[39]

Soon, Stewart begged his sister Estelle Axton to mortgage her house so he could upgrade their label's studio equipment.[40] A copyright issue with the Satellite name forced a change and Stewart used the first two letters of Stewart's and Axton's last names to become Stax in 1960.[41]

The neighborhood surrounding the studio was turning into a poor, all–Black ghetto, and Memphis itself was still staunchly segregated. As late as 1971, in fact, the city would choose to close its public swimming pools in the middle of the summer rather than allow Black and white kids to swim together.[42]

To provide some steady income for the cash-strapped label, Axton opened up a record store in the former movie concession area, which became the Satellite Record Shop. Axton's store became known as the place to get "Black" records that were unavailable at the mainstream stores. Further, Axton let neighborhood kids hang out without buying anything, also unlike other stores.[43] A Black keyboardist named Booker Jones and white kids such as buddies bass player Duck Dunn and guitarist Steve Cropper became regulars.[44] Those three would soon form three-quarters of Booker T and the MGs, Stax's legendary house band. The kids hanging out at Satellite also provided Stax a live focus group (not unlike what the audience for Dewey Phillips's radio show had provided for early Sun Records).[45]

Stewart was looking for a pop sound, but after three years in the business, he had little to show for it and nothing near a hit.[46] In 1960, popular local musician-deejay-comedian Rufus Thomas and his 16-year-old singing daughter, Carla, came into Stax and recorded the R&B/pop single "Cause I Love You." Stax finally saw its first hit and at just the right time.[47] Stewart then hooked up with Jerry Wexler of giant Atlantic Records.[48]

Yet from the start, Stax was a virtual racial oasis. As Estelle Axton had seen Stax, "We never saw color, we saw talent. That was what was so great about being over there [removed from the segregated, white downtown]."[49] The first Black employee at Stax, John Gary Williams and later of the Mad Lads, recalled first approaching the old theater as a young teen:

> I went in there when Jim Stewart and Chips Moman were fanning the cobwebs out of the Capitol Theater. I said, "What y'all doing?" [Jim] said, "We're gonna have a record company." I said, "Well I can sing." He said, "Come back when you get good." I didn't leave. I stayed there and he never said nothing else. He never said, "go away." Jim was one of those hardcore guys—horn-rimmed glasses, pumped hair. When we see shit like that—ooh look out! But, he wasn't like that. He was a business person minding his own business.[50]

Cropper and Dunn had formed a popular local band in high school, the Royal Spades, along with baritone saxophonist Don Nix, trumpeter Wayne Jackson, singer Ronnie Angel, and keyboard player Jerry "Smoochy" Smith. When the group met novice saxophonist Packy Axton, they weren't in need of another horn. What Axton did have, however, was a mother and an uncle who owned a studio and a record label. He was welcomed into the band.[51] Some of those musicians would become the Mar-Keys (named for the movie marquee still affixed to the Stax building).

The Mar-Keys breakout was the instrumental single "Last Night" (1961). "Last Night" was a simple song in a Black R&B style and, as author Robert Gordon put it, where "frat-house meets cathouse."[52] It has a horn blast on the first beat, a strong drumbeat, farfisa organ, and a deliberate rhythm, as if they are still gathering their recollections of a party that had gone long into the night. The song's only spoken words come at two breaks in the middle, both with former Satellite Records clerk Floyd Newman simply speaking an *oooh*, followed by the title of the song, and then the sax and the rest of the band starting back up. In the studio, the song was refined into its final form by committee, with a mix of white and Black musicians.[53] This was also two years before the Kingsmen had a major hit with the similarly styled garage rock/frat anthem "Louie, Louie."

In June 1961, "Last Night" surprisingly went to number two on the R&B chart and number three on the pop chart, selling one million copies, according to Stewart.[54] At the time, multiracial groups weren't even accepted at most music venues, thus touring groups had to be comprised either of all-white or all–Black musicians.[55]

The next year, bandleader Booker Jones lured ace drummer Al Jackson away from another gig with a healthy salary at Stax and joined up with Cropper and Dunn to solidify Booker T and the MGs. In 1962, that group recorded the landmark instrumental jam "Green Onions," which was built on a sound and feel similar to "Last Night" but taken to a new level of musicianship.

Stax also featured the Memphis Horns. Horn player Wayne Jackson would recall that they "couldn't even conceive of a job that much fun."[56] Stax artists would have a raw, Memphis-roots music feel, and they would be synonymous with a strong emphasis on the low end, horns where background vocals or guitars might normally be, keyboard and sax solos, and a significant gospel influence.[57]

The next major discovery was soul singer Otis Redding from Macon, Georgia. Redding rolled into Stax unannounced and was signed after auditioning with a single song. Redding was the son of a part-time preacher, raised on gospel, and enamored with the smooth soul-pop of Sam Cooke and the Pentecostal-infused rock and roll of Little Richard. "These Arms of Mine" launched Redding's career in 1963, charting as high as number 85 on the pop chart.[58]

Redding did not necessarily have the greatest vocal range, but he could convey a range of emotions like few others, from immense strength to the most heartfelt vulnerability and everything in between. He was also an expert arranger and songwriter. Stewart would describe Redding thusly: "Otis was totally creative, totally positive. Everybody wanted to be there when Otis walked in. It was like magic."[59] David Ritz noted that "Redding's open-throated singing became a standard for the decade's great soul artists."[60]

Perhaps Redding's finest moment, and the song that Stewart felt defined Stax, was the 1966 hit "Try a Little Tenderness." It's the slowest of soul numbers, an impossibly restrained ballad, until the uncontainable Redding starts to burst out.[61]

Stax became the center of soul music, cranking out hits and soul classics. Redding was joined by the writing and production team of Isaac Hayes and David Porter, as well as artists Wilson Picket ("In the Midnight Hour"), Sam & Dave ("Hold On! I'm Comin'," "Soul Man," "Knock on Wood"), the Staples Singers ("Respect Yourself," "I'll Take You There"), and others. In 1965, Stax brought in Al Bell, a confident, big personality who further transformed Stax from a regional mom-and-pop operation—sister-brother, actually—into a national force.[62]

In the mid- and late 1960s, the Lorraine Motel was a hangout for the Stax family. It was also where visiting artists from out of town stayed while recording. The Lorraine's coffee shop was the only public place in Memphis where Black and white personnel were allowed to hang out together, for one thing. Songwriting sessions were conducted there as well, day and night. The pool at the Lorraine was also popular because the Stax studio didn't have air-conditioning.[63]

Up until the early '70s, when Isaac Hayes would become a crossover star, most white people in Memphis scarcely knew Stax existed. In their 1967 Stax tour in Europe, crowds had gone wild for the entire Stax lineup, shocking the Stax folks.[64] That success led to the Stax performances at the Monterey Pop Festival, where Stax and Redding especially broke through to white crowds and what Redding called the "Love Crowd." Redding and Booker T and the MGs continued to successfully tour on the psychedelic circuit.[65]

Then, in December 1967, a charter plane carrying Redding and most of the Stax group the Bar Kays crashed in a lake just outside Madison, Wisconsin, killing four of the Bar Kays, the pilot, and Redding. Redding was dead at 27 years of age, devastating his wife, Zelma, four young kids, and the Stax community. Immediately prior to Redding's death, he had recorded his and Cropper's "Sittin' on the Dock of the Bay," which would be released posthumously and would become his signature song.[66]

13. James Brown and Soul Brothers and Sisters, 1954–1960s

Stax moved forward and continued to build on the crossover success of Redding and the rest of their lineup. Bell still had the entire label poised for even greater heights. This, however, meant a more corporate approach and the end of Stax's tight family atmosphere that had defined the label to that point. Bell had the entire Stax roster work on a 28-album mega release. Where Hayes, Porter, Cropper, Dunn, Jackson, and Jones and others had always had huge input on company decisions, they were now being marginalized. Further, the MGs were being limited in their own career options. When Cropper was given a 10-percent cut of the East Memphis Publishing Company and Jones nothing, Jones wanted out.[67]

The loss of Redding, the social ills of the nation, and soon, and another enormous tragedy in their own backyard would all further combine to ensure that Stax would never be the same.

14

Cultural Checkpoints: War, Assassinations, and Chaos, ca. 1968

This chapter is an accounting of the major social and political events of a wild year, 1968, in the United States and elsewhere and how the story of rock intertwined in those stories.

The Great Society Stalls. By 1968, President Johnson's push for social programs was stalling out in Congress, and many on the left were losing faith in him.[1]

The Tet Offensive. In January 1968, while Johnson and the U.S. military continued to assure the American public that the enemy was on the run and victory near, the North Vietnamese and Viet Cong forces (the communist guerrilla army) launched a massive surprise offensive called the Tet Offensive. Militarily, the U.S. and South Vietnamese response was swift and victorious, but politically and psychologically, it was a disaster for the ongoing war effort and further evidence of a lack of any progress toward an end of the conflict. Later the same month, General Westmoreland requested 206,000 more troops.[2]

Johnson Loses Cronkite. In February 1968, venerated *CBS Nightly News* anchor Walter Cronkite concluded a special broadcast on the Tet Offensive with comments that seemed to both reflect and help cement the nation's collective view of the war effort: "To say that we are mired in stalemate seems the only realistic, yet unsatisfactory, conclusion."[3]

My Lai Massacre. A shocking military cover-up was exposed, where in March 1968, ranking officers for Charlie Company of the Americal Division's 11th Infantry Brigade had authorized a "search and destroy" mission on the village of My Lai, which was considered to be a stronghold of communist forces. U.S. soldiers proceeded to slaughter 504 unarmed villagers, all children, women, and the elderly; many women were raped before being killed.[4]

14. Cultural Checkpoints: War, Assassination, Chaos, ca. 1968

Martin Luther King Slain in Memphis. Throughout Martin Luther King, Jr.'s, activism in the civil rights movement, the threats to his life remained constant. King had even addressed the topic, and never in more stark terms, in his "I've Been to the Mountaintop" speech the night before his assassination in Memphis on April 4, 1968.

King was never directly linked to any communist efforts but early on the civil rights movement had been funded by socialist sources. In a country bent on battling a monolithic communism and maybe not so in tune with the realities of Black America, this was enough to make King a threat to a nation's status quo in the eyes of J. Edgar Hoover and others.[5]

By the mid-'60s, as writer Michael Eric Dyson later summarized, King had increasingly "butted heads with the soft, safe image manufactured for him. The more he protested poverty, denounced the Vietnam War, and lamented the unconscious racism of most whites, the more he lost favor and footing in white America."[6] By 1967, universities had stopped asking him to give lectures, and financial support for his cause had dried up.[7]

In April 1968, Martin Luther King was called to Memphis and the site of a contentious strike among a predominantly African American sanitation workers' union. King had originally planned on staying at a more upscale hotel, but when questioned about that choice, he switched to the modest, home away from home for Stax, Lorraine Motel.[8]

On April 4, King briefly stood out on the balcony of the Lorraine. Next, as *Time* magazine described it, "a white sniper's bullet cut down Dr. Martin Luther King Jr., pre-eminent voice of the just aspirations and long-suffering patience of black America."[9] After a two-month manhunt, King's killer, James Earl Ray, was captured at London's Heathrow Airport. Ray pled guilty and was sentenced to 99 years in prison. There was no hard evidence that Ray had coconspirators.[10]

As Harvard professor Cornel West later put it, "When Martin died something died in the soul of black people. We haven't gotten over it."[11] The message seemed to be, if a man of profound Christian faith and nonviolent principles and solely dedicated to bringing about change in that vein ended up being gunned down, what hope was there for any other African American?

The killing was so momentous that *Time* described it at the time as "an act of outrage that at first blush seemed to threaten the onslaught of race war."[12] Memphis was immediately placed under curfew and riots and looting broke out in some 100 cities across the country. National Guard troops patrolled Memphis, Detroit, Washington, and Baltimore.[13]

In Boston, in the first 24 hours after King's death, the city was on edge, though there was little violence. On April 5, James Brown was scheduled to perform at the Boston Garden. Given that there were full-scale riots in larger cities across the country, there was little reason to believe that Boston would be different. Boston's new mayor, 38-year-old Kevin White, helped to negotiate both for the show to proceed and also to have it on live TV as well so that people would have a reason to stay in.[14]

Brown wanted to defuse the situation, and when he took the stage with the (white) mayor, he told the crowd, "And look, this is swingin' cat. Okay, yeah, give him a big round of applause, ladies and gentlemen. He's a swingin' cat." The mayor then implored the crowd to honor and follow King's nonviolent credo before Brown launched into "Mr. Dynamite." Boston saw minor skirmishes that night but no more.[15]

Brown also supported Nixon to great controversy and despite claims of Uncle-Tom-ism. Brown believed that African American individualism and hard work alone could change their fate. Detractors asserted that Brown didn't appreciate the country's economic realities or understand the impact of Nixon's dismantling of Johnson's Great Society programs.[16]

Nonetheless, Brown also produced the affirmative Black Pride anthem "Say It Loud, I'm Black and I'm Proud." The mainstream would still see him as a threat to the American way of life.[17] By the end of the '60s, Brown would come to be known as "Soul Brother Number One."[18] Said minister and civil rights activist Al Sharpton, "Where other artists were black, Nat King Cole, Sam Cooke, even the Motown acts, were able to cross over as blacks to mainstream. James Brown made mainstream crossover to black. He made us acceptable as we were, which was a big deal."[19]

Most public figures praised King in the days after his death, though the riots added to the feeling of national upheaval. Others cast the event in negative political terms. Prominent conservatives effectively blamed King for his own death. Governor Reagan called King's murder "a great tragedy that began when we began compromising with law and order and people started choosing which laws they'd break."[20] South Carolina senator Strom Thurmond claimed that such a lawless act of assassination was a result of King's own movement being rooted in disobeying laws.[21] Georgia's sitting governor Lester Maddox called King an "enemy of our country."[22]

The *Chicago Tribune* editorialized on the riots, conflating King's nonviolent resistance with the looting and rioting that had erupted: "Moral values are at the lowest level since the decadence of Rome," the editors argued. "If you are black, so goes the contention, you are right, and you must be indulged in every wish."[23]

There was a deep grieving period and a lull in the civil rights movement, and many activists would move into the political arena.[24]

The president's riot commission stated that there was "a need for new programs, laws and attitudes for the poor African American community."25 The commission concluded, "There can be no higher priority for national action and no higher claim on the nation's conscience."26 None of the commission's proposals would be completed.27

King's assassination completely upended Stax Records as well. Before that day, race had been relegated to a virtual non-issue within the confines of the studio and the offices of Stax. But with King's death, Black people in the neighborhood began to see Stax in a different light. Instead of a symbol of the promise of America and integration, some Black people now questioned this company in the middle of their neighborhood making money off something so deeply ingrained in Black culture: soul music. Part of the problem, according to Steve Cropper, was that "I think just the fact that the public thought that Stax was solely a white-owned record company. Al Bell was part owner of the company."28

James Brown and comedian Jerry Lewis on the *Jerry Lewis Show*, 1969 (NBC-TV promotional).

For the first time, racial resentment materialized within the company as well, primarily a distrust of the white players from some of Stax's newer Black members.29

Locals began haranguing first the white personnel on their way into the studio from their cars every morning and then Black personnel as well. Sam and Dave were shaken down for money by local gang members.30 The FBI came in and ran a sting.31

Stax would find its footing again in the '70s. Stax producer/songwriter and then star Stax performer Isaac Hayes redefined soul music again with the 1969 release of the album *Hot Buttered Soul*. Hayes transformed soul by building the songs up with complex string arrangements and funky basslines. His shaved black head shown on the album cover came to symbolize both the growing Black soul sound and the Black Power movement going forward.[32]

Riots and Student Movements around the World. The year 1968 saw student movements not only in the United States but also in France, Germany, Czechoslovakia, Argentina, Japan, and Mexico, when younger leftists challenged old-guard, right-aligned governments.

In May in Paris, what started as a small student protest against the government at one of France's elite universities, the Sorbonne, spread within days to include millions of French workers in a general strike. The protest paralyzed the country and nearly brought down the government.[33]

Robert Kennedy Assassinated. In June '68, Senator Robert Kennedy, the frontrunner for the Democratic Party presidential nomination, was gunned down at the Ambassador Hotel in Los Angeles by a 22-year-old Palestinian sympathizer.[34]

Johnson Quits and Upheaval at the Democratic Convention in Chicago. In August 1968, President Johnson, being vilified by America's left-leaning youth for giving them the Vietnam War, surprisingly quits his presidential campaign. In 1968 alone, the supposedly "winding down" war had seen the deaths of over 14,500 U.S. troops and now 28,000 overall, while deaths of Vietnamese were into the millions, and there was no end in sight.

The left-leaning youth also saw the old guard of the Democratic Party as lacking the will to meaningfully alter an unjust, corporate-dominated economic system and to move toward peace, while two Kennedys and King were dead. Yet the counterculture's ability to rally and protest in numbers had also energized the left.[35]

In January 1968, Abbie Hoffman and Jerry Rubin's Yippies organized a couple of thousand protesters to congregate and illegally camp out in downtown Chicago during the Democratic National Convention. There was protesting in the streets, lighting garbage cans on fire, and windows being broken.[36] Leary and Hoffman spoke to the crowd, and poets gave readings. The uniting event was a rock show, but many acts bailed out due to the threat of anarchy. Still, protest music was provided by Country Joe and the Fish and folk singers Judy Collins and Phil Ochs, and rock music from the Fugs.[37]

Mayor Richard Daley ordered police to crack down on anti-war protesters.[38] As the nation watched on national television for three nights, the area around the convention erupted in violence. The Chicago police used nightsticks and tear gas to clear things out. Some "long hairs" were dragged out of hotels and beaten.[39] The Chicago convention shook America up further, and it was a blow to the Democrats' hope for a strong unified image in support of nominee Hubert Humphrey.

Rubin, Hoffman, Bobby Seale, and five others were convicted of conspiracy, inciting to riot, and related charges and became known as the "Chicago Seven" (after Seales's case was separated).[40] The convictions were all later either dismissed or remanded due to judicial errors, while prosecutors would decline to retry any of the remaining charges.[41]

Nixon Elected President. In November 1968, Nixon, running on a platform of "law and order" and ending the war, narrowly defeated Hubert Humphrey in the presidential election with 43.4 percent of the popular vote to Humphrey's 42.7 percent.[42]

Post–'68 Haight-Ashbury. Back in the Haight district in 1969, the hippies had one more cause before the end of the decade. Locals turned an economically depressed lot on the South Campus section of Berkeley into a park, both for a community space and to provoke authorities. The hippies cited the same doctrine that Europeans had used in taking over North America: that land should be put to its highest economic use and not left unproductive.[43] On May 15, a rally was held at noon on campus of between 2,000 and 6,000 hippies, and there was a confrontation with police.[44] Some demonstrators threw rocks at the police; the police launched tear gas, and some fired birdshot into groups of people.[45] A police car with an officer inside was overturned. The officer pulled his revolver to escape the angry crowd.[46] A demonstrator was shot in the back while fleeing down the street. Bricks and chunks of concrete were tossed from rooftops toward officers below.[47] Two African American bystanders—each only observing the mayhem, one from a rooftop and the other from a window—died from gunshot wounds.[48] Reagan brought in the National Guard that occupied Berkeley for 17 days.[49]

During the same time as the riot, John Lennon and new bride Yoko Ono were conducting what they called Bed-Ins for Peace for two weeks. The couple sat up in a bed in a hotel suite in Montreal and spoke to the press to promote nonviolent protests against wars and other new ways to promote peace.[50] Lennon supported the park but also warned the activists, "The students are being conned! It's like the school bully: He aggravates you and aggravates you until you hit him, and then they kill you."[51]

In 1972, a crowd in Berkeley tore the fence down, but the city refused to take it over as a park; it would fall into disrepair for some time.[52]

Late '60s Pop Culture

Film. In 1968, Hollywood launched the cutting edge of sci-fi, one year before the moon landing, with the Stanley Kubrick adaptation of Arthur C. Clarke's book *2001: A Space Odyssey* (1968). The year also saw Roman Polanski's psychological/paranoia and occult-based horror classic

Rosemary's Baby (1968) and George A. Romero's genre-defining zombie movie *Night of the Living Dead* (1968), subtly implicating the masses in their support of Vietnam, among other things.

TV. Rowan and Martin's Laugh-In was a groundbreaking and hip countercultural sketch comedy hit.

Top-40 Music. Among the top-ten hot singles for 1968 were the Beatles' "Hey, Jude," the top single of the year, the relaxed Stax soul of Otis Redding's "(Sittin' On) The Dock of the Bay," the flower power of the Rascals' "People Got to Be Free," and Cream's psych-blues-rock "Sunshine of Your Love."

15

The Beatles Come Full Circle, 1968–1970

In early 1968, after the release of *Magical Mystery Tour*, the Beatles, with wives and girlfriends and a group including actor and musician friends, traveled to India for several weeks to study transcendental meditation with Maharishi Mahesh Yogi. That practice included meditation and reciting Hindu mantras and raising one's spiritual consciousness. The four Beatles even gave up drugs during their stay.[1] George Harrison explained his mindset at the time and something he referred to as "Christ-consciousness" in an interview with *International Times*:

> Christ said "The Kingdom of Heaven is Within," and he said, "The Kingdom of Heaven is AT HAND," which to my understanding means it's just 'ere, lads, you know, it's—at hand means like this, like this—ashtray, it's right in front of you. And the Kingdom of Heaven is within, so, why don't the Christians like, go within?[2]

Starr and wife, Maureen, left India after a week, Harrison and Patty Boyd left a couple of weeks later to spend time with Ravi Shankar and make music, and Lennon and McCartney left after a couple of months.[3]

At one point, the band members became disillusioned with the yogi. For one thing, the yogi seemed remarkably cold and unconcerned when the group received the devastating news that band manager and close friend Brian Epstein had died. The group had also then believed the yogi had made sexual advances toward two female guests, though that was later discovered to be a misunderstanding. In any event, the Beatles came to embrace meditation, especially Harrison, and the time in India was an especially productive time for songwriting.[4]

The Beatles—Stage Four (A Reality Check)

While the Beatles had hit a creative peak with *Revolver* and *Sgt. Pepper's*, which had spilled into the *Magical Mystery Tour*, their output over their final three studio albums would be stellar as well. The White Album (1968) saw the band still exploring far afield from the pop-rock that they had redefined. It is a wildly ambitious double album in which the band members pushed and challenged one another. As Starr explained, "While we were recording the 'White Album,' we ended up being more of a band again, and that's what I always love. I love being in a band."[5] But the recording of the album also showed the first signs of the Fab Four breaking into four distinct entities, too, in personal conflicts and disparate musical directions.

The album includes everything from classic blues-based rock ("While My Guitar Gently Weeps"), aching ballads ("Julia"), retro-rock ("Back in the U.S.S.R."), music hall ("Honey Pie"), even proto-heavy metal ("Helter Skelter"), and an unsettling musique concrète collage ("Revolution 9"). Along with the help of George Martin and engineers, the end result is a sprawling effort but one of the more interesting of rock releases.

Thematically, Dirk Dunbar called the White Album the Beatles' fourth stage in which the group dreamed of a better future, but they were also looking to deflate their near-mythological status and bring matters back to earth:

> An acceptance of life in the mainstream, the fourth stage of the Beatles' lyrics negates their hallucinogenic visions of utopia in favor of individuality and political and spiritual freedom. White album songs such as "I'm So Tired" and "Yer Blues"—in which Lennon screams that he wants to die—reflect the group's inner turmoil and the painful end of their surrealistic dream, and the Beatles began to dismiss their own myth.[6]

Lennon would later explain, "If the Beatles of the sixties had a message, it was to learn to swim. Period. And once you learn to swim, swim. The people who are hung up on the Beatles and the Sixties dream missed the whole point."[7] In that vein, on "Glass Onion" Lennon pokes fun at the Beatles cult by making numerous lyrical references to previous Beatles songs and intentionally providing fodder for those inclined to overanalyze those lyrics and put too much importance in their meaning.[8]

The Beatles' critical take on corporate greed, "Piggies," was controversial in some right-wing quarters.[9] Similarly, "Back in the U.S.S.R." raised alarms with other right-wing folks, including the John Birch Society, due to its seemingly communist-friendly lyrics.[10] McCartney, the songwriter, however, later explained that aside from being a fun nod to both Chuck Berry's "Back in the U.S.A." and the Beach Boys' "California Girls," the song was a "hands across the water" moment. McCartney knew that the Beatles especially and rock music in general were hugely popular and influential with the citizens of the Soviet Union, yet those people could only get Beatles records on the black market (they were one of the hottest items), and no local or foreign rock and roll bands could even perform in the U.S.S.R.[11] Thus, the song as well as its sound effect of a jet landing were gestures of inclusion.[12]

The Beatles—Stage Five (Back Home)

The Beatles' last two albums were *Abbey Road*, released in 1969, and *Let It Be*, released in 1970. *Let It Be* was actually recorded first, but the release was delayed when it had been decided that more production work was needed, handled by Phil Spector.[13] Therefore, *Abbey Road* was the last collection of songs the group actually recorded. The two albums generally combined to form what Dunbar saw as the group's fifth and final thematic stage, a return home:

> The use of home and sun to depict a cosmic return centers the group's ecological lyrics and culminates on their last albums, *Abbey Road* and *Let It Be*.... "Get Back" ... [and] the joyousness of returning home is redundantly expressed in the refrain of "Two of Us," which describes two friends embarked on life's journey, standing alone in the sun, going nowhere in particular, but having fun getting there.[14]

Further, whereas the sun is referenced in more literal terms in earlier songs ("Good Day Sunshine," "It's All Too Much"), Dunbar noted, "The million suns in 'Across the Universe' shine limitless love and in 'Here Comes the Sun' and 'Sun King' the sun is the cosmic force that issues in a reunion of humans and nature."[15] Otherwise, *Let It Be* would close out with a theme of peaceful resolution and coming home, e.g., "Golden Slumbers."

Let It Be is often considered to be the Beatles' least-great album, though it produced some classic songs, including the title track, "I've Got a Feeling," and "Get Back." Indeed, as to the Lennon-written "Across the Universe," few songs match it as a spiritual account of a majestic, benevolent universe. Lennon quotes a Hindu mantra, inspired by his time in India, and he describes love as a force that unites everything in the universe. Lennon once offered an interesting insight into his creative process when writing the song's lyrics:

> They were purely inspirational and were given to me as boom! I don't own it, you know; it came through like that.... It's like being possessed; like a psychic or a medium. The thing has to go down. It won't let you sleep, so you have to get up, make it into something, and then you're allowed to sleep. That's always in the middle of the bloody night, when you're half-awake or tired and your critical facilities are switched off.[16]

Abbey Road produced some more of the Beatles' greatest individual songs, including "Come Together" and the Harrison-written gems "Something" and "Here Comes the Sun." There was also the more pure, childlike fun with "Octopus' Garden" and, echoing the heavy blues-rock being made by Eric Clapton, then with Cream, and Jimi Hendrix, "I Want You (She's So Heavy)." All of that was followed with a remarkable and seamless 16-minute, eight-song medley that closed out the album, and thus the Beatle phenomenon.

At that time, infighting over personal relations, creative direction, and business decisions were taking a toll on the four. The unity and intense chemistry that had served the group so well was now cracking. Lennon and Harrison were growing tired of competing with McCartney to get songs on each album, and the four were split in two as to who would handle their business affairs for them. The Lennon and McCartney partnership was something like a marriage in which it seemed that at least one of the pair, here Lennon, needed more room to work out his own issues and to fully grow.[17] For a long time afterward, it would be popular to blame Yoko Ono for interfering with the Fab Four and causing the band's end. In retrospect and per subsequent accounts of all four band members, it seems clear that Ono more represented Lennon's new direction in life than being any root cause of dissension.[18] Indeed, the entity that was the Beatles simply seemed to have run a natural course.

In the *Abbey Road* medley, for example, "You Never Give Me Your Money" starts as McCartney's somber lament of a time of innocence gone and notes the group's business squabbles. But the song also beautifully acknowledges that a dream had actually come true as well, and it then even references a children's nursery rhyme to underscore the innocence. In the same vein, "Golden Slumbers" literally starts to put the enterprise to rest, and it, too, is actually an old nursery rhyme that McCartney had written new music for.[19]

In the hard rock track "Polythene Pam," Lennon's sneering, punkish *ya-ya-yas* is a statement from a somewhat jaded, now-29-year-old music vet, in direct contrast with the optimistic but maybe a bit naive *ya-ya-yas* of their earlier selves. Lennon doesn't negate that early idealism and unbridled joy, but he seems to be acknowledging that life can certainly get much more challenging and more complicated as it goes on.

In "Carry That Weight," McCartney alludes to his last efforts to keep the band together. Again, however, the group also seems to be moving forward and appreciating the experience before moving on to "The End." Music writer Richie Unterberger summarized the medley:

> The aura of vague impending gloom, though, is immediately swept away as the track segues into the uplifting "The End," as if the burden of "Carry That

Weight" has been magically removed—for the conclusion of the Abbey Road album, at any rate.[20]

On "The End," each of the four members take a short turn with solos. At that point, each had become excellent musicians but had rarely engaged in showy solos. Instead, each had consistently played in a way that enhanced and served the songs themselves. Here, each lets loose, and all are quite spectacular, yet no one overreaches.

Once that flurry settles, and although the Beatles did not necessarily have a "message," "The End" closes rather majestically with a harmonized line that finds a simple equanimity in the universe, where shared love balances everything.[21]

That line is followed by the sort of cute, tacked-on, 23-second "Her Majesty." The addition has drawn complaints for being superfluous—or for McCartney insisting on having the last word. Yet, the blurb also serves to undermine any idea of overstating the importance of whatever "message" the band had just left behind, beyond simply inspiring people to decide what the "message" was for themselves.

Woodstock

In the late '60s, Paul Kantner had started an early and successful head shop in Brooklyn and then successfully promoted a rock concert in Miami.[22] In 1969, Kantner began promoting a new music festival, billed as "Three Days of Peace and Music." The festival would be on April 15–17, on a farm next to Woodstock, New York, an hour and a half from New York City.[23]

Some of the biggest acts of the time—including the Beatles, the Stones, Bob Dylan, and Joni Mitchell—were not available for various reasons. Still, the lineup was an unprecedented collection of top rock and folk acts, including the Who, Joan Baez, Jimi Hendrix, the Grateful Dead, Ravi Shankar, Country Joe and the Fish, up-and-comers like Richie Havens and Santana, and a dozen others.

Kantner, expecting to make a nice profit, had presold 180,000 tickets, but double that showed up.[24] Unarmed off-duty police provided security, but fans tore down fences anyway, making the event "free."[25] Everyone could see the elevated platform and hear the music from a system boasting two 70-foot speaker towers.[26] There were apparently no fights, assaults, or homicides.[27]

Woodstock would be considered a massive success and a milestone in twentieth-century pop culture history. The hippies were clearly no longer, as some said, "a small number of oddballs"—it was a bona fide cultural movement.[28] Pulling off Woodstock signaled that the youth of America, or a massive swath of them at least, could actively create their own vision of a new future and a new sense of community. It was the sort of mobilization of the masses normally only seen with countries' competing sports teams or their armies.

16

"Do What Thou Wilt" (or *Partying with the Stones!*), 1968–Early '70s

As the '60s progressed, the rock and roll–fueled Western-youth movement largely continued to abandon a view of the church as the central arbiter of morality, thus leaving a void of sorts. The countercultural movement was reevaluating the meaning of a lot of things, such as the life goals of middle-class respectability and more superficial measures of success. And if there was a God, the counterculture was questioning whether church leaders had an exclusive hotline to His word. This while nuclear bombs hung over everyone's head. The door was thus wide open to all manner of religious and spiritual philosophies. Members of the counterculture variously embraced the teachings of Jesus, mysticism, and writers such as Aldous Huxley, Carl Jung, Sri Mahatar Babaji, and Sri Paramahansa Yogananda or simply none of the above.

As to certain occult and paganist practices, the background is that these beliefs had existed before, or otherwise alternatively to, the Protestantism and Catholicism that established the dominant religious narratives throughout Western culture for centuries. A hope was that returning to such paths could better open up new ways to become more in tune with a natural spiritual state and find answers to the biggest mysteries of life and the universe. This, as opposed to conforming to what was perceived as a rigid, hierarchical, and exploitive status quo that simply wasn't working. One result of this would be that one of the odder individuals of the twentieth century would enter the story of rock and roll.

Aleister Crowley's (1875–1947) story is a tangent in the rock narrative, but it also provides significant context for some of hard rock's philosophical underpinnings and its extreme limits, as well as also connecting to the stories of giants the Rolling Stones, the Beatles, Led Zeppelin, and Black Sabbath.

Crowley was an accomplished mountaineer and an author and poet. He was also a proud drug abuser and sexual deviant, a shameless and phenomenally narcissistic self-promoter, an infamous black magician, and the founder of his own religion.[1] Crowley had a run of notoriety in the United Kingdom in the 1920s. A tabloid once called him "The Wickedest Man in the World," and he even billed himself as "The Great Beast 666" for greater notoriety.[2] Despite his towering flaws, he left enough of a legacy that his likeness was added to London's National Portrait Gallery in 2003.[3]

Crowley was born in 1875 in Royal Leamington Spa in the United Kingdom. Crowley's father inherited a small fortune from family brewery interests, which Crowley would inherit as a young man. Crowley's parents were also members of the Plymouth Brethren, an extreme sect of Christian fundamentalism that, as Crowley put it, anticipated "the imminent end of the world with smug satisfaction."[4] As a child, he was restricted to reading only the Bible, and he often expressed a deep hatred for his parents. He would soon rebel totally against his oppressive upbringing.[5]

At around the turn of the century, while in college, Crowley was searching for religious alternatives. At that time, many others were seeking the same.[6] Charles Darwin's theory of evolution, advanced in 1859 in his *On the Origin of Species by Means of Natural Selection*, highlighted modern science's steady undermining of biblical proclamations asserted as literal scientific fact. During England's Victorian era (1837–1901), in fact, the nation had seen a massive decline in religious belief—that is, the "Victorian crisis of faith"—that lasted throughout the century.[7] By the start of the twentieth century, many sought new, more direct connections with a spiritual world. In part emboldened by that modernizing world and technologies like the miraculous-seeming wireless Morse code (1897) (i.e., radio waves), it could be a short jump to seances and other occult practices.[8]

Crowley joined an occult group called the Hermetic Order of the Golden Dawn in 1898, whose curriculum included Hermetic Qabalah, astrology, occult tarot, geomancy, and alchemy.[9] Members of the order sought to achieve an emotional/psychological state called entering the "Abyss," described as being beyond the "mystical realm" of "good and evil where 'all is one.'" There, seekers would either become one "or plummet into madness."[10]

In 1904, while honeymooning in Cairo, Egypt, Crowley claimed that he had channeled a supernatural entity named Aiwass that guided him in writing what Crowley titled *The Book of the Law*.[11] Crowley declared a new age, one of the "crowned and conquering child," which he believed to be the Egyptian god Horus. He also believed that only a few special people, including himself, would enjoy total freedom in their actions.[12] This was the start of Crowley's religion, Thelema (Greek for "will"). In *The*

16. "Do What Thou Wilt"... 1968–Early '70s

Aleister Crowley, 1934 (Wide World Photos, Library of Congress).

Book of the Law, Crowley further famously declared that the only rule for its followers would be to "Do what thou wilt," meaning that individuals should work to align themselves with what he called a "True Will."[13] Crowley believed that embracing one's personal inclinations was to be "emancipated from all limitations," which he considered to be one's highest good.[14]

Because Crowley explicitly did not believe in the stories of the Bible, he did not believe in Satan and thus was not a Satanist. He would, however, for promotional purposes, call himself "The Great Beast 666." Crowley also later wrote a poem called *Hymn to Lucifer* in which he portrayed the fallen angel not as "the Devil" but as a pantheistic, prefall Lucifer, and as described in the Bible, a "Morning Star" and "bringer of light." To Crowley, life was about rebelling against all constraints; the final line of the poem, in fact, is "The Key of Joy is Disobedience."[15]

Crowley's life would be filled with a wild array of events, including occult practices and leading some sects, extreme hedonism, including sadomasochism, the regular solicitation of prostitutes, sex with both men and women, and heavy drug use, including alcohol, cocaine, and heroin.[16] To Crowley, higher acts of rebellion and sin, or just writing about them, only heightened his sense of freedom.[17] In his poetry book *White Stains*, he expounded on topics such as bestiality, necrophilia, coprophagia, and urophagia, while in another book he suggested sex with the crucified Christ. The point for Crowley was simply, he said, "excess in all directions."[18] As he further wrote, "I want none of your faint approval or faint dispraise. I want blasphemy, murder, rape, revolution, anything good or bad, but strong."[19]

Crowley deemed his practices "magick," with the "k" meant to distinguish what he was doing from the show business version of the supernatural.[20] To Crowley, magick was "the art of causing change to occur in accordance with will" and included heightening his senses through sexual orgasms and having visions.[21]

Crowley's conception of love seemed to exclusively mean the act of sex and how it made him feel and with little apparent distinction between love and lust. He also once explained his view of women: "Morally and mentally women were for me beneath contempt. They had no moral ideals."[22]

As to drugs, in his sacred text, Crowley instructed, "To worship me take wine and strange drugs whereof I will tell my prophet, & be drunk of; they shall not harm ye at all."[23] Yet he would also struggle with terrible drug and alcohol addictions his entire life.[24]

In short, Crowley believed that his own often-cryptic writings were the total truth.

Crowley passed in a boarding house near Hastings, England, in 1947, his death hastened by chronic heroin use.[25] Isherwood wrote that in the end, Crowley had been "largely forgotten by the countrymen he had once so shocked."[26] In the end, his myth had unraveled greatly, and he was seen more as a warped individual and of far less import than he had seemed to believe.

A purposefully crafted bad-boy image that shocked the British establishment, murky teachings, and a "Do What Thou Wilt" philosophy certainly had its attraction, however. Crowley was even the prototype for several dark magician characters in films of the 1950s and '60s, including *Night of the Demons*, *The Devil Rides Out*, and *The Dunwich Horror*.

Those influenced by Crowley's beliefs, to varying degrees, included the founder of the Church of Scientology, L. Ron Hubbard, and Timothy Leary. One of Leary's autobiographies, *Confessions of a Hope Fiend* (1973), even took its title from two of Crowley's works, *Confessions* and *Diary of a Drug Fiend*.[27]

Crowley's image as the ultimate, mystical rebel figure also happened to fit into some of the most bombastic and iconoclastic aspects of the rock and roll of the time. He explored the human psyche, human will, ego, and some form of spirituality, albeit all from a wildly hedonistic perspective. But this being a strange and confused time, people wanted answers and resolution to life's uncertainties, and for many, organized religion was not proving satisfying.

16. "Do What Thou Wilt"... 1968–Early '70s

What is good and evil *really*? Why was human sexuality such a source of shame? What were the true limits or guidelines to life's pleasures? If Western society was so morally "good," why was it so greedy and exploitive of others, and why was it preparing for nuclear Armageddon? Options were open.

As to the Beatles' connection to Crowley, they were likely introduced to him through a popular occult book that had spoken positively of Crowley and that had hit British bookstores in March 1967, a couple of months before the photo shoot for *Sgt. Pepper's*.[28] Paul McCartney later said that John Lennon was being "bold and brassy" when he stumped for not only Crowley to appear on the iconic cover of *Sgt. Pepper's* but also Hitler, Christ, and Gandhi. Of those, only Crowley was used, which was also a massive boost for his profile.[29]

Lennon's push for Crowley seemed to reflect a desire for *any* alternatives to what the establishment had to offer, and Lennon also seemed to have a muddled understanding of Crowley's actual writings and lifestyle. In an interview with *Playboy* magazine, Lennon was quoted as saying, "The whole Beatle idea was to do what you want ... do what thou whilst, as long as it doesn't hurt somebody."[30] Crowley was, however, more obsessed with rebelling for the sake of rebelling as opposed to being self-actualized. He also seemed to be out of touch with any moral compass, with little to no concern about harming others (especially women), and he was tremendously *self*-destructive.

McCartney was unimpressed with Crowley. He once stated that Crowley was the one who took his mix of the dark arts and hedonism "to its extreme, and by doing so, showed that it doesn't work. I believe we owe him a debt of thanks for this."[31]

It would seem that Lennon and other rock and rollers were simply looking to get past the establishment's manipulations in a quest for some answers, or as Lennon would later sing solo, "Gimme Some Truth" (1971). Pre-rock life had seemed to be about grooving along to "The Woody Woodpecker Song" and "How Much Is That Little Doggie in the Window?" and that hardly seemed like *living*. For many, if sex, drugs, and rock and roll were all a part of getting more connected to the universe, all the better.

The Rolling Stones' connection to Crowley and the occult was in part tied to filmmaker Kenneth Anger. Anger's story is also a bit tangential in rock's story, but he indeed had some interesting ties to some key figures of this era.

Anger has been called the first avant-garde filmmaker as well as being cited as an important influence by prominent directors such as Martin Scorsese, David Lynch, and John Waters.[32] As a young man, Anger (b. 1927) started creating films that were short, dialogue-free, and surrealistic, dealing with erotica and pagan and occult themes.[33] His films would explore many moral issues that organized religion tended to dismiss out of hand, especially around sexuality. Anger was gay at a time when homosexuality was closeted and illegal in California (until 1976).[34] His first film, *Fireworks* (1947), included homosexual themes and violent homophobia. The film got Anger arrested on obscenity charges, though California's courts deemed it to be art rather than pornography.[35]

Anger was living in San Francisco when he made *Scorpio Rising* (1961), a film portraying biker and homoerotic themes, Nazi iconography, and clips from a third-rate religious film depicting Jesus. It is startling imagery; Anger described it as "a death mirror held up to American culture."[36]

Anger became a devout follower of Thelemic practices in the '50s and produced several Crowley-themed films depicting various pagan gods.[37] In the mid–'60s, he began work on the film *Lucifer Rising*, which was inspired by Crowley's poem *Hymn to Lucifer*, casting Lucifer as "the original rebel" and a symbol of a freedom untainted by the church.[38] Anger later told film critic Roger Ebert that the film, which also coincided with the age of Aquarius, depicted "the beginning of the pagan age and the end of Christianity."[39]

Anger began to recruit young men to play Lucifer in the film and found handsome aspiring musician Bobby Beausoleil.[40] Beausoleil also formed a jazz group specifically to record the soundtrack for the film.[41] He and Anger had a falling out, and Beausoleil moved on to join one of the communes in Haight-Ashbury around the time of the Summer of Love (more on that shortly). The film's completion was delayed.[42]

Later, Anger used footage shot for *Lucifer Rising* for his next short film, *Invocation of My Demon Brother* (1969). *Invocation* starred Anger himself and Beausoleil as well as featuring performance footage from Anger's new friends Mick Jagger and Keith Richards, and with Jagger's brother Chris and Richard's girlfriend Marianne Faithfull in acting roles.[43] Anger had tried to cast Jagger as Lucifer in the film, which Jagger seriously considered before passing.[44] Jagger did, however, compose an electronic piece for the film with a Moog synthesizer.[45]

Lucifer Rising would essentially be finished in 1972, though it would not be widely distributed until 1980 when Beausoleil was finally able to finish the score. In the film, Anger depicts volcanic eruptions and fiery lava, a beautiful, topless Faithfull as an Egyptian goddess. Beausoleil is shown covered in blood holding a bloody sword before slinking into a bath. There is a contemporary image of Lucifer/the Devil, a picture of Crowley hangs on a wall, and a flying saucer is seen.

There was friction during the shoot, and by the time *Lucifer Rising* was released, Anger had supposedly "cursed" most of the people involved in the film. Faithfull was deeply mired in a heroin addiction at the time.[46]

Richards and Pallenberg were close with Anger at one point, and Richards admittedly "dabbled" in black arts with Pallenberg, along with doing a lot of heroin. "It's something everybody ought to explore," Richards once explained.[47] He would also say, "When we were just innocent kids out for a good time, they were saying 'They're evil, they're evil.' Oh, I'm evil, really? So that makes you start thinking about evil."[48]

Ultimately, the Stones' excursion into the world of the occult was relatively short lived, and they would downplay the depth of their involvement with Anger. According to Faithfull, "The only reason that the Stones were not destroyed by the ideas they toyed with is that they never took them as seriously as their fans."[49]

Certainly, though, some of that philosophy is evidenced in the Stones' work of the time. There was the more obvious, such as the title of their 1967 album, *Their Satanic Majesty's Request*—actually a humorous play on the language used in British passports, replacing "Britannic" with "Satanic," while on their 1969 album *Let It Bleed*, one writer noted, for example, that the Stones "ambivalently explored drug addiction, rape, murder and predation."[50]

Of course, the Stones were capable of soulful and melodic music with honest, emotional depth throughout their career. Earlier on, it was the loss of innocence in "As Tears Go By" (1966), the wondrously psychedelic "She a Rainbow" (1967), and beautiful ballads like "Ruby Tuesday" (1967) and "Wild Horses" (1971). But by 1968, fear and chaos seemed to be coming to a head all around the world. If the possibly fiery end of the world was not imminent, it could certainly seem an inevitable result of the human condition. Jagger recalled "a very rough, very violent era. The Vietnam War. Violence on the screens, pillage and burning."[51] So now what?

Instead of "All You Need Is Love," the Stones responded with "Gimme Shelter" on 1969's *Let It Bleed*. According to Jagger, this was "a kind of end-of-the-world song, really. It's apocalypse."[52] It is the eeriest, yet most affecting, of rock songs. It captured the existential dread of the times and embraced it head-on.

The guitars on "Shelter" are unsteady but still powerful and ominous. Jagger is accompanied by soul singer Merry Clayton, who gives her own legendary performance. The lyrics are often unclear, which adds to the unease as well, and Richard's open tuning gives the feeling that nothing is holding them all down. Not until a few verses in do Clayton's words start to crystallize about a world seemingly teetering on the edge of mayhem, rape, and murder.

The song's crescendo comes with Clayton singing so powerfully that twice you hear her voice break; it is passion but also with some desperation. Jagger and Clayton end the song suggesting a response of if not love, a more physical intimacy, in the face of imminent apocalypse.

"Sympathy for the Devil" from 1968 is another iconic Stones song. That track opens with both Watts and a conga player knocking out a relentless tribal beat. Jagger unleashes some jungle yells, yet Nicky Hopkins's piano brings the song to London, very much in the here and now.

Jagger starts to sing from the perspective of a mysterious character whose identity as the Devil quickly becomes apparent. In that role, Jagger proclaims that he has been present at all of humanity's worst moments, referencing the murder of Jesus, the killing of Czar Nicholas and his entire family in the Russian Revolution of 1917, and so on. And the Devil, according to Jagger's narrative, has even existed in people that society considers to be the most dignified among us. To the Stones, the so-called Devil is not so much something or someone to look down on; it is an aspect of human nature, and it always has been. In this sense, to try to demonize the "other" as evil would be a cop-out and disingenuous. The message is to be careful of who you vilify because after all, to paraphrase Jagger, we are him and he is we. Hence, some *sympathy* for the Devil and thus us. That's how Jagger was seeing it anyway.

The song is not intended as an *evil* view of the world but as a blunt rejection of the Judeo-Christian historical perspective and its too-neat delineation of good and evil. It is an attempt to make sense of the apparent duality of human nature. To many in the counterculture, "us versus them" had too often been used by those in power as a weapon to keep someone else down. "Sympathy for the Devil" reflected the view that some were no longer accepting a suspect establishment's declarations as to what was moral.

As "Sympathy" winds down, the Stones have no apparent reservations in embracing their darker sides. Richards tears off one of his most searing solos: his own, modern, electric, rock take on Robert Johnson's Delta blues. Jagger is lost in the rhythm, shouting, and far from showing any signs of letting up, he yells to the band to go further. The band is loose and fiery, almost lost in a trance, as if trying to reconcile the good and evil in all of us, and right now.

If one accepts that certain desires and the potential for bad acts are a part of all of us, the Stones' perspective could be, in a way, liberating. That is, there is no longer a need to pretend to be pious and perfectly moral or even to cast judgment on others. Instead, just do your thing, presumably try not to hurt others, and live life to its fullest. The Stones had already proclaimed such a message in a previous song, "I'm Free" (1965).[53]

Despite "Sympathy" and a bit of a public furor upon its release, Jagger denied that the Stones were Satanists. He explained, "We didn't want to really go down that road. And I felt that song was enough. You didn't want to make a career out of it."[54]

A somewhat surprising highlight of the Stones' oeuvre, and perhaps showing the real reach of the group's talent, is a song with no blues in it at all, the disarmingly elegant "You Can't Always Get What You Want." With "Hey, Jude," the Beatles had opened the door to orchestral elements. With the help of the London Bach Choir and as the song title demonstrated, even the Stones could make a certain sort of peace with the end of the '60s.

Even without Satan, it was a wild, rather brutal ride being in, or even just *around*, the Rolling Stones. It was a life maxing out on sex, drugs, rock and roll, incredible wealth, fame, youth and invincibility, and with virtually no one to answer to. When Richards was being questioned on the witness stand by a British prosecutor in a marijuana possession trial in 1967, he had famously testified, "We are not worried about petty morals."[55] That may not have come out *quite* how Richards meant it or it may, but the point was made. They were not going to be talked down to by an establishment they didn't respect.

Toward the end of the '60s, writer Steve Appleford summarized the Stones status:

> [As] members of a new kind of royalty where no whim was too ridiculous to be seriously considered, they were worshipped by young girls and Decca's accountants alike, celebrated in these innocent days before the drug raids, the divorces, the deaths and decay, and their eventual fate as rootless tax exiles.[56]

Thus, they had become the first real *rock stars*.

As to love songs, the Stones learned their lessons from the soul music masters, and there were classics such as "Angie" (1973) and "Beast of Burden" (1978). Commentator Martha Bayles, however, noted a difference in the original soul music and its religious roots, and "rock" or classic rock's interpretations. Bayles opined that "large numbers of white rock artists" were "either ignorant of or indifferent to the religious background of soul" and "perceived its enthusiasm to be wholly erotic," while many Black performers "did their best to reinforce that perception."[57]

When Jagger and Richards wrote about women and relationships, though, and unlike the Beatles' three primary songwriters, romance was much less of a priority. Even "Beast of Burden" is very much a plea for sex. Also, in Jagger's lyrics, the man always had the upper hand.[58] In fact, he had frequently said that "all women are groupies."[59] As Richards observed, "Mick's attitude towards women is that they are cattle. They are goods. That's his basic attitude."[60] Certain of Jagger's lyrics became part of an underlying rock trend of misogyny—for example, "Bitch," "Under My Thumb," "Little T&A," and "Stupid Girl."

The songs "Some Girls" and "Brown Sugar," though intended as homages of sorts, made much maligned stereotyped references to Black women. As to "Brown Sugar," Jagger was apparently referring to his then-girlfriend, African American actor Marsha Hunt, but Jagger also references sex with slave women and cunnilingus, among other things. As Jagger would later state, "God knows what I'm on about on that song. It's such a mishmash. All the nasty subjects in one go."[61]

And the Stones were not exactly conservative in their personal lives. Jagger has had eight children by five women. Richards slept with the girlfriends of two bandmates and that of the band's first manager.[62] Jones and Wyman could very possibly be identified as sex addicts. When Wyman was 52, he married his 18-year-old girlfriend, Mandy Smith, whom he had been courting since she was 13 and, according to her, sleeping with since she was 14.[63]

As to the Stones and drugs, Jagger sometimes explicitly referenced the same in song. In "Let It Bleed," Jagger references cocaine, and in "Dead Flowers" he references being in pain and heroin and another girl bringing relief.[64] Richards established his immense and prolific talent over the decades, yet while also developing a reputation as a massive drug user that would make him the poster child for rock and rollers and extreme drug use.[65]

The Stones were living it to the hilt, but the consequences of that life added up fast as well.

Guitarist Brian Jones didn't make it out of the '60s. His 27-year life was filled with trouble and tragedy—beginning well before he joined the band—though he left an inspired musical legacy. Jones had helped set the band's course early on with his blues roots, his flamboyant style, and as a talented multi-instrumentalist. But Jones also had mounting personal problems, especially drug and alcohol dependency. This kept him from keeping up with Jagger and Richards, as the pair moved forward with their own vision for the band.[66] A major blow came when Jones's girlfriend, Anita Pallenberg, left him for Richards.[67]

In June 1969, the rest of the Stones asked the struggling Jones to leave the band, and Mick Taylor was brought in to replace him. Less than a month later, Jones drowned in a swimming pool while under the influence of alcohol and drugs (rumors of foul play have since been debunked).[68]

But life both in and even just around the band could be quite destructive. In 1987, Bill Wyman would reflect, "This life is incredibly destructive. You overcome it but the scars are still there. You still have bad dreams."[69] While still a relatively young man, the apparent toll of the lifestyle led to Richards variously being referred to as "Mr. Unhealthy" and looking like "an unresurrected Christ."[70] In 1971's "Sway," Jagger would sing of waking up to his mind breaking up and that a demon had got a hold of him.[71] Richards had this observation of Jagger navigating the rock star life:

> It's hard going for that front man gig Mick does. It's hard being out front. You gotta be able to make it work: You gotta actually believe you're that semidivine when you're out there, then come off stage and know you ain't. And that's the problem: Eventually the reaction time gets slower. You still think you're semidivine when you're in the limo and semidivine at the hotel, until you're semidivine for the whole goddam tour.[72]

A defining moment for the Stones came in December 1969 with the band's surreal and tragic performance at the Altamont Speedway Free Festival. The Stones spearheaded organizing the show and headlined, with guests the Grateful Dead, Jefferson Starship, and others. Joel Selvin's 2017 book *Altamont: The Rolling Stones, the Hells Angels, and the Inside Story of Rock's Darkest Day* provided an in-depth treatment of the concert. Selvin lays out the Stones' and Jagger's various misguided decisions regarding the concert, including the Stones hurrying their planning for the show so that they could get their own concert film out before the Woodstock film. In sum, a bad venue had been selected lacking proper food, sanitation, and security for a staggering 300,000 concertgoers. The Stones had also, in fact, hired the Hell's Angels biker gang as event security, not realizing that the U.S. chapter was far more violent than the U.K. contingent they were familiar with, as well as being utterly ill-prepared for such a massive event.

The bikers got drunk and high and harassed and beat on concertgoers with pool cues and fists throughout the day. They even knocked out Marty Balin of Jefferson Airplane.[73] As the day went on, the crowd became more and more agitated and the Hell's Angels more violent.[74] One observer noted that the only time the mood settled had been when country-rock band Flying Burrito Brothers performed.[75]

During the Stones' set, members of the Hell's Angels had already been targeting 18-year-old concertgoer Hunter Meredith, one of a small minority of African Americans in attendance, there with his white girlfriend. Members of the biker gang had punched him in the face and several chased him.[76] Eventually, Meredith had grabbed a gun and, high on methamphetamine, moved toward the stage, an apparent danger.[77] The bikers stabbed him in the chest and then brutally stomped him. The bikers though later acquitted, also reportedly prevented anyone from getting Meredith medical help in time that likely would have saved his life.[78] Some had believed that "Sympathy for the Devil" was playing at the time of the killing and thus may have spurred the violence, though that song had been played three songs prior.[79]

Altamont also had an LSD-related drowning and a hit and run that killed two festivalgoers.[80] In sum, the concert became the obvious dark contrast to the wonder of Woodstock, and it is generally considered to mark the official "end" of the '60s and its idealism.[81] It was a disturbing enough event that Jagger formally swore off the occult and burned all of his occult books afterward.[82]

Moving into the 1970s, the Stones' album *Exile on Main Street* (1972) is legendary as the Stones' and one of the genre's greatest albums. In sum, although there is none of the band's true signature hits, the double album is a raw rock and roll ("Rocks Off") amalgamation of the band's influences from Chess, Delta blues ("Ventilator Blues"), country ("Tumbling Dice"), and soul ("Happy"). It's as wild ("Rip This Joint") and as sexually charged ("Hip Shake Thing") as a Saturday night in a southern juke joint or roadhouse. Jagger was backed by slide guitar, horns, sax, and washboard rhythms, as it balances between tense and loose, darkness and joy. The strong sexual energy also comes with strong gospel and spiritual uplift ("Let It Loose" and "Shine a Light").

The record is also legendary for the extreme decadence occurring during its recording in the South of France. The documentary, initially unreleased, covering the 1972 tour supporting the album *Cocksucker Blues*, depicted Jagger snorting cocaine, Richards using heroin, and the Stones cheering on a couple as they have sex on their tour plane.[83] Band friend and journalist Stanley Booth said of his time covering that tour, "It was an ugly scene full of amyl nitrate, Quaaludes, tequila sunrises, cocaine, heroin, and too many pistoleros, and it left me with more material than I could ever use."[84]

Another remarkable story of the life of a Stone comes from 1976, when Richards brought his six-year-old son Marlon on the road with him. Father and son shared the life-on-the-road experience, from fancy hotel suites to places at the bar.[85] At times, Richards would be driving under the influence of heroin, and Marlon would have to warn his dad when they were coming to a border crossing so he could, as Richards would recall, "pull over, have a shot and either dump it or re-sort your shit."[86]

As to the Stones' impact on people in general, Richards had his own illuminating perspective:

> The Rolling Stones destroy people at an alarming rate. Something about us makes them come face-to-face eventually with themselves, sometimes for the better, sometimes in the worst possible way. Maybe that ultimately is the most important thing about the Stones. For some unknown reason, they strike at a person at a point and in a position that they don't even know exists.[87]

Not to suggest direct causation on the part of the members of the Stones, but the list of casualties of those around them and trying to keep up with them is long. Those in the Stones' inner circle that saw addictions spiral out of control include first manager Andrew Loog Oldham and former sax man Bobby Keys, along with the early drug deaths of Jones's and Richards's close friend and country-rock guitar icon Gram Parsons, not to mention an array of mental breakdowns and attempted and completed suicides by various girlfriends, wives, and wives' paramours.[88]

But the group members themselves moved on. Some of their best work was still ahead of them. The music could be beautiful and inspiring, though the group's hedonistic bent would regularly come through, too. They did not have a lot of use for romantic love or necessarily have a lot of faith in the universe ultimately being particularly benevolent. All of this placed them squarely as the yin to the Beatles' yang. Whether always entirely accurate or not, the Beatles would be associated with the peace and love of the '60s and, along with Woodstock, optimism for the future. The Stones would earn their own status as a revered but very different kind of musical institution. In 2003, and to Richards's disdain, Jagger and only Jagger would be knighted by Prince Charles, whereas the queen declined to partake in the ceremony.[89]

17

Transitions and Strange Days, End of the '60s

The rock and rollers and counterculturalists did not necessarily have a clear blueprint to fully effect the change envisioned in places like Detroit, Memphis, the Haight, and London moving forward into the '70s. There were certain victories, times of great unification, and even personal growth, yet also serious fallout and repercussions in pushing some things too far. Hard lessons were learned on the fly. The sometimes exhilarating '60s were coming to an end and there would still be some letdowns and stark reality checks.

Writer Greil Marcus identified certain records as "end-of-the-decade warnings" in Bob Dylan's *John Wesley Harding*, the Velvet Underground's *White Light/White Heat* (1968), the Rolling Stones' *Let It Bleed* (1969), John Lennon's *Plastic Ono Band* (1970), and Sly and the Family Stone's *There's a Riot Goin' On* (1971).[1] The Beatles' "Day in the Life" had been one dramatic, creative crescendo. But where to go from there?

By 1969, the hippies in the Haight were getting older and some left for new neighborhoods or out of the city.[2] Even the members of the Grateful Dead moved to homes in rural Marin County and built a studio there.[3] Not until the mid–Naughts would the Haight become a vibrant neighborhood again.[4]

Many hippies remained committed to a "back to the land" life and moved to rural locales in Northern California, Oregon, and Washington and to other communes near Taos, New Mexico, and southeastern Colorado. In the Northeast, hippies from New York moved into upstate New York and others to Vermont.[5] Influenced by people like nineteenth-century essayist, poet, and philosopher Henry David Thoreau, these new communities would involve some of the earliest efforts at solar power, organic foods, and other ecological concerns.[6]

It is also no coincidence that Silicon Valley sprouted near Haight-Ashbury, and at least some of the hippie mindset found its way into Silicon

Valley's culture.[7] The legendary cofounder of tech giant Apple Computers, Steve Jobs (1955–2011), for example, was born and raised in the valley. He also once said that taking LSD was one of the "two or three most important things" he had ever done in his life.[8]

Darkness

One of the most disturbing stories of the '60s also has strong ties to the story of the Haight and rock and in at least a couple of different ways.

Charles Manson was born in 1934 in Cincinnati, Ohio, to a troubled 16-year-old Kathleen Maddox and an unknown father.[9] Kathleen left her child with family members in Kentucky, Ohio, and West Virginia and was otherwise in and out of motels. Manson later claimed that his mother once tried to sell him at a bar when he was five.[10]

A young Manson began a crime spree of stealing cars and armed robbery still as a youth, followed by his and another inmate raping a fellow juvenile detainee.[11] Manson then spent most of the rest of his teens and 20s in institutions.[12] There, Manson learned about controlling women from pimps, a later occupation, and he read L. Ron Hubbard's teachings of Scientology as well as Dale Carnegie's *How to Win Friends and Influence People*, clinging to Carnegie sections on persuasion like "Everything You or I Do Springs from Two Motives: The Sex Urge and the Desire to Be Great."[13]

In December 1967, Manson begged prison authorities to not release him to the free world, but his request was denied. Manson, then 32, went to live in Haight-Ashbury.[14] At that point, the Haight already had a mix of idealists, free spirits, and the not-so-stable, including lots of adrift and vulnerable youth. Manson began to use mental manipulation and LSD to collect hangers-on who came to worship him as a guru, especially preying on troubled, deeply insecure, and young girls. With pliable, sexually "open" young women at his command, he attracted more male followers, forming what would become known as the "Manson Family."[15]

Manson's deranged motive and vision was that he and his family of about 100 would initiate a race war, hide out until the war was over, and then he and his "family" alone would repopulate the planet.[16] To avoid trouble, Manson moved his group to a ranch in the desert.[17]

Manson was also an aspiring songwriter, believing this was how he could reach a mass audience. He held a psychotic delusion that the Beatles were communicating with him personally through the White Album (e.g., locusts, referenced in biblical prophesies, are actually beetles, thus "Beatles"[18]) and that "Helter Skelter" was the name for the coming race war (actually, the name came from an amusement park ride and, otherwise, the song was McCartney's attempt to outdo the Who for the wildest rock song ever).[19]

In 1969, former Kenneth Anger colleague Bobby Beausoleil became friends with Manson associate Gary Hinman and then Manson himself.[20] As Anger later recalled of Beausoleil,

> I knew him when he was 19, and although he was, in quotes, a "bad boy," he was so immature. Manson just overwhelmed him. Manson is part of the complete moral and anarchic chaos we're in for. It will last for 1,500 years, until a new system comes along.[21]

In the summer of 1969, Beach Boy Dennis Wilson picked up some of Manson's young female followers hitchhiking, and for a short time, the "family" actually lived with Wilson on the California ranch he was leasing.[22] Wilson even used one of Manson's odd songs, changing the title and some of the music and lyrics, and recorded it as a B-side for the Beach Boys ("Never Learn Not to Love").[23] Once Wilson started to realize what he had gotten himself into, however, and afraid, he simply left the ranch and let the landlord deal with evicting his guests.[24]

Around the same time, on July 31, 1969, Beausoleil, accompanied by Manson "right-hand" man Bruce Davis, tortured and stabbed Gary Hinman to death, the first of the Manson-related murders. It was thought to have either been ordered by Manson, who may or may not have been present, or been part of a drug deal gone bad. The words "Political Piggy" were written in Hinman's blood on the wall at the murder scene in an attempt to confuse police, while a bloody paw print was left to try to deflect blame to the Black Panthers.[25] Beausoleil was caught and sentenced to life in prison, where he would finish the soundtrack for Kenneth Anger's *Lucifer Rising*.[26]

On August 9, a week before Woodstock, Manson's followers carried out his orders to kill the occupants of the home at 10050 Cielo Drive in Benedict Canyon, a neighborhood in Beverly Hills.[27] This had been the home of Terry Melcher, a music executive who had recently rejected his music. Although it turned out Melcher had moved out several months before, Manson assumed it would still be inhabited by someone newsworthy, and therefore the plan proceeded. Manson's group committed the gruesome, ritualistic stabbing and shooting deaths of pregnant actress Sharon Tate, wife of director Roman Polanski, who was not at home, and four of Tate's friends. The words "Pig," "Rise," and "Healter Skelter" (*sic*) were written in blood on the walls.[28]

The next day, Manson directed the murders of Leno and Rosemary LaBianca in Los Feliz.[29] At that time, the very idea of a "serial killer" was not even in the country's consciousness.[30] It was shocking and even worse than random violence in that it seemed motivated only by the darkest and most deranged of impulses.

On Friday, December 5, 1969, Manson's groupies were identified as being responsible for the Tate murders. Los Angeles was wracked with fear, with an eye out for deranged, long-haired types.[31] That Saturday was Altamont.[32]

Manson and his "family" members were eventually convicted and Manson spent the remainder of his life in prison.[33] Manson's name remains synonymous with the worst of humanity. Unlike other serial killers and mass shooters who have since gained infamy, Manson's ability to order others to carry out killings for him and under entirely delusional motives is virtually unprecedented.

Spaced Out

On July 11, 1969, five days before NASA launched Apollo 11 for its anticipated, manned moon landing on July 20, British musician David Bowie released the single "Space Oddity." Some originally thought the song a novelty to cash in on the spectacle of Apollo 11. While space travel had in fact captured the world's consciousness at the time, the song was written the year before. It had actually been inspired by the Stanley Kubrick film *2001: A Space Odyssey* as well as a breakup Bowie had gone through at the time. Some suspected drugs may have had some influence on the song, though those who knew Bowie at the time didn't recall him yet being heavily into drugs, as he would be later.[34]

"Space Oddity" marks the odd timing both of the end of what seemed to be the most socially turbulent of decades, while humankind was also miraculously becoming space travelers for the first time. It is a very odd pop hit. Bowie sings the story of a fictitious astronaut, Major Tom, and the song has eight parts, starting with a ground control countdown and a liftoff. The song also starts with a very earthbound acoustic guitar, but as the song goes on, it gives way to an alien-sounding stylophone—a small, stylus-operated synthesizer. Early Bowie collaborator John "Hutch" Hutchinson said of Bowie, "Most musicians make songs with structures that have been used before—his songs have a structure that he dreams up himself."[35] Here, especially, that uniqueness and lack of familiarity are used to maximum effect.

As Major Tom gloriously launches into space, all is well. Despite the profundity and danger of the situation, however, the press asks inane questions: Who is his favorite football team? Then the spacewalk goes terribly wrong. The major's line breaks, and he is sent drifting off into deep space.

Tom says goodbye to his wife via radio. It's a true nightmare scenario that was for the first time in human history a real possibility: floating weightlessly in space for eternity. Yet somehow, Major Tom still seems to be finding some kind of peace. Some have suggested that given the major's "'inability to connect' with others emotionally," he may have preferred to not come back.[36] And while the technology that put Major Tom into outer space exceeded the wildest dreams of humankind throughout the ages, he ends up stuck in a space capsule that is, as Bowie sang, now functionally little more than a metal can.

The stylophone then hits higher and higher notes representing a disappearing radio signal until there is silence. It is an oddly moving song. Instead of complete distress at the possibility of spinning off into deep space, Bowie embraces the angst but also the wonder of it all. It is tense but liberating. Of further note, the hit song manages to capture perhaps the ultimate oxymoron: feelings of alienation are universal.

"Space Oddity" was such a moving and modern encapsulation of space travel that British television used it as the background music for its coverage of the actual moon landing. Bowie would later joke, "Nobody had the heart to tell the producer: 'Um ... but he gets stranded in space, sir.'"[37]

From "Space Oddity," Bowie would soon become a "Starman" and his famous alter ego, the androgynous, bisexual, and interstellar messenger Ziggy Stardust, on *The Rise and Fall of Ziggy Stardust and the Spiders from Mars* (1972). At a time of great transition and uncertainty, Bowie looked spaceward. On that album is arguably Bowie's best and defining song, "Life on Mars?" Bowie, along with longtime guitarist Mick Ronson and Yes keyboardist Rick Wakeman on piano, effortlessly bridges British dance hall and rock and roll, while connecting to the cosmos. The song ultimately sounds, as the BBC put it, "like a cross between a Broadway musical and a Salvador Dali painting."[38]

The underlying tale in Bowie's lyrical puzzle finds the female protagonist, inspired by a real-life ex-girlfriend, being "disappointed with reality," as Bowie would later say, and finding pop culture artificial and redundant.[39] She believes there must be more to life, more out there—maybe on Mars?—and Bowie reaches for it.

Ongoing Assimilation

While Black pop stars had crossed over into mainstream success, especially at Stax and Motown, continued assimilation would be a challenge. In the United States, more and more young African Americans were graduating from college, joining the middle class, and even joining corporate America. But assimilation had another side to it. The major labels that ran the music business, like in any industry, answered only to their bottom line. Black pop performers aspiring for the top level of success needed to have a look and sound that the labels believed would max out their investment—that is, what would be most accepted in the white mainstream. Further, assimilation also meant that consumer dollars that had been going to local Black-owned record stores and music venues were now going to larger corporate-owned interests.[40]

Additionally, mainstream assimilation also meant music less geared to the day-to-day, real-world lives of working-class and poor Blacks. To illustrate, at the end of the '60s, in film, Bahamian American Sidney Poitier, charismatic and dignified, was the first Black star getting leading roles. In contrast, at around the same time came the classic so-called *blaxploitation* films, such as *Sweet Sweetback's Baadasssss Song* (1971), *Shaft* (1971), and *Super Fly* (1972). These films were tougher and more soulful looks into urban Black life and featured heroic and virile Black revolutionaries as the leads with Melvin Van Peebles, Richard Roundtree, and Ron O'Neal, respectively. The films were popular and iconic but were too gritty and too Black-centric to become more a part of the popular mainstream. As music writer Nelson George summarized of the films, they showed Black activists to be ineffectual, and "once-vital black neighborhoods of America were controlled by corrupt or at best indifferent police and cynical criminals of every color with only black supermen ... able to survive."[41] The soul soundtracks of the films were even more successful and iconic, with hit songs such as Isaac Hayes's "Shaft" theme song and Curtis Mayfield's "Pusherman."

18

A Generation Gap, Late '60s–Early '70s

At the end of the '60s, much of the youth generation was fed up with what it saw as a top-down moralizing antithetical to its views of freedom and individuality. Following oppressive and overly formal societal codes was, as one writer put it, "abdicating the individual's responsibility for self-realization."[1] Politically, many further saw unfettered capitalism as both insatiable and immoral and certain socialist ideals as providing moral and spiritual benefits, or at least some balance. With the rise of rock and roll, the mainstream's popular music of only a generation or two before had been rendered all but irrelevant to a generation. As such, rock music and a generation gap were firmly in place.

An older generation, however, believed that too much freedom was dangerous, and that the youth had crossed a line. Further, that older generation believed that being anti–Western establishment capitalism and Christianity was tantamount to communism in the form of the U.S.S.R. and China and thus, totalitarian, godless, and inherently anti-individual freedoms.

With few politicians or others in positions of power reflecting the youth movement's wants and needs, rock musicians, in some ways by default, became leaders and heroes for many.

As the '60s wound down, certain key issues and conflicts were brought into focus. This could partly be embodied by the terms "sex," "drugs," and "rock and roll," of which a brief summation follows.

Sex

Fornicating in the Middle of the Road. Or Not.

Many kids of the '60s had felt sexually repressed, with the very topic of sex often taboo. But sexuality was now at least being acknowledged.[2]

On the one hand, many rock and rollers lived and played the sex, drugs, and rock and roll ethos to the hilt. Allen Ginsberg spoke in a Boston church, preaching the taking of LSD, smoking pot, and practicing "sexual liberation," including what he saw as the positive societal outcome of having "orgies in the parks."[3] Timothy Leary was a bit less extreme when he said, "Millions of Americans [are] writing their own Declarations of Independence."[4]

Conservative author Roger Kimball, however, described the 1960s as "an era that is presented as The Last Good Time."[5] Robert Pattison wrote, "Freedom was abundant, but limits and responsibility are vague or nonexistent," thus "the individual rock fan continually defines herself, now using reason, now discarding it, as feeling dictates."[6]

Still, while Paul McCartney had written the intentionally over-the-top White Album song "Why Don't We Do It in the Road?", his answer to his own song's question was actually quite conservative: "Well, the answer is we're civilised and we don't."[7]

Black Bear Ranch

The story of one countercultural commune of the time offers some insights into communal living and the tensions between "free love," morality, and self-realization.

Black Bear Ranch sat on 80 acres deep in the wilderness in far–Northern California. Black Bear was started in 1968 by 50–100 adults loosely united by their countercultural beliefs and a desire for back-to-nature communal living. The ranch had been in part funded by the proceeds of a large LSD transaction, an anonymous donor, and some supporters in the entertainment industry.[8]

Black Bear's communal arrangement meant sharing everything and led to extremely loose social boundaries, including sexual. In the beginning, the commune actually briefly had a rule *prohibiting* sleeping with the same person two nights in a row in an effort to be, in commune members' views, utterly free and unencumbered.[9] As captured in the documentary film *Commune* (2005), this arrangement was quickly found to be unworkable. Whatever the group's goals, the rule led to what frequent ranch resident and actor-activist Peter Coyote later referred to as a mood of "murder over the orange juice." By this, Coyote meant that in the morning when a significant other returned from a night with another, and despite the consensual nature of the arrangement, rage and jealousy often lurked right below the surface. Something as mundane as spilled orange juice could then result in an outburst of anger that had nothing to do with the juice.

Other otherwise warmly nostalgic former residents recalled this phase as resulting in "tremendous emotional wreckage," rampant jealousy, and a lack of fulfillment. One person related the following:

> The most memorable relationship that I had at Black Bear was with Catherine and Catherine was a total free soul from Chicago. We lived together in one of the cabins. I was walking up to the cabin, it was illuminated from within by this wonderful light. It was three or four kerosene lamps and it was a beautiful light. The sun had just set, the stars were beginning to come out and as I looked over, framed in the two doors was Catherine naked with, um, some other man whose name I forget [laughing]—terrible that I forget his name! But they were standing and embracing and, um, when I first looked at it I thought what a beautiful picture and then suddenly it hit me that it was Catherine! [laughs] … and I just totally flipped out.[10]

Catherine would recall having had several genuine "loves" at the ranch but also "all the pain that we all had to go through."[11]

Still, another ranch couple, Majah and Cedar Seeger, experienced the anti-monogamy phase very differently. The Seegers did experience the same emptiness as the others, but as Cedar told it some 30 years later, "Once we realized and acknowledged that, that's when we became a couple which kind of bucked the trend at the Ranch at that time. But we came together for reasons that were based on … they weren't based on need, they were based on choice and that made it powerful."[12] An apparent lesson—at least for the Seegers—would seem to be that promiscuity could be ugly and grow old fast, but reflexively marrying too soon might not have led to the couple's development either. The two came out of Black Bear more fully aware and as what certainly appeared to be a solidly married couple, deeply in love, 30 years later.

Drugs

Cops and Dopers: *Dragnet*

Dragnet is one of the most famous and iconic police procedural TV shows ever, having had multiple iterations on radio and TV dating from the 1950s and then on TV again from 1967 to 1970 (a film in the '90s spoofed the original iterations). The constant was Sergeant Joe Friday, played by series creator Joe Webb. Friday was America's favorite no-nonsense, unflappable detective, along with various, equally buttoned-up partners. Friday and *Dragnet* embodied everything noble and efficient about the establishment's view of law enforcement. In its late–'60s run, the show was regularly in the top 30 in ratings, while Webb established the show's conservative voice. In sum, Friday regularly and sternly lectured stand-ins for the hippie counterculture about their wayward lifestyles and their failure to properly conform to the establishment's conceptions of God, patriotism, and the law.[13]

The show was ostensibly based on true stories: "Only the names have been changed to protect the innocent," as the show's intro reminded every week. Sometimes, however, the show set up fictitious "debates" between misguided representatives of the counterculture and the all-knowing, always-right Friday and partner. In one 1967 episode, "The Prophet," the show utilized a deranged Timothy Leary-ish, LSD-proponent-turned-cult-leader to make its points.[14] Friday is investigating the leader for giving LSD to schoolkids. The initial confrontation turns into a debate about illegal drugs. Friday cites as fact an actually debunked story of an LSD user who had stared at the sun so long that he was blinded and pulled his own eyes out.[15]

But, the freak asks, why is pot illegal? Because, Friday explains and again falsely, pot induces "dangerous hallucinations," and if that was not convincing enough, "What gives you a privilege greater than God?" The cult leader responds, "What about liquor?" Friday replies, also with no basis, that alcohol does *not* lead to anything, but pot is a sure gateway to LSD and heroin. Friday declares, "Marijuana is the flame, heroin is the fuse, LSD is the bomb." Case closed.

In another episode, "The Big High," Friday and his partner are hot on the lead of a marijuana dealer.[16] An informant tells them about a "weed party" happening in the city. The duo and uniformed police officers arrive at the residence, they knock, but no one responds. Officers kick the door in, but despite the commotion, three pot smokers are still sitting in their living room, zonked out and utterly oblivious.

It has been well established that people can get "burned out" and lethargic smoking pot, and marijuana can have serious negative effects on the brains of users, to be sure, especially of younger people.[17] But presumably for just about anyone who has ever actually smoked marijuana, as depicted, the scene might less resemble a "weed party" than perhaps a *lobotomy* party.

The shocking twist comes when it turns out that one of the pot smokers is a mother of an infant, whom she has mindlessly left in the bathtub to drown. Although show producers always assert that the stories are true, the tragedy seems almost infinitely more likely to have been a result of the use of alcohol, heroin, or a legal prescription sedative.

Earlier in the episode, a misguided proponent of marijuana tells Friday, "In a couple of years, things may change when all the kids grow up and start wearing ties and go into the [voting] polls. Marijuana's gonna be like liquor: packaged and taxed and sold right off the shelf." The cocksure Friday replies, "I doubt it, Mr. Shipley."[18]

Lou Reed Scoring Heroin in Harlem

Where *Dragnet*'s depiction of the realities of pot and LSD use rang false, Lou Reed provides an entirely different and illuminating take on heroin and addiction. With the possible exception of Keith Richards, no rock musician is more closely associated with drug use and heroin especially, and even the glamorizing of it, than Reed, even if that was never either's intent. Whereas the song "Heroin," from Velvet Underground's 1967 debut, captures the feeling and the enticing but horrific ability of the drug to negate the pains, fears, and burdens of living, "Waiting for the Man" captures the process of *being* a heroin addict.

The song starts with an upbeat rhythm, but it is also a relentless, grinding blues-rock workout. John Cale steadily hits his piano with his fists along with Moe Tucker's hammering drums. Reed's delivery is almost deadpan but oddly carefree.[19]

It's a simple story Reed tells and a partly, if not completely, autobiographical first-person account of a young white man heading to predominantly Black Harlem to score. Nothing outrageous actually happens, but Reed paints a rather dark tale with clarity and a keen sense of humor.

Reed illustrates some important aspects of life as a junkie trying to score. First, he makes it clear from the start that this addict, prescoring, feels bad, dirty, and barely even feels alive.[20] Second, Reed conveys the inequality of power in this particular business. That is, the "Man," or drug dealer, is *never* on time—and definitely never early—but this purchaser will gladly wait anyway and as long as it takes. And he will never complain.[21] It is a tough market for consumers.

Once Reed's character is in Harlem, he sings of being confronted by an African American man who messes with the white addict so far out of his element and by himself. The Black man, apparently sizing up the outsider, asks him if he is there to mess with the women in Harlem—that is, Black women. Reed's character respectfully explains that he has no such intention, that he is only waiting for his "Man." Reed sings as though he is very much on edge but still upbeat, despite being confronted with a real prospect of physical violence of some sort. There is no fear here with the addict, however; Reed, or at least his character, has a tunnel-vision of sorts. Just like the relentless rhythm of the song, Reed will not be deterred. As an addict close to scoring, he has no fear except not scoring. It is a sort of fearlessness but not born out of faith but of addiction and nihilism.

The world of the addict is indeed upside down compared to most at least semifunctioning human beings. Anything but the drug becomes secondary and can and will wait, including commitments to one's partner, which Reed also mentions. The addict will put anything and everything off until tomorrow. The rhythm grinds on, and at the end of the song, Reed is already singing about waiting for his man the next time. The drug—and escaping the pains of withdrawal and whatever real-life personal demons—are his only concerns. It is an untenable cycle.

In Sum

The counterculture-versus-establishment conflict of the '60s has reverberated ever since, though in different permutations. Roger Kimball lamented a societal failure to counteract what he saw as a negative impact of the counterculture: "All it takes is a look at the highly eroticized advertisements festooning billboards, or the sorts of graphic sexual fare available even on network television today."[22] One can certainly place blame on the counterculture for more liberal social standards and a more brazenly sexual popular culture, all a by-product of very real freedom and personal autonomy. But Kimball is describing, for example, corporate America, too, and it's capitalizing off all pop culture trends, including the liberal sexuality he bemoans in its greenlighting of TV, film, and ad campaigns. For that matter, corporate interests have disregarded moral outcomes even when it has meant societal devastation to further include everything from cigarettes to alcoholic beverages to environmental collapse and so on. Thus, although Kimball has points, which have long been echoed by others, there is little to suggest that the counterculture, as a monolithic entity, had zero morals or even that it was demonstrably worse than the establishment. The counterculture made a genuine, largely good faith attempt to increase the "peace and love" in the world, for better and for worse, and in ways at which the establishment often failed.

Hippies sometimes declared that as Jesus wore sandals, had long hair, was utterly anti-materialism, loved all unconditionally, and spoke of peace, love, and accepting the marginalized, they were more in his footsteps than the establishment.[23] Whether that is entirely accurate or not, one could perhaps imagine Him, say, *humming along with* "All You Need Is Love."

19

Cultural Checkpoints: Protests, Imagining a Different World, and a Left-Right Divide Solidifies, Mid-'69–Early '70s

The '60s culminated with various protests, protest songs, non-protest songs, and a solidifying of a left-right, socio-political divide in the West and the United States in particular. Also, a solo John Lennon's anthem would inspire a range of responses, but also afford a rather remarkable assessment of rock's continued role in the arc of Western civilization, and on both the broadest *and* most personal levels.

The Stonewall Uprising

In 1969, homosexuals were effectively "closeted" across the United States, or otherwise risked all forms of familial, social, religious and workplace excommunication, criminal charges, and physical violence. In New York City, gay people had a few safe, public taverns and clubs where they could be themselves.[1]

The Stonewall Inn in Greenwich Village was the most well-known gay bar, and the only one that tolerated men dancing with one another.[2] The local police's relationship with the owners of most gay clubs, however, which was often the mob, shifted with the political winds, and police could decide to conduct raids without warning.[3] Patrons could be arrested for, for example, not wearing at least three articles of gender-appropriate clothing or dancing with men, and they were regularly assaulted whether they cooperated or not.[4]

In the early morning hours of June 28, 1969, such a raid sparked a nerve in the crowd. A spontaneous resistance broke out, with about 400 protesters jeering police, and throwing debris and bottles. Surrounded, the police initially had to barricade themselves inside the tavern and call for reinforcements.[5] With rage and frustration finally boiling over, the protesters circled around the block for hours before dissipating.[6] The evening effectively heralded the beginning of the gay rights movement. The officer in charge of the Stonewall raid observed that afterwards, members of the gay community "were not submissive anymore."[7]

Massive Antiwar Demonstration in Washington, D.C.

In November of 1969, as many as half a million people conducted what is believed to be the largest anti-war demonstration in U.S. history. Politicians, including Eugene McCarthy, George McGovern and Charles Goodell, spoke while folk singers Peter, Paul and Mary, Arlo Guthrie and Pete Seeger performed. Seeger led a crowd of 500,000 in singing John Lennon's solo song, "Give Peace a Chance."[8]

Kent State Killings and a Hard Hat Riot

Outraged by Nixon's announced expansion of the war effort to send troops to fight communist forces in Cambodia, a crowd of student anti-war protesters at Ohio's Kent State University faced off with National Guardsman on May 4, 1970. Protesters refused to disperse and some threw rocks and empty tear gas canisters at the Guardsmen. Apparently, feeling threatened, though the impetus was unclear, twenty-nine of the guardsmen fired 67 rounds at the crowd over a period of 13 seconds, killing four students and wounding nine others.[9]

Four days later, students gathered to protest in the Wall Street section of New York City, outside City Hall. A lasting image came when hundreds of hard-hatted construction workers got past a police line and chased the peace protestors down. A lunchtime crowd of mostly suited Wall Street workers lined the streets behind the police barricades, cheering the workmen.[10] The workers proceeded to beat and kick the protesters and swat them with their helmets. The hard hats chanted "All the way, U.S.A." and "Love it or leave it." The onlooking police appeared to allow the violence.[11]

Protest Songs

In June of 1970, Crosby, Stills, Nash & Young released the Neil Young–penned folk-rock song "Ohio," whose chorus echoed the number killed in Ohio. Despite being banned from AM radio for directly challenging Nixon in the lyrics, the song peaked at number 14 on the U.S. *Billboard Hot 100*. The song also memorialized the event and lodged it into listeners' consciousnesses for decades to come.[12]

At the same time, there was a rightwing backlash to the student unrest; a national poll found that most Americans blamed the students for initiating the conflict, for not dispersing, and ultimately causing the deaths of their own.[13]

Other major protest songs of the time included Lennon's "Give Peace a Chance" (1969); Richie Havens' live "Handsome Johnny" (1967), an iconic moment from Woodstock; and reggae star Jimmy Cliff's "Vietnam" (1970).

"What's Going On"

Motown had largely been about soothing pop-soul music that took listeners away from their problems along with bringing the pop music sounds of African Americans into more white homes. Marvin Gaye had thus made his music mostly detached from social issues, but by the end of the '60s, he was becoming more and more affected by the same.[14]

Even further, Gaye also had a slew of more personal problems hitting him all at once. He felt confined within Motown, where Barry Gordy controlled how the music was made, and he felt trapped in a tumultuous marriage to Gordy's daughter, Anna Gordy. Then, his singing partner Tammi Terrell (e.g., "Ain't No Mountain High Enough") was diagnosed with a brain tumor that would take her life by 1970.

As to his family, Marvin had not had much contact with his younger brother Frankie, who was serving in the army in Vietnam. When Frankie returned home, however, the brothers had a long conversation about the war experience that left both men in tears (and which later became the basis for a song).[15] Gaye was also long tormented by his relationship with his own father, Marvin Gay, Sr., a former Pentecostal minister, and the man who would eventually shoot his son dead in 1984.[16]

By 1969, Gaye was at times depressed and suicidal and decided to shift focus in music from love songs to songs that could "reach the souls of people."[17] Gaye ditched his previous clean-cut, Motown image, grew a beard, and replaced his dress suits and sweaters with sweatsuits as he set out in a new direction.[18]

Gaye talked to Renaldo "Obie" Benson of the Four Tops about a song Benson had started called "What's Going On." Gaye transformed the song with a new melody and new lyrics.[19] The finished product starts with an easy sax and the sounds of a house party and a feel-good, forget-your-troubles vibe, but something else is indeed going on. It is accessible pop but heavier and a little jazzier than the usual Motown track. Gaye starts in with his strong, smooth baritone, and refers to family members as stand-ins for different parts of America: brothers are dying, mothers are grieving, and he asks fathers—who also symbolize the powers that be—to neither escalate conflict at home nor continue to wage war abroad.[20] Gaye also effortlessly eases into a sometimes-piercing falsetto, and from hope to anguish, in the face of war, poverty, riots, and assassinations. Back-up singers provide a call-and-response.

Unlike a typical protest song, this is not a demand for a specific political act, and nor is it a question, hence the absence of a question mark in the title. Gaye's hope is that providing an unvarnished and deeply personal view of his part of the world, simply providing a reality check, will touch the highest good in others. It is direct plea for love and decency that he thought might be the best hope for more badly needed change.

The song was released the first week of January of 1971, and it became Motown's fastest-selling single ever, hitting number one on the Hot Soul Singles Chart, and number two on the Billboard Hot 100.[21] The album of the same name was released that May, with the title track the first song. After that, Gaye wanted to "keep the rhythm going throughout like the heartbeat of a late-night party."[22] Gaye moves through the issues confronting Black Americans like a guide, illuminating poverty, returning vets, heroin (a master to enslaved addicts), ecology, and faith, as he goes.

The album reached number six on the pop charts and charted for over a year, and it was nominated for two Grammy Awards in 1972.[23] Both the single and the record have proven to be timeless accounts of America and Black life, and are widely regarded as all-time classics.[24]

"Imagine"

In September of 1971, John Lennon released his solo album *Imagine*, which included the iconic title song. In the decades since, "Imagine" has resonated world-wide, even being highlighted in two Olympic ceremonies, being used at large charity events, and providing comfort in times of crisis.[25] The song is especially relevant to this book for three reasons: first, as a unique song; second, as a synthesis of post–'60s, countercultural ideals; and, third, as an insight into Lennon and issues of mental health. As such, it requires a special analysis.

As to the song itself, Lennon sings and accompanies himself on piano, backed by bass, drums, and strings, with production by Phil Spector. It is a slow, almost sluggish-seeming ballad at first, but with a deceptively powerful melody. Lennon's lyrics offer up a utopian world-vision of peace and unity. However, instead of a direct demand for action, he simply suggests a particular viewpoint, that is, like "What's Going On," it, too, is a *non*-protest song. The notion of offering a message as a suggestion was inspired by one of wife–Ono's poems (she received a co-writing credit, retroactively).[26]

The song's lyrics represent Lennon's attempt to move past, and even negate, what he sees as barriers preventing world peace and unity: nationalism, greed, and religion. Lennon does not, however, offer specific ideologies to replace these ideas, and many took the song as particularly disrespectful to Western views of patriotism, capitalism, and Christianity. This was especially so given that at the time of the song's release, the Cold War was at the forefront of people's minds, and the Soviets had, though unofficially, ended religion, and done away with the specific "ownership of capital for private *gain*."[27] Many right-of-center in the West saw "Imagine" as an atheistic and communist anthem, and loathed Lennon for it.[28]

In "Imagine," Lennon expressed some bold ideas on these most contentious of issues. He then sang it all in such a casual manner that it can be easy to overlook and misconstrue the full implications of the lyrics. There is a lot there.

To start with, while "Imagine" can be seen as atheistic, Lennon, himself, in fact, professed a belief in an afterlife and in God. He once explained: "I believe in God but not as one thing, not as an old man in the sky. I believe that what people call God is something in all of us."[29] So, if Lennon was not atheist, then why didn't he set forth a specific conception of God in "Imagine"? Arguably, he did, though not in name. That is, the entire premise of "Imagine" is a belief that every human being has the power to help create a veritable Heaven on earth, which reflects Jesus's words when he said, "The kingdom of God is within you."[30] That is, the song is rooted in the sentiments of *freewill, faith,* and *love,* all also Biblical concepts, and all *aspects of* a higher power. For better or worse, Lennon did not explicitly make that connection for listeners. Yet, by not aligning "Imagine" with a specific religion, it retains a more universal message of peace and love. Thus, contentious for many, but hardly radical.

Perhaps even more disconcerting for many is the suggestion to imagine that there is no Heaven or Hell. This can, however, be interpreted not as actually negating an afterlife, but, in part, simply as a call to live in the moment. This also matches the song's deliberate pace and feel. In this sense, the suggestion is to do good deeds, *with intention* and for personal fulfillment, and not solely as a bargain for later reward or to avoid punishment.

Also, though, Lennon explained, and specifically with regard to "Imagine," his problem with religion was when it became a divisive, "my-God-is-bigger-than-your-God thing."[31] For example, this would include the notion that Christians go to Heaven forever, and everyone else is brutally tortured for all eternity. In other religions, such as Hinduism and in Buddhism, or for anyone that subscribes to "universal salvation," there can be an afterlife where misdeeds have severe consequences, but it is not an *eternal* damnation.[32] And there is also the seeming contradiction between eternal torture and Jesus's consistent message of loving thy enemy and forgiveness. So, this lyric, too, is most certainly and understandably controversial, but it would also seem to be conveying a not altogether unreasonable viewpoint.

Many were further dubious of the song's suggestion of a world without private possessions. Even a decidedly left-leaning person like folk-legend Joan Baez, for example, would express her misgivings about the line to audiences before performing "Imagine" live. And there was, of course, the awkward fact that Lennon, himself, was a very wealthy man.[33] (Although Lennon would change the lyrics when singing "Imagine" live to acknowledge that he, too, struggled with the concept.[34])

Still, as an ideal, this, too, was in line with the teachings of spiritual masters throughout history, including Jesus, who stated: "If you want to be perfect, go, sell your possessions and give to the poor, and you will have treasure in heaven. Then come, follow me." And, also famously: "Again I tell you, it is easier for a camel to go through the eye of a needle than for someone who is rich to enter the kingdom of God."[35] So, it is an extreme goal, but, again, hardly radical. And if Lennon having possessions made him a hypocrite, he was at least acknowledging and promoting the same ideals that Jesus had set forth.

Of further note, Lennon did also express support for certain communist ideals.[36] Yet, while "Imagine" is an explicit call for people of any class, low and high, to choose a new world, Marxism specifically distinguishes the *proletariat* from the ruling class. Even the peaceful, anti-communist Czech revolution of 1989, for example, adopted "Imagine" as its anthem. Thus, the song speaks in broader terms than a specific religious, political or economic model, and it is really about striving to overcome greed.

As to the third and final point, there is an interesting mental health backstory to "Imagine" that provides insight into Lennon's inner world and mental health issues more broadly.

Again, and from Lennon's perspective, the timing of "Imagine" is crucial. As the '60s ended, many had lost faith in a lot of things. For Lennon, despite active civil rights, youth, and peace movements; his own band having achieved staggering success; and his own early solo efforts with protest songs like "Give Peace a Chance" (1969) and "Power to The People"

(March 1971), the Vietnam War continued; nuclear bombs were still being stockpiled; corporate greed still controlled the economy; and Nixon was in his second term in the White House. And, despite an acknowledged greatness of Jesus, self-identifying Christians did not seem to be willing or able to act to change any of the above. Thus, Christianity was being seen as ineffectual in some very real and practical ways. As such, Lennon was not buying the professed conception of God of others to fix humanity and the world. With "Imagine," Lennon was simply recalibrating his previous hopes that rock and roll and the counterculture, alone, could save the world.

Even further, it is not coincidental that "Imagine" was written the year after Lennon's work with psychologist Dr. Arthur Janov, the progenitor of *primal scream therapy*. Lennon had always had anger issues and sometimes even a mean streak. He later publicly acknowledged and apologized for previous incidents of domestic abuse.[37] He and Ono both were drawn to try Janov's practice.

Participants in primal therapy (Janov later dropped the "scream" from the name) get in touch with deeply-repressed feelings, including rage and grief, from earliest childhood traumas, and literally scream or otherwise emote so as to clear out those blockages in their psyche (and not to be confused with choosing to get irate over *present-day* life challenges). It is one of the most introspective and painful forms of therapy, and its main cathartic elements are embraced in some other modalities as well.[38] (A note: despite skepticism in the mental health fields, ongoing advances in neuroscience, immunology, and epigenetics increasingly support Janov's approach.[39])

Lennon had nothing but praise for Janov and primal therapy.[40] In fact, the experience directly inspired his classic, 1970 album, *John Lennon / Plastic Ono Band*, which included the previously mentioned "Mother." (Ono released her own Janov-inspired *Plastic Ono Band* album as well.[41]) The therapy helped Lennon develop a more personal conception of God, which he also sang about on that record.[42]

At this point in Lennon's life, he was, again, letting go a lot of things from the '60s, including the idea that a rock revolution would completely transform society. On the last track of *Plastic Ono Band*, the exasperated dirge, "God," Lennon sang that he only really still believed in two things: himself and the love he shared with Ono. Considering that his conception of love was well beyond just boy-girl attraction, and was a spectacular, intergalactic one that extended "Across the Universe," as he sang in that song, it would seem fair to say that, for Lennon, concepts of love and God were interchangeable, i.e., as in the Bible, "God is love."[43]

In the end, whether "Imagine" could have been better worded or not, it is a rather bold attempt to reconcile the relationship between humans and the universe/God, while offering a glimmer of hope.

Despite Lennon's not insubstantial ego, the song is also a quite humble effort. "Imagine" is Lennon letting go of the notion that anyone will necessarily change their viewpoint of anything just because they hear one of his songs. A few years since Beatlemania, Lennon was now understanding the very human limits of his influence. All he could do was sing, and suggest that people imagine something better, and hope for the best from his fellow humans.

Nixon Speaks to the "Silent Majority"

Addressing the nation on TV in April of '70, and tiring of the peace movement and its anti-patriotic tone and social disruption, Nixon called for the American people to support his policy in Vietnam: "Tonight, to you—the great silent majority of my fellow Americans—I ask for your support." Nixon hit a nerve and received an enormous response, including thousands of letters of support, sparking his reelection.[44]

COINTELPRO

Hoover's Counter Intelligence Program, COINTELPRO, zeroed in on the Black Panthers, as well as Martin Luther King and other activist groups, with Hoover's explicit goal to dismantle the Panthers. The campaign culminated in December 1969 with a five-hour police shootout at the group's Southern California headquarters and an Illinois state police raid in Chicago in which Black Panther leader Fred Hampton was killed.[45]

It would later be revealed that the FBI used numerous unlawful practices in the program including agent provocateurs, sabotage, misinformation, and even lethal force. The bureau director apologized for "wrongful uses of power."[46]

While COINTELPRO hurt the Panthers, internal frictions and the dissolution of the party's main leadership brought the organization to an end by the mid-'70s.[47]

The First Earth Day

In 1965, Lyndon Johnson had told Congress: "This generation has altered the composition of the atmosphere on a global scale through ...

a steady increase in carbon dioxide from the burning of fossil fuels."[48] By April of 1970, the environmentalism movement started to gain momentum and Wisconsin Senator Gaylord Nelson promoted a nonpartisan and nondenominational, national teach-in on environmental issues, leading to the first Earth Day celebration.[49]

A Shift in Television

The older generation's favorite musical/variety show, *The Lawrence Welk Show*, playing old-time (pre-rock) pop music, closed out a 20-year run in 1971. *Mod Squad*, which would run from 1968 to 1973, was a successful, hip drama with an early interracial cast.

Pentagon Papers Published

Former U.S. Marine Corps officer Daniel Ellsberg leaked a classified governmental report, "The Pentagon Papers," detailing the United States' covert policy on Vietnam from 1945 to 1967, to *The New York Times*. Presidents Truman, Kennedy, and Johnson were all exposed as having misled the American public as to the degree of U.S. involvement in Vietnam. This included Johnson's plans to escalate the war while telling the American public the precise opposite during the 1964 presidential election, and more misinformation under Nixon. The U.S. Supreme Court ruled against the government and the *Times* continued publication in June of 1971.[50]

Unlike any other time in American history, a youth generation had lost trust in its own government.

ERA Approved by Senate

In March of 1972, the Senate approved the Equal Rights Amendment. Despite strong national support for equal rights under the law regardless of gender, 38 states needed to ratify the amendment over the next 10 years, though only 35 would.[51]

Nixon Wins Reelection

Nixon's presidential campaign platform relied on a good economy, a nation tired of upheaval, a promise to end the war in Vietnam, and foreign affairs successes. In November of 1972, Nixon trounced the democratic

Party's presidential nominee, the U.S. Senator from South Dakota, George McGovern.

Roe v. Wade Decided

In January of 1973, the U.S. Supreme Court held that women have a right to abortion and defined different levels of state interest for regulating abortion in the second and third trimesters of pregnancy. *Roe vs. Wade* was a landmark for a right to obtain an abortion, while also catalyzing an anti-abortion, "pro-life" movement, versus the "pro-choice" camp, and a raging debate that would play a crucial role in American politics for decades to come.

Last U.S. Troops Leave Vietnam

A cease-fire agreement is signed in March of 1973, and the North Vietnamese would take over Saigon in 1975.[52] The war would ultimately cost the United States over a trillion dollars (in 2023 dollars) and 58,220 lives.[53]

Arab Oil Embargo

In October of 1973, the Organization of the Petroleum Exporting Countries (OPEC) stopped selling oil to any nation that had supported Israel in its "Yom Kippur War" with Egypt, Syria and Jordan. The move contributed to one of the worst recessions in U.S. history. President Nixon insists that the United States can be energy independent by 1980.[54]

Watergate and Nixon Resignation

The Washington Post directly ties Nixon to the burglaries of the Watergate Hotel in 1972, as well as the office of political rival Daniel Ellsberg's psychiatrist to obtain and disclose his personal mental health records in 1971.[55] The operations were financed through illegally laundered campaign contributions as part of a Nixon re-election effort.[56]

On August 9, 1974, facing likely impeachment and removal by Congress for his role in covering up the Watergate scandal, President Nixon resigned. The image of Nixon declaring "I am not a crook" and subsequent departure from the White House by helicopter became defining images, and symbols of America's immense distrust of its politicians, even at its highest level.[57]

The Christian Right and Liberalism Continue to Define and Assert Themselves

Part of the conservative backlash to the '60s countercultural upheaval grew into what would become collectively referred to as the Christian Right. That collective was comprised of various leaders across multiple denominations, including the Rev. Jerry Falwell, a Fundamentalist with rigid and literal interpretations of the Bible, and Pentecostal televangelist, Pat Robertson. By 1976, one-third of Americans identified themselves as born-again Christians.[58]

Such religious conservatives were united in a belief that America was in a downward, moral death spiral that only conversion to Christianity could halt. They believed that pre-marital sex, and all forms of sexual contact without the primary purpose to achieve pregnancy, were sins; homosexuality was a crime against God; all abortion murder; and that both women and men had God-ordained, natural roles in society, i.e., a wife stayed home to raise children while the father earned the wages and was the head of the household. The Christian Right further believed that the courts were forcing religion out of public schools, and that a "liberal" media and rock and roll music were corrupting America's youth.[59]

The political left was further establishing their own beliefs and agendas as well. Pre-marital sex between consenting adults was seen as largely okay, though attitudes varied from simply more open attitudes toward sex, such as with Alex Comfort's illustrated *The Joy of Sex* (1972), to the more promiscuous.[60]

Self-help and New Age spiritual practices also came to the fore in dealing with various emotional, psychological and spiritual issues, and for many filling a role often previously filled by organized religion. This included programs such as the therapy/seminars for EST (Erhard Seminars Training), and the growth of a self-help book industry that had started with the Norman Vincent Peale's (Christian-based) *The Power of Positive Thinking*, and followed by works such as Robert M. Pirsig's *Zen and the Art of Motorcycle Maintenance* (1974), and M. Scott Peck's *The Road Less Traveled* (1978).

One of the best summations of this conflicted point in American social, cultural, and political history is found in Paul Cowan's *Tribes of America* (1979). Cowan, a *Village Voice* journalist in New York, examined certain hot-button issues of the time such as the separation of church and state, state's rights, and race, all of which have continued to resonate ever since. In one example, Cowan reported in the early '70s about the State of West Virginia's Department of Education and its decision to revamp and modernize the state's textbooks. The basic idea was to no longer stress rote memorization, but instead get kids to think and ask questions. It was also, however, as Cowan put it, the promotion of "the classic liberal assumption" that children should "grow beyond the confines of his culture."[61] This effectively meant questioning long-held familial, cultural, and religious traditions of West Virginians.

To many, the state's efforts reflected a lack of respect and appreciation for the "Heartland," which was seen as a common problem with elite journalists and politicians.[62] Cowan wrote that too often Christianity was being perceived as "on a par with Greek myth."[63] For example, some parts of the new school texts made light of biblical stories through comical representations, such as through a *New Yorker*–styled cartoon of Adam and Eve and Mark Twain's humorous "Adam's Diary."[64]

Cowan also cited a funding proposal for the training of teachers, signed by West Virginia's superintendent of schools, in which teachers were called "agents" for guiding the "culturally lost" of Appalachia.[65] Cowan further questioned how one could "outlaw school prayer and still pretend that secular humanism—momentarily our national creed—does not carry its own deep assumptions about religion."[66] To take that and other cultural touchstones away from rural West Virginia kids risked leaving them "adrift."[67] Finally, Cowan noted that while he had once regarded the region's "profound respect for the stability of religion, of ceremony, of family life" as "old-fashioned and bourgeois" customs, through covering the story had come to increasingly respect them.[68]

In September of 1974, when the new texts, considered "blasphemous" by many, were introduced into public schools, chaos erupted. A wing of a school board building was blown up with dynamite; cars and homes were firebombed; and school buses were shot at, and all done by self-identifying Christians.[69] As Cowan summarized, "Dynamite wasn't the answer. But neither was a kind of cultural imperialism indifferent to the fact that 81 percent of the district opposed the textbooks. It was, in a word, complicated."[70]

Moving forward, there would be similar problems such as forced busing to integrate schools, and ongoing white flight to the suburbs and the impact of that on states' funding of city programs and schools. Economically, jobs left unionized areas and cities, while corporate America began a long, ongoing search for ever cheaper labor. The result of it all was a country that had been divided by a hippie youth and an establishment, continued to be divided by right and left, white and Black, and now even the rural/suburbs versus the cities.

20A

Prog and Full Arenas (Also, Jesus Freaks), Early '70s

Entering the '70s, the Beatles were no more, though each of the four former members began successful solo careers, and the Rolling Stones were self-proclaimed but accurately "The World's Greatest Rock & Roll Band."[1] Also, the Beatles incredible success with the grand experimentation of *Sgt. Pepper's*, the creative heights of artists like Phil Spector and Motown, guitar heroism from the likes of Hendrix and Clapton, and the dynamic sounds of vocalists like Aretha Franklin brought the rock and roll genre to new levels of both commercial success as well as artistic credibility. This would all, however, almost naturally go hand in hand with new levels of egos and excesses as well.

One outcome was the spawning of a new rock subgenre: progressive or "prog" rock. In prog, the scope of rock music would be further expanded through classically trained instrumental techniques, avant-garde and experimental influences, and symphonic ambitions. Some of the best of the genre included the groups Procol Harum and Pink Floyd as well as the works of the Moody Blues (e.g., *Days of Future Passed*, 1967), Captain Beefheart (e.g., *Trout Mask Replica*, 1969), King Crimson (e.g., *In the Court of the Crimson King*, 1969), and the psych-chamber-pop of the Zombies (e.g., *Odessey and Oracle*, 1968), among others.

Critics of the genre, however—and there were more than a few—also saw a lot of artists overreaching and an overly ambitious music sometimes disconnected from the raucous and spontaneous energy that had made rock music special in the first place.[2]

Further, corporate labels and radio had also perfected the sale of rock records and concert tickets and the money was flowing in for everyone. Thus, rock and roll and those with the boldest and hardest-hitting rock music that most spoke to the mainstream could now be taken to stadium levels of extravagance. For many of the biggest rock groups, those royalty checks, a whole lot of drugs, and "hot-and-cold-running groupies" were part of a "rock star" lifestyle.[3]

Great music continued to be made, but instead of young delinquents with guitars who didn't take themselves too seriously, sometimes rock's bombast and self-importance could overtake its authenticity.

The stage was set for those who would follow in the steps of the British Invasion and the ongoing soul and funk genres, as well as ambitious experimentalists, more audacious rock groups, and some softer rock.

While not addressed in this book, by the late '70s, rock and R&B would both be brought back to earth and to the streets with the rise of rap music out of the Bronx and punk rock out of the Bowery in Manhattan and then in London. Those developments would be something of a reset and help launch the original rock and roll phenomenon on a whole new trajectory going forward.

An interesting development that *is* briefly covered here and that speaks directly to the intersection of rock music, religion, and authority is the advent of Christian rock.

Christian Rock

When rock and roll first took off in the '50s, church leaders saw it and Christian music as diametrically opposed to one another. In 1958, Martin Luther King, Jr., for example, had stated that he believed that rock music and gospel were "totally incompatible" and that rock also furthered negative stereotypes of African Americans.[4] Yet by the mid-'60s, King protégé Andrew Young was declaring that rock and roll had done "more for integration than the church."[5]

The rise in popularity of rock and the Beatles in the mid-'60s made it even tougher for parents to convince their children that the four lovable lads who made "I Wanna Hold Your Hand" and "All You Need Is Love" were up to no good.

Still, matters like the overwhelming popularity of the Beatles and Lennon's Jesus comment spurred many church leaders and churchgoers to be more fervent and more proactive in ensuring that Christians not be lulled into confusing any popular music with Christian music. If songs that did not speak directly to Christ or had sexually aggressive rhythms were not welcome in church services, why would any self-respecting Christian need them in their lives?[6]

But the door going from rock to the church was not necessarily locked. The Byrds' country-rock record *Sweethearts of the Radio* (1968), for example, included a cover of the Louvin Brothers' bluegrass gospel song "The Christian Life."[7] In 1969, Norman Greenbaum had a number three hit on the Billboard pop chart, selling over 2 million copies, with his hard rock gospel song and ode to a friendship with Jesus, "Spirit in the Sky." The also popular Doobie Brothers had a similarly themed hit in 1972 with a gospel cover song, "Jesus Is Just Alright" ("alright" meaning good and not merely acceptable).[8]

Indeed at least *some* fans of rock were in the church, some wavered in and out, and the Jesus People movement, aka "Jesus Freaks," was thriving. Certainly, many hippies were searching for if not some kind of spiritual connection, then some greater meaning in their lives.

The experience of Barry McGuire, singer of the 1965 landmark countercultural hit "Eve of Destruction," illustrates one path through that conundrum. After McGuire's smash hit and then his release of two quality rock albums, he was cast as a lead in the hit Broadway musical *Hair* in 1968. *Hair* was the first rock musical, producing mainstream hits "Age of Aquarius" and "Let the Sunshine In." The story is about a community of hippies in the East Village in New York City and their search for self-actualization and freedom in a time of social turmoil, as well as dealing with the Vietnam draft.

McGuire found something else while doing the production, though. He later explained, "The very lifestyle that we were promoting was killing us all. I looked around me I saw my friends, one, two, three at a time goin' down: drug overdose, suicide, sexually transmitted diseases."[9] McGuire left the production and kept searching and listening to the various gurus, lecturers, and religious figures around at the time. At one point, he recalled a friend telling him that he belonged to the "Guru of the Month Club."[10] Finally, in 1971, McGuire recalled that "truthfully, just out of bored, sarcastic curiosity," he picked up a book called *The Life and Times of Jesus Christ*:

> For the first time in my life, I stopped looking at Christians; I stopped looking at denominations, organizations, Catholics, Protestants, ya know, all this stuff that goes on in His name.... I fell on my face on the floor of that house in Stone Canyon. I said, "God, I don't know why, how; if I wake up alive tomorrow I'll follow You wherever You lead me."[11]

McGuire still wasn't completely enamored with all of the establishment-type Christians he saw, but he was changed: "Within a week I was on a Greyhound bus out of Hollywood, and I've never looked back, except in awe and wonder at how He revealed Himself to me in my state of mind at that time."[12] After his conversion, McGuire became a gospel artist and continued to make albums in the Christian category throughout the '70s.[13]

In the late '60s and early '70s came Larry Norman, the original "Jesus Rocker" and the father of what would become known as contemporary Christian music (CCM). Norman was born in Texas in 1947 before he and his family moved to San Francisco when he was three. His parents became involved in a predominantly Black Pentecostal service there, and Norman was singing gospel music by five.[14]

As a young adult, after a stint with the psychedelic group People!, Norman went solo and released the first major label mix of modern rock and gospel with *Upon This Rock* in 1969.[15] Norman explained his thinking behind the record:

> "Upon This Rock" was written to stand outside the Christian culture. I tried to create songs for which there was no anticipated acceptance. I wanted to display the flexibility of the gospel and that there was no limitation to how God could be presented.[16]

One writer noted Norman's potential for broader appeal given "his haggard appearance, sly wit, and street savvy."[17] The debut managed to feel of the times and even hip, bringing in folk and psychedelic influences, along with more straightforward rock and gospel. Norman also steered clear of dogma while still carrying an unapologetic Christian message with songs like "You Can't Take Away the Lord" and "Forget Your Hexagram."[18] Some of his lyrical topics included protesting racism and poverty and trying to raise awareness of problems such as sexually transmitted diseases.

Despite mainstream critical praise—*Billboard* called Norman the most important songwriter since Paul Simon—the debut sold poorly. The record would, however, find a niche following when it was picked up in Christian bookstores and found an audience.[19] Norman instantly became the focal point of the Jesus People counterculture movement, even while the Christian establishment largely denounced him.[20]

In 1972, Norman put together his defining record, a standout rock album and the real godhead, if you will, of the Christian rock genre: *Only Visiting This Planet*. Norman continued to unapologetically sing of his faith but while loving rock and roll music unapologetically, too. Hence the best and best-known song on the record is "Why Does the Devil Get All of the Good Music?" Other songs, such as "I've Got to Learn to Live without You," could have fit in at the very top of the charts of the early '70s.

The Jesus People and their Jesus movement grew quickly, including landing a 1971 *Time* magazine cover with a pop art picture of Jesus,[21] and in 1972, a weeklong revival called Explo '72 was described as the Christian Woodstock.[22] Fans sometimes called themselves "born again Jesus freaks."[23]

From these beginnings, a CCM genre would develop. In that community, there would long be a debate about how often Jesus's name should be invoked and how strongly faith should be professed in any given song. Norman, however, believed that the fact that he was a Christian, alone, meant everything he did was from a Christian perspective and therefore was Christian music.[24] The Christian music–rock conundrum continued to be framed by traditionalists as a struggle between popularity and commercial success, both considered to be secular constructs, versus music solely and specifically tailored to church goals.[25] At the same time, as Norman's current website explains, the fact that his record sold to the mainstream at all and drew rave reviews from the secular press was "all the more proof to Christians that Larry was doing the work of Satan."[26]

In 1975, Norman started his own label, Solid Rock Records, and procured top talent. The label set the tone for the CCM industry.[27]

Prominent televangelists James Robison and Jimmy Swaggart openly disparaged Christian rock music, with Swaggart once calling Norman's music "spiritual fornication."[28] Swaggart even published a book called *Religious Rock 'n' Roll: A Wolf in Sheep's Clothing*. (Ironically, Swaggart, cousin to and raised alongside rock pioneer Jerry Lee Lewis, would see his career crash due to sex scandals in the 1980s and early 1990s.[29])

In Norman's personal life, he could rub people the wrong way, and his behavior could be erratic. He also allegedly fathered a child out of wedlock and was then not involved in raising the child, which did not help his standing in those Christian quarters.[30]

A couple of side notes. In 1978, future U.S. vice president under Donald Trump and evangelical Christian Mike Pence had his religious conversion at a Christian music festival where Norman headlined in 1978 (Pence has given few details of that particular day). Also noteworthy, in 1975, Bob Dylan would form a personal bond with born-again evangelical Jimmy Carter over their discussions of Christianity; Carter quoted Dylan lyrics during his 1976 presidential campaign. Dylan then made headlines in 1979 by stating that he had become a "born again" follower of Jesus (more on that later) and followed with four gospel-themed albums.[31]

Norman continued to gain acclaim and acceptance over the years, including being inducted into the Gospel Music Hall of Fame in 2001.[32] Prominent rockers such as Black Francis of the Pixies, Van Morrison, John Mellencamp, and U2 have all cited Norman as a direct influence. In 2008, Norman died of heart failure at age 60.[33]

20B

A Very Special '70s Cultural Checkpoint: The Sitcom

Coming out of the upheaval of the '60s, the establishment's goal continued to be to maintain order and normalcy. The idea remained that if people could maintain the status quo, most Americans could live reasonably affluent and pleasant lives, or certainly the appearance of it.

In American pop culture, nothing reflected and idealized normalcy like the family sitcom. The shows *Ozzie and Harriet*, *Father Knows Best*, and *Leave It to Beaver* in particular were all relatively popular in their original runs in the 1950s and into the mid–'60s and then continued on in long runs in syndication. All three shows became most popular precisely during and shortly after some of the nation's most painful and awkward upheaval. The sitcom family format became an American TV standard and in many ways serves as a proxy for the idealized view mainstream America had for itself: middle-class affluence and complacency, where no one rocks the boat. In other words, pretty much the opposite of what rock and roll stood for.

The *Brady Bunch* had picked up the sitcom torch during its original run from 1969 to 1974. The show garnered mostly negative reviews at the time and it was not an exceptionally high-rated program.[1] Despite being seen by critics as heavily clichéd, "bland," and often, at best, "high camp fun," the show would remain popular in reruns for decades to come.[2] Sean Griffin of the Museum of Broadcast Communications explained the show's later success in syndication:

> Many children who grew up with the show came from families of divorce, or were "latch-key" children with both parents working. Consequently, some of those amused at the naivete of the series also admittedly envy the ideal nuclear family that they never had and that the Bradys represent.[3]

It was not hard to see the allure of such drama-free living. Baby boomers and Gen Xers spent untold hours watching the Bradys in rerun perpetuity. An op-ed columnist for the *Boston Globe* once wrote, "I knew that beige split-level as well as my own house" and adding, "We Gen-Xers might have been latch-key kids, but we had Mike and Carol [the Brady parents] to come home to."[4] While acknowledging that the show had its shortcomings, the Museum of Broadcast Communications declared, "Yet, the program stands as one of the most important sitcoms of American 1970s television programming, spawning numerous other series on all three major networks, as well as records, lunch boxes, a cookbook, and even a stage show and feature film."[5]

Although the *Brady Bunch* was never meant to be confused with *Macbeth*, its being representative of mainstream entertainment and its outsized role in the lives of so many Americans makes it worth further analysis, especially in relation to its counterpoint, rock and roll.

As many already know, the premise of the show was laid out in the iconic opening credit sequence of every episode. The lyrics of the earworm theme song played over a nine-square grid, each square showing the face of one of the nine main characters. The Bradys were a melded family. A single, widowed mother with three daughters had married a single, widowed man with three sons. They were comfortably middle class and white and lived in sunny Southern California.

Show topics, like many sitcoms, never crossed into anything serious, such as dealing with any form of domestic strife, drug or alcohol use, anxiety around sexual issues, serious shortcomings at school, any significant disrespect by a child toward a parent or vice versa, or any of the myriad controversial outside, social topics of the time. As examples, in one episode, daughter Jan has an allergy and thinks it is the dog, but it is just the dog's flea powder. A family camping trip starts out with the boys and girls divided, but it all works out. Marcia double-books two dates for the same night.

The only effort the show's creators made to deal with some of the chaos of the times came in a single episode when eldest son Greg "rebelled" by becoming a buffoonish caricature of a hippie. That is, he seemed to briefly lose his mind, although he is not on any drugs. By the end of the episode, all was well. No lesson was learned or experienced, and there is no suggestion as to why Greg lost his mind. But everything is completely fine.

Whether intended to be serious art or not, the Bradys came to epitomize the notion of a surreal, sometimes quite inane, alternate world of domesticity being accepted as "normal." In fact, two popular feature-length film spoofs of the show in the '90s were derived entirely from that premise.[6]

As an example, the Bradys' live-in housekeeper, Alice, was always the wisecracking comedian of the group, good for a laugh every episode ("Oh,

20B. A Very Special '70s Cultural Checkpoint: The Sitcom

The Brady Bunch, 1973 (PictureLux).

Alice!"). In reality, though, and as specifically pointed out in the films, nothing Alice ever said *was* particularly funny. Odd, lighthearted, and with comic *intentions*, yes, but never actually humorous. From the original show: Alice: [who has just tripped] "My foot played a game of Chinese checkers ... and lost."[7] Yet the Bradys, and the soulless laugh track, guffawed every time.

More important, the Brady characters had a surprising lack of depth, even by sitcom standards. The characters were scarcely *one*-dimensional, let alone three. Peter was, well, the middle son, and one time, his voice cracked. Marcia was pretty and pleasant. Cindy had cute curls. She had a doll she liked. And so on.

Perhaps the most fascinating thing about the Brady family is that they somehow avoided any discussion of the most crucial topics of all. Not that the show was going to deal with tragedy on a regular basis, but two tragedies were the basis for the show's very existence. That is, all of these school-age children had suffered the most horrific of losses: the death of a parent at a young age. If the show's iconic opening credit sequence established *anything*, it was that this was the story of two separate families suddenly thrown together. Yet the only time the characters ever mention one of the dead parents is ever so briefly and vaguely in the pilot episode.

In Carol Brady's case, this came as an ambiguous reference to some previous trauma: "A few years ago, I thought it was the end of the world," but that's it. Then, when Bobby is afraid to display a picture of his deceased mother, his dad steps in:

> **MIKE:** I don't want you to forget your mother and neither does Carol.
> **BOBBY:** Gee, that's swell! I really like this picture but I didn't want to upset my new mom.
> **MIKE:** You know something? Your mother would be very proud of you right now.[8]

Apparently, someone really did want Bobby to just forget mom forever and to not upset anyone. Mom was never mentioned again. (As an aside but to be thorough, the actor playing the father, Mike Reed, was a closeted gay man his entire life; the Brady's family dog disappeared and was never mentioned again; the Bradys' lawn was clearly Astroturf; and in the pilot, on the day of their wedding, Mike and Carol discuss tranquilizers as a fine way to calm nerves.)

While the *Brady Bunch* is just a sitcom, it may still be a fair encapsulation of the cost of stability and conformity at the expense of emotional and psychological depth and authenticity. Bobby Brady, for example, is fictitious, but he actually does represent real-life kids who learned to gloss over the toughest and most unpleasant issues in life. Psychologically speaking, simply avoiding those anxieties and pains means that those issues don't go away, and may hinder people in their lives moving forward. At some point, the young Bobby Bradys of the world will likely need to pay the piper and deal with such matters. In that sense, Bobby Brady and Lou Reed's addict/protagonist in "Waiting for the Man" are not entirely different from each other.

21

Rock Gods, a Possible Alternate Route to Heaven, and Egos, 1969–1979

The '60s had established rock music's considerable power and potential. The Beatles were "modern mythical heroes," and songs like "Across the Universe" and the Stones' "Sympathy for the Devil" had opened the door for rock to directly address moral, spiritual, and even religious matters previously seen as being in the sole purview of religious authorities. Also, the blues-based guitar heroes, e.g., Hendrix, Clapton, and Jeff Beck, were channeling a new, amplified, and powerful version of rock.

At the same time, socially and politically, key issues, civil rights and a war in particular, would be done for the time being, and the passion and righteousness that went with those causes had very much cooled off. Author Jon Savage described the youth of the early '70s as having "gorged on sixties excess but lacking the idealism with which that excess had been inaugurated."[1]

As to sex, the ideals of elevating sex as an expression of love and liberating it from shame in the Free Love era continued, but now it was more just teenage hormones, rock and roll, and hedonism driving things. As to drugs, except for the addictions associated with the obviously harder drugs like heroin, drugs were good. Thus, neither sex nor drugs had much in the way of limits being placed on them. Some rock bands, especially harder rock bands, would further push almost everything to the maximum, in volume, sonic power, ambitions, as well as in decadent offstage living. And pushing and even crossing such lines is exciting as well as being one way to find one's true limits.

With all of the above in mind, the next phase in hard rock belonged to Led Zeppelin. The British quartet would become the best, biggest, heaviest, and most successful rock band of the '70s.

Led Zeppelin

Led Zeppelin consisted of lead guitarist Jimmy Page, singer Robert Plant, the two primary songwriters, along with drummer John Bonham and bassist John Paul Jones.[2] Plant was born in 1948, the oldest of two in a comfortably middle-class, Catholic home in West Brompton in the country's industrial Midlands. Plant's father was a civil engineer, his mother a homemaker.[3]

The Midlands was a place full of legends of old battles involving Romans, Angles, and Saxons, with stories sometimes passed on to Robert by his father and his grandfather. Plant became infatuated with the local lore and places like the ancient woods of Uffmoor Wood and Clent Hills. The region had in fact inspired the writings of another local, J.R.R. Tolkien; Plant became a huge fan of Tolkien as well.[4]

Plant discovered rock and roll when he heard Elvis for the first time at age ten; he would impersonate Presley while singing in his living room.[5] From there, and like Jagger and Richards, Plant would start his own search for the source of that music and discovered bluesmen like Sonny Boy Williamson II and Robert Johnson. Johnson's emotional power and his sexuality were especially strong pulls for the teenaged Plant. The young singer struck out on his own to pursue his musical ambitions, leaving home at just 16, and started singing in clubs.[6]

Jimmy Page was born in 1944 in the London borough of Hounslow and was an only child.[7] Page's father had a respectable office job, while his mother was a doctor's secretary. Page's introduction to rock had also come with Elvis, though he was drawn to Elvis's guitarist, Scottie Moore. Page took to the guitar himself, and then he, too, became a rabid blues/R&B/Chess Records fan.[8]

In 1962, Page became a regular at Alex Korner's Marquee in London as part of the die-hard blues scene.[9] At the Marquee, a record collector's grapevine ensured that records from the likes of blues guitarists such as Johnson, Albert King, and Freddie King all got around.[10]

Page was only 19 when he became a studio session ace for a range of acts as well as a producer. He would also become a member of the Yardbirds, a band that had counted fellow guitarists Eric Clapton and Jeff Beck as members. In his time as a session man, Page further picked up on Indian music and the sitar before the Beatles, and he was in tune with the local, traditional British folk music scene.[11]

Bassist John Paul Jones was also a leading studio guitarist playing with a who's who of British rock and pop before joining Led Zeppelin along with being a top-rate arranger and keyboardist.[12] Page and Jones connected with each other and were told about Plant, who was singing with

21. Rock Gods ... Route to Heaven, and Egos, 1969–1979   193

Band of Joy at the time. Plant had power, mystique, raw sex appeal, and vocal range and would all help to redefine the rock front man. Plant joined the pair and brought his drummer, Bonham, along from his group.[13]

Bonham was a powerhouse and also one of rock's greatest musicians; *Modern Drummer* magazine would later rank him behind only jazz man Buddy Rich among all-time greats.[14] Led Zeppelin formed in 1968.

The group's trademark sound would be blues-based but amplified and often sonically overwhelming. Still, a large portion of their songs were acoustic, and they had a remarkable gift for melodies. The group was so deeply indebted to the Delta blues, in fact, that they would later have to retroactively give proper royalties and writing credits on songs such as "Whole Lotta Love," "The Lemon Song," and "Bring It on Home."[15]

Led Zeppelin could be transcendent—though this was definitely not Summer of Love–type stuff. Plant's lyrics drew from his Midlands lore but also mysticism, the occult, and tales of fantasy, including Tolkien's books, and he told of faraway lands, such as an Indian outpost, "Kashmir." Looking back years later, Page jokingly summarized the band's outlook at the time: "Fuck the sixties. We're going to chart the new decade!"[16]

The band was also particularly bold sexually. Plant had flowing, curly blond hair and wore open shirts and scarves and tight jeans; early on, one music writer even called him "prissy."[17] But Plant wailed like a Viking across the frozen tundra, as he had on the "Immigrant Song," and they explored anguish, love, and lust in "Dazed and Confused," with Plant referencing wanting sex 25 hours a day and the seemingly otherworldly power women could have over men.[18]

The rock audience took to the band quickly. The self-titled debut reached the U.S. top ten two months after its release in 1969, while *Led Zeppelin II* (1969) and *Led Zeppelin III* (1970) each hit number one.[19] Many critics, however, initially couldn't see beyond the band's overwhelming heaviness. As late as 1973, one *Rolling Stone* critic had already grown weary of them, calling them "Limp Blimp," while noting the inferiority of the grand and melodic effort of "Stairway to Heaven" off their fourth album.[20]

That 1971 fourth release, in fact, untitled but what became known as "Led Zeppelin IV," actually became theirs, and one of rock's, crowning achievements. It would become the fifth best-selling album in the United States of all time and ultimately sold 37 million copies worldwide.[21]

On "Stairway," Zeppelin redefined blues-based guitar rock altogether. Page starts with a disarmingly pretty, acoustic–Brit-folk melody, accompanied by flute, while Plant expands on themes of folk mysticism and paganism, conjuring images of pipers and a May queen. The middle section adds electric guitars, and the electric riffs take over for the last third of the song. While Page delivers one of rock's greater solos, Plant belts out the dramatic conclusion of some epic, cosmic journey. The lyrics are enigmatic, though at one point, Plant refers to a familiar woman and, at another, asserts that one can change their direction along the road of life.

At the end of the song's eight-minute running time, the band reels it back into a contemplative Plant who sings the title chorus and finally ends the song. The group actually seemed to have made some sort of connection to "Heaven," and whatever exactly the "Stairway" might symbolize to listeners, they did so through references to Celtic mythology and Tolkien and not explicitly to Christianity. In band biographer Stephen Davis's words, the song "expressed an ineffable yearning for spiritual transformation deep in the hearts of the generation for which it was intended."[22] It was *the* '70s rock anthem, and for a long time it was the single most-played pop song on the radio despite its running time.[23]

On the same album, the blues-rock blast of "Rock and Roll" updated the sound of Chuck Berry and the essence of rock guitar. "Black Dog" was complex but blistering and further showcased Plant's bold sexual style. "Going to California" showcased a strongly melodic, British-folk-gone-Southern-Cal bent.[24]

The group continued to branch out over their last four regular studio albums through 1979. They ably added strains of funk ("The Ocean") and reggae ("D'yer Maker"), along with more melodic and pop sensibilities ("The Rain Song" and "Fool in the Rain"). "No Quarter" was an ingenious experiment in slow, sonic effects that went beyond the scope of the blues or what was becoming known as heavy metal.

With their deep, heavy blues, strong sexual energy, and cryptic pagan and occult themes, Led Zeppelin possessed perhaps the most powerful mystique rock has known. In the early '70s, in fact, Page had begun reading up on the occult, especially Aleister Crowley's works. The phrase "Do what thou wilt" was inscribed on the vinyl for *Led Zeppelin III*.[25] Page and Kenneth Anger became friends through their shared interest in Crowley, and Page purchased Crowley's former home at Loch Ness in Scotland. The guitarist reportedly invited Anger to exorcise a previous occupant's ghost.[26] Although Page didn't stay at the estate much, he was filmed in and around it in the band's concert film *The Song Remains the Same*.[27] Page mostly avoided answering questions about his specific beliefs on the occult: "I don't really want to go on about my personal beliefs or my involvement in magic."[28] That ambiguity, however, seemed to only contribute to the band's mythos.

Anger later hired Page to produce the soundtrack for *Lucifer Rising*, but the pair had a falling out.[29] In another bizarre turn of events, Manson murderer Bobby Beausoleil completed the score while still in prison, and his music would replace Page's in the final cut.[30]

It was not a coincidence that Led Zeppelin's powerful brand of rock and roll came about when it did. The group's sound seemed to rise above or otherwise overwhelm the challenges in the lives of their fans, the majority being working-class white males, facing some particularly insecure times.

A rock-inspired youth generation were unified on some things but not everything. Generally speaking, the lives and perspectives of white males, especially middle-, working-class, and poor ones, were shifting apart from those of many college kids, intellectuals, hippies, females, people of color, and LGBTQ-identifying individuals.

It has long been a challenge in every society when its working-class men are under-earning, underemployed, under-satisfied, or feeling undervalued. In modern Europe, such times often dovetailed with colonization, wars, and mass emigration to the United States.[31] In the United States, there was Western expansion as well as war. After having enjoyed immense and continuous economic growth since the end of World War II, an energy crisis, war debt, increasing world competition in manufacturing (such as steel), and some economic policy missteps by Nixon all fueled spikes in both unemployment and inflation in the United States. Between 1973 and 1975, the U.S. economy formally entered a recession that impacted working-class white people in a way it had not since the Depression.[32] Manufacturing jobs were leaving overseas, unions were in decline, and automation was robbing people of pride in workmanship. For the first time since the Great Depression, Americans faced an economy that could result in a lower standard of living for its youth.[33]

These economic troubles also coincided with the seismic changes in the cultural landscape, with civil rights, feminism, a push for the ERA, and even gay rights all coming to the fore. Thus, the economic and cultural landscapes, including views on matters as fundamental as masculinity, femininity, sexuality, and race, were all changing rapidly.

In a new modern era, long-accepted notions of masculinity and, for example, power in the household and elsewhere were now sometimes being seen as domination. At work, what was once seen as strong leadership could be seen as part of an outdated patriarchy. In short, traditional societal institutions, norms, and values were starting to be seen as relics of an unjust time that perpetuated injustices. White males may not have been the most sympathetic demographic, but they, and especially middle-class, working-class, and poor ones, were facing their own significant life challenges, including no less than being asked to redefine conceptions of their identities and their place in society.

It was in this context that Led Zeppelin struck a nerve. Robert Christgau wrote positively of Led Zeppelin, observing that the group's "chest-thumping megalomaniac grandeur" and a "self-aggrandizement that made no demands on everyday life was exactly what the times called for."[34] It was a heady time for hard rock, but along with that success, egos also seemed to hit a crescendo. Led Zeppelin led the way and became the biggest rock band on the planet, eventually selling over 300 million units, which were mostly full-length albums given the group's aversion to singles.[35] They even leased a jet airplane for touring and put their band logo on the tailfin. Their 1973 U.S. tour set numerous attendance records, concluding with selling out Madison Square Garden three nights in a row.[36]

On that financial front, much credit went to the band's confrontational manager, Peter Grant. Grant used the group's immense drawing power to leverage unprecedented terms from concert venue owners, altering the music industry in the process.[37]

The group's live performances were epic as well. Along with their sheer power, they and all of the hard rock bands of the time were taking full advantage of the increased capabilities of arena sound systems and placing an increasing premium on high volumes. Loudness reflected a bolder sound but also served to make listeners assert themselves emotionally to match that energy, or otherwise be overwhelmed by it. The notion of call-and-response became more of a "one-way conversation." Stacks of Marshall amps became the norm for every serious rock band, and bands tried to outdo one another in decibels.[38]

Otherwise, "Dazed and Confused" could become a 40-plus-minute jam, while Bonham's drum solos could run as long as 30 minutes.[39] An era-defining image is Jimmy Page in front of a stadium full of fans, dressed in a white leather suit, shirtless, with a colorful dragon image on the back and running down his leg. Sometimes Page is seen playing what seemed almost cartoonishly excessive at the time and even for rock: a guitar with two necks.

In the group's concert film *The Song Remains the Same* (1976), Plant is shown backstage pondering a comment someone had made about the band's music and its seeming connection to an ancient time. Plant responds, "It's right though, isn't it? That feeling that's left everybody—the cosmic energy! Everybody goes 'Yaaa!' Bam! [mimics striking a guitar chord]." One evening out and about in Hollywood during the band's heyday, Plant, standing on a balcony overlooking the Sunset Strip, famously declared, "I am a golden god!"[40]

Thus, Led Zeppelin emphatically proved that rock and roll bands could be unapologetically hard and heavy, break almost any taboos and yet still call the shots in the establishment's corporate world.[41] The barbarians were in the gates and having a great time.

The group would also become well known for some of the more outlandish tales of rock and roll excesses. They rode motorcycles down hotel hallways, threw televisions out windows, and indulged in plenty of groupies, including one infamous and at least partially true story concerning a young woman and a fish caught from a balcony at Seattle's Edgewater Inn.[42] Page also had his 14-year-old girlfriend, Lori Mattix, "hidden away" in hotel rooms.[43] And there was wildly excessive use of alcohol by Bonham and Page's cocaine and heroin addictions.[44] All of this became part of the band's and rock and roll's still-growing mythos.

This era of hard rock has often been identified as misogynistic and for some fairly obvious reasons. Clearly, in many ways groupies were disposable, and there was an inherent power differential of such elevated (the vast majority) male rock stars, both on- and offstage.

However, *some* of that misogyny was misunderstood. National Public Radio (NPR) music writer Ann Powers, for example, noted that although "feminists and conservatives alike developed a view of hard rock in particular as irredeemably misogynist," there has also been some reassessment of the female groupies' place in that era. In retrospect, those women "typically had few regrets about their time on the rock scene."[45] Famed "super groupie" Pamela Des Barres, for example, who had relationships with some top stars including Page, considered herself a "muse" to "musical geniuses."[46]

Led Zeppelin's take on the blues, rock, and sexuality was fairly unique. As Powers further noted, Plant was not your typical "smooth soul crooner or a growling bluesman."[47] Plant provided a distinct new sexuality to hard rock that spared white, hard rock fans the discomfort they "still felt toward overt black sexuality."[48] One male fan of the era summarized by saying that "Dazed and Confused" "turned the sexual act into something very Cecil B. DeMille: orgasm as mystical experience."[49]

Led Zeppelin thus definitively marked a point of rock's peak extremes, both with powerful music and themes, and in finding where those outer limits of sex, drugs, and rock and roll existed, assuming they did. They, along with other bands of the time, established new high-water marks for the power of rock but also in offstage antics that would become a new standard, de rigueur for many, in destructive and debauched behavior.

Music journalist Charles Murray had his own take when discussing the difference between Led Zeppelin's extreme takes on the blues and some of the original songs they covered and were inspired by. Specifically, Murray examined Muddy Waters' electric-blues classic "You Need Love" and Led Zeppelin's heavy, proto-metal version, and one of their signature songs, "Whole Lotta Love." The latter is generally considered one of the great hard rock songs of all time.[50]

All four members of Led Zeppelin bring immense power to the song, along with backward echoes and other effects for a true sonic assault.

Bonham pulverizes. Jones's bass is low and relentless. Page goes wild. Plant wails passionately. It is certainly not your typical love song.

Underlying the sonic drama is an account of a couple in the act of making love. Really, though, it is about the protagonist male and specifically his sexual climax. Toward the climactic end of the song, Plant bluntly equates the number of inches of sexual penetration to the amount of love he has to give.[51] And although Murray seems to have missed out on some of Led Zeppelin's charms, he is not *entirely* wrong in observing differences between the two songs:

> The former is a seduction ... warm and solicitous: [Muddy Waters] suggests that the woman to whom he is singing is both sexually inexperienced and starved of affection, and volunteers to remedy both conditions.... Led Zeppelin, by contrast, come on like thermonuclear gang rape.... The woman is strictly an abstract, faceless presence, she is an essential part of the intercourse kit, but not as an individual. Love, in this context, is a euphemism for something measurable with a ruler.[52]

Certainly, in the '70s, rock's ego and its libido had been fully unleashed.

Led Zeppelin's brand of rock and their view toward sex was vastly influential and part of a larger trend. Many hard rock bands of the '70s and '80s would be even more blunt. The music varied from fun, exciting, and extremely well-done odes to the joy of sex to otherwise simply being crude, clichéed, and misogynist. Examples of all of the above are numerous but include songs like Ted Nugent's "Wang Dang Sweet Poon Tang" ("poon tang" being slang for female genitalia), Kiss's "Love Gun" and "Lick It Up," Van Halen's "Bottoms Up!" and into the '80s, aptly named Whitesnake's "Slide It In," Motley Crüe's "Girls, Girls, Girls," and so on. Certain of these bands would sometimes be labeled under the partly humorous and rather crude nomenclature of "cock rock."[53]

To complete the Led Zeppelin story, in the mid- and late '70s, band members would also endure tragedies (of which some wanted to blame on the band's occult connections[54]). In 1975, Plant and his then-wife Maureen, survived a serious car accident in Greece, and then in 1977, Plant's five-year-old son Karac died from a viral infection.[55] Jimmy Page's addictions took hold in the late '70s, though he would bounce back.[56]

As to John Bonham, on September 24, 1980, early on in a day of band practice at a British studio, he began drinking quadruple vodka screwdrivers. He continued to drink into the evening, ultimately consuming some 40 units (i.e., the equivalent of 40 one-ounce shots) of alcohol. Bonham then fell asleep and was put to bed on his side. After midnight, however, Bonham vomited and fatally asphyxiated.[57] The band chose to disband instead of continuing without him.[58]

Led Zeppelin would reunite for several one-off shows with Plant, Page, and Jones and twice with Bonham's drummer son, Jason. Jones continued to collaborate with others as well as produce and arrange with notable success with acts including Dusty Springfield, Lenny Kravitz, and R.E.M. Page stayed active with numerous collaborations.

Plant has continued with a stellar solo career as well, continuously taking unexpected paths from covering rock oldies to utilizing synthesizers to an award-winning, laidback, collaborative album of folk and blues with bluegrass star Alison Krauss.[59]

Led Zeppelin all but redefined hard rock and heavy metal for most that came afterward. Hip-hop acts, too, would regularly mine Bonham and Page's best beats and riffs for samples.[60]

Black Sabbath

Also important at this point was Birmingham, England's Black Sabbath, who formed in 1970. Sabbath had similarities with Led Zeppelin in sheer heaviness and in some lyrical themes. Sabbath would become known as the founding fathers of the genre of heavy metal, which Zeppelin was also an important factor in.

Sabbath was less bluesy than Zeppelin and more focused on establishing the use of extreme, pummeling rhythms that effectively, as one writer put it, "crushed the bouncy rhythms of popular rock."[61] In part, heavy metal would be the voice of brewing frustration and deep-seated anger and even rage. Black Sabbath would also give a voice to that aspect of the rock culture looking to make a "connection between life and the cosmos" without the need for approval from the establishment or organized religion's perceived dogma.[62]

Around the 1940s, Birmingham was the United Kingdom's extremely gritty, heavily industrialized, second-largest city.[63] (For reference, it was also the brutal, 1920s and '30s setting of the partly reality-based HBO gangster series *Peaky Blinders*.[64]) The city was badly bombed during the war, and for many residents, postwar life was lived in vast bombed-out slums lacking basic amenities.[65]

Future Sabbath front man John "Ozzy" Osbourne (b. 1938) came from those slums and from a family plagued by alcoholism, violence, suicide, and other mental health problems.[66] Like so many others, when Osbourne heard the Beatles on British radio and on TV in 1962 and '63, he would recall that "everything changed" and that "for the first time I felt as though my life had meaning."[67] All of the band members—drummer Bill Ward, bassist Terence "Geezer" Butler, and lead guitarist Tony

Black Sabbath performing in Amsterdam, the Netherlands, 1971 (Photograph by Gijsbert Hanekroot/Redferns).

Iommi—started with tough working-class jobs in Birmingham. Osbourne worked at a slaughterhouse and then as a car-horn tester (his trainer was near deaf), while Iommi lost the tips of two fingers in a sheet metal factory accident, which altered his playing style.[68]

Sabbath's musical influences included the heavy blues rock and psychedelic guitars of Clapton, Beck, and Hendrix and the fury of MC5. Other building blocks of metal would be hard and heavy Sabbath contemporaries like Blue Cheer, Vanilla Fudge, UFO, and Montrose.

Butler was also the band's primary lyricist and drew from Aleister Crowley (a side note: a solo Osbourne would later write the song "Mr. Crowley," clearly unimpressed by the black magician[69]), horror films, black magic–themed novels, and sometimes positively from his Catholic faith.[70] Butler and Osbourne had taken the band name from the title of the 1963 Boris Karloff horror film.[71] The first song on the band's self-titled 1970 debut album, also "Black Sabbath," set the tone not only for the band's career but for most every heavy metal band to follow, as well as similar genres, like goth.

The song sounds like the musical equivalent of the best, most menacing, gothic horror movie ever; there are even church bell and thunderstorm sound effects. By song's end, it is a galloping rocker, the rhythm tracking the Devil's hot pursuit. Despite Osbourne's plea to God for help earlier in the song, the people are on the run from Satan, terrified.[72] In short, the rest of that debut album, along with five more standout albums released over the next five years, became the basic text of heavy metal.

Black Sabbath created sludgy, sonic heaviness, but they could also cut through it all with fast tempos and wailing guitar workouts on songs like "Iron Man" and "Paranoid." Osbourne was a remarkably compelling vocalist, and he captured the power and mystery of the songs without becoming a caricature. As author Ian Christe described it, "Ozzy Osbourne delivered these lyrics as if in a trance, reading messages of truth written in the sky."[73]

Other lyrical themes included society's failure to stop its slide toward nuclear apocalypse ("Wicked World," "Electric Funeral," "Children of the Grave"), sci-fi/fantasy tales ("Behind the Wall of Sleep," "Into the Void"), and battling depression/mental health issues ("Paranoid"). "Iron Man" was the tale of an awakening hero whose story spoke to fans lacking empowerment in a world where innocence seemed lost.

In metal, there would be few love songs, though Sabbath did have some moving ballads of love ("Sabbra Cadabra") and heartbreak ("Changes").[74]

From the beginning, the band's very name suggested at the least a certain lack of reverence for the church and conjured a pseudo-occultist image. Along with some drug-referencing lyrics, the band became obvious targets for both the mainstream press and the religious right. Yet Butler, for example, noted that everyone in the band believed in God. This even while the group continued to take up the counterculture's challenge to the notion that the church was the infallible, final word on everything under the sun.

At Sabbath's core, they wrestled with good and evil in a world in which they saw the powers that be as untrustworthy and self-destructive. On another signature song, "War Pigs," the band explicitly declares who they see as doing the actual work of Satan: the generals and politicians sending young people off to war again and again. And on "After Forever," Butler actually asserts his Catholic perspective with lyrics explicitly acknowledging that the only way to love is through God.[75]

Of course, Sabbath also pushed boundaries. In one particular song, "Lord of This World," Osbourne sings from Satan's point of view, although the song pretty clearly puts Satan and his followers in a negative perspective. The song comments on humanity's apparent lack of faith and its moral confusion and thus serves as a challenge and a warning to listeners.

Also fueling detractors was band members' abuse of drugs and alcohol and song references to the same.⁷⁶ In the 1971 song "Sweet Leaf," for example, Osbourne extolls the virtues of marijuana, and in 1972 was the homage to cocaine, "Snow Blind."⁷⁷

In the late '70s, Osbourne began doing solo work, while also having increasingly severe addiction problems, leading to his being kicked out of the band in 1979.⁷⁸ Sabbath would continue, and Osbourne would have a highly successful solo career.⁷⁹ Both continued to contribute to the success of the heavy metal genre in the ensuing decades.

Rock and roll continued to push things to all kinds of new extremes. Few in the '70s would much more embody rock's intensities and extremes than Ted Nugent.

The Nuge

Ted Nugent was born in 1948 in Detroit, the second of four kids. His father, Ward, was an army drill instructor. In Ted's words, Ward raised the Nugent kids with a "militantly rigid hand, both literally and figuratively."⁸⁰ Nugent would once say that he had "hated" his father in his younger years but later expressed appreciation.⁸¹

At nine, Nugent got his first guitar and started "beating on it and making noise." Nugent soaked in everything Chuck Berry ever did as well as the works of early guitar stars Duane Eddy and Lonnie Mack.⁸² Nugent also connected with nature at an early age and learned to hunt for food, which became an integral part of his life and even his onstage persona for the rest of his life.⁸³

Nugent's father despised rock and roll, calling it "the devil's music."⁸⁴ Still a teen, Nugent formed the Lourds, who covered early rock and R&B groups but, as Nugent recalled it, "a little faster, a little whiter, and a little less soulfully than the original versions."⁸⁵

Nugent formed the Amboy Dukes in 1964, playing a fast, intense version of rock and R&B and moved back to Detroit with his group.⁸⁶ They became best known for the loud, fuzzy, psychedelic hit "Journey to the Center of the Mind," a defining song of the genre and one that put Nugent and his guitar on the map. Ironically, while Nugent would long be the rare, proudly drug- and alcohol-free rocker, at the time he wasn't even aware that the song depicted an inward journey with the assistance of LSD.⁸⁷

Nugent continued to embrace his primal instincts on the group's moderately successful early '70s albums: *Survival of the Fittest* (1971), *Call of the Wild* (1973), and *Tooth, Fang & Claw* (1974). The sound shifted into harder rock, and Nugent became a supercharged Chuck Berry–meets- …

Tarzan?, sometimes appearing onstage in a loincloth and swinging on a rope out over the crowd.[88]

Nugent was an exciting performer but would also court controversy. He described at the time as having a "dual life" as a family man with a wife and two kids, but on tour he transformed into the Motor City Madman, as he would be nicknamed. His spontaneous "motormouth" raps onstage often touched on the sexual nature of his music or humorous topics, such as the power of his guitar to, as he put it, "blow the balls off a charging rhino at 60 paces."[89]

Nugent went solo, and his self-titled solo debut in 1975 produced the hits "Stranglehold" and "Hey, Baby," putting him all over the radio. With his 1976 and '77 releases *Free for All* and *Cat Scratch Fever*, respectively, and the title tracks of each especially, Nugent produced some of the more popular hard rock tracks of the decade and some wild and memorable guitar riffs. Lyrically, it was sex, confrontations, love, the outdoors, more sex, and rock and roll.

Nugent impacted an array of hard rock but also punk musicians in his wake. Two so influenced were the seminal hard-core punk icons in Henry Rollins, vocalist for Black Flag, and friend Ian MacKaye, the singer for Minor Threat and then Fugazi. Rollins explained, "[We] would read about the Nuge and the thing that really rubbed off on us was the fact that he didn't drink or smoke or do drugs.... [Nugent's performance] was the craziest thing we'd ever seen onstage and here's this guy saying, 'I don't get high.' We thought that was so impressive."[90] In the early '80s, this would help spur something called the clean-and-sober "straight edge" movement in the punk scene, the name taken from a MacKaye-written song with Minor Threat noting the personal benefits of being alcohol- and drug-free.[91]

Along with Nugent's long-held "vengeance" toward his father and authority figures, his other major musical inspiration was clear. As Nugent put it, "I was a wang-dang addict, I was addicted to girls. It was hopeless. It was beautiful."[92] This take on sex was not uncommon in the world of hard rock at the time, of course, but he was one of the most outspoken and direct. In a VH1 TV special, in fact, Nugent acknowledged having had several relationships with underage girls in the '70s and acknowledged gaining the support of their parents, seeming to suggest having paid them money to do so.[93] When Nugent was 30, his girlfriend was Hawai'i-native Pele Massa, who at 17 was too young to legally marry. Nugent worked with Massa's parents to become her legal guardian so that they could be together.[94]

In 1981, at 32, Nugent wrote the song "Jailbait." Referring to a 13-year-old girl in the song, he asks a police officer to not handcuff him but handcuff the girl so that they could both have their way with her.[95]

The penultimate example of Nugent's mix of inspirations may be "Stranglehold." *Guitar World* magazine named Nugent's solo in the song as one of the top 50 of all time, and it was a hit.[96]

Nugent wrote the lyrics, though most of the song is sung by Derek St. Holmes. There is a mystery with the song; the one verse Nugent speaks includes a line suggesting he has the key to immortality, and you almost believe him. The song's sexual nature comes in the chorus and the repeated sexually-charged invitation to a lover in spoke-sung lines. Yet, oddly, that is followed by a line about smashing someone's face. According to Nugent, it is all a part of his passions for living life, regardless of any obstacles. As he explained, "Hence, 'I crushed your face' to this day, this song is without question THE sexiest, grinding pure animal love song of all time."[97] Nugent has further explained that "the ultimate human beings, warriors of the U.S. Military, use this soulful soundtrack for inspiration to kill bad guys, and Kirk Gibson played it just prior to hitting that famous bottom of the 9th homerun, and the Chicago Blackhawks play it every night before attacking the ice to kick maximum ass on their hockey opponents."[98] Thus vengeance, sexual attraction to women, and love, but also an apparent domination of women, are all inextricably linked in Nugent's mind.

Nugent has also diversified his career beyond rock, becoming an outspoken political conservative (a decided minority in the larger world of rock performers), a hunting and outdoors enthusiast, and a gun-rights advocate. He has also hosted his own radio show and a *Ted Nugent Spirit of the Wild* PBS video series, and he has been on a board of directors for the National Rifle Association.[99]

Some of his more memorable pronouncements include his take on LSD use:

> Should a kid going to a Grateful Dead concert who's caught with sugar-cube-encrusted LSD go to prison for life with no parole? Of course not. But should that guy get caned? Yeah. And should he go to prison in an overcrowded cell where a huge, unclean black man will fuck him in the ass every night? Yeah. Now, that sounds cruel, doesn't it? Well, tough fucking shit.[100]

Nugent is more notorious, however, for his commentary regarding Democratic politicians and even drawing investigation by the Secret Service when he stated that if Barack Obama was elected president, "I will be either dead or in jail by this time next year" and that Obama should "suck on his machine gun," among other things.[101]

At the same time, Nugent has attempted to make a distinction in racial matters between African Americans he considers "blood brothers" versus many others he does not. Nugent actually named his 2013 tour his "Black Power" tour, as he wanted to get his message on race out.[102] He explained to an audience at one of those shows:

21. Rock Gods ... Route to Heaven, and Egos, 1969–1979   205

> For 50 years, for 50 years, I've been celebrating where I come from, for 50 fucking years every night on stage. I've been celebrating, we all come from black America's soul music, every night on stage for 50 fucking years. I say celebrate the Black blood brothers. Celebrate Howlin' Wolf and Muddy Waters, [inaudible], James Brown.[103]

Last, Nugent has also expressed his own take on the problems of African Americans. From his radio show in 1994:

> Those big uneducated greasy black mongrels on there, they call themselves rap artists. Excuse me? During a bad bloody case of diarrhea, I got more soul than those guys do at the peak of their life. That's not music.... No wonder James Brown went to prison, no wonder Wilson Pickett went to jail, no wonder Chuck Berry went to jail. They're embarrassed by their black brothers.[104]

In any event, in the end, Nugent's primal energy, his biggest hits, and his guitar work have left a mark on rock's history.

Kiss

One could hardly talk about rock's extremes and its spectacle without talking about Kiss. Gene Simmons and Paul Stanley, two Jewish kids from New York City, became cofounders and chief co-songwriters for the group.

Stanley (Stanley Eisen) was born in 1952 to two Jewish parents who had fled Europe and the Nazis during the war. Simmons (Chaim Witz) was born in 1949 in Israel to two Hungarian emigrants. Simmons's uncle and his mother, Florence Klein, were the only two of their family to survive the concentration camps. When asked about her experience in 1994, Klein responded, "My dear, I can never unlock that door and bring up those memories, because if I did, I would go crazy and never come back."[105]

Simmons recalled an early childhood in Israel in a bullet-ridden house and extreme poverty with rationed milk and bread. When he was eight, he and his mother emigrated to New York City, while his father remained in Israel with children from another mother.[106]

Both Simmons and Stanley became converts to rock music in the '60s after experiencing the Beatles and the British Invasion.[107] Simmons played bass and sang some of the songs, Stanley was lead singer, and in 1973, they added lead guitarist Ace Frehley and drummer Peter Criss. In pre-punk New York, the group was heavily inspired by the garish glam of the New York Dolls and the wild theatrics and hard rock of Alice Cooper.[108]

All four members adopted elaborate and futuristic, horror- or sci-fi-inspired stage costuming, including cod pieces and eight-inch platform shoes for Simmons and iconic, personalized, black-and-white makeup, plus silver for Frehley. Simmons was the Demon, Stanley the Starchild, Frehley the Spaceman, and Criss the Cat. For years, fans didn't even know what they actually looked like sans makeup. Next, a manager showed them some potential special effects, including fire breathing—a natural for a demon—so Simmons began to blow fire at shows as well as having fake blood dribble out of his mouth to go with over-the-top lights and pyrotechnics.[109]

Kiss was rock and roll comic book superheroes come to life in concert. Their breakout fourth album, *Kiss Alive!*, was recorded live with partly augmented crowd sounds. They also produced a number of fist-pounding arena anthems, including "Rock and Roll All Night" and "Detroit Rock City," and even scored a power ballad hit with "Beth." They were utterly irresistible to their rabid, largely adolescent, male cult following dubbed the "Kiss Army."[110]

The group's outrageousness and party-all-the-time lyrics made them hard for many to take seriously, and critics would largely dislike them for a time. Still, Kiss was a major touchstone for a great many adolescent rockers entranced by the type of extreme, whacked-out, sing-along spectacle that was Kiss. The band has even been name-checked in the lyrics of at least three songs by esteemed acts, Cheap Trick, Weezer, and Wilco, a rather unique honor in and of itself.[111]

Kiss also unabashedly embraced their rock god status, further portraying themselves as sex gods in songs like "Ladies' Room," "Room Service," and "Love Gun." The cover for the *Love Gun* album depicts the four band members standing with a dozen women literally at their feet. Simmons matter-of-factly described his real-world life as being a "24-hour whore."[112]

Simmons has long been the band's very outspoken spokesperson and has bluntly stated his own view of the rock and roll spectacle: "Rock and roll is all about gimmicks.... If people think of Kiss as performers first and musicians or anything else later, that's wonderful."[113] He does not drink or take drugs, and he has been in a long-term, mostly very *non*-monogamous marriage with former-model Shannon Tweed, with whom they have two kids. Simmons has also managed to otherwise be the over-the-top, mega-ego rock star, and proudly so. In fact, Simmons has long taken pride in at least two things: the massive commercialization of every aspect of his band and having had thousands of different sex partners.

As to the first, in 1977, a Gallup poll declared Kiss the most popular rock band in the world. With a mostly younger cult following and the band's imagery, merchandising became wildly profitable. Simmons spearheaded the licensing of comic books, pinball machines, makeup and masks, board games, a live-action TV movie, lunch pails, T-shirts, action figures, Kiss clothes for your pets, all the way to—why not?—Kiss coffins, all of which netted millions.[114]

As to the second matter, Simmons has proudly announced that at one point, he had sexual intercourse with, by his count, 4,600 different women. He also said that for a long time, he took and saved Polaroid photographs of each and every one.[115]

Into his 50s and 60s, Simmons's views have stayed consistent. In February 2002, as one example, Simmons was the subject of a notorious interview on the NPR radio show *Fresh Air* with interviewer Terry Gross. Simmons gave his unique philosophies on life and made a lewd come-on:

* * *

TG: Are you trying to say that all that matters to you is money?

GS: I will contend and you try to disprove it, that the most important thing as we know it, on this planet in this plane is in fact money. Want me to prove it?

TG: Go ahead.

GS: The first thing you need besides air, which so far is free, and by the way if you went scuba diving, you're paying for air. The other thing besides that is food. That's what we need to survive. I don't know what other tool I would use besides money to buy it. Although, as woman, of course, you have the ability to sell your body, then get the money, and then with that get food. But ultimately money is a part of it.

TG: You *are* weird. [laughing]

GS: Really? How do you get food?

TG: Well not by selling my body, but….

GS: …but that's a choice you have that I don't, but getting to the money part, money is the single most important thing on the planet, including the notion that, uh, love gives you everything, that's a load of hogwash, because although I subscribe to the romantic notion of life.[116]

* * *

TG: Now let's get to the studded cod piece [a piece of fabric that covers a man's groin area]. Do you have a sense of humor about that? I mean does that seem funny to you or …

GS: No. It holds in, it holds in my manhood, otherwise it would be too much for you to take. You'd have to put the book down and confront life and the notion is, "If you want to welcome me with open arms, I'm afraid you're also going to have to welcome me with open legs." [paraphrasing a lyric from the Who's 1981 hit song "You Better You Bet"].

TG: That's a really obnoxious thing to say.

GS: No it's not. Its— Why should I say something behind your back that I can't tell you to your face?

TG: Has it come to this? Is this the only way that you can talk to a woman? To do that shtick?

GS: Let me ask you something, why is it shtick when all women have ever wanted since we crawled out of caves is, "Why can't a man tell me the truth and speak to me plainly." So if I do that, you can't have it both ways.
TG: So you really have no sense of humor about this, do you?
GS: Oh, I'm laughing all the way, you know where to …
TG: Oh, to the bank, right?
GS: Well of course.[117]

Legacy-wise, a perceived relative lack of a high level of songwriting and musicianship, though very possibly also due to Simmons's public comments, may have kept them out of the Rock & Roll Hall of Fame for a long time. In 2014, they were finally inducted due to fan voting and a deeply committed fan base.[118]

22

The Big Power Pop Stars, 1972–1977

The Beatles' early songs had been inspired by the first wave of '50s rockers, in channeling the spirit of Little Richard, being buoyed and fortified both by a backbeat and blues-based rock guitars à la Carl Perkins and Chuck Berry, and drawing from the structured and melodic love songs of Buddy Holly and Motown. On tracks like "I Want to Hold Your Hand" and "I Saw Her Standing There," Lennon and McCartney were fearless in declaring their joy and feelings of love. Those songs announced that they would no longer settle for blasé love relationships, and they forged an immense emotional depth in pop music.

In the early and mid–'60s, other groups were producing similarly styled music. So-called "beat bands" included the Hollies, the Zombies, the Easybeats, and the Small Faces.[1] In a 1967 interview, the Who's Pete Townshend used the term "power pop" to describe his band's song "Pictures of Lily" as well as in reference to similar songs by the Small Faces and the Beach Boys, specifically for the latter's "Fun, Fun, Fun."[2]

In Townshend's description, "power" essentially referred to a strong beat, power chords, and chiming guitars, while the "pop" would refer to traditional song structures with melodies, harmonies, and hooks. Thematically, the referenced songs are also expressions of love or bliss, or often the longing for the same, and sometimes longing for the unattainable. "Pictures of Lily," in fact, was a boy pining for the girl on his pin-up calendar only to find out by the end of the song that the calendar is old and the model long since deceased. "Fun, Fun, Fun" refers to a future date of fun.

In the '70s, certain bands arose that were indebted to that early Beatles catalog and the beat bands, and Townshend's term was resurrected to formally label a new musical genre. Certain groups set the parameters for the genre like Badfinger (e.g., "No Matter What," "Come and Get It") and the Raspberries ("Go All the Way," "Tonight," "Overnight Sensation" ["Hit Record"]), who had success though for relatively short runs. Others of the era included the Records ("Starry Eyes"), 20/20 ("Yellow Pills"), Marshall Crenshaw ("Someday, Someway"), and certain Todd Rundgren singles (e.g., "I Saw the Light").

In a 2010 essay on power pop, Pulitzer Prize–winning novelist Michael Chabon specifically identified songs of the genre as being "inherently happy" yet also always possessing a conflicting "sadness, yearning, and despair."[3] As Chabon described it, power pop embodies an "unfulfilled longing" for something one could not have or is off in the future. It is always something "only perfect as long as it is deferred," such as in the above-mentioned songs, such as "Tonight" or "Someday, Someway."[4] Where rock's harder acts were going big in attaining pleasures or otherwise seeking the answers to life's most epic questions, power pop acts were simply yearning for an idealized love and bliss.

Chabon also noted that something of a thread of suicide and depression seems to run through power pop and even some of its key acts. For example, two of the four members of Badfinger, Peter Ham and Tom Evans, committed suicide; there was the sudden, fatal, single-car accident of the troubled Chris Bell of Big Star; and in the '90s, the suicide of singer Jim Ellison of Material Issue.[5]

This *longing* issue perhaps also correlates with the genre's, generally speaking, lack of major commercial successes. For one thing, unfulfilled longing and hopeless romanticism are not usually seen as being all that "cool" and certainly not in relation to the swagger that often defines rock and roll—for example, Elvis, Mick Jagger, and Robert Plant. Also, and by definition, power pop's traditionalism never fits with the latest musical trends of any given era either. In the '70s and beyond, hard rock was more epic and heavier, prog rock was more ambitious and complex, punk was a primal assault, and post-punk and hip-hop would abandon traditional song structures altogether. As power pop chronicler Ken Sharp summarized, "Power pop is the Rodney Dangerfield of rock 'n' roll. It is the direct updating of the most revered artists—the Who, the Beach Boys, the Beatles—yet it gets no respect."[6]

Starting in the late '70s, Rockford, Illinois's Cheap Trick brought excitement and a harder and more substantive sound to the genre with a string of highly regarded albums. Cheap Trick's songs were less yearning and longing and instead powerful and assertive, without sacrificing any of their pop melodicism. Their famous concert album *Live at Budokan* (1978), which includes genre-defining classics "I Want You to Want Me" and "Surrender," is arguably as good as live rock and roll gets.

Cheap Trick had something the early Beatle records had: a confidence to declare their wants and be vulnerable but be okay no matter the outcome. This, as opposed to, for example, Badfinger's Pete Ham explicitly

22. The Big Power Pop Stars, 1972–1977

Cheap Trick, from left: Rick Nielsen, Bun E. Carlos, radio DJ Rodney Bingenheimer, unidentified, Tom Petersson, and Robin Zander backstage after a gig ca. 1977 at the Whisky in Los Angeles, California (Photograph by Jeffrey Mayer).

singing in "Without You" that he *cannot* survive without his lover or, otherwise, those already mentioned songs of longings that will never be requited. On "I Want You to Want Me," singer Robin Zander sounds joyous as well as extremely confident that the object of his desire may well want him as much as he wants her. Indeed, this is made clear by the thousands of girls at the Nippon Budokan arena heard screaming in response to Zander every time he makes the request of the song title. Clearly, even if Zander's love is entirely unrequited, he'll be fine, one way or another. The same went for John Lennon on "I Want to Hold Your Hand" and Paul McCartney on "I Saw Her Standing There." Thus, power pop was often about longing, but it also did not *always* have to be fixed on unattainable happiness.

Rounding out the power pop genre in the late '70s and early '80s were songs like the Knack's hit "My Sharona" (1979), which was so far on the "pop" side of the genre's spectrum that its hook all but swallowed the entire song. At the same time, the band epitomized a "skinny tie" trend of similar MTV-/top-40-friendly acts like Tommy Tutone ("867-5309/Jenny") and the Romantics ("What I Like about You").[7] The Plimsouls also had success and produced a new wave/power pop hit with "A Million Miles Away" (1983).

Along with all of the above, the early and mid-'70s rock band Big Star would rather quietly alter the genre's trajectory altogether.

Big Star

Michael Chabon called Big Star's "September Gurls" "the pocket history of power pop," and it has in fact become one of the genre's great anthems.[8] The title and lyrics reference birth months and thus apparently astrology, while Alex Chilton otherwise blissfully sings of a love that he once had before but wants again.

Big Star, however, was a different breed of power pop (though they never identified themselves as power pop). They had great traditional songcraft, but they were also soulful and would push the limits of the genre.

Big Star's original run was short lived, with almost no commercial success whatsoever, yet their catalog would live on and make them a legendary band. Their first three albums would not only do much to shape power pop down the road, but they would have a massive influence on '80s indie rock and beyond.

Big Star had the requisite Beatles influence but also country-rock and folk influences such as from the Byrds, fringe elements drawn from their local Memphis music scene, and the influence of drug culture. And although the band members were white and grew up in Memphis in the late 1950s and '60s, they were possibly more influenced by the soul of Stax than Sun Records' rockabilly stars.

At the band's most melodic—that is, "Thirteen," "Ballad of El Goodo," and "September Gurls"—they rival the best of the Beatles. At their heaviest and darkest—for example, their entire third album, *Third/Sister Lovers*—they are as edgy and as challenging as Velvet Underground. Thematically, they can also at times be akin to gospel.

Big Star developed a cult following possibly only exceeded in the annals of rock history by the Velvets. Two groups of die-hard Big Star fans were two of the most crucial bands of the '80s indie rock movement, R.E.M. and the Replacements, followed by a slew of others acts (e.g., alt-country stars Wilco, Ryan Adams). In the '90s, there would be a slew of bands collectively referred to as a power pop revival, though it might better be thought of as a Big Star revival (e.g., Teenage Fanclub, the Posies, Matthew Sweet, and others). Even though successful, those bands, too, were often marked by a commercial underappreciation.

All of this influence came despite the fact that Big Star's original run lasted about two years, their three albums initially sold less than 30,000 copies *combined*, and they only had 11 live shows with either the original three or four members of the group.[9]

Alex Chilton was born in Memphis in 1950, the youngest of four. Chilton's father was a jazz musician who brought the records of jazz greats Charles Mingus, Dave Brubeck, and Glenn Miller into the Chilton home as well as the sounds of Ray Charles, Stax, and other R&B artists.[10]

Chilton's parents regularly socialized at the family home hosting impromptu parties with local musical types and musicians traveling through Memphis. This meant lots of live jazz in the Chilton home, but as Alex later recalled, it also meant a lot of heavy drinking and "a lot of crazy people all the time."[11]

Chilton idolized his brother Reid who, older by ten years, had introduced Alex to rock and roll. At 17, Reid had a freak fatal accident when he had a seizure while taking a bath, which led to him drowning. Alex was with his mother when they discovered his body.[12] The Chilton family, devastated, would not speak of Reid with family friends again in the coming years. It was the first and worst of gross injustices that would shape Alex's life.[13]

At 16, in 1967, Alex's love of music and singing at a talent show led him to hook up with a local group called the Box Tops. Chilton was already a soulful singer, sounding far beyond his years. With the song "The Letter," Chilton and bandmates captured the story of an intense long-distance love affair, at a time when soldiers were far away in Vietnam, and surprisingly topped the pop charts with a number one hit. Other successes followed with "Cry like a Baby" hitting number two, along with some minor hits.[14]

Despite the strong showing, Chilton and the Box Tops had a negative experience with the music industry. Band management dictated much to Chilton on what to sing and even how to sing it, and he was quickly feeling used and trapped within his own group. Further, while the Box Tops were selling plenty of records, they saw relatively little money, and they toured on shoestring budgets.[15]

An early gig with the Doors in 1968 showed Chilton that times were indeed changing and that rock was going in a very different direction than the more traditionally structured pop songs that had been his forte to that point.[16]

In an aside, but another sign of the times, a brief stay in California with Beach Boy Dennis Wilson led to crossing paths with the Manson family. Chilton once picked up groceries for them, and another time, he woke up on a couch next to Manson.[17]

Barely into his 20s, Chilton had already had a taste of big-time success and had been out to see the broader world, including the then-thriving folk/folk-rock scene in New York.[18] Disheartened with the music industry, however, Chilton quit in 1970 and moved back to Memphis.[19]

At the time, Chilton's friend in Memphis, singer/guitarist/songwriter Chris Bell, was playing with bass player Andy Hummel and drummer Jody Stephens. Chilton joined them, envisioning he and Bell as a songwriting duo in the mold of Lennon and McCartney.[20] The four adopted the name Big Star, taken from the name of a Memphis grocery chain with a store near the studio. The name also matched Bell's vision for the band's future, and it seemed to ironically reflect Chilton's lackluster experience as a "big star." In the same vein, their 1972 debut record would be named *#1 Record*.

Even while rock was generally going to a variety of other new directions, Chilton and Bell continued to embrace classic song structures, melodies, harmonies, and jangling guitars. The debut did otherwise have some fire on it, such as on "Don't Lie to Me," while on Bell's "Feel," he sings of a breakup that feels near fatal. Most of the album, though, is relatively upbeat with much emotional depth.

"Thirteen" is an all-time great ballad, played on an acoustic guitar with a brilliant melody and sung by Chilton with stark vulnerability. Chilton wrote the song upon reflecting on his own life at 13 and two particular life-altering memories: seeing the Beatles on the *Ed Sullivan Show* and experiencing love for the first time.[21] Lyrically, add in some rebellion against a parent, a reference to the power of rock and roll (and to the Rolling Stones), an apparent sexual innuendo, and it is an almost perfect distillation of the wonder of early adolescence.

Other tracks include "In the Street," which Cheap Trick covered (and modified a bit) as the theme of the popular TV show *That 70s Show* in the '90s, which would provide the band some rare mainstream exposure.

The Chilton-penned "Ballad of El Goodo" is another standout ballad. The song is a statement of resilience, including one verse directly opposing the Vietnam draft, but it is also noteworthy as a rare claiming of the word of God in rock and roll.[22]

The song is built around a pretty guitar lead and Chilton's heart-on-his-sleeve vocals. That gives way to Stephens's pounding drums, Hummel's descending bassline, and Chilton's steely resolve and faith. Chilton alludes to people being lined up, an apparent reference to body bags, and his own staunch refusal to obey orders to serve in Vietnam. Chilton also explicitly invokes the name of God as being on his side in the matter.[23]

Again, it is a remarkable thing to evoke in the world of rock and roll; even Brian Wilson had been wary of putting "God Only Knows" on *Pet Sounds*.[24] Sure, religious conservatives of the '60s and early '70s, such as the widely influential Reverent Norman Vincent Peale (author of the 1950s bestseller *The Power of Positive Thinking*) had chided those who avoided the draft, but so what? Why did the establishment get to decide what it was that God wanted? Although Chilton was not religious, though Bell would embrace Christianity a couple of years later, "Ballad of El Goodo" was one of four songs in just three albums in which the group would explicitly invoke, or earnestly grapple with, God, the Lord, Jesus, or one's soul as a song's topic. That is four more occurrences than most rock bands.[25]

Also of note are two tracks from *#1 Record*, the Bell-written and -sung "Try Again" and Chilton's "Watch the Sunrise." The songs are consecutive tracks on the album, and although there is no reason to think that they were written to work in tandem, the effect is striking.

"Try Again" is a direct reference to the Lord and a raw, poignant effort by Bell, who sings lead and plays an acoustic rhythm guitar. Chilton plays a mournful steel guitar and harmonizes. Without any drum to keep time and Bell's drawn-out, heart-wrenching vocals, a very human struggle is made real. Bell is singing directly to the Lord to help him work through a painful, trying time, and it is not clear how it will end.

Chilton's "Watch the Sunrise" follows and almost seems to suggest that the faith and patience in the previous song have been rewarded, or at least for Chilton it has. An acoustic guitar opens again but it is upbeat until the notes cascade down and fall away, as if releasing the residual tension of "Try Again." The song reasserts itself with the title chorus. It is another beautiful song as well as measured and clearheaded. Chilton seems to be appreciating the moment, but he also seems wise enough to not believe he has life permanently beat.

Critics could hardly praise *#1 Record* enough. *Rolling Stone* called it "exceptionally good," noting that "even the prettiest tunes have tension and subtle energy to them, and the rockers reverberate with power." *Billboard* wrote, "Every cut could be a single."[26]

Unfortunately, commercially the debut went nowhere. It was recorded in 1972 at Ardent Studios, as were all three of Big Star's main albums, and with a distribution deal through Stax. Stax had just switched from their small independent distribution deal to a very different situation at Columbia.[27]

First, Columbia bypassed Stax's usual distribution channels—the smaller, Black-owned, mom-and-pop stores in Black neighborhoods—in favor of the bigger department stores. Second, Columbia did not push the Stax releases with the major retailers to ensure that Stax artists did not cut into the sales of their already established R&B stars, such as Sly and the Family Stone, the Isley Brothers, and Earth Wind & Fire. If Stax's major Black stars were getting lost, the offbeat white rock group Big Star was all but invisible.[28]

Bell was already drinking a lot at that point, using pills like the sedative Mandrax, and injecting the opioid Dilaudid.[29] He had put his all into *#1 Record*, not only performing but writing, recording, producing, and mixing. When his high hopes met with commercial failure, he became further depressed and manic. According to numerous people close to him, he was also wrestling with his sexuality.[30] As Bell fell deeper into drinking and drugs, he became more challenging for his bandmates to deal with.[31] He then became suicidal and was hospitalized for a time.[32]

Bell and Chilton, who was also known to be difficult to work with, were butting heads over the direction of the next album. At one point, Hummell and Bell had a fistfight at the studio. In November 1972, Bell quit the band. Soon after, bassist Andy Hummel also quit, permanently leaving the music business for a regular family life.[33]

Now with just three members, Big Star recorded their second album, *Radio City* (1974). The album had a different feel. Bell's harmonizing was gone, for one thing, though the record did include some of his writing contributions. The critical reception, however, was much the same: Cashbox would call it "excellent material," while *Billboard*, most ironically in retrospect, called it "a highly commercial set."[34]

Radio City has some more edgy moments, reflecting Chilton dealing with some of his life disappointments, such as "You Get What You Deserve," and more underlying tension, such as "Mod Lang," in which he exhibits a troubled state of mind.

Chilton closes the album with the pop genius of "September Gurls" and the short but exceptional, solo-acoustic, "I'm in Love with a Girl." Overall, the songwriting and Chilton's vocals make *Radio City* an equal to the debut.

At that point, however, Stax was falling apart, and incredibly, *Radio City* also would fall through the cracks. This time, Stax and Columbia were again battling each other, with Stax again on the losing end. Columbia wouldn't release Stax from their distribution deal to keep them from becoming major competitors. Stax, and thus Big Star, received virtually no promotion, and *Radio City* did just a little better than the debut, which is to say, no one but impressed music critics knew who they were. Stax went bankrupt the following year.[35]

Worse still, the *Radio City* tour was plagued by logistical problems, such as all of the band's equipment being stolen in Syracuse and alcohol and drug abuse taking a greater toll on Chilton.[36]

The third Big Star album would not even get a proper release or even a proper title when first completed in 1975. It would alternatively be referred to by either *Third* or *Sister Lovers* or the hybrid moniker *Third/Sister Lovers* due to it being the third album and for the fact that Chilton and Stephens were dating sisters at the time.[37]

On *Third*, legendary Ardent producer Jim Dickinson let Chilton do his thing on what would become a uniquely dark, beautiful, and often brutal vision. At this point in Chilton's life, he was established, at least within the industry, as a top singer and songwriter. He had experienced childhood trauma and loss, been chewed up by the recording industry once before he was 18, and then two more surefire albums fell off the face of the earth despite his best efforts. His friend and former collaborator was having horrible personal problems and had left the group.[38] His volatile and drug- and alcohol-plagued relationship at the time with girlfriend Lesa Aldridge was falling apart.[39] His record company, Stax, was in bankruptcy. Amazingly, the recordings for *Third/Sister Lovers* capture all of the above.

At the time, Chilton was also taking large amounts of Valium, Seconal, and Demarol (Memphis had a pill culture), later noting, "Whatever was there I drank it or took it." He also later summarized, "I think that to say that it's a fairly druggy sort of album that is the work of a confused person trying to find himself or find his creative direction is a fair statement about the thing."[40] The end result has variously been described as "stark" and rife with "pure desperation and often perverse destruction" but also possessing a "haunting brilliance."[41] Upon hearing Chilton's effort, legendary Atlantic records executive Jerry Wexler stated, "This record makes me feel very uncomfortable."[42]

Slow songs like "Kangaroo" and the strikingly named "Holocaust" are augmented by microphones placed in intentionally odd places, noisy solos, and seemingly random inclusions of strings and accordions.[43] Chilton explores a discomfiting world; it is visceral and it is as beautiful as it is bleak. Chilton seems all but shattered at times, and he is able to express precisely that. On "Night Time," Chilton bluntly sings of possibly wanting out altogether. As disjointed as the whole affair is and although the point is not always immediately clear, it all still has soul.

Third/Sister Lovers includes some pop gems as well, such as "Kizza Me" and "Thank You Friends." Some measure of relief comes later on with the lovely but off-kilter "Take Care." The very last song, a cover of Jerry Lee Lewis's "Whole Lotta Shakin' Goin' On," is a ragged tribute to the group's Memphis roots.

One of the more well-known tracks off the album is "Jesus Christ." The vaguely upbeat and melodic-enough Christmas song is sung from the perspective of Christmas Day. It is arguably one of rock's better Christmas songs. Chilton's intentions with the song, however, are not entirely clear. Along with the fact that he did not identify as Christian, having, in his words, only briefly explored it, Chilton would downplay the religious aspect of the song.[44] He did, however, note that he wrote the song partly in response to Bell having become a born-again Christian after leaving the band.[45] Chilton certainly does not sing the song like a convert, though music writer Stewart Mason suggests that "the simple, catchy chorus ... trumps" any implied sarcasm, making "Jesus Christ" a song "that appeals to believers and nonbelievers alike."[46] Chilton perhaps buys into Jesus but while retaining myriad reservations.

Third was Chilton's vision, and it would also be considered an act of commercial suicide. Atlantic did not even know what to make of the record and refused to release it at all. The release would then not come until 1978, four years after Big Star had ceased. With *Third*, Chilton's rejection by the music industry had all but been reciprocated. However, a cult following began around Big Star, and their records that *were* out there in the United States and Europe became highly sought after.[47]

In the meantime, Chris Bell's older brother David took him to Europe, hoping a change of scenery would help him, and Chris recorded solo material there. Then, prior to Chris's recordings being released, on December 27, 1978, Bell was at a party in Memphis. Though not inebriated, he may or may not have been using pills, and at one point he had reportedly been ranting about the music industry.[48] Bell left the party, drove, clipped a curb, and crashed his Triumph into a utility pole, killing him instantly.[49] The Memphis music scene and Chilton were devastated.[50]

In the '80s, Chilton laid low, moving to New Orleans to get away from the music industry and to get off booze and drugs. He took odd jobs, once working a dishwashing gig at a restaurant.[51]

Most of Chilton's solo records and collaborations would be unconventional and critically hit and miss. Chilton's clear anti-commercial streak certainly carried on; his second solo record, for example, was titled *Like Flies on Sherbet*. Chilton explained in a 1985 interview:

> Somewhere along the line I figured out that if you only press up a hundred copies of a record, then eventually it will find its way to the hundred people in the world who want it most.[52]

In 1992, Bell's unreleased demos were finally collected and posthumously released as the album *I Am the Cosmos*. The release featured the brilliant title track and the heart-wrenching "You and Your Sister," among others, all bringing Bell overdue recognition.[53]

In 1993, Chilton was talked into a Big Star reunion by members of a fraternity at the University of Missouri, which resulted in a live album. Stephens rejoined, but with Bell gone and Hummel not wanting to participate, Chilton brought on devout Big Star disciples Ken Stringfellow and Jon Auer of the Seattle-area band the Posies. The new Big Star continued to tour off and on over the next couple of decades and recorded one new studio album in 2005.[54]

Stephens would become the manager at Ardent Studios. Although Chilton has not become a household name, he would eventually receive widespread recognition and praise from fans, critics, and peers alike before his untimely death from a heart attack in 2010.[55]

23

Rockers, Dancers, Disco, and Disco's Demolition, 1970s–1980

One reason that rock and roll had been such a phenomenon in the 1950s in the first place was that it liberated the physical bodies of the West and in America, especially those of European descent. This was certainly evidenced in the initial shock and revulsion with Elvis "The Pelvis" Presley's gyrating dance moves on television, yet quickly followed by his mass acceptance and idolization. For a variety of reasons, though, things changed and rock and roll changed. Dancing would not necessarily continue to be a major part of the rock movement and all of its various offshoots and subgenres, and certainly not as paired-off dancing couples. This chapter, then, is a story of rock, dance, sexuality, race, and disco music, as well as disco's subsequent demolition.

Postwar mid-'50s America was, to many, not only conformist but emotionally and physically stilted. Cultural historian Barbara Ehrenreich saw the country, or really the white mainstream, as "frozen over and brittle—not only physically immobilizing but also as emotionally restrained," while rock and roll and dancing to rock had "thawed this coolness."[1]

In the United States, there had already been a history of solo social dancing in African American culture, from clogging to tap dancing. There had also been more sexually evocative dances, including hip- and shoulder-rolling dances and the shimmy, aka the hootchy-kootch, which came out of African American social clubs in the 1910s and '20s.[2]

In the jazz age of the '20s and '30s, more daring dancers took to the jitterbug, and swing dancing was popular. By the '40s, however, in the mainstream white culture, social dancing "cooled down" as big band jazz faded out. Further, with more and more people living in the suburbs, there were fewer trips to ballrooms.[3]

With the rise of rock music in the '50s and its exciting beat came popular variations of swing dancing, now called rock and roll dancing. This often took place at "sock hop" dances held in high school gymnasiums (shoes were removed to spare the hardwood floors) and set to fast-paced songs like Bill Haley and the Comets' "Rock around the Clock" (1955) and Danny and the Juniors' "At the Hop" (1957). In 1960, things further shifted in the mainstream with Chubby Checker's smash-hit cover version of Hank Ballard's "The Twist." Checker's version launched the hip-swiveling national dance sensation of the same name that lasted into 1961.[4]

The early leader of the Black Panther Party, Eldridge Cleaver, opined that the twist in particular had allowed white people to feel "exhilarating and soothing new sensations" and "release from some unknown prison in which their Bodies had been encased."[5] The twist also afforded a certain physical and sexual closeness for boys and girls, though without the tensions of the physical touching and trying to determine what was enough and what was too much—something dance chaperones often tried to police.[6] That was followed by a slew of similar dance crazes and moves, like the Watusi, the frug, and the swim, and similarly themed songs, such as the Isley Brothers' "Twist and Shout."[7]

That dance phase faded out after a few years. As the '60s progressed, the rise of folk rock and the British Invasion saw rock become a white-dominated genre distinguishable from other subgenres of rock and roll more conducive to dancing, specifically R&B, soul, and funk. Those genres would also be more associated with Black and Latino audiences. In 1962, folk stars Peter, Paul, and Mary's debut record, for example, actually came packaged with a note explicitly asking listeners to *not* dance to the music so that they could focus on the messaging.[8] The Beatles, after having famously covered the Isleys' "Twist and Shout" early on in 1963, soon became a high-minded studio band no longer focused on the teen-pop milieu associated with dance hits.

Many rock fans of the time saw rock music as substantive and as inspiration for social movements and protest, while most dance music was, in contrast, seen as frivolous pop music. By the late '60s, hippie types at rock shows, and sometimes under the influence of drugs like marijuana or LSD, were less dancing and more engaged in "free-wheeling ecstatic movements."[9] By the end of the '60s, fans at live rock shows were observed not necessarily moving or dancing to the music at all but instead, as *Billboard* wrote in 1968, "just digging."[10]

There are a lot of theories as to why, and to again speak in the broadest of generalizations, white males in particular would no longer dance the same way. For one thing, since the twist, males no longer led, and dancing was often left to the spontaneous movements of each individual. The mostly white rockers and rock fans of the era were not as prone to letting it loose on the dance floor while, white males, as a whole, came to be seen as lacking a certain physical fluidity. Stephen Morris, a drummer from the dance-friendly band New Order that arose in the '80s, was not alone in his belief that "it takes [the psychoactive drug] ecstasy to make a white man dance."[11] Also in the '80s, star and Black comedian Eddie Murphy would joke about the general inability of white people to dance: "Y'all be trying ... do y'all listen to the words or the beat?"[12] Respected rock writer Chuck Klosterman once spoke for many other white male rockers when he wrote, "If I am sober enough to drive, I am too sober to dance."[13]

Again, there isn't necessarily one explanation as to how this came to be. One explanation is that as the people in dominant and seemingly (consciously or not) superior positions in American society, white males already had other avenues of social fulfillment and expression besides dance. It has also been theorized that an aversion to dancing reflected a desire to avoid the risk of looking or feeling out of control, and thus many white males otherwise took to "stolidity and physical reserve."[14] This would also, in part, mean a distancing from those groups generally not in such positions of power and opportunity that did embrace dance, specifically including African Americans, Latinos, women, and gays.

In soul, and even more so in funk, dance would remain central to the music experience. The most visible example would be the famed weekday afternoon television show *Soul Train*, which first aired in the U.S. in 1971. The show was the Black-populated version of the *American Bandstand* format, with young couples dancing to the top acts of the day and live acts performing.[15]

In the African American community, James Brown especially had reshaped dance into something intensely powerful, masculine, and important both as individual expression and as an act of self-determination. Such physical expressions were not only derived from African traditions but that physical freedom had been vital to those enslaved or otherwise deprived of agency over their own lives and bodies. Contemporary writer Ta-Nahesi Coates explained the impact of both James Brown's and Michael Jackson's dancing: "black kids, historically, grow up in conditions where all you have to control is your body to demonstrate power," and thus "'body control' becomes a measure of power."[16]

By the '70s, post–British Invasion rock, and especially hard rock performers, were mostly white, male, and heterosexual (or presented as such) with a predominantly similar fan base. This was essentially the Western mainstream. Certain powerhouse groups were enormously popular such as the Who with their windmill-power chords, Led Zeppelin and Viking wails, and the Stones who, in a bit of self-parody, took to including a 20-foot inflatable penis as part of their stage show for a time.[17]

Those rockers were not necessarily consciously avoiding dance rhythms but simply embracing the powerful, guitar-based, often sexualized rock and roll that they loved. Dancing just wasn't in the equation. Still, the channeling of rock to its harder elements and most epic scale came at the exclusion of other possible directions and influences, such as dance music and those styles generally favored by the non-white rocker crowd. As music critic Robert Christgau further observed, "Three crucial elements got shortchanged in the process: black people, politics, and Pop-with-a-capital-P, Pop in the Andy Warhol sense."[18]

In many ways, rock's relationship with dancing reflected its relationship with the body and sex, and that relationship had shifted. Again, the hippie notion of "free love" had originally meant to be not only an embracing of sexual pleasure but, ideally, an elevating of society's view of sex to something more open, less shameful, and more loving. What was more often being carried forward, however, was a much less nuanced pursuit of instant gratification and carnal pleasure modeled in songs like the Rolling Stones' "Let's Spend the Night Together" (1967) and "Brown Sugar" (1971), the Doors' "Light My Fire" (1967), and Led Zeppelin's "Whole Lotta Love" (1969).

To further reiterate, at this point, rock and rock and roll had no actual *limits*. It lacked the sexual subtleties of the blues or R&B and instead possessed an "I will do whatever I want" and "if it feels good, do it" bravado befitting what had become world-beating rock stars.[19] This was all empowering in many ways, yet and again, it also crossed into all sorts of excesses, narcissism, and even misogyny. Thus, hard rock was trending more "Whole Lotta Love" or "Stranglehold," as opposed to, in soul music for example, Otis Redding's passionate but patient "Try a Little Tenderness," Gladys Knight's empowered "If I Were Your Woman," or the Spinners' vulnerable but self-assured "I'll Be Around."

And rock stars were almost expected and even encouraged to live these values out in the grandest ways possible as fans vicariously lived through them. With unlimited bank accounts and no bosses or nine-to-five schedules to otherwise interfere with one's wants, as one writer described it, rock stars had a "license to … act out our most rebellious, Bacchanalian fantasies."[20]

The biggest bands leased their jets for tours and ate lobster thermidor in what could sometimes amount to flying cocaine sex parties. Many stars had underage girlfriends, and like Ted Nugent, Steven Tyler became legal guardian of his 16-year-old girlfriend.[21] The Stones even promoted their *Black and Blue* (1976) album with a billboard depicting an abused and bound woman next to Jagger, with the caption, "I'm Black and Blue from the Rolling Stones—and I love it!"[22] It would all get to a point by the late '70s that David Lee Roth, the front man for L.A.-area superstars Van Halen, would institute an infamous "grid system" to locate girls in the audience he liked. He would then send crew members directly to them to invite the girls backstage after the show.[23] Again, rock had no real limits.

Also of note, in a post–Jimi Hendrix world, the lead guitar had come more squarely to the forefront of rock. Lead guitarists were seen as guitar gods whose soaring solo excursions could scarcely ever be considered as "too much." And it was not hard to see how the climactic guitar solos had phallic and often orgasmic implications.

In short, '70s hard rock had very much come to be about exhibiting an oft-extreme masculinity and being exceedingly assertive and especially sexually.

Rock actually had a long tradition of challenging certain other traditional roles of masculinity. Little Richard had been rock and roll's first gender-bending act in the '50s, and he had been followed into the '70s by others such as the sometimes cross-dressing but heterosexual sex symbol Mick Jagger; the also gender-bending and at one point bisexual-identifying—but married to a woman—glam rocker David Bowie; the glam/arena rocker Freddie Mercury of Queen; and the flamboyant Elton John.

As to homosexuality, Richard, Mercury, and John had identified as gay, though Richard publicly vacillated as to his sexual identity throughout his life, while Mercury and John remained "in the closet" throughout the '70s for fairly obvious reasons. Straight rocker Rod Stewart, for example, had his reputation badly "tarnished" by a widespread false rumor in the '70s as to his sexuality, possibly started by a disgruntled former manager.[24]

At that time in the '70s, in the world of hard rock and much of the mainstream, any performer who appeared as too effeminate was seen as weak and would have no place in rock and roll, and openly gay was mostly unacceptable at that time. Instead, these rockers utilized either the inherent bombast of rock or camp, which was safer but still entertaining.[25] Mercury expressed his own dynamic personality with a supreme confidence that he used to command arenas like few others. John sported show-stopping outfits and equally wild trademark eyeglasses but that came across as fun expressions of his immense talent.

Perhaps most important, both Mercury's and John's music aligned with what was not only great music but music that possessed what the world of rock approved of as essentially being masculine. That is, the hard rocker was, as Ann Powers wrote, "hard-hitting and risk-taking"; Queen's "Keep Yourself Alive" could thus be an example.[26] Writer Richard Dyer similarly noted that rock utilized "repeated phrases" that "trap you in their relentless push," something embodied by John's "Crocodile Rock."[27]

At the time, rock was putting little value in dancing, subtlety, modesty, contemplation, or passivity, all of which was seen as fit for pop music or maybe soft rock.[28] Again, though not necessarily consciously, these values also reflected issues of gender and race.

For a typical hormone-addled, sexually anxious, adolescent, white heterosexual male of the '70s, that some of hard rock music's most talented performers were also incredibly bold with their sexuality made them natural heroes. Powers, again, explained, for example, that "Led Zeppelin's white male rock fans heard a new expressiveness about sex emerging from an ideal version of themselves."[29] That is, the Mick Jaggers, Robert Plants, and David Lee Roths of the world were definitely not worrying about getting a date, whether some girl might dump them, or when they might next engage in sexual relations. These rock gods were clearly also sex gods, and they were worshipped.

In sum, if one was extremely talented, the music was appropriately masculine, and if one was more boldly flamboyant, as opposed to being soft or feminine, a performer could be accepted by rock and roll fans.

So, then, what did happen to the dance tradition through all of this? What about those other descendants of the original '50s rock and roll revolution, those not dominated by the highly sexualized world of white male rock stars and that *were* often centered in dance?

Coming into the '70s, soul music was continuing to come into its own. This especially included the innovative works of Isaac Hayes in Memphis and his *Hot Buttered Soul* (1969), along with the sweet Philly Soul sound of Philadelphia International Records (PIR), with its string arrangements and positivity coming out of an often tough urban landscape.

Some R&B, soul, and funk was also becoming more defined by a danceable four-on-the-floor beat, a steady bass drum, strings, horns, and synthesizers and with little emphasis on the lead guitar.[30] Crucial proto-disco, like the O'Jay's "Love Train" (1972), a *Billboard* number one in March 1973, and MFSB's (Mother Father Sister Brother) album *Love Is the Message*, the same year, came out of PIR.[31]

Further, despite some groups having great success blending funk and rock, including Sly and the Family Stone, Stevie Wonder, Rufus, and Parliament-Funkadelic, radio programmer "narrowcasting" largely kept those records off the biggest "white" radio stations and restricted them to "Black" radio. Plus, the corporate consolidation of the record industry meant that Black acts like Rufus, for example, could be pushed into releasing more pop-oriented fare.[32] A virtual restratification of music continued.

For various other social reasons and cultural traditions, it was Black, female, gay, and Latino communities in particular that would be disco's early proponents and main music makers. The most danceable soul and funk was popular at African American clubs in New York and elsewhere but also in New York's underground gay dance clubs and where other new sounds were coalescing.

Before the Stonewall uprising (1969), New York's gay clubs had been badly needed social spaces for the city's gay community. These were places of brief respite and refuge from lives on society's furthest fringes, dominated by the constant threat of oppression, violence, and arrest. Author Edmund White described the clubs of the time as "temples to despair."[33]

But Stonewall was the key moment in a sea change in attitude of gay communities. One result was that the gay nightclubs would become the popular homes of the first discotheques.[34]

The term "discotheque" itself (roughly French for disc/record + library) had originally come from the underground jazz dance clubs under and immediately after Nazi occupation in Paris.[35] Gay clubs in New York such as the Loft in the Bowery and the Gallery and the Paradise Garage, both in SoHo, became the first "discos."[36] Popular deejays like David Mancuso at the Loft and then Francis Grasso at Sanctuary tended to select soul and funk records with "a strong and heavy groove" for dancing and learned to manipulate the emotional peaks and valleys of the dance floor.[37] Deejays also learned to reduce the time between songs more and more and to seamlessly start the next song at the same beats per minute to keep the crowd moving.[38] The clubs featured immersive sound systems, throbbing beats, futuristic pulsing light shows, and wall-to-wall bodies.[39] One writer present, Andrew Kopkind, described a feeling where "the world is enclosed in this hall, that here is only *now*, in this place and time."[40] The experience was also enhanced by alcohol and drugs, including poppers, LSD, Quaaludes, and MDA.[41] Thus, such clubs became a whole new kind of "refuge" and an alternate world.

Still, more substantive gay rights and more solid mainstream acceptance were years away. Even the slightest public expression of homosexuality was deemed offensive and threatening enough to elicit a strong backlash. The most prominent leader of the antigay movement at the time was pop singer and product spokesperson Anita Bryant, who warned America, "Homosexuals cannot reproduce, so they must recruit."[42]

And, of course, the impact of the civil and women's rights movements from the '60s were a shock to the status quo and were presenting new dynamics to contend with throughout society.[43]

In sum, the long unquestioned notion that white males would always completely dominate society's positions of power was shifting.

The early '70s were a downtime for many African Americans as well, with the end of the civil rights era, the return of Vietnam vets to civilian life, and the "rust-belting" of American manufacturing in the Northeast and Midwest.[44] Some prominent soul music of the era was referred to as music of "worry," such as Sly and the Family Stone's *There's a Riot Goin' On* (1971), the O'Jay's *Back Stabbers* (1972), and Funkadelic's *Cosmic Slop* (1973).[45]

The developing disco genre was first and foremost geared for dancing. For example, disco producers often pushed the vocals to the background, sometimes to simply serve as an "echo of the beat," and entire verses might be removed in editing.[46] Otherwise, it was also flamboyant and futuristic music, sometimes with a synthetic feel and sophisticated arrangements, and it could be repetitive.[47] As such, many of these characteristics simply did not translate well to those not on a dance floor, and the genre would be misunderstood by a great many.

For many minority communities, being bright and flamboyant was a form of free expression and reflected a refusal to be quiet or invisible, and a freedom that came with self-acceptance of one's sexuality. To that point, fitting into society had often really meant being compliant and content with occupying the bottom of the power and economic food chains and, for gay people, being "in the closet" altogether. In the world of disco, flamboyance, futurism, and a synthetic feel represented a new way forward and a promising and exciting future.

Disco was also repetitive. As to repetition, disco vocalists often intentionally used a repetitive and seemingly monotonous style.[48] This, as author Tim Lawrence explained, followed "in the tradition of gospel" and "emptied words of their meaning in order to open the self to spiritual inspiration."[49] Thus, songs like Gloria Gaynor's "Never Can Say Goodbye" or Andrea True's "More More More" were hypnotic and trance inducing. Further, disco and disco dancing was also more about a "whole-body eroticism," as opposed to a rock demographic and that genre's "phallic eroticism."[50]

Last, as to elevating the singer or lead guitarist to a godlike status as in rock, disco instead elevated each individual dancer on the dance floor. Disco was a "utopian disco diversity"—a theme in songs like "Love Train" and Sister Sledge's "We Are Family." According to Nadine Hubbs, disco was "ultimately triumphant, transcendent—but on a human, not monumental, scale."[51] Thus, whereas to some, disco was feather light, for many marginalized in society, *everything* about disco was affirming and significant.

From 1973 to 1977, disco grew in exposure via soul-rooted hits like Barry White's Love Unlimited Orchestra's "Love's Theme" and MFSB's "TSOP (The Sound of Philadelphia)," with both hitting number one on the

Billboard Hot 100 in 1974. The sound was further rounded out by works like the Funkadelic arm of George Clinton's funk enterprise and songs like "Cosmic Slop" (1973), while the Hues Corporation went to number one with "Rock the Boat" (1974), as did Gloria Gaynor's cover of "Reach Out (I'll Be There)" in 1975. Heatwave released the anthemic "Boogie Nights" in 1977.

In the mid–'70s, disco records received increasing radio play and sales. Although disco songs tended to be created and written by producers, certain acts became stars, including Donna Summer (e.g., "Hot Stuff," "Last Dance"), Chic ("Le Freak"), the Village People ("YMCA," "In the Navy"), and KC & the Sunshine Band ("Boogie Man").[52] And disco was also a platform for strong women performers, and Summer, Gaynor (e.g., "I Will Survive"), Chaka Khan ("I'm Every Woman"), and Grace Jones ("I Need a Man") all became big stars.

By 1976 and 1977, most record companies had jumped on board with disco, and disco hits were all over *Billboard*'s top-ten singles chart.[53] Although disco started with mostly all Black performers, more and more white artists took to it. Even rockers such as the Rolling Stones, Rod Stewart, and the Grateful Dead were cutting disco tracks.[54]

With its growth out of the underground, the next phase of disco was in glittering and often exclusive clubs, especially Manhattan's legendary and high-profile Studio 54. That club was a disco playground for glamorous jet-setting celebrities, from top models to Diana Ross to Andy Warhol, and with lots of sex and cocaine for good measure. Disco thus became associated in the public eye with glitzy, high-end, decadent glamour and celebrity and a world about as far removed from the lives of middle- and working-class, white heterosexual males as could be.

Donna Summer, Portland, Oregon, 1976 (Keystone Press/Alamy Stock Photo).

Then, in late 1977, the film *Saturday Night Fever* was released, starring John Travolta. The film depicted Travolta as Tony Manero, a white, straight, slick, handsome, and masculine twenty-something character looking to use his dancing talent and disco to escape his working-class struggles. For the Brooklynite, the music, the stylish clothes, and the flashy dance moves at a local disco were an opening for him to leave his life behind and become a star in a very different world in Manhattan. The film was based on a story in a magazine that turned out to be fabricated, but that didn't alter the film's impact.

The film's soundtrack included major disco hits from the Trammps, KC and the Sunshine Band, and several from the Bee Gees, whose "Stayin' Alive" became a ubiquitous smash hit. The Bee Gees were a white, Australian-born brother group that had transitioned from a Beatles-influenced pop act to disco. They would far and away become the genre's biggest sellers.

Saturday Night Fever was a sensation and the second highest grossing film of all time at the time. Its soundtrack, too, went to number one, and for fifteen years, it was the top-selling album of all time.[55]

The film's depiction of disco scenes did not really resemble what discos had looked like at that time. The paired-off dancing of men and women with the male leading, for example, did not reflect what was really a more "free-form, improvised dancing," and floor-clearing solos, as in Travolta's showcase scenes, would have been out of place.[56] Nonetheless, spurred by the film, disco had a huge cultural impact, and its central figure was now a handsome, smooth, white, ladies' man in a signature white suit, in Travolta.

The film actually led disco club owners and patrons across the nation to attempt to re-create and mimic those movie scenes. While the late '70s economic recession had ramped up anxieties even further, disco was everywhere. Chains of discos had popped up by the thousands in shopping centers across the United States. One result was that a cliché of self-absorbed, uncool disco fanatics took shape.[57] For many, this left even more of a lasting negative impression of disco and the entire scene, perhaps best embodied by *The Simpsons* TV show's clueless, cringe-inducing, recurring character, Disco Stu. And like every other popular musical genre ever, corporate interests ensured that the mainstream was quickly glutted with the product, and everything from third-generation Philly Soul to the bizarro-novelty-hit-gone-number one, "Disco Duck" (1978).[58]

Thus, it was already pretty clear that disco was wearing out its welcome and running out of steam commercially. In fact, the entire peak of the disco craze lasted only two years, but the backlash would be remarkably swift and strong.

Despite and very much because of disco's mainstream successes, an enormous groundswell of anti-disco fervor smoldered over the last years of the '70s. This was especially so among young, working-class, white rock fans, a demographic already finding itself "lost in a new culture of women's liberation, Black rights, sexual liberation and Studio 54-inspired androgyny and materialism."[59] Indeed, the slogans "Disco Sucks" and even "Death to Disco" became popular with rock fans and rock deejays and appeared on hats, T-shirts, and bumper stickers.[60]

In December 1978, early shock-jock and Chicago rock-radio deejay Steve Dahl was forced out of his job at WDAI radio to make way for a disco format. An angry Dahl switched to Chicago's WLUP and used his disgust and resentment toward disco as part of his on-air appeal.[61]

One of Dahl's bits was to begin to play a disco record and then drag the needle over it, making a horrible scratching noise, and then play the recording of an explosion as if he had just blown the record up. Dahl immediately connected with a legion of younger, white, suburban male rock fans.[62] Dahl would be the focal point of anti-disco sentiment, though similar sentiments were being expressed across the country.[63]

In July 1979, the Chicago White Sox baseball team asked Dahl to be part of a promotion for a doubleheader on July 12, 1979. The team was having a middling season and was looking to boost attendance and interest by connecting with Dahl and his younger, suburban, white, male fan base. The White Sox ownership, the Veeck family, already well-known for publicity stunts, contacted Dahl and set up a promotion. Attendees would get discounted tickets if they brought a disco record. Dahl would then actually blow up all of the collected disco records in a dumpster on the field in between games.[64]

Neither the Veecks nor Dahl had any idea how popular the offer would be. On a night the team could expect to draw 20,000 paying fans, the crowd well exceeded Comiskey Park's capacity of 47,795.[65] Dahl and his crew did an on-field presentation after the first game, with Dahl in military garb, and then conducted the climactic explosions in center field. Dahl left the field, but bedlam ensued, the crowd went wild, and thousands took to the field. As one witness reported, "The place went bonkers.... People started jumping out of the stands," and the field was damaged. Some climbed down the tall yellow foul poles. In the end, 39 people were arrested, and the White Sox had to forfeit the second game.[66]

At the time, the night was an embarrassment for the White Sox and for baseball. But with disco just about at the end of its run as a pop sensation, the night helped accelerate its complete demise as a viable commercial entity by 1980. Because no one was hurt and the cause of hating an already declining pop trend seemed so innocuous, the Disco Demolition incident has largely been recalled rather warmly and comically in retrospect.

There was more to the night, however. It was not hard to see that almost all of the actors at the stadium were white males and that the disco genre was extremely popular among Blacks, women, Latinos, and homosexuals.[67] In fact, one Comiskey Park usher on the night of Disco Demolition was African American Vincent Lawrence, who later became a pioneering deejay in house music, a direct descendant of disco. Lawrence noted that a great many rock fans did not or could not make a very basic distinction in the records they brought to destroy: "A lot of the records were not disco records but BLACK records—Marvin Gaye, Stevie Wonder."[68] And as Chic's Nile Rodgers later recalled, "It felt to us like Nazi book-burning, this is America, the home of jazz and rock and people were now afraid even to say the word 'disco.'"[69] To author John-Manuel Andriote, "My take on what happened [at Comiskey Park] was that it was a boiling-over of testosterone from white straight men who saw disco—and the whole club scene—as threatening to their masculinity."[70]

The revolt against disco reflected the continuing racial stratifications of rock. The mainstream was used to defining what "good" music was, and music that did not fit that definition was "bad." One result, again from Robert Christgau, was that "in the official rock pantheon the Doors and Led Zeppelin are Great Artists while Chuck Berry and Little Richard are Primitive Forefathers and James Brown and Sly Stone are Something Else."[71]

Yet Dahl, and others, have always vehemently denied that Disco Demolition had any racist or homophobic motivations.[72] In a 2016 interview, Dahl noted that "we didn't blow up Jimi Hendrix records, we didn't blow up the Chi-Lites, we didn't blow up David Bowie. It was really just about the music."[73] Dahl would add, "It was a moment to say, 'the music you revere is great, and you are okay just as you are. Don't be pressured to wear a costume to win a girl or impress others. You're fine.' Who doesn't like to hear that?"[74]

Dahl further wrote in his 2016 memoir, "No kid, just figuring out who he was and where he was going, would be prepared to have his assimilated rock-and-roll identity stripped from him. If the resistance was furious, it was because they were not prepared to shuck the rock and roll, which had sheltered them in their transition from kid to adult."[75]

Again, such challenges for white males came at the same time that many minority groups were stepping up in the social strata and also being helped up by left-leaning intellectuals and liberals in positions of power. This transformation contributed to the feeling, as Paul Cowan had reported on in places like West Virginia and Boston, that many in power were no longer aligned with or sympathetic to the interests of white males.

In the end, disco's societal saturation and Travolta's Tony Manera becoming the apparent new model for men marked its end. White males still dominated society in almost every other way, of course, and again, disco's moment in the sun was completely over after that two-year stretch. Yet, middle- and working-class, heterosexual white males were terrified and had felt that their very identities were being, as Dahl put it, "stripped" of them. That is, mainstream society would expect white males to conform their very being to this new status quo, or otherwise risk severe marginalization and be made social outcasts. Dahl and crew and the millions like them across the nation knew that they would never be able to meet this new standard foisted on them, and they would never be accepted in such a social structure.

Of course, if one accepts that this was a devastating development, that Disco Demolition and the "death to disco" response was completely natural, that raises another question: What was life like for everyone who wasn't a white, male, heterosexual fan of rock in every other year *but* 1978 and 1979?

And disco didn't completely disappear. Given the genre's roots in marginalized communities, it was not a coincidence that disco's biggest anthem was Gloria Gaynor's "I Will Survive." The Bee Gees, to the annoyance of some, were inducted into the Rock & Roll Hall of Fame in 1997, as was Donna Summer in 2013. Disco's subsequent influence has been rather broad and influenced not only leading rock acts of the time but more current pop stars like Daft Punk and Lady Gaga and R&B stars such as Justin Timberlake and Bruno Mars.

Conclusion

From its inception, rock has been a great equalizer. It started with severely marginalized Americans, the Black bluesmen and their alleged "Devil's music," gospel and the "holy roller"–labeled Pentecostals, and rural whites and their so-called hillbilly music, all combining into something deeply personal and across broad, traditional divides. Its place in this greater arc of Western civilization has been to help society continue to move forward in many ways, even while sometimes stumbling badly. But the arc has continued.

Through the 1960s and '70s, rock and roll entertained millions, while simultaneously inspiring and reflecting change and upheaval. Some traditional establishment values were exposed as facades concealing hypocrisy, greed, inequality, and denial. Old norms were thus ignored and rules broken, sometimes in inspired ways and other times with harsh consequences for the rocker.

Rock music and its attendant ethos was often almost diametrically opposed to the establishment values of the time. From the beginning, rock had been bent on breaking out of stifling parental, moral, and religious authority, from demands to "Turn down that damn music!" to rules forbidding premarital sexual relations and underage drinking, and despite admonitions to "Honor thy father and mother."[1]

On the positive side, and as to the sex, drugs, and rock and roll equation. Starting with sex, to the rocker, mid-century America was failing to engage in meaningful discussions of sexual desires, angst, and experiences. At the least, rock helped break a door down in establishing that not every sexual thought or act need be shameful or denied.

As to drugs, the rock and countercultural revolution made alcohol and marijuana "casual drugs." Alcohol was already mainstream, of course, but it became less stigmatized, even for youth.[2] Marijuana came with its own drawbacks, though it could hardly be argued to be more problematic than alcohol. As such, at the least, an openness toward pot was a victory against establishment hypocrisy and scare tactics, which the kids had not been buying into anyway. In the years since, marijuana has steadily continued on the road to widespread legality in the twenty-first century.

Rock also helped open a door for hallucinogens, which had altered and expanded the consciousnesses of many, while others at least had some laughs and some interesting "trips." Decades later, hallucinogens would finally find legal acceptance and again be seriously studied in the medical world. By the 2010s, they were part of highly promising treatments for various psychological ailments, including depression and addiction.[3]

On the other side of that same equation, the rock revolution's sometimes total disregard of existing establishment values brought its own set of problems. A notion of sex as "free love" was often taken to soul-numbing extremes in a worship of the flesh and nasty emotional entanglements, not to mention unwanted pregnancies and venereal diseases.

As to drugs, a veritable who's who of the classic rock–era artists and their fans maxed out on drugs and alcohol, some even dying, while many more would eventually find their way to rehabs and AA meetings in search of sobriety.

Also, rock music helped to facilitate the integration of Western society more broadly and, on deeper personal levels, ways the West would never turn back from. This is an enormous achievement, though of course not to be confused with entirely *resolving* immense racial issues and divisions.

All in all, rock and roll would continue to be an incredibly powerful cultural force in Western life and continue to be, as argued here, the single most illustrative and helpful vehicle for understanding the ongoing arc of Western civilization.

These trends and dynamics continued to play out through the '80s and '90s, and more aspects of Western civilization would be uniquely illuminated. Would the fringe rock subgenres of metal, punk, and hip-hop grow in popularity? Yes. Massively. What would happen with rock's ever-increasing bombast and ego? See, for example, hair metal and grunge. What about Dr. Janov and rage and rock and roll? A hint: in 2013, at 89, Janov would acknowledge being a serious fan of fringe-thrash-metal-maniacs-turned-superstars Metallica.[4] Other mental health concerns? There would be high-profile suicides and many rock stars would deal with emotional and psychological traumas through therapy; some top bands would even hire group therapists to all but live with them. Drugs and addiction? Drugs continued to be used, of course, but at the same time in 2015, singer-songwriter Bill Withers remarked to the audience at the Rock & Roll Hall of Fame induction ceremony that it felt like "the largest AA meeting in the Western Hemisphere."[5] These are the stories of artists like Kool Herc, the Ramones, Cheap Trick, Suicidal Tendencies, Prince, Public

Enemy, Metallica, Teenage Fanclub, Pearl Jam, Oasis, and many more. But those stories are for another time.

Since about 1997, rock music stopped being the West's dominant musical genre, culturally and commercially. That year saw the end of the most direct influence of the classic rock titans, especially the British Invaders, particularly with the end of grunge and Britpop, and the release of Radiohead's post-rock masterpiece *OK Computer*. And rock may well never be dominant again. Still, rock and roll changed the world, profoundly and permanently, and its musical, cultural, emotional, and even spiritual impact continues to reverberate. Indeed, the "strange," "loose," "strong," and "bold" rock and roll music of the 1950s, '60s, and '70s could scarcely have better validated Alexis de Tocqueville's prognostications for the United States, as noted at the start of this book. The same forces that seem to push this greater arc of Western civilization along, that resulted in Protestantism, democracy, freedom of the enslaved and the segregated, and psychoanalysis, all also led to the rock and roller. Like few other times in history, though, this era of rock and roll helped address so much angst as well as both to open a door to that spirit inside every individual *and* unite people at the same time.

So, while rock music has inspired and entertained and it can even be classified as "important," how exactly has it stacked up over the years against its original rival, the authority of the 1950s Western establishment? What about rules and morals? There is, in fact, more to the establishment than just coercion, dogma, and the price of doggies in windows. Rejecting *everything* about the establishment prior to rock and roll is akin to rejecting *any* morals or any semblance of authority and structure.

Of course, rock and roll *can* be moral! Part of its beauty is its flexibility, wide-open nature, and capacity to help people find common ground. Many major acts, such as R.E.M. and Bruce Springsteen, have produced entire catalogs of morally respectable rock music. Plus, as just a few examples, John Lennon and George Harrison certainly had extremely positive views of Jesus, while others have strongly identified as Christian, such as Larry Norman, U2, and many others. Bob Dylan had his Christian conversion and his gospel albums. In 1997, Dylan also said this:

> Here's the thing with me and the religious thing. This is the flat-out truth: I find the religiosity and philosophy in the music. I don't find it anywhere else. Songs like "Let Me Rest on a Peaceful Mountain" or "I Saw the Light"—that's my religion.[6]

Even the oft-acerbic Lou Reed's last words on his deathbed were, "Take me into the light!" To that, friend and writer Michael Azzerrad noted, "I think maybe the guy knew it all along."[7] To the more extreme religious hardliner, of course, this will not spare a rocker from eternal damnation. That is just the risk the rocker takes.

Finally, to further reconcile the rebellious nature of rock and roll with establishment morality, it may be helpful to look to something often seen as central to the traditional establishment moral perspective: family relations or "family values."

Rock's sometimes reckless dynamics can indeed run counter to basic moral guideposts that help to form a bedrock of healthy familial and social structures. Rock's inherently freewheeling nature definitely makes it highly imperfect (or "perfectly imperfect," as Sam Phillips put it[8]). Over the years, however, the parental generation, imperfect themselves, have sometimes crossed lines and enforced unjust and irrational rules. That is, notions of morality have sometimes been seen as being twisted by authority figures to justify some ugly behaviors. Thus, to the rocker, the "honor" in "Honor thy father and mother" need not be understood as treating parents and a parental generation with *blind obedience* but with some basic level of *decency* and respect. In some cases, rebellion has absolutely been the most rational of choices. To otherwise read "honor" as blind obedience means that at times even the objectively very worst of authoritative decisions will be presented as akin to being the word of God, and that is clearly a problem.

As part of the arc of Western civilization, rock has not been a cure all, nor has it necessarily provided a clear blueprint for the future. But it has been a highly positive development. It's just that freedoms are messy. The only thing certain in life is that human imperfection will be a part of the process.

In sum, rock and roll has thus provided a soundtrack to the lives of millions but also helped people of the West and the world in navigating all sorts of struggles, for better and for worse but mostly for the better. Rock music and the spirit that it taps into can continue to benefit anyone who feels trapped in their life, whether by a rigid status quo or any other oppressive form of authority. Rock and roll can provide the inspiration to create a new way of living, if, of course, one is ready to take a bold risk, have some faith, and really *feel* it.

Chapter Notes

Epigraphs

1. Maureen Cleave, "How Does a Beatle Live? John Lennon Lives like This," *London Evening Standard*, March 4, 1966, 10.
2. Martin Huxley, "Aerosmith: The Fall and the Rise of Rock's Greatest Band," in *Aerosmith: The Fall and the Rise of Rock's Greatest Band* (New York: St. Martin's, 1995), 171.
3. Martha Bayles, *Hole in Our Soul: The Loss of Beauty and Meaning in American Popular Music* (Chicago: University of Chicago Press, 1996), 236n67.
4. David Leaf, dir., *The Night James Brown Saved Boston* (Shout Factory, 2008).
5. Bob Spitz, *The Beatles: The Biography* (New York: Little, Brown, 2005), 25.

Chapter 1

1. Alexis de Tocqueville, *Democracy in America*, ed. Harvey Claflin Mansfield (Chicago: University of Chicago Press, 2000), 184.
2. James A. Cosby, *Devil's Music, Holy Rollers and Hillbillies: How America Gave Birth to Rock and Roll* (Jefferson, NC: McFarland, 2016).
3. William Strauss and Neil Howe, "The New Generation Gap," *The Atlantic*, August 15, 2017, https://www.theatlantic.com/magazine/archive/1992/12/the-new-generation-gap/536934/.
4. Graham Lock, "The Fall Land on Their Feet," *New Music Express*, March 24, 1979, 37.
5. Robin Weiss, "The 'Rules' of Psychotherapy," *New York Times*, November 22, 2014, https://opinionator.blogs.nytimes.com/2014/11/22/the-rules-of-psychotherapy/.
6. Peter Guralnick, *Lost Highway: Journeys and Arrivals of American Musicians* (New York: Back Bay Books, 2012), 335; "American Masters: Good Rockin' Tonight: The Legacy of Sun Records," Episode 16, no. 5, PBS, November 28, 2001.
7. Gwar, YouTube channel, accessed November 27, 2020, https://www.youtube.com/channel/UCJF9MkMFCglAnMTts8dy3_Q.
8. Suzanne Raga, "13 Variations on 'Sex, Drugs, and Rock 'n' Roll' from around the World," Mental Floss, April 4, 2016, https://www.mentalfloss.com/article/77888/13-variations-sex-drugs-and-rock-n-roll-around-world. ("The first identified use of the phrase as we know it was in a 1969 LIFE magazine piece, which declared, 'The counter culture has its sacraments in sex, drugs and rock.' Two years later, a writer for the Spectator, a British magazine, also attempted to wrap his head around 'kids these days,' saying, 'Not for nothing is the youth culture characterized by sex, drugs and rock 'n' roll.'" A modern update of "wine, women, and song.")
9. Brian P. Conniff, "The Enduring Catholic Imagination of Bruce Springsteen," *America*, April 19, 2018, https://www.americamagazine.org/arts-culture/2018/04/18/enduring-catholic-imagination-bruce-springsteen.
10. "Heartland Rock Music Artists," AllMusic, accessed November 27, 2020, https://www.allmusic.com/subgenre/heartland-rock-ma0000012246/artists; Bruce Springsteen, *Hammersmith Odeon*,

London '75, liner notes (New York: Legacy Recordings, 2006), CD & DVD.
  11. "R.E.M. Biography, Songs, & Albums," AllMusic, https://www.allmusic.com/artist/rem-mn0000325459/biography.
  12. "U2—I Still Haven't Found What I'm Looking For," Genius, accessed November 27, 2020, https://genius.com/U2-i-still-havent-found-what-im-looking-for-lyrics.
  13. Richard Milner, "The Truth about the Christian Background of U2," Grunge, April 26, 2022, https://www.grunge.com/844162/the-truth-about-the-christian-background-of-u2/.
  14. Cosby, *Devil's Music*, 198–99.
  15. Michael T. Bertrand, *Race, Rock, and Elvis* (Urbana: University of Illinois Press, 2005), 16.
  16. David Willey, "Vatican 'Forgives' John Lennon," BBC News, November 22, 2008.
  17. Cosby, *Devil's Music*, 3.
  18. Victor Bockris, *Transformer: The Lou Reed Story* (London: Harper, 2014), 177.

Chapter 2

  1. Quoted in Eric Frederick Goldman, *The Crucial Decade: America, 1945–1955* (New York: Knopf, 1956), 218.
  2. Quoted in Goldman, *The Crucial Decade*, 218.
  3. Matthew 5:39 and 5:44.
  4. Albert Einstein, interview with Alfred Werner, *Liberal Judaism 16* (April–May 1949), as cited in Ralph Keyes, *The Quote Verifier: Who Said What, Where, and When* (New York: St. Martin's, 2006), 284.
  5. *The Atomic Café* (London: New Video Group, 2002) [DVD].
  6. David Mikkelson. "Who Was the First TV Couple to Sleep in the Same Bed?" Snopes, September 22, 2022, https://www.snopes.com/fact-check/early-to-bed/.
  7. Peter Conrad and Joseph W. Schneider, *Deviance and Medicalization: From Badness to Sickness* (St. Louis: Mosby, 1980), 61.
  8. Molly Wellmann, *Handcrafted Cocktails the Mixologist's Guide to Classic Drinks for Morning, Noon & Night* (Cincinnati: F.W. Media, 2013), 59; E. Freye, *Pharmacology and Abuse of Cocaine, Methamphetamines, Ecstasy and Related Designer Drugs: A Comprehensive Review on Their Mode of Action, Treatment of Abuse and Intoxication* (Dordrecht: Springer, 2009), 112.
  9. W.J. Rorabaugh, *American Hippies* (Cambridge: Cambridge University Press, 2015), 15–16.
  10. Michael Watts, "John Peel: 'If Something Has Me Confused, I Want to Play It on the Radio,'" *The Guardian*, September 30, 2015, https://www.theguardian.com/music/2015/sep/30/john-peel-1971-interview-melody-maker-michael-watts-rocks-backpages.
  11. Cosby, *Devil's Music*.
  12. Glenn C. Altschuler, *All Shook Up: How Rock 'n' Roll Changed America* (Oxford: Oxford University Press, 2003), 23.
  13. Cosby, *Devil's Music*, 128–29.
  14. Cosby, *Devil's Music*, 137–41.
  15. "Western Swing," *Encyclopædia Britannica*, accessed November 27, 2020, https://www.britannica.com/art/Western-swing; "Honky Tonk Music Genre Overview," AllMusic, accessed November 27, 2020, https://www.allmusic.com/style/honky-tonk-ma0000002648; "Bluegrass," *Encyclopædia Britannica*, accessed November 27, 2020, https://www.britannica.com/art/bluegrass-music.
  16. Cosby, *Devil's Music*.
  17. Bertrand, *Race, Rock, and Elvis*, 153.
  18. Cosby, *Devil's Music*, 159.
  19. Peter Guralnick, *Last Train to Memphis* (New York: Black Bay Books, 1995), 75.
  20. Cosby, *Devil's Music*, 147.
  21. Cosby, *Devil's Music*, 147.
  22. Cosby, *Devil's Music*, 135.
  23. "Billy Haley," AllMusic, https://www.allmusic.com/artist/bill-haley-mn0000077870/biography.
  24. Cosby, *Devil's Music*, 151.
  25. Guralnick, *Last Train to Memphis*, 400.
  26. "1950s: TV and Radio," Encyclopedia.com, accessed November 27, 2020, https://www.encyclopedia.com/history/culture-magazines/1950s-tv-and-radio; Altschuler, *All Shook Up*, 91.
  27. Altschuler, *All Shook Up*, 6.
  28. Altschuler, *All Shook Up*, 6.
  29. Jason Ankeny, "Pat Boone," All Music, accessed November 27, 2020, http://www.allmusic.com/artist/pat-boone-mn0000131681/biography.

30. Altschuler, *All Shook Up*, 77.
31. James Baldwin and Esquire Editors, "James Baldwin: How to Cool It," *Esquire*, October 9, 2017, https://www.esquire.com/news-politics/a23960/james-baldwin-cool-it/.
32. Dave Laing, "Sam Phillips," *The Guardian*, July 31, 2003, http://www.theguardian.com/news/2003/aug/01/guardianobituaries.artsobituaries.
33. Guralnick, *Lost Highway*, 330.
34. Cosby, *Devil's Music*, 169–71.
35. Cosby, *Devil's Music*, 139.
36. Rob Bowman et al., *According to the Rolling Stones* (London: Phoenix, 2013), 15.
37. Altschuler, *All Shook Up*, 131n1.
38. Cosby, *Devil's Music*, 195.
39. Cosby, *Devil's Music*, 201.
40. Cosby, *Devil's Music*, 24.
41. Rorabaugh, *American Hippies*, 32.
42. Ankeny, "Pat Boone."
43. Bruce Weber, "TV Emperor of Rock 'n' Roll and New Year's Eve Dies at 82," *New York Times*, April 18, 2012.
44. Altschuler, *All Shook Up*, 114.
45. Altschuler, *All Shook Up*, 77.
46. Cosby, *Devil's Music*, 24.
47. "Phil Spector," AllMusic, accessed December 17, 2020, https://www.allmusic.com/artist/phil-spector-mn0000694967/biography.
48. Robert Pattison, *The Triumph of Vulgarity: Rock Music in the Mirror of Romanticism* (Oxford: Oxford University Press, 1997), 195.

Chapter 3

1. Rorabaugh, *American Hippies*, 32.
2. Kim Newman, *Wild West Movies: Or How the West Was Found, Won, Lost, Lied about, Filmed and Forgotten* (New York: Bloomsbury, 1990).
3. Stephen Kiss, "On TV Westerns of the 1950s and '60s," New York Public Library, December 1, 2012, https://www.nypl.org/blog/2012/12/01/tv-westerns-1950s-and-60s; Rorabaugh, *American Hippies*, 35.
4. John Robert Greene, *America in the Sixties* (New York: Syracuse University Press, 2010).
5. Greene, *America in the Sixties*, 25.
6. Greene, *America in the Sixties*, 99.
7. Greene, *America in the Sixties*, 30.
8. "Bay of Pigs," Encyclopedia.com, https://www.encyclopedia.com/history/latin-america-and-caribbean/cuban-history/bay-pigs.
9. Department of State, Office of the Historian, "The Cuban Missile Crisis, October 1962," accessed November 27, 2020, https://history.state.gov/milestones/1961-1968/cuban-missile-crisis.
10. Department of State, Office of the Historian, "The Cuban Missile Crisis, October 1962," accessed November 27, 2020, https://history.state.gov/milestones/1961-1968/cuban-missile-crisis.
11. Rorabaugh, *American Hippies*, 17.
12. Rorabaugh, *American Hippies*, 17.
13. Rorabaugh, *American Hippies*, 17.
14. Rorabaugh, *American Hippies*, 17.
15. Rorabaugh, *American Hippies*, 20.
16. Rorabaugh, *American Hippies*, 20.
17. Rorabaugh, *American Hippies*, 20.
18. David Lance Goines, *The Free Speech Movement: Coming of Age in the 1960's* (Berkeley: Ten Speed Press, 1993), 49.
19. Greene, *Life in America during the 1960s*, 74–76.
20. Clayborne Carson and David L. Lewis, "Martin Luther King, Jr.," *Encyclopaedia Britannica*, accessed November 27, 2020, https://www.britannica.com/biography/Martin-Luther-King-Jr.
21. Clayborne Carson and David L. Lewis, "Martin Luther King, Jr.," *Encyclopaedia Britannica*, accessed November 27, 2020, https://www.britannica.com/biography/Martin-Luther-King-Jr.
22. Martin Luther King, Jr., "I Have a Dream," American Rhetoric, accessed November 27, 2020, http://www.americanrhetoric.com/speeches/mlkihaveadream.htm.
23. Greene, *Life in America during the 1960s*, 43–47.
24. Malcolm X, "I Have a Nightmare (I Charge the White Man)," Genius, https://genius.com/Malcolm-x-i-have-a-nightmare-i-charge-the-white-man-annotated.
25. Rorabaugh, *American Hippies*, 109.
26. Rorabaugh, *American Hippies*, 32.
27. Rorabaugh, *American Hippies*, 91.
28. Rorabaugh, *American Hippies*, 91.
29. Shaunacy Ferro, "Did Penicillin Kickstart the Sexual Revolution?" *Popular Science*, January 28, 2013, accessed

November 27, 2020, https://www.popsci.com/science/article/2013-01/did-penicillin-kickstart-sexual-revolution/; Rorabaugh, *American Hippies*, 91.
30. Rorabaugh, *American Hippies*, 18.
31. War Graves Commission, *Annual Report 2014–2015*, accessed November 27, 2020, https://issuu.com/wargravescommission/docs/ar_2014-2015?e=4065448/31764375.
32. Derek Brown, "1963: The Profumo Scandal," *The Guardian*, April 10, 2001, https://www.theguardian.com/politics/2001/apr/10/past.derekbrown.
33. http://www.edwardianteddyboy.com/.
34. "Teddy Boys: Britain's Original Teenage Subculture," Huck Magazine, accessed November 27, 2020, http://www.huckmagazine.com/art-andculture/photography-2/teddy-boys-britains original-teenage-subculture.
35. The Edwardian Teddy Boy—Notting Hill Teddy Boys 1955, accessed February 13, 2023, http://www.edwardianteddyboy.com/page12.html.
36. The Edwardian Teddy Boy—Notting Hill Teddy Boys 1955.
37. The Edwardian Teddy Boy—Notting Hill Teddy Boys 1955.
38. "Angry Young Men," *Encyclopaedia Britannica*, accessed November 27, 2020, https://www.britannica.com/topic/Angry-Young-Men.
39. Brown, "1963: The Profumo Scandal."
40. "Lady Chatterley's Lover: A Raunchy Rival to Poldark," *The Guardian*, September 6, 2015, https://www.theguardian.com/tv-and-radio/shortcuts/2015/sep/06/how-raunchy-is-lady-chatterleys-lover.
41. Brown, "1963: The Profumo Scandal."
42. Fleix Allen, "What Was the Profumo Affair and What Did Lord Denning's Inquiry into the Scandal Reveal?" *The Sun*, December 18, 2019, https://www.thesun.co.uk/news/4730042/profumo-affair-john-profumo-lord-denning-inquiry-scandal.
43. Allen, "What Was the Profumo Affair?"
44. Accessed November 27, 2020, http://www.churchsociety.org/issues_new/church/stats/iss_church_stats_attendance.asp#Sources; accessed November 27, 2020, http://www.christian-research.org/anglican-uk/anglican-england.html; "Statistics," Latin Mass Society, accessed November 27, 2020, https://lms.org.uk/statistics.
45. Keith Richards, *Life* (London: Weidenfeld & Nicolson, 2010), 31.

Chapter 4

1. Paul Du Noyer, *Liverpool—Wondrous Place: From the Cavern to the Capital of Culture* (London: Virgin Publishing, 2012), 1.
2. "*Time* 100," accessed November 27, 2020, http://205.188.238.181/time100/artists/profile/beatles.html.
3. Jonathan Gould, *Can't Buy Me Love: The Beatles, Britain, and America* (New York: Crown, 2008), 214.
4. Gary Trust, "We're No. 1! 'Billboard #1 Gospel Hits' Debuts atop Gospel Albums Chart," *Billboard*, January 22, 2015, https://www.billboard.com/music/the-beatles/chart-history/billboard-200.
5. Dirk Dunbar, *Renewing the Balance* (Parker, CO: Outskirts Press, 2017), 169.
6. Spitz, *The Beatles*, 15.
7. Spitz, *The Beatles*, 18.
8. Spitz, *The Beatles*, 15.
9. Gould, *Can't Buy Me Love*, 41, 127.
10. Stephen Guy, "Fun and Fear," Liverpool Museums Blog, accessed November 27, 2020, http://blog.liverpoolmuseums.org.uk/2010/02/fun-and-fear.
11. Gould, *Can't Buy Me Love*, 43.
12. Mark Lewisohn, *Tune In. The Beatles: All These Years* (New York: Crown Archetype, 2013), 33.
13. Bayles, *Hole in Our Soul*, 168.
14. Spitz, *The Beatles*, 26, 21.
15. Spitz, *The Beatles*, 25.
16. Spitz, *The Beatles*, 29.
17. Spitz, *The Beatles*, 28.
18. Spitz, *The Beatles*, 21.
19. Spitz, *The Beatles*, 19.
20. David Sheff, interview with John Lennon and Yoko Ono, *Playboy*, January 1981, https://www.playboy.com/read/john-lennon-yoko-ono-interview/.
21. Lewisohn, *Tune-In*, 111, 115.
22. The Beatles, *The Beatles Anthology* (New York: Chronicle Books, 2000), 13.
23. Bruce Eder, "Lonnie Donegan Biography," AllMusic, accessed November 27,

2020, https://www.allmusic.com/artist/lonnie-donegan-mn0000277549/biography.
24. Spitz, *The Beatles*, 112.
25. Spitz, *The Beatles*, 85.
26. Spitz, *The Beatles*, 40–41.
27. Spitz, The Beatles, 90–91.
28. Barry Miles, *Paul McCartney: Many Years from Now* (New York: Holt Paperbacks, 1998), 21.
29. Miles, *Paul McCartney*, 538.
30. Spitz, *The Beatles*, 34.
31. Spitz, *The Beatles*, 34.
32. Lewisohn, *Tune-In*, 220 [Berry], 131 [audition], 650 [Robinson and Motown].
33. Lewisohn, *Tune-In*, 11–12 [Everlys, Holly], 408 [Brill Building].
34. Spitz, *The Beatles*, 148.
35. "Paul McCartney Reacts to BTS Singing 'Hey Jude,'" *The Late Show with Stephen Colbert*, accessed November 27, 2020, https://www.youtube.com/watch?v=475Yc5YlqAU&t=315s; Spitz, *The Beatles*, 147.
36. *Fresh Air*, October 8, 2010.
37. *Fresh Air*, October 8, 2010.
38. Philip Norman, *John Lennon: The Life* (New York: Anchor, 2009), 120.
39. Norman, *John Lennon*, 120.
40. Mark Lewisohn, *The Complete Beatles Chronicle* (Nevada City, CA: Harmony Books, 1992), 18.
41. Spitz, *The Beatles*, 207.
42. Spitz, *The Beatles*, 198.
43. Spitz, *The Beatles*, 305.
44. Lewisohn, *Tune-In*, 398.
45. Lewisohn, *Tune-In*, 221–22.
46. Spitz, *The Beatles*, 209.
47. Spitz, *The Beatles*, 217.
48. "It's Been a Hard Day's Hamburg," *The Independent*, June 13, 2009, https://www.independent.ie/entertainment/music/its-been-a-hard-days-hamburg-26543444.html.
49. Mark-Lewisohn-The-Complete-Beatles-Recording-Sessions-1988-pdf.
50. Mark Lewisohn, *The Complete Beatles Recording Sessions: The Official Story of the Abbey Road Years 1962–1970* (London: Octopus Publishing, 2018), 6.
51. Gould, *Can't Buy Me Love*, 168.
52. Gould, *Can't Buy Me Love*, 168.
53. Dirk Dunbar, "The Evolution of Rock and Roll: Its Religious and Ecological Themes," *Journal of Religion and Popular Culture* 2, no. 1 (2002).
54. Gould, *Can't Buy Me Love*, 215.
55. Spitz, *The Beatles*, 63.
56. The Beatles, *The Beatles Anthology*, 105.
57. Accessed November 27, 2020, http://www.edsullivan.com/artists/the-beatles.
58. Spitz, *The Beatles*, 460.
59. Norman, *John Lennon*, 319.
60. The Beatles, "Adelaide," accessed November 27, 2020, https://www.thebeatles.com/story-tags/adelaide.
61. Spitz, *The Beatles*, 584.
62. Dunbar, *Renewing the Balance*, 169.
63. Accessed November 27, 2020, http://content.time.com/time/covers/0,16641,19660415,00.html.
64. Spitz, *The Beatles*, 544.
65. Bob Dylan, *Chronicles, Vol. 1* (New York: Simon & Schuster, 2005), 28.
66. Dylan, *Chronicles, Vol. 1*, 98.
67. Edna Gundersen, "Dylan Is Positively on top of His Game," *USA Today*, September 10, 2001.
68. Hardeep Phull, *Story behind the Protest Song: A Reference Guide to the 50 Songs That Changed the 20th Century* (Santa Barbara: Greenwood, 2008), 30.
69. Quoted in John Bauldie's sleeve notes for *The Bootleg Series Volumes 1–3 (Rare & Unreleased) 1961–1991*, https://www.npr.org/2000/10/21/1112840/blowin-in-the-wind; Andry Greene, "50 Years Ago Today: Bob Dylan Premiered 'Blowin' in the Wind,'" *Rolling Stone*, April 16, 2012, https://www.rollingstone.com/music/music-news/50-years-ago-today-bob-dylan-premiered-blowin-in-the-wind-201983/.
70. Brian Naylor, "'Blowin' in the Wind' Still Asks the Hard Questions," NPR, October 21, 2000, https://www.npr.org/2000/10/21/1112840/blowin-in-the-wind.
71. John Bush, "Blowin' in the Wind by Bob Dylan—Track Info," AllMusic, accessed February 13, 2023, https://www.allmusic.com/song/blowin-in-the-wind-mt0013150448.
72. Ezekiel 12:1–2.
73. Naylor, "'Blowin' in the Wind' Still Asks the Hard Questions."
74. Philip Pullulla, "Pope Opposed Bob Dylan Singing to John Paul in 1997," *Reuters*, March 8, 2007, https://www.reuters.com/article/us-pope-dylan/pope-opposed-bob-dylan-singing-to-john-paul-in-1997-idUSL0862623620070309.
75. Spitz, *The Beatles*, 534.
76. Aristotle, *Metaphysics*, Book I,

Chapter II, Internet Classics Archive, http://classics.mit.edu//aristotle/metaphysics.html [Aristotle]; C. G. Jung, *Letters of C. G. Jung: Volume I, 1906–1950*, 31 [Jung]; and 2 Corinthians 13:5.

77. Dunbar, *Renewing the Balance*, 170.

78. Milak Gilmore, "Beatles' Acid Test: How LSD Opened the Door to 'Revolver,'" *Rolling Stone*, August 25, 2016, https://www.rollingstone.com/music/music-news/beatles-acid-test-how-lsd-opened-the-door-to-revolver-251417/.

79. Rorabaugh, *American Hippies*, 52.

80. Stephen Thomas Erlewine, "Bringing It All Back Home—Bob Dylan: Songs, Reviews, Credits," AllMusic, accessed February 13, 2023, https://www.allmusic.com/album/mw0000193642/Overview.

81. Paul Williams, *Bob Dylan Performing Artist: The Early Years 1960–1973* (San Francisco: Underwood Miller, 1990), 131–32.

82. Bob Dylan, *Chronicles*, Vol. 1, 90.

83. Gerard Herzhaft, "Catfish Blues," in *Encyclopedia of the Blues* (Fayetteville: University of Arkansas Press, 1992), 442; Alan Lomax, *The Land Where the Blues Began* (York, UK: Methuen, 1993), 410.

84. "500 Greatest Songs of All Time," *Rolling Stone*, September 15, 2021, https://www.rollingstone.com/music/music-lists/500-greatest-songs-of-all-time-151127/bob-dylan-like-a-rolling-stone-2-54028/.

85. "Eddie Sedgwick," Biography, accessed November 27, 2020, https://www.biography.com/personality/edie-sedgwick.

86. Hank Kalet, "Bob Dylan: Highway 61 Revisited," Pop Matters, February 6, 2004, https://www.popmatters.com/dylanbob-highway61mft-2495871353.html.

87. Sol Stern, "Sorry, Jann Wenner, Rock 'n' Roll Didn't Make Us Free," *Daily Beast*, October 29, 2017, https://www.thedailybeast.com/sorry-jann-wenner-rock-n-roll-didnt-make-us-free?source=TDB&via=FB_Page.

88. Stanley Booth, *The True Adventures of the Rolling Stones* (Chicago: Chicago Review Press, 2000), 5.

89. Accessed November 27, 2020, http://www.liverpoolmuseums.org.uk/maritime/exhibitions/blitz/blitz.asp.

90. Adam Edwards, "RIP Jumping Jack Flash Senior," *The Telegraph*, November 14, 2006, http://www.telegraph.co.uk/culture/music/rockandjazzmusic/3656537/RIP-Jumping-Jack-Flash-senior.html.

91. Edwards, "RIP Jumping Jack Flash Senior."

92. Edwards, "RIP Jumping Jack Flash Senior."

93. Edwards, "RIP Jumping Jack Flash Senior."

94. Booth, *The True Adventures of the Rolling Stones*, 5.

95. Booth, *The True Adventures of the Rolling Stones*, 5.

96. Victor Bockris, *Keith Richards: The Biography* (Boston: Da Capo, 2003), 20.

97. Bockris, *Keith Richards*, 20.

98. Bockris, *Keith Richards*, 18.

99. Booth, *The True Adventures of the Rolling Stones*, 12.

100. Booth, *The True Adventures of the Rolling Stones*, 13.

101. Richards, *Life*, 77–78.

102. Richards, *Life*, 77–78.

103. Booth, *The True Adventures of the Rolling Stones*, 54.

104. Mick Jagger et al., *According to the Rolling Stones* (San Francisco: Chronicle Books, 2003), 15.

105. Bockris, *Keith Richards*, 46.

106. Bockris, *Keith Richards*, 160.

107. "Brian Jones," *Rolling Stones*, accessed November 27, 2020, http://www.rollingstones.com/artist/brian-jones.

108. Booth, *The True Adventures of the Rolling Stones*, 19.

109. Jagger et al., *According to the Rolling Stones*, 50.

110. *Life* 127, Jann S. Wenner, "John Lennon: The Rolling Stone Interview, Part One," *Rolling Stone*, January 21, 1972, https://www.rollingstone.com/music/music-news/john-lennon-the-rolling-stone-interview-part-one-160194.

111. Jagger et al., *According to the Rolling Stones*, 41.

112. Jagger et al., *According to the Rolling Stones*, 62.

113. Jagger et al., *According to the Rolling Stones*, 25.

114. Jagger et al., *According to the Rolling Stones*, 107.

115. Steve Appleford, *Rolling Stones: It's Only Rock and Roll, Song by Song* (Collingdale, PA: Diane, 1997), 12.

116. Appleford, *Rolling Stones*, 29.

117. Geoffrey Giuliano, *Behind Blue*

Eyes: The Life of Pete Townshend (Lanham, MD: Cooper Square Press, 2002), 37.

118. Ira A. Robins, "The Who," *Encyclopaedia Britannica*, accessed November 27, 2020, https://www.britannica.com/topic/the-Who#ref667143.

119. Robins, "The Who."

Chapter 5

1. Greene, *Life in America during the 1960s*, 125.

2. Greene, *Life in America during the 1960s*, 14.

3. "Nazis Take Czechoslovakia," History.com, accessed November 27, 2020, https://www.history.com/this-day-in-history/nazis-take-czechoslovakia.

4. "Battlefield Vietnam," PBS, accessed November 27, 2020, https://www.pbs.org/battlefieldvietnam/history.

5. "LBJ," PBS, accessed November 27, 2020, http://www.pbs.org/wgbh/americanexperience/features/primary-resources/lbj-michigan.

6. "Goldwater Suggests Using Atomic Weapons," History.com, accessed November 27, 2020, http://www.history.com/this-day-in-history/goldwater-suggests-using-atomic-weapons.

7. "Gulf of Tonkin," History.com, accessed November 27, 2020, https://www.history.com/topics/vietnam-war/gulf-of-tonkin-resolution-1.

8. Greene, *Life in America during the 1960s*, 124.

9. "Battlefield Vietnam," PBS.

10. Greene, *Life in America during the 1960s*, 126.

11. Accessed November 27, 2020, http://www.vietnamgear.com/war1965.aspx; accessed November 27, 2020, http://www.americanwarlibrary.com/vietnam/vwatl.htm.

12. Charles Perry, *The Haight-Ashbury: A History* (New York: Wenner Books, 2005), 49.

13. "Vietnam," *Encyclopaedia Britannica*, accessed January 12, 2023, https://www.encyclopedia.com/history/encyclopedias-almanacs-transcripts-and-maps/american-soldier-vietnam.

14. Accessed November 27, 2020, https://brookfieldinstitute.org/viet-nam; Christian G. Appy, *Working-Class War: American Combat Soldiers and Vietnam* (Salem: University of North Carolina Press, 1993), 19; accessed November 27, 2020, http://michiganintheworld.history.lsa.umich.edu/antivietnamwar/exhibits/show/exhibit/draft_protests/the-military-draft-during-the-.

15. Zach Schonfeld, "How Creedence Clearwater Revival Became the Soundtrack to Every Vietnam Movie," Pitchfork, February 20, 2018, https://pitchfork.com/thepitch/how-creedence-clearwater-revival-became-the-soundtrack-to-every-vietnam-movie.

16. John Fogerty, "John Fogerty Shares Inspiration behind 'Fortunate Son,'" May 8, 2013, https://www.youtube.com/watch?time_continue=1&v=6g9wY9L-PwM.

17. Fogerty, "John Fogerty Shares Inspiration."

18. Fogerty, "John Fogerty Shares Inspiration."

19. Fogerty, "John Fogerty Shares Inspiration."

20. Katherine Q. Seeyle, "Cheney's Five Draft Deferments during the Vietnam Era Emerge as a Campaign Issue," *New York Times*, May 1, 2004, http://www.nytimes.com/2004/05/01/us/2004-campaign-military-service-cheney-s-five-draft-deferments-during-vietnam-era.html; accessed November 27, 2020, http://thehill.com/blogs/ballot-box/presidential-races/290105-trump-got-five-draft; Randall Chase, "Biden Deferred, Disqualified from Vietnam Duty," SFGate, September 1, 2008, https://www.sfgate.com/news/article/Biden-deferred-disqualified-from-Vietnam-duty-3196927.php-deferments-during-vietnam.

21. David Lauter, "Clinton Releases '69 Letter on ROTC and Draft Status," *LA Times*, February 13, 1992, http://articles.latimes.com/1992-02-13/news/mn-2993_1_vietnam-war/2; Steven M. Gillon, *The Pact: Bill Clinton, Newt Gingrich, and the Rivalry that Defined a Generation* (Oxford: Oxford University Press, 2008), 21.

22. George Lardner, Jr., and Lois Romano, "At Height of Vietnam, Bush Picks Guard," *Washington Post*, July 28, 1999, https://www.washingtonpost.com/wp-srv/politics/campaigns/wh2000/stories/bush072899.htm.

23. Seeyle, "Cheney's Five Draft

Deferments"; Chase, "Biden Deferred, Disqualified from Vietnam Duty."

24. Eric Schechter, "How I Got out of the Vietnam Draft—And Why That Still Matters," *Time*, September 16, 2014, https://time.com/3378546/vietnam-draft.

25. Greene, *Life in America during the 1960s*, 59.

26. Greene, *Life in America during the 1960s*, 57.

27. "Selma to Montgomery March," History.com, accessed November 27, 2020, http://www.history.com/topics/black-history/selma-montgomery-march.

28. Greene, *Life in America during the 1960s*, 108–9.

29. Greene, *Life in America during the 1960s*, 108–9.

30. "How Did the Vietnam War Affect America," accessed November 27, 2020, https://thevietnamwar.info/how-vietnam-war-affect-america.

31. Greene, *Life in America during the 1960s*, 108.

32. "Mario Savio," American Rhetoric, accessed November 27, 2020, https://www.americanrhetoric.com/speeches/mariosaviosproulhallsitin.htm.

33. Accessed November 27, 2020, https://freespeech.berkeley.edu/timeline.

34. Perry, *The Haight-Ashbury*, 103.

Chapter 6

1. Jack Kerouac, "About the Beat Generation," 1957, published as "Aftermath: The Philosophy of the Beat Generation," *Esquire*, March 1958; accessed November 27, 2020 ["weary"], https://www.britannica.com/art/Beat-movement.

2. Rorabaugh, *American Hippies*, 22.

3. Rorabaugh, *American Hippies*, 29; Jesse Hamlin, "How Herb Caen Named a Generation," SFGate, November 26, 1995, https://web.archive.org/web/20140808044256/http://www.sfgate.com/entertainment/article/HOW-HERB-CAEN-NAMED-A-GENERATION-3018725.php.

4. Stephen Prothero, "On the Holy Road: The Beat Movement as Spiritual Protest," *Harvard Theological Review* 84, no. 2 (April 1991).

5. Rorabaugh, *American Hippies*, 26.

6. Rorabaugh, *American Hippies*, 24.

7. Rorabaugh, *American Hippies*, 25.

8. Rorabaugh, *American Hippies*, 26.

9. Rorabaugh, *American Hippies*, 3.

10. Rorabaugh, *American Hippies*, 28.

11. Rorabaugh, *American Hippies*, 29.

12. Rorabaugh, *American Hippies*, 3.

13. Bob Dylan, quoted in John W. Whitehead, *Grasping for the Wind: The Search for Meaning in the 20th Century* (Grand Rapids: Zondervan, 2001).

14. David Fear, "Sundance 2017: Grateful Dead Doc 'Long Strange Trip' Is Heartbreaking Tribute," *Rolling Stone*, January 24, 2017, https://www.rollingstone.com/movies/movie-news/sundance-2017-grateful-dead-doc-long-strange-trip-is-heartbreaking-tribute-113939/.

15. Alice Echols, *Scars of Sweet Paradise: The Life and Times of Janis Joplin* (New York: Picador, 2000), 68.

16. Echols, *Scars of Sweet Paradise*, 18–19.

17. Joseph A. Rodriguez, *City against Suburb: The Culture Wars in an American Metropolis* (Westport, CT: Praeger, 1999), 40.

18. "Allen Cohen and the S.F. Oracle," accessed November 27, 2020, http://www.rockument.com/blog/haight-ashbury-in-the-sixties/allen-cohen-and-the-s-f-oracle.

19. Rorabaugh, *American Hippies*, 4.

20. Perry, *The Haight-Ashbury*, 5.

21. Rorabaugh, *American Hippies*, 6.

22. Rorabaugh, *American Hippies*, 6–10.

23. Rorabaugh, *American Hippies*, 6–10.

24. Rorabaugh, *American Hippies*, 10.

25. Rorabaugh, *American Hippies*, 9.

26. Rorabaugh, *American Hippies*, 2, 100.

27. Rorabaugh, *American Hippies*, 9.

28. Rorabaugh, *American Hippies*, 11.

29. Perry, *The Haight-Ashbury*, 72–73.

30. A. M. White et al., "Using Death Certificates to Explore Changes in Alcohol-Related Mortality in the United States, 1999–2017," *Alcoholism: Clinical and Experimental Research* 44, no. 1 (2020).

31. Rorabaugh, *American Hippies*, 50; Joshua Clark Davis, "The Business of Getting High: Head Shops, Countercultural Capitalism, and the Marijuana Legalization Movement," *The Sixties: A Journal of Politics, Culture and Society* 8, no. 1 (2015).

32. Perry, *The Haight-Ashbury*, 72–73.
33. Perry, *The Haight-Ashbury*, 246.
34. Rorabaugh, *American Hippies*, 38.
35. Albert Hofmann, *LSD: My Problem Child* (Oxford: Oxford University Press, 2018), 15.
36. Albert Hofmann, "LSD—My Problem Child," accessed November 27, 2020, https://www.hallucinogens.org/hofmann/child1.htm.
37. Rorabaugh, *American Hippies*, 38.
38. Maia Szalavitz, "The Legacy of the CIA's Secret LSD Experiments on America," *Time*, March 23, 2012, http://healthland.time.com/2012/03/23/the-legacy-of-the-cias-secret-lsd-experiments-on-america.
39. Amanda Fielding, "Celebrating Bicycle Day," Oxford University Press Blog, April 19, 2013, https://blog.oup.com/2013/04/bicycle-day-lsd-albert-hoffman.
40. Perry, *The Haight-Ashbury*, 250.
41. Daniel Wacker et al., "Crystal Structure of an LSD-Bound Human Serotonin Receptor," *Cell*, January 26, 2017, https://www.cell.com/cell/fulltext/S0092-8674(16)31749-4.
42. https://www.britannica.com/science/cocaine; https://www.britannica.com/science/heroin.
43. Carl Jung, *Man and His Symbols* (New York: Dell Publishing Co., 1968).
44. Rorabaugh, *American Hippies*, 44.
45. Rorabaugh, *American Hippies*, 39.
46. Rorabaugh, *American Hippies*, 39.
47. Rorabaugh, *American Hippies*, 41.
48. Rorabaugh, *American Hippies*, 42.
49. Rorabaugh, *American Hippies*, 42.
50. Rorabaugh, *American Hippies*, 42.
51. Perry, *The Haight-Ashbury*, 119.
52. Rorabaugh, *American Hippies*, 45–46.
53. Rorabaugh, *American Hippies*, 49.

Chapter 7

1. Perry, *The Haight-Ashbury*, 259.
2. Rorabaugh, *American Hippies*, 14.
3. Richie Unterberger. "The Charlatans," AllMusic, accessed November 27, 2020, https://www.allmusic.com/artist/the-charlatans-mn0000805332/biography.
4. Rorabaugh, *American Hippies*, 46.
5. Rorabaugh, *American Hippies*, 44.
6. Rorabaugh, *American Hippies*, 51.
7. Perry, *The Haight-Ashbury*, 12, 51.
8. Rorabaugh, *American Hippies*, 51–52.
9. Blair Jackson, *Garcia: An American Life* (New York: Penguin Books, 1999), 11.
10. Jackson, *Garcia*, 32–33.
11. Perry, *The Haight-Ashbury*, 36.
12. Jason Ankeny, "Phil Lesh," AllMusic, accessed November 27, 2020, https://www.allmusic.com/artist/phil-lesh-mn0000848187/biography; Timothy Monger, "Bob Weir," AllMusic, accessed November 27, 2020, https://www.allmusic.com/artist/bob-weir-mn0000077175/biography; "Ron Pigpen McKernan," AllMusic, accessed November 27, 2020, https://www.allmusic.com/artist/ron-pigpen-mckernan-mn0000826981/biography; Rachel Sprovtsoff, "Bill Kreutzmann," AllMusic, accessed November 27, 2020, https://www.allmusic.com/artist/bill-kreutzmann-mn0000061608/biography.
13. Rorabaugh, *American Hippies*, 52.
14. "Drummer Bill Kreutzmann on Drugs, Money and the End of the Grateful Dead," PBS, July 6, 2015, https://www.youtube.com/watch?v=MEdhlX-hdNk.
15. Jann Wenner and Charles Reich, "Dawn of the Dead," February 20, 1972, excerpted in *Grateful Dead: The Ultimate Guide* (New York: Rolling Stone, 2021), 26.
16. Dennis McNally, *A Long Strange Trip: The Inside History of the Grateful Dead* (New York: Crown/Archetype, 2007), 42–43.
17. Perry, *The Haight-Ashbury*, 137.
18. Rorabaugh, *American Hippies*, 14.
19. Rorabaugh, *American Hippies*, 9.
20. Wenner and Reich, "Dawn of the Dead," 26.
21. "Grateful Dead," accessed November 27, 2020, https://www.rockhall.com/inductees/grateful-dead.
22. Rorabaugh, *American Hippies*, 145.
23. Rorabaugh, *American Hippies*, 145.
24. Rorabaugh, *American Hippies*, 54, 145.
25. Rorabaugh, *American Hippies*, 145.
26. Perry, *The Haight-Ashbury*, 40.
27. Perry, *The Haight-Ashbury*, 41; Rorabaugh, *American Hippies*, 55.
28. Rorabaugh, *American Hippies*, 55.
29. Perry, *The Haight-Ashbury*, 40.
30. Perry, *The Haight-Ashbury*, 41; Rorabaugh, *American Hippies*, 55.

31. Perry, *The Haight-Ashbury*, 41.
32. Perry, *The Haight-Ashbury*, 41.
33. Rorabaugh, *American Hippies*, 56.
34. Perry, *The Haight-Ashbury*, 150.
35. Perry, *The Haight-Ashbury*, 50.
36. Perry, *The Haight-Ashbury*, 50.
37. Perry, *The Haight-Ashbury*, 87; accessed November 27, 2020, http://www.diggers.org/overview.html; Gail Dolgin and Vicente Franco, *American Experience: The Summer of Love*, PBS, 2007.
38. Barry McGuire, "Eve of Destruction," accessed November 27, 2020, https://genius.com/Barry-mcguire-eve-of-destruction-lyrics.
39. Thomas Forte, "History 118: U.S. History since 1877," April 19, 2017, https://blogs.dickinson.edu/hist-118pinsker/2017/04/19/2895/.
40. Perry, *The Haight-Ashbury*, 92, 121.
41. Perry, *The Haight-Ashbury*, 96.
42. Perry, *The Haight-Ashbury*, 175.
43. Rorabaugh, *American Hippies*, 116–17; Wilhelm Reich, *The Sexual Revolution: Toward a Self-Regulating Character Structure* (New York: Farrar, Straus and Giroux, 1986); "Wilhelm Reich," *Encyclopaedia Britannica*, accessed December 26, 2020, https://www.britannica.com/biography/Wilhelm-Reich.
44. Jeffer Berner, "The 'Now Generation,'" *San Francisco Sunday Examiner-Chronicle*, July 9, 1967, Datebook, 28.
45. Perry, *The Haight-Ashbury*, 35.
46. Rorabaugh, *American Hippies*, 56.
47. Michael R. Frontani, *The Beatles: Image and the Media* (Jackson: University Press of Mississippi, 2007), 122.
48. Joe S. Harrington, *Sonic Cool: The Life & Death of Rock 'n' Roll* (Milwaukee: Hal Leonard, 2002), 191 [baroque]; Peter Lavezzoli, *The Dawn of Indian Music in the West* (New York: Continuum, 2006), 171 [sitar popularity].
49. Rorabaugh, *American Hippies*, 57.
50. Rorabaugh, *American Hippies*, 59.
51. Rorabaugh, *American Hippies*, 84.
52. Perry, *The Haight-Ashbury*, 6.
53. Rorabaugh, *American Hippies*, 72.
54. Spitz, *The Beatles*, 666.
55. Gilmore, "Beatles' Acid Test."
56. Dunbar, *Renewing the Balance*, 170.
57. Spitz, *The Beatles*, 670.
58. David Horn, *Bloomsbury Encyclopedia of Popular Music of the World, Volume 11* (London: Bloomsbury, 2017), 36.
59. Spitz, *The Beatles*, 600.
60. Spitz, *The Beatles*, 604.
61. The Beatles, "Eleanor Rigby," accessed November 27, 2020, https://genius.com/The-beatles-eleanor-rigby-lyrics.
62. Matthew 18:3.
63. *Berkeley in the Sixties*, accessed November 27, 2020, https://films.com/ecTitleDetail.aspx?TitleID=33589&r=SR.
64. Norman, *Lennon*, 434.
65. "Yellow Submarine," accessed November 27, 2020, https://www.the-paulmccartney-project.com/song/yellow-submarine.
66. William Blake, *William Blake: Selected Poems* (New York: Penguin Classics, 2006).
67. Rorabaugh, *American Hippies*, 75.
68. Rorabaugh, *American Hippies*, 60.
69. Rorabaugh, *American Hippies*, 178.
70. "Allen Cohen and the S.F. Oracle," accessed November 27, 2020, http://www.rockument.com/blog/haight-ashbury-in-the-sixties/allen-cohen-and-the-s-f-oracle.
71. W.J. Rorabaugh, "How Hippies Created Today's American Culture," History News Network @myHNN, October 3, 2015.

Chapter 8

1. "Lou Reed about Velvet Underground and Andy Warhol," YouTube, June 6, 2008, https://www.youtube.com/watch?v=UD3rXg9R8BI.
2. "500 Greatest Albums List (2003)," *Rolling Stone*, May 31, 2009, https://www.rollingstone.com/music/music-lists/500-greatest-albums-of-all-time-156826/the-velvet-underground-and-nico-the-velvet-underground-52023.
3. Simmy Richman, "The Velvet Underground: The Velvet Revolution Rocks On," *The Independent*, February 12, 2017.
4. Bockris, *The Life and Death of Andy Warhol*, 36–41.
5. Victor Bockris, *The Life and Death of Andy Warhol* (New York: Bantam Books, 1989), 15–16.
6. Bockris, *The Life and Death of Andy Warhol*, 4–5.
7. Bockris, *The Life and Death of Andy Warhol*, 4–5.
8. "Jackson Pollock," accessed

November 27, 2020, https://www.jackson-pollock.org.

9. Accessed November 27, 2020, http://mengnews.joins.com/view.aspx?aId=2873516.

10. UCLA Student Newspaper, quoted in George Cotkin, *Feast of Excess: A Cultural History of the New Sensibility* (Oxford: Oxford University Press, 2015), 17.

11. Bob Dylan, "Visions of Johanna," accessed November 27, 2020, https://genius.com/Bob-dylan-visions-of-johanna-lyrics.

12. Elijah Wald, *How the Beatles Destroyed Rock 'n' Roll: An Alternative History of American Popular Music* (New York: Oxford University Press, 2011), 235; Jonathan Eisen, *The Age of Rock: Sounds of the American Cultural Revolution* (New York: Random House, 1969), 2.

13. Bockris, *The Life and Death of Andy Warhol*, 491.

14. Bockris, *The Life and Death of Andy Warhol*.

15. Lili Anolik, "Andy Warhol and Edie Sedgwick: A Brief, White-Hot, and Totally Doomed Romance," *Vanity Fair*, December 6, 2017, https://www.vanityfair.com/style/2017/12/andy-warhol-and-edie-sedgwick-a-brief-white-hot-and-totally-doomed-romance.

16. Andy Warhol and Pat Hackett, *Popism: The Warhol Sixties* (Boston: Mariner Books, 2006), 285.

17. Steven Watson, *Factory Made: Warhol and the Sixties* (New York: Pantheon, 2003) xii.

18. Anthony DeCurtis, *Lou Reed: A Life* (New York: Little, Brown, 2017), 99.

19. Rachel Nuwer, "Andy Warhol Probably Never Said His Celebrated 'Fifteen Minutes of Fame' Line," *Smithsonian Magazine*, April 8, 2014, https://www.smithsonianmag.com/smart-news/andy-warhol-probably-never-said-his-celebrated-fame-line-180950456.

20. Bockris, *The Life and Death of Andy Warhol*, 169–72.

21. Bockris, *The Life and Death of Andy Warhol*, 203.

22. Anne Morra, "Salvador Dalí Has Left the Building," *Inside/Out*, September 29, 2011, https://www.moma.org/explore/inside_out/2011/09/29/salvador-dali-has-left-the-building/; Brian Dillon, "Undone in Three Minutes," *The Guardian*, January 24, 2009, https://www.theguardian.com/artanddesign/2009/jan/24/andy-warhol-screen-tests-susan-sontag-lou-reed-salvador-dali.

23. Canes Lions Learnings, "Cannes Moments: Lou Reed on the Genius of Andy Warhol," YouTube, July 24, 2013, https://www.youtube.com/watch?v=2BKorJi_RBg.

24. Vaipan, "The Life of Andy Warhol (Documentary—Part Two)," YouTube, January 7, 2019. https://www.youtube.com/watch?v=PVJwdnamIVc.

25. Jan Greenberg and Sandra Jordan, *Andy Warhol, Prince of Pop* (New York: Laurel Leaf, 2007), 84.

26. Bockris, *The Life and Death of Andy Warhol*, 354–55.

27. Anolik, "Andy Warhol and Edie Sedgwick."

28. Liz Jobey, "Solanas and Son," *The Guardian*, August 24, 1996, T10ff.

29. Andy Warhol and Pat Hackett, *Popism the Warhol 60s* (New York: Harper & Row, 2003), 108.

30. Warhol and Hackett, *Popism the Warhol 60s*, 222.

31. Frederick Neuhouser, *Foundations of Hegel's Social Theory: Actualizing Freedom* (Cambridge, MA: Harvard University Press, 2003), 160.

32. Merrill Reed Weiner, "A Family in Peril: Lou Reed's Sister Sets the Record Straight about His Childhood," Cuepoint, April 13, 2015, https://medium.com/cuepoint/a-family-in-peril-lou-reed-s-sister-sets-the-record-straight-about-his-childhood-20e8399f84a3.

33. Weiner, "A Family in Peril."

34. Weiner, "A Family in Peril."

35. "The Velvet Underground," Rock & Roll Hall of Fame, accessed February 11, 2023, https://www.rockhall.com/inductees/velvet-underground.

36. Weiner, "A Family in Peril."

37. Daniel Bates, "How Lou Reed Was Given Electroshock Therapy Aged Just 17," *Daily Mail*, September 8, 2015, http://www.dailymail.co.uk/news/article-3222881/How-Lou-Reed-given-electroshock-therapy-aged-just-17-sexuality-New-York-psychiatric-hospital-described-hell-Queens.html.

38. Chris Colin, "Lou Reed," *Salon*, May 16, 2000, http://www.salon.com/2000/05/16/reed_3.

39. Legs McNeil, *Please Kill Me: The*

Uncensored Oral History of Punk (New York: Grove, 1996), 2–3.

40. Weiner, "A Family in Peril."
41. Bates, "How Lou Reed Was Given Electroshock Therapy."
42. Lou Reed, "Kill Your Sons," Genius, accessed November 27, 2020, https://genius.com/Lou-reed-kill-your-sons-lyrics.
43. "Rock and Roll Heart," documentary on the life of Lou Reed on YouTube, American Masters.
44. Chris Baker, "Lou Reed's Lasting Legacy at Syracuse University: A Criminal, a Dissident and a Poet," Syracuse.com, October 31, 2013, https://www.syracuse.com/entertainment/2013/10/lou_reed_syracuse_university.html.
45. "Angus MacLise," AllMusic, accessed April 10, 2021, https://www.allmusic.com/artist/angus-maclise-mn0000756247/biography.
46. Nelson Algren, *A Walk on the Wild Side* (Ashland, OR: Blackstone Audio, 2010).
47. Victor Bockris and Gerard Malanga, *Up-tight: The Velvet Underground Story* (London: Omnibus Press, 1996 [1983]), 13.
48. Joe Harvard, *The Velvet Underground and Nico* (New York: Continuum, 2004), 129.
49. Richie Unterberger, "The Velvet Underground Biography, Songs, & Albums," AllMusic, accessed February 13, 2023, https://www.allmusic.com/artist/the-velvet-underground-mn0000840402/biography.
50. Stephen Holden, *Rolling Stone*, May 25, 1972, 68.
51. "Lou Reed on the *Charlie Rose Show*, April 12, 1998," YouTube, accessed November 27, 2020, https://www.youtube.com/watch?v=LE3qo9sNgDs.
52. "January 29, 1965," *Time*, accessed November 27, 2020, http://content.time.com/time/covers/0,16641,19650129,00.html.
53. Chris Jones, "Review of *The Velvet Underground—The Velvet Underground & Nico (Deluxe Edition)*," BBC Music, 2002, accessed October 28, 2013, http://www.bbc.co.uk/music/reviews/fq4h.
54. Bockris and Malanga, *Up-tight*, 8.
55. Bockris and Malanga, *Up-tight*, 10.
56. Cannes Lions Learnings, "Lou Reed."
57. J.J. Murphy, *The Black Hole of the Camera: The Films of Andy Warhol* (Berkeley: University of California Press, 2012), 153.
58. Murphy, *Black Hole of the Camera*, 153.
59. "Nico," AllMusic, accessed November 27, 2020, https://www.allmusic.com/artist/nico-mn0000868306/biography.
60. Bockris and Malanga, *Up-tight*, 34.
61. DeCurtis, *Lou Reed*, 99.
62. DeCurtis, *Lou Reed*, 99.
63. "Lou Reed about Velvet Underground and Andy Warhol," YouTube, June 6, 2008, https://www.youtube.com/watch?v=UD3rXg9R8BI.
64. DeCurtis, *Lou Reed*, 73.
65. Alexis Petridis, "*The Velvet Underground: The Velvet Underground & Nico Super Deluxe*—Review," *The Guardian*, October 18, 2012, https://www.theguardian.com/music/2012/oct/18/velvet-underground-nico-super-deluxe-review.
66. Martin Torgoff, *Can't Find My Way Home: America in the Great Stoned Age, 1945–2000* (New York: Simon & Schuster, 2004), 156.
67. Torgoff, *Can't Find My Way Home*, 156.
68. Torgoff, *Can't Find My Way Home*, 156.
69. Bockris and Malanga, *Up-tight*, 65.
70. Bockris and Malanga, *Up-tight*, 7.
71. Torgoff, *Can't Find My Way Home*, 158.
72. DeCurtis, *Lou Reed*, 91.
73. Warhol and Hackett, *Popism*, 170.
74. Bockris and Malanga, *Up-tight*, 88.
75. Bockris and Malanga, *Up-tight*, 88.
76. "Are You Happy Being a Schmuck? Lou Reed, Sydney 1975," YouTube, July 12, 2017, https://www.youtube.com/watch?v=bx-mH9ZjnuM&t=5s.
77. Howard Sounes, *Notes from the Velvet Underground: The Life of Lou Reed* (London: Transworld, 2018), 191.
78. "Lou Reed about Velvet Underground and Andy Warhol."
79. Greg Kot, "The Velvet Underground: As Influential as the Beatles?" *The Guardian*, October 21, 2014, http://www.bbc.com/culture/story/20131125-do-the-velvets-beat-the-beatles.
80. Jim DeRogatis, *Let It Blurt: The Life and Times of Lester Bangs, America's Greatest Rock Critic* (New York: Crown, 2000), 210.

81. Irvin and McLear 2007, p. 80.
82. Tyler Wilcox, "The Unlikely Making of the Velvet Underground & Nico," *Pitchfork*, March 13, 2017, https://pitchfork.com/thepitch/1463-the-unlikely-making-of-the-velvet-underground-nico.
83. Joe Harvard, "Velvet Underground and Nico," in *33 1/3 Greatest Hits, Volume 1*, ed. David Barker (London: Bloomsbury, 2006).
84. *The Mojo Collection*, 4th ed. (Edinburgh: Canongate Books, 2007), 80.
85. Joe Coscarelli, "Art of the Rolling Stones: Behind That Zipper and That Tongue," *New York Times*, June 8, 2015, https://www.nytimes.com/2015/06/08/arts/music/art-of-the-rolling-stones-behind-that-zipper-and-that-tongue.html.
86. Bockris and Malanga, *Up-tight*, 77; Booth, *The True Adventures of the Rolling Stones*.
87. Bockris and Malanga, *Up-tight*, 63.
88. Bockris and Malanga, *Up-tight*, 61.
89. Richie Unterberger, "The Velvet Underground Biography, Songs, & Albums," AllMusic, accessed February 13, 2023, https://www.allmusic.com/artist/the-velvet-underground-mn0000840402/biography.
90. "Chelsea Girl," AllMusic, accessed November 27, 2020, https://www.allmusic.com/album/chelsea-girl-mw0000651868.
91. Unterberger, "The Velvet Underground."
92. Ben Beaumont-Thomas, "David Bowie: Lou Reed's Masterpiece Is Metallica Collaboration Lulu," *The Guardian*, April 20, 2015, https://www.theguardian.com/music/2015/apr/20/david-bowie-lou-reed-masterpiece-metallica-lulu.
93. DeCurtis, *Lou Reed*, 436.
94. Laurie Anderson, "Laurie Anderson's Farewell to Lou Reed: A Rolling Stone Exclusive," *Rolling Stone*, November 6, 2013, https://www.rollingstone.com/music/music-news/laurie-andersons-farewell-to-lou-reed-a-rolling-stone-exclusive-243792/; "Lou Reed and Laurie Anderson Wed," *People*, April 25, 2008, https://people.com/celebrity/lou-reed-and-laurie-anderson-wed.
95. McNeil, *Please Kill Me*, 4.

Chapter 9

1. Rorabaugh, *American Hippies*, 132.
2. Joan Didion, *Slouching toward Bethlehem* (New York: Farrar, Straus and Giroux, 1968), 121–22.
3. "Vietnam War U.S. Military Fatal Casualty Statistics," National Archives, accessed November 27, 2020, https://www.archives.gov/research/military/vietnam-war/casualty-statistics.
4. Perry, *The Haight-Ashbury*, 24.
5. Perry, *The Haight-Ashbury*, 26–27.
6. Perry, *The Haight-Ashbury*, 32.
7. Rorabaugh, *American Hippies*, 112.
8. Greene, *Life in America during the 1960s*, 139.
9. Charles B. Reich, "Grening in America," quoted Greene, *Life in America during the 1960s*, 160.
10. Didion, *Slouching toward Bethlehem*, 84.
11. Perry, *The Haight-Ashbury*, 154.
12. Perry, *The Haight-Ashbury*, 154.
13. Perry, *The Haight-Ashbury*, 153.
14. Rorabaugh, *American Hippies*, 167.
15. Rorabaugh, *American Hippies*, 169.
16. Benjamin Ramm, "Why Thousands of Teens Ran away from Home in the 1960s," BBC, June 15, 2017, https://www.bbc.com/culture/article/20170615-when-all-the-children-ran-away.
17. Rorabaugh, *American Hippies*, 97.
18. Rorabaugh, *American Hippies*, 96.
19. Rorabaugh, *American Hippies*, 71.
20. Rorabaugh, *American Hippies*, 106.
21. Rorabaugh, *American Hippies*, 132.
22. Rorabaugh, *American Hippies*, 92.
23. Rorabaugh, *American Hippies*, 116.
24. Rorabaugh, *American Hippies*, 31.
25. Rorabaugh, *American Hippies*, 92.
26. Rorabaugh, *American Hippies*, 91.
27. Rorabaugh, *American Hippies*, 176, 190.
28. Rorabaugh, *American Hippies*, 66–67.
29. Rorabaugh, *American Hippies*, 122.
30. Rorabaugh, *American Hippies*, 125.
31. Rorabaugh, *American Hippies*, 125.
32. Rorabaugh, *American Hippies*, 119.
33. Rorabaugh, *American Hippies*, 118.
34. Rorabaugh, *American Hippies*, 122, 120.
35. Rorabaugh, *American Hippies*, 129.
36. "Ken Kesey," Biography.com,

August 5, 2000, https://www.biography.com/writer/ken-kesey.

37. Perry, *The Haight-Ashbury*, 43.

38. "Allen Cohen and the S.F. Oracle," Rockument, accessed November 27, 2020, http://www.rockument.com/blog/haight-ashbury-in-the-sixties/allen-cohen-and-the-s-f-oracle.

39. Rorabaugh, *American Hippies*, 55.

40. Perry, *The Haight-Ashbury*, 268.

41. Perry, *The Haight-Ashbury*, 142.

42. Allen Cohen, chapter 8, in "The Summer of Love: Excerpt from the Memoir of Allen Cohen," 269. *Reading the Twentieth Century: Documents in American History*. Donald W. Whisenhunt.

43. "Home—PMC—NCBI," National Center for Biotechnology Information, U.S. National Library of Medicine, accessed February 11, 2023, https://www.ncbi.nlm.nih.gov/pmc/.

44. Perry, *The Haight-Ashbury*, 143; Didion, *Slouching toward Bethlehem*, 108–9.

45. Perry, *The Haight-Ashbury*, 143.

46. "Allen Cohen and the S.F. Oracle."

47. Rorabaugh, *American Hippies*, 171.

48. Rorabaugh, *American Hippies*, 171, 172.

49. Rorabaugh, *American Hippies*, 172.

50. Rorabaugh, *American Hippies*, 63n29.

Chapter 10

1. Robert Hart, "Hard to Imagine," *Touchstone Magazine*, accessed March 21, 2021, https://www.touchstonemag.com/archives/article.php?id=23-05-009-v.

2. Accessed November 27, 2020, http://www.churchsociety.org/issues_new/church/stats/iss_church_stats_attendance.asp#Sources; accessed November 27, 2020, http://www.christian-research.org/anglican-uk/anglican-england.html; "Statistics," Latin Mass Society, accessed November 27, 2020, https://lms.org.uk/statistics.

3. "Catholicism," Encyclopedia.com, accessed November 27, 2020, https://www.encyclopedia.com/philosophy-and-religion/christianity/protestant-denominations/catholicism.

4. "Catholicism," Encyclopedia.com.

5. "Second Vatican Council," Encyclopedia.com, accessed November 27, 2020, https://www.encyclopedia.com/philosophy-and-religion/christianity/roman-catholic-and-orthodox-churches-councils-and-treaties/second-vatican-council.

6. Accessed June 10, 2019, https://web.archive.org/web/20110610203034/https://www.aei.org/basicPages/20031124161414312.

7. Tobin Grant, "The Great Decline: 60 Years of Religion in One Graph," June 16, 2014, https://religionnews.com/2014/01/27/great-decline-religion-united-states-one-graph.

8. Lydia Saad, "Churchgoing among U.S. Catholics Slides to Tie Protestants," Gallup, June 9, 2009, https://news.gallup.com/poll/117382/church-going-among-catholics-slides-tie-protestants.aspx; Frank Newport, "In U.S., Four in 10 Report Attending Church in Last Week," Gallup, December 24, 2013, https://news.gallup.com/poll/166613/four-report-attending-church-last-week.aspx.

9. Accessed November 27, 2020, http://www.time.com/time/magazine/article/0,9171,835309-2,00.html#ixzz1K5yHNuJt.

10. John Elson, "Is God Dead?" *Time*, April 8, 1966, https://content.time.com/time/subscriber/article/0,33009,835309,00.html.

11. Gould, *Can't Buy Me Love*, 341.

12. Maureen Cleave, "How Does a Beatle Live? John Lennon Lives like This," *London Evening Standard*, March 4, 1966, http://www.beatlesinterviews.org/db1966.0304-beatles-john-lennon-were-more-popular-than-jesus-now-maureen-cleave.html.

13. Norman, *John Lennon*, 447.

14. Weber, *The Beatles*, 181.

15. Gould, *Can't Buy Me Love*, 341.

16. "The Beatles Banned Segregated Audiences, Contract Shows," BBC, September 18, 2011, https://www.bbc.com/news/entertainment-arts-14963752.

17. Gould, *Can't Buy Me Love*, 340.

18. Gould, *Can't Buy Me Love*, 346.

19. Norman, *John Lennon*, 454.

20. Norman, *John Lennon*, 454.

21. Fred Bronson, *The Billboard Book of Number One Hits* (New York: Billboard Books, 2003), 201.

22. Accessed November 27, 2020, https:

//abcnews.go.com/Entertainment/john-lennon-killer-mark-david-chapman-considered-killing/story?id=11658475.

23. Perry, *The Haight-Ashbury*, 115.
24. Rorabaugh, *American Hippies*, 72.
25. Perry, *The Haight-Ashbury*, 155–56.
26. Jordan Runtagh, "Beatles' 'Sgt. Pepper' at 50: Meet the Runaway Who Inspired 'She's Leaving Home,'" *Rolling Stone*, May 27, 2013, https://www.rollingstone.com/feature/beatles-sgt-pepper-at-50-meet-the-runaway-who-inspired-shes-leaving-home-124697.
27. Steve Huey, "The Piper at the Gates of Dawn," AllMusic, accessed November 27, 2020, https://www.allmusic.com/album/the-piper-at-the-gates-of-dawn-mw0000191309; Toby Manning, *The Rough Guide to Pink Floyd* (London: Rough Guides, 2006), 71.
28. Richie Unterberger, "Syd Barrett," AllMusic, accessed December 19, 2022, https://www.allmusic.com/artist/syd-barrett-mn0000044874/biography.
29. Danny Goldberg, "All the Human Be-in Was Saying 50 Years Ago, Was Give Peace a Chance," The Nation, January 16, 2017, https://www.thenation.com/article/archive/all-the-human-be-in-was-saying-50-years-ago-was-give-peace-a-chance/.
30. Goldberg, "All the Human Be-in."
31. Rorabaugh, *American Hippies*, 63.
32. Rorabaugh, *American Hippies*, 66.
33. Rorabaugh, *American Hippies*, 66.
34. Perry, *The Haight-Ashbury*, 137.
35. Rorabaugh, *American Hippies*, 84.
36. Rorabaugh, *American Hippies*, 73.
37. Perry, *The Haight-Ashbury*, 165.
38. Perry, *The Haight-Ashbury*, 213.
39. *Billboard*, December 30, 1967, https://books.google.com/books?id=aSgEAAAAMBAJ&printsec=frontcover&rview=1&source=gbs_ge_summary_r&cad=0#v=onepage&q&f=false.
40. Perry, *The Haight-Ashbury*, 229.
41. Runtagh, "Beatles' 'Sgt. Pepper'"; Perry, *The Haight-Ashbury*, 173.
42. Rorabaugh, *American Hippies*, 73.
43. Jefferson Airplane, "White Rabbit," accessed November 27, 2021, https://jeffersonairplane.com/tag/white-rabbit.
44. Rorabaugh, *American Hippies*, 74.
45. Perry, *The Haight-Ashbury*, 198.
46. Perry, *The Haight-Ashbury*, 198.
47. Accessed November 27, 2020, http://www.thesmokinggun.com/sites/default/files/assets/jimihendrixbuster.jpg.
48. "Jimi Hendrix," Biography.com, accessed November 27, 2020, https://www.biography.com/musician/jimi-hendrix.
49. Rorabaugh, *American Hippies*, 74.
50. "Jimi Hendrix," Biography.com.
51. Rorabaugh, *American Hippies*, 74.
52. Perry, *The Haight-Ashbury*, 201.
53. Spitz, *The Beatles*, 576.
54. Kenneth Womack, *The Beatles Encyclopedia: Everything Fab Four* (Santa Barbara, CA: ABC-CLIO, 2014).
55. "50 Years Ago This Week: The Beatles Change the World," *Time*, September 18, 2017, http://time.com/4935871/1967-beatles-cover.
56. David Simonelli, *Working Class Heroes: Rock Music and British Society in the 1960s and 1970s* (Lanham, MD: Lexington Books, 2012), 107.
57. Richard Poirier, *The Performing Self: Compositions and Decompositions in the Languages of Contemporary Life* (New Brunswick, NJ: Rutgers University Press, 1992), 137.
58. For the 1968 Grammy Awards, see "10th Annual GRAMMY Awards," GRAMMY.com, archived from the original on April 14, 2014. For the first rock LP to receive Album of the Year, see Glausser 2011, p. 143.
59. Rorabaugh, *American Hippies*, 78.
60. "500 Greatest Albums List (2003)," *Rolling Stone*.
61. Spitz, *The Beatles*, 674–81.
62. Carl Bernstein, "There's Never Been Anything like the Beatles' New 'Band,'" *Washington Post*, June 18, 1967, ProQuest Historical Newspapers, accessed June 6, 2017.
63. Rorabaugh, *American Hippies*, 78; Gavin Edwards, "The Beatles Make History with 'All You Need Is Love': A Minute-by-Minute Breakdown," *Rolling Stone*, August 28, 2014, https://www.rollingstone.com/music/features/the-beatles-make-history-with-all-you-need-is-love a minute-by-minute-breakdown-20140828.
64. Rorabaugh, *American Hippies*, 145.
65. Perry, *The Haight-Ashbury*, 216–17.
66. Perry, *The Haight-Ashbury*, 216–17.
67. Perry, *The Haight-Ashbury*, 143.
68. Rorabaugh, *American Hippies*, 146.
69. Perry, *The Haight-Ashbury*, xiii.

Chapter 11

1. Marshall Frady, *Martin Luther King, Jr: A Life* (New York: Penguin, 2005), 18.
2. David Zirin, *People's History of Sports in the United States: 250 Years of Politics, Protest, People, and Play* (New York: New Press, 2009), 143.
3. Krishnadev Calamur, "Muhammad Ali and Vietnam," *The Atlantic*, June 4, 2006, https://www.theatlantic.com/news/archive/2016/06/muhammad-ali-vietnam/485717/.
4. Calamur, "Muhammad Ali."
5. Perry, *The Haight-Ashbury*, 206.
6. Perry, *The Haight-Ashbury*, 214.
7. Perry, *The Haight-Ashbury*, 221.
8. Perry, *The Haight-Ashbury*, 220.
9. Perry, *The Haight-Ashbury*, 226.
10. Perry, *The Haight-Ashbury*, 229.
11. Athan G. Theoharis et al., *The Central Intelligence Agency: Security under Scrutiny* (Santa Barbara: Greenwood, 2005), 49, 175, 195, 203, 322; Robert Justin Goldstein, *Political Repression in Modern America: From 1870 to 1976* (Champaign: University of Illinois Press, 2001), 456.
12. "Operation Chaos," *New York Times*, June 11, 1975, http://www.nytimes.com/1975/06/11/archives/operation-chaos.html?_r=0.
13. Accessed November 27, 2020, http://www.gcrg.org/bqr/10-2/bcd.html.
14. James Lawrence Powell, *Dead Pool: Lake Powell, Global Warming, and the Future of Water in the West* (Oakland: University of California Press, 2008); Booth, *The True Adventures of the Rolling Stones*, 109; Ryan Cooper, "The Sierra Club Was Once the Victim of a Politically Motivated IRS Attack," *Washington Monthly*, May 15, 2013, http://washingtonmonthly.com/2013/05/15/the-sierra-club-was-once-the-victim-of-a-politically-motivated-irs-attack.
15. Perry, *The Haight-Ashbury*, 212.
16. Perry, *The Haight-Ashbury*, 212.
17. Greene, *Life in America during the 1960s*, 114–15.
18. Greene, *Life in America during the 1960s*, 115.
19. Rorabaugh, *American Hippies*, 147, 149.
20. Rorabaugh, *American Hippies*, 149.
21. Robert F. Kennedy, "Remarks at the University of Kansas, March 18, 1968," JFK Library, accessed November 27, 2020, http://www.jfklibrary.org/Research/Research-Aids/Ready-Reference/RFK-Speeches/Remarks-of-Robert-F-Kennedy-at-the-University-of-Kansas-March-18-1968.aspx.
22. Matthew Dallek, "The Conservative 1960s," *The Atlantic*, December 1995, https://www.theatlantic.com/magazine/archive/1995/12/the-conservative-1960s/376506.
23. "Black Power," U.S. History, accessed November 27, 2020, https://www.ushistory.org/us/54i.asp.
24. "Black Panther Party," *Encyclopaedia Britannica*, accessed November 27, 2020, https://www.britannica.com/topic/Black-Panther-Party.
25. "Black Panther Party," *Encyclopaedia Britannica*; "Huey P. Newton," *Encyclopaedia Britannica*, accessed November 27, 2020, https://www.britannica.com/biography/Huey-P-Newton.
26. "Black Panther Party," *Encyclopaedia Britannica*.
27. "Black Panther Party," *Encyclopaedia Britannica*.

Chapter 12

1. Lloyd Price, *sumdumhonky* (Beverly Hills: Cool Titles, 2015), 6, 10.
2. Price, *sumdumhonky*, 12.
3. Price, *sumdumhonky*, 2.
4. Accessed November 27, 2020, https://www.popmatters.com/rock-pioneer-lloyd-price-has-a-couple-of-stories-to-tell-2495463952.html.
5. Peter Guralnick, *Careless Love: The Unmaking of Elvis Presley* (New York: Back Bay Books, 2000), 285, 314, 323; Price, *sumdumhonky*, xiv.
6. "Rock and Roll; Renegades; Interview with Lloyd Price," Open Vault, accessed November 27, 2020, http://openvault.wgbh.org/catalog/V_526618E785CF478CB0497C99EA6DA357.
7. Price, *sumdumhonky*, 38.
8. Price, *sumdumhonky*, 62–63.
9. Peter Guralnick, "How Did Elvis Get Turned into a Racist?" *New York Times*, August 10, 2007, http://www.nytimes.com/2007/08/11/opinion/11guralnick.html?pagewanted=all&_r=0.

10. Erika Doss, *Elvis Culture: Fans, Faith, and Image* (Lawrence: University Press of Kansas, 1999), 72–73.

11. "How Big Was the King? Elvis Presley's Legacy, 25 Years after His Death," *CBS News*, August 7, 2002.

12. Doss, *Elvis Culture*, 73, 108–9.

13. Eli Yamin, *So You Want to Sing the Blues: A Guide for Performers* (Lanham, MD: Rowman & Littlefield, 2018), 150.

14. Cosby, *Devil's Music*, 42–84.

15. Lomax, *The Land Where the Blues Began*, prologue; James C. Cobb, *The Most Southern Place on Earth: The Mississippi Delta and the Roots of Regional Identity* (Oxford: Oxford University Press, 1989), 108–9.

16. Vann R. Newkirk II, "The Great Land Robbery," *The Atlantic*, September 2019, https://www.theatlantic.com/magazine/archive/2019/09/this-land-was-our-land/594742.

17. Newkirk, "The Great Land Robbery."

18. Victoria W. Wolcott, *Remaking Respectability: African American Women in Interwar Detroit* (Chapel Hill: University of North Carolina Press, 2001), 94–130.

19. Paul Cowan, *The Tribes of America* (New York: Doubleday, 1979), 94.

20. B.B. King and David Ritz, *Blues All around Me: The Autobiography of B.B. King* (New York: Avon Books, 1996), 284–85; Kevin Carter and W. Speers, "B.B. King's Gift to the Pope: His Guitar 'Lucille,'" Philadelphia City Archives, December 19, 1997.

21. Lynn Norment, "B.B. King Talks about Love, the Blues, and History," *Ebony*, February 1992, 46.

22. Nelson George, *The Death of Rhythm & Blues* (New York: Penguin, 2003), 107.

23. Clarence Page, "How White Fans Saved B.B. King's Blues," *Chicago Tribune*, May 15, 2015, accessed November 27, 2020, http://www.chicagotribune.com/news/opinion/page/ct-bb-king-blues-page-perspec-0504-20150515-column.html.

24. Page, "How White Fans."

25. "Where's the Blues in the Black Community," Houston Press, accessed November 27, 2020, http://www.houstonpress.com/music/wheres-the-blues-in-the-black-community-6531188AA.

26. "Where's the Blues."

27. B. Brian Foster, *I Don't Like the Blues: Race, Place, and the Backbeat of Black Life* (Chapel Hill: University of North Carolina Press, 2020), 45.

28. Foster, *I Don't Like the Blues*, 84.

29. W.C. Handy, *Father of the Blues: An Autobiography* (New York: Da Capo, 1991), 74.

30. John Bush, "W.C. Handy," AllMusic, accessed November 27, 2020, https://www.allmusic.com/artist/wc-handy-mn0000195430/biography.

31. Author's personal observations, 2012; "Google Maps Search," Google Maps, accessed February 11, 2023, https://www.google.com/maps/@34.1458732,-90.5361643,377m/data=!3m1!1e3.

32. "Corrections Corporation of America Announces Third Quarter 2008 Financial Results," November 6, 2008, https://www.globenewswire.com/news-release/2008/11/06/1222911/0/en/Corrections-Corporation-of-America-Announces-Third-Quarter-2008-Financial-Results.html.

33. "Tutwiler, Mississippi," Wikipedia, accessed November 27, 2020, https://en.wikipedia.org/wiki/Tutwiler,_Mississippi#Demographics.

34. Author's personal observations, 2012.

Chapter 13

1. *Cincinnati Enquirer*, August 8, 1994, 27.

2. "Ray Charles," *Encyclopaedia Britannica*, accessed December 25, 2020, https://www.britannica.com/biography/Ray-Charles.

3. Lindsay Planer, "I Got a Woman," AllMusic, accessed November 27, 2020, https://www.allmusic.com/song/i-got-a-woman-mt0034438533.

4. "James Brown," Biography.com, accessed November 27, 2020, https://www.biography.com/people/james-brown-9228350.

5. "James Brown," *Encyclopaedia Britannica*, accessed November 27, 2020, https://www.britannica.com/biography/James-Brown-American-singer.

6. Don Rhodes, *Say It Loud! The Life of James Brown, Soul Brother No. 1* (Guilford, CT: Lyons Press, 2014), 25.

7. Richie Unterberger, "James Brown," AllMusic, November 27, 2020, https://www.allmusic.com/artist/james-brown-mn0000128099/biography.
8. "James Brown," *Encyclopaedia Britannica*.
9. George, *The Death of Rhythm & Blues*, 99.
10. Unterberger, "James Brown," All Music.
11. Unterberger, "James Brown," All Music.
12. Unterberger, "James Brown," All Music.
13. "Funk," *Encyclopaedia Britannica*, accessed November 27, 2020, https://www.britannica.com/art/funk.
14. Accessed November 27, 2020, https://rockhall.com/inductees/james-brown/bio/#sthash.IwG0SdGq.dpuf.
15. George, *The Death of Rhythm & Blues*, 99; Roger Horrocks, *Male Myths and Icons: Masculinity in Popular Culture* (New York: Palgrave Macmillan, 1995), 140.
16. Charlie Gillett, *The Sound of the City: The Rise of Rock and Roll* (New York: Da Capo, 1996), 233.
17. Stephen Thomas Erlewine, "How Hall & Oates Bared Their Soul," Cuepoint, accessed November 27, 2020, https://medium.com/cuepoint/70s-scenario-how-hall-oates-walked-along-the-red-ledge-to-discover-their-x-static-voice-5cb5b01d4d6f.
18. "Grammy Awards 1966," accessed November 27, 2020, http://www.awardsandshows.com/features/grammy-awards-1966-241.html.
19. Jon Landau, "Rock 1970—It's Too Late to Stop Now," RS, December 2, 1970, in Charles Nanry, ed., *American Music from Storyville...* 250.
20. Richard Delgado, *Critical White Studies: Looking behind the Mirror* (Philadelphia: Temple University Press, 1997), 273.
21. Matt Simmons, *Fat, Drunk, and Stupid: The Inside Story behind the Making of* Animal House (New York: St. Martin's Griffin, 2014), 33–41.
22. Simmons, *Fat, Drunk, and Stupid*, 80; "How Playing a Fake Singer Turned Otis Day into a Real R&B Star," Slate, February 10, 2015, https://youtu.be/fjKi_LAeQR0.
23. Wald, *How the Beatles Destroyed Rock 'n' Roll*, 220–21.
24. John Landis, dir., *Animal House* (Universal Pictures, 1978).
25. Alice Echols, 2011, *Hot Stuff: Disco and the Remaking of American Culture*. W.W. Norton and Company. 58.
26. Joseph Vogel, "How Michael Jackson Made 'Bad,'" *The Atlantic*, September 10, 2012, https://www.theatlantic.com/entertainment/archive/2012/09/how-michael-jackson-made-bad/262162.
27. Wald, *How the Beatles Destroyed Rock 'n' Roll*, 240.
28. Wald, *How the Beatles Destroyed Rock 'n' Roll*, 240.
29. "Berry Gordy," Motown Museum, accessed November 27, 2020, https://www.motownmuseum.org/story/berry-gordy.
30. Paul Justman, dir., *Standing in the Shadows of Motown* (Artisan Entertainment, 2002).
31. "The Sound of Young America," BBC, accessed November 27, 2020, https://www.bbc.co.uk/programmes/b0074sn6.
32. Gillett, *Sound of the City*, 211.
33. Gillett, *Sound of the City*, 212.
34. "Berry Gordy," Motown Museum.
35. Ben Whalley, prod., *Motor City's Burning: Detroit from Motown to the Stooges* (BBC, 2008).
36. Mark Kurlansky, *Ready for a Brand New Beat: How "Dancing in the Street" Became the Anthem for a Changing America* (New York: Riverhead Books, 2014), 117.
37. Kurlansky, *Ready for a Brand New Beat*, 186.
38. Kurlansky, *Ready for a Brand New Beat*, 101.
39. "Stax History," accessed November 27, 2022, https://www.staxrecords.com/pages/history2.
40. Rob Bowman, *Soulsville, U.S.A.: The Story of Stax Records* (New York: Schirmer, 2010), 5.
41. https://www.staxrecords.com/pages/history2, accessed November 27, 2020.
42. *Stax 50th Anniversary Celebration*, liner notes (Santa Monica: Universal Music).
43. Bowman, *Soulsville*, 10.
44. Accessed November 27, 2020, http://www.amazon.com/Booker-T/e/B001LHZW40/ref=ntt_mus_dp_pel; Bowman, *Soulsville*.
45. Bowman, *Soulsville*, 10.

46. Bowman, *Soulsville*, 9.
47. Bowman, *Soulsville*, 16.
48. Bowman, *Soulsville*, 13.
49. Bowman, *Soulsville*, 21.
50. Bowman, *Soulsville*, 71.
51. Bowman, *Soulsville*, 22.
52. Robert Gordon, *It Came from Memphis: The Legendary Sounds from Memphis*, liner notes (London: Manteca, 2005).
53. Bowman, *Soulsville*, 30.
54. Bowman, *Soulsville*, 27.
55. Bowman, *Soulsville*, 26.
56. Gordon, R. *Respect Yourself: Stax Records and the Soul Explosion*, (New York: Bloomsbury Publishing, 2015), 201.
57. *Stax 50th Anniversary Celebration*.
58. Bowman, *Soulsville*, 42.
59. Bowman, *Soulsville*, 105.
60. "Otis Redding," *Encyclopaedia Britannica*, accessed November 27, 2020, https://www.britannica.com/biography/Otis-Redding.
61. Otis Redding, "Try a Little Tenderness," Genius, accessed November 27, 2020, https://genius.com/Otis-redding-try-a-little-tenderness-lyrics.
62. *Stax 50th Anniversary Celebration*.
63. Bowman, *Soulsville*, 95.
64. Bowman, *Soulsville*, 115.
65. Bowman, *Soulsville*, 123.
66. "Otis Redding," *Encyclopaedia Britannica*.
67. Bowman, *Soulsville*, 186–87.

Chapter 14

1. Greene, *Life in America during the 1960s*, 79.
2. History.com Editors, "William Westmoreland—History," History.com, accessed February 12, 2023, https://www.history.com/topics/vietnam-war/william-westmoreland.
3. "Mired in Statement," accessed November 27, 2020, http://www-personal.umd.umich.edu/~ppennock/doc-Cronkite.htm.
4. Greene, *Life in America during the 1960s*, 128.
5. King Encyclopedia, "Federal Bureau of Investigation (FBI)," Martin Luther King, Jr., Research and Education Institute, May 21, 2018, https://kinginstitute.stanford.edu/encyclopedia/federal-bureau-investigation-fbi.
6. Michael Eric Dyson, *April 4, 1968: Martin Luther King Jr.'s Death and How It Changed America* (New York: Civitas Books, 2008), 54.
7. Dyson.
8. Kyle Scott Clauss, "49 Years Ago Today, James Brown Saved Boston," *Boston Magazine*, April 5, 2017, https://www.bostonmagazine.com/news/2017/04/05/james-brown-saved-boston-king/.
9. Clauss, "49 Years Ago Today."
10. Clauss, "49 Years Ago Today."
11. "The Night James Brown Saved Boston," New England Historical Society, April 4, 2020, https://www.newenglandhistoricalsociety.com/the-night-james-brown-saved-boston/.
12. "Time Looks Back: The Assassination of Martin Luther King, Jr.," *Time*, April 4, 2013, https://swampland.time.com/2013/04/04/time-looks-back-martin-luther-kings-assassination/.
13. Bowman, *Soulsville*, 145; "Time Looks Back."
14. "The Night James Brown Saved Boston."
15. Clauss, "49 Years Ago Today."
16. *James Brown: The Godfather of Soul* (New York: Da Capo Press, 2003).
17. George, *The Death of Rhythm & Blues*, 103–4.
18. Nelson George and Alan Leeds, eds., *The James Brown Reader: Fifty Years of Writing about the Godfather of Soul* (New York: Plume, 2008).
19. David Leaf, dir., *The Night James Brown Saved Boston* (David Leaf Productions, 2008).
20. Rick Perlstein, *Nixonland: The Rise of a President and the Fracturing of America* (New York: Scribner, 2009), 257.
21. Perlstein, *Nixonland*, 257.
22. Perlstein, *Nixonland*, 257.
23. Perlstein, *Nixonland*, 258.
24. Dyson, *April 4, 1968*.
25. "An Hour of Need" and "The Assassination," *Time*, April 12, 1968.
26. "An Hour of Need" and "The Assassination."
27. Marcus Casey and Bradley Hardy, "50 Years after the Kerner Commission Report, the Nation Is Still Grappling with Many of the Same Issues," Brookings Institution, March 9, 2022, https://www.brookings.edu/

blog/up-front/2018/09/25/50-years-after-the-kerner-commission-report-the-nation-is-still-grappling-with-many-of-the-same-issues/.
28. Bowman, *Soulsville*, 147.
29. Bowman, *Soulsville*, 190.
30. Bowman, *Soulsville*, 147.
31. Bowman, *Soulsville*, 147.
32. Jason Birchmeier, "How Buttered Soul," AllMusic, accessed November 27, 2020, http://allmusic.com/album/hot-buttered-soul-r9077/review.
33. "Events of May, 1968," *Encyclopaedia Britannica*, accessed December 25, 2020, https://www.britannica.com/event/events-of-May-1968.
34. Kenneth T. Walsh, "How Robert F. Kennedy's Death Shattered the Nation," *U.S. News*, June 5, 2015, https://www.usnews.com/news/articles/2015/06/04/how-robert-f-kennedys-death-shattered-the-nation.
35. "The Vietnam War and Its Impact," American Foreign Relations, accessed November 27, 2020, http://www.americanforeignrelations.com/O-W/The-Vietnam-War-and-Its-Impact-Nixon-s-peace-with-honor.html; Rorabaugh, *American Hippies*, 132.
36. Rorabaugh, *American Hippies*, 153.
37. Rorabaugh, *American Hippies*, 152.
38. Rorabaugh, *American Hippies*, 153.
39. Rorabaugh, *American Hippies*, 154.
40. Rorabaugh, *American Hippies*, 154.
41. Bruce A. Ragsdale, *The Chicago Seven: 1960s Radicalism in the Federal Courts*, 2008, https://www.fjc.gov/sites/default/files/trials/chicago7.pdf.
42. Leon Wildes, "Nixon Administration Targets John Lennon," Utne Reader, accessed November 27, 2020, https://www.utne.com/politics/nixon-targets-john-lennon-ze0z1710zols.
43. Rorabaugh, *American Hippies*, 160.
44. Rorabaugh, *American Hippies*, 161.
45. Rorabaugh, *American Hippies*, 161.
46. Rorabaugh, *American Hippies*, 161.
47. Rorabaugh, *American Hippies*, 161.
48. Rorabaugh, *American Hippies*, 162.
49. Rorabaugh, *American Hippies*, 162.
50. Rorabaugh, *American Hippies*, X.
51. Rorabaugh, *American Hippies*, 161.
52. Rorabaugh, *American Hippies*, 161.

Chapter 15

1. Perry, *The Haight-Ashbury*, 226.
2. "You Can't Even Say What It Is," *International, Times*, August/September, 1969.
3. Spitz, *The Beatles*, 756.
4. The Beatles, *The Beatles Anthology*, 285–86.
5. Staff, "The Day Paul McCartney Made Ringo Starr Quit the Beatles," Far Out Magazine, August 22, 2020, https://faroutmagazine.co.uk/ringo-starr-paul-mccartney-quit-the-beatles/.
6. Dunbar, *Renewing the Balance*.
7. "*Playboy* Interview with John Lennon and Yoko Ono," Beatles Interviews, accessed November 27, 2020, http://www.beatlesinterviews.org/dbjypb.int3.html.
8. "'I Am the Walrus' History," accessed November 27, 2020, http://www.beatlesebooks.com/walrus.
9. Nicholas Schaffner, *The Beatles Forever* (New York: McGraw-Hill, 1978), 115.
10. Jon Wiener, *Come Together: John Lennon in His Time* (Urbana: University of Illinois Press, 1991), 63.
11. Pavel Aksenov, "Beatles for Sale: The Vinyl Underground in the USSR," BBC News, October 5, 2012, https://www.bbc.com/news/entertainment-arts-19827438.
12. Joan Goodman, "*Playboy* Interview with Paul McCartney," *Playboy*, December 1984.
13. Richie Unterberger, "Let It Be," AllMusic, accessed November 27, 2020, https://www.allmusic.com/album/let-it-be-mw0000192939.
14. Dunbar, *Renewing the Balance*.
15. Dunbar, *Renewing the Balance*.
16. David Sheff, *All We Are Saying: The Last Major Interview with John Lennon and Yoko Ono* (New York: St. Martin's Griffin, 2000).
17. Spitz, *The Beatles*, 846–50.
18. Spitz, *The Beatles*, 844–54.
19. Stephen Thomas Erlewine, "Abbey Road," AllMusic, accessed December 7, 2019, https://www.allmusic.com/album/abbey-road-mw0000192938.
20. Richie Unterberger, "Magic Mystery Tour," AllMusic, accessed November 27, 2020, https://www.allmusic.com/album/magical-mystery-tour-mw0000651227.

21. The Beatles, "The End," Genius, https://genius.com/The-beatles-the-end-lyrics.
22. Rorabaugh, *American Hippies*, 84.
23. Rorabaugh, *American Hippies*, 84–85.
24. Rorabaugh, *American Hippies*, 85.
25. Rorabaugh, *American Hippies*, 85.
26. Rorabaugh, *American Hippies*, 85.
27. Rorabaugh, *American Hippies*, 87.
28. Rorabaugh, *American Hippies*, 87.

Chapter 16

1. Gary Lachman, *Aleister Crowley: Magick, Rock and Roll, and the Wickedest Man in the World* (Los Angeles: Tarcher-Perigree, 2014), 22; Aleister Crowley, *Confessions of Aleister Crowley* (London: Penguin, 1989), 34.
2. Lachman, *Aleister Crowley*, 15.
3. Lachman, *Aleister Crowley*, 22; Crowley, *Confessions*, 15.
4. Crowley, *Confessions*, 40.
5. Lachman, *Aleister Crowley*, 24.
6. Lachman, *Aleister Crowley*, 50.
7. Fyfe, A., & van Wyhe, J. (n.d.). Victorian Science & Religion. https://www.victorianweb.org/victorian/science/science&religion.html.
8. "Guglielmo Marconia," *Encyclopaedia Britannica*, accessed November 27, 2020, britannica.com/summary/Guglielmo-Marconi; https://www.scienceandmediamuseum.org.uk/objects-and-stories/telecommunications-and-occult.
9. Francis King, *Modern Ritual Magic: The Rise of Western Occultism* (Stockholm: Prisma, 1989), 42–43, 61.
10. Richard Kaczynski, *Perdurabo, Revised and Expanded Edition: The Life of Aleister Crowley* (Berkeley: North Atlantic Books, 2010), 67.
11. Kaczynski, *Perdurabo*, 542.
12. Kaczynski, *Perdurabo*, 542.
13. Lachman, *Aleister Crowley*, 19.
14. Lachman, *Aleister Crowley*, 118.
15. Aleister Crowley, "Hymn to Lucifer," Genius, accessed January 19, 2023, https://genius.com/2156018?.
16. "Aleister Crowley, "All That's Interesting," accessed November 27, 2020, https://allthatsinteresting.com/aleister-crowley; Lachman, *Aleister Crowley*, 28.

17. Kaczynski, *Perdurabo*, 46.
18. Kaczynski, *Perdurabo*, 17–18.
19. Kaczynski, *Perdurabo*, 17–18.
20. Kaczynski, *Perdurabo*, 46.
21. Accessed November 27, 2020, https://www.esquire.com/uk/culture/news/a5483/kenneth-anger.
22. Kaczynski, *Perdurabo*, 43.
23. Crowley, *Confessions*, 396.
24. Lachman, *Aleister Crowley*, 219, 238.
25. Lachman, *Aleister Crowley*, 314.
26. Lachman, *Aleister Crowley*, 277.
27. John Carter, *Sex and Rockets: The Occult World of Jack Parsons* (Port Townsend, WA: Feral House, 2005), 149.
28. Richard Cavendish, *The Black Arts: A Concise History of Witchcraft, Demonology, and Other Mystical Practices throughout the Ages* (Los Angeles: Tarcher-Perigree, 1968), 2.
29. "Iconic Sgt. Pepper," *Rolling Stone*, accessed November 27, 2020, http://www.rollingstone.com/music/features/beatles-iconic-sgt-pepper-art-10-things-you-didnt-know-w474057; Roger Hutchinson, *Aleister Crowley: The Beast Demystified* (Edinburgh: Mainstream Publishing, 2006).
30. Kaczynski, *Perdurabo*; Lachman, *Aleister Crowley*, 326.
31. Lachman, *Aleister Crowley*, 13.
32. Gary Lachman, "Kenneth Anger: The Crowned and Conquered Child," in *Anger: Magick Lantern Cycle*, DVD lined booklet (London: British Film Institute), 19; Bill Landis, *Anger: The Unauthorized Biography of Kenneth Anger* (New York: Harper, 1995), 195.
33. Landis, *Anger*, 14.
34. Mended in Senate April 21, 1975 amended in Assembly March 3, 1975. (n.d.). https://www.unmarriedamerica.org/Archives/1975-CA-Consenting-Adults-Act/1975-AB489-CA-Consenting-Adults-Act.pdf.
35. J. Hoberman and Jonathan Rosenbaum, *Midnight Movies* (New York: Harper & Row, 1993).
36. Landis, *Anger*, 104–13.
37. Landis, *Anger*, 23, 72–81.
38. Landis, *Anger*, 140; Isaiah 14:4–14 (KJV); accessed November 27, 2020, https://www.esquire.com/uk/culture/news/a5483/kenneth-anger.
39. Roger Ebert, "Interview with Kenneth Anger: Interviews: Roger Ebert," ac-

cessed February 11, 2023, https://www.rogerebert.com/interviews/interview-with-kenneth-anger.
40. Landis, *Anger*, 141–42.
41. Landis, *Anger*, 145.
42. Landis, *Anger*, 158, 145.
43. Landis, *Anger*, 166.
44. Hoberman and Rosenbaum, *Midnight Movies*.
45. Landis, *Anger*, 162–67, 170–74.
46. Landis, *Anger*, 162–67, 170–74.
47. Philip Norman, *Mick Jagger* (Milan: Mondadori, 2013), 553.
48. Steve Appleford, *The Rolling Stones: It's Only Rock and Roll: Song by Song* (New York: Schirmer, 2000), 77.
49. Marianne Faithfull and David Dalton, *Faithfull: An Autobiography* (New York: Cooper Square Press, 2000), 187.
50. Richie Unterberger, "Let It Bleed by the Rolling Stones—Track Info," All Music, accessed February 11, 2023, https://www.allmusic.com/song/let-it-bleed-mt0007209859.
51. "Mick Jagger Remembers," *Rolling Stone*, accessed November 27, 2020, https://web.archive.org/web/20070613021207/http://www.rollingstone.com:80/news/coverstory/mick_jagger_remembers/page/3.
52. "Mick Jagger Remembers."
53. The Rolling Stones, "I'm Free," Genius, accessed November 27, 2020, https://genius.com/The-rolling-stones-im-free-lyrics.
54. Appleford, *The Rolling Stones*, 77.
55. "The Stones Fight the Law and the Law Wins," History.com, accessed November 27, 2020, https://www.history.com/this-day-in-history/the-stones-fight-the-law-and-the-law-wins.
56. Appleford, *The Rolling Stones*, 33.
57. Bayles, *Hole in the Soul*, 271.
58. Booth, *The True Adventures of the Rolling Stones*, 30.
59. Christopher P. Andersen, *Jagger Unauthorized* (New York: Dell, 1994), 123.
60. Appleford, *The Rolling Stones*, 77.
61. Appleford, *The Rolling Stones*, 107.
62. Booth, *The True Adventures of the Rolling Stones*, 140.
63. Bill Wyman and Richard Havers, *Rolling with the Stones* (New York: DK, 2002), 487, 496–97.
64. The Rolling Stones, "Let It Bleed," Genius, accessed November 27, 2020, https://genius.com/The-rolling-stones-let-it-bleed-lyrics; The Rolling Stones, "Dead Flowers," Genius, https://genius.com/The-rolling-stones-dead-flowers-lyrics.
65. Jon Dolan, "Keith Richards' Wildest Escapades: 19 Insane Tales," *Rolling Stone*, December 18, 2019, https://www.rollingstone.com/music/music-lists/keith-richards-wildest-escapades-19-insane-tales-from-a-legendary-life-169242/gunning-for-trouble-1973-68192.
66. Richie Unterberger, "Brian Jones," AllMusic, https://www.allmusic.com/artist/brian-jones-mn0000618445/biography.
67. Keith Richards, *Life*, 212–15.
68. Paul Trynka, *Brian Jones, the Making of the Rolling Stones* (New York: Viking, 2014), 323–36.
69. "Portrait of Bill," accessed April 5, 2011, http://www.timeisonourside.com/bill2.html.
70. Craig Brown, "Keith Needs Mick to Stay Cool," *The Telegraph*, March 1, 2008, https://www.telegraph.co.uk/comment/columnists/craigbrown/3555591/Keith-needs-Mick-to-stay-cool.html. ["Mr. Unhealthy"]; Stanley Booth, *Keith: Standing in the Shadows* (New York: St. Martin's Griffin, 1996), 4 ["an unresurrected Christ"].
71. The Rolling Stones, "Sway," Genius, accessed November 27, 2020, https://genius.com/The-rolling-stones-sway-lyrics.
72. Bockris, *Keith Richards*, 214.
73. Rorabaugh, *American Hippies*, 88.
74. Philip Norman, "The Rolling Stones' Darkest Hit 'Sympathy' for the Devil Turns 50," *Daily Mail*, December 5, 2018, https://www.dailymail.co.uk/news/article-6465489/The-Rolling-Stones-Sympathy-Devil-50-blamed-murder-fire-macabre-events.html.
75. Anthony Scaduto, *Mick Jagger: Everybody's Lucifer* (Philadelphia: David McKay, 1974).
76. Joe Selvin, "The Dark Truth about Mick Jagger and His Notorious Gig," *Daily Mail*, August 20, 2016, https://www.dailymail.co.uk/news/article-3750676/The-dark-truth-Jagger-Altamont.html.
77. "The Altamont Festival," *Encyclopaedia Britannica*, accessed November 27, 2020, https://www.britannica.com/topic/The-Altamont-festival-1688314#ref709728.

78. "The Altamont Festival."
79. Norman, "The Rolling Stones' Darkest Hit."
80. Norman, "The Rolling Stones' Darkest Hit."
81. "The Altamont Festival."
82. Norman, *Mick Jagger*, 555.
83. "The Trouble With 'Cocksucker Blues,'" *Rolling Stone*, November 3, 1977, https://www.rollingstone.com/music/music-news/the-trouble-with-cocksucker-blues-237858.
84. Mick Brown, "True Adventures of the Rolling Stones: Author Stanley Booth Interview," *Rolling Stone*, April 19, 2012, http://www.telegraph.co.uk/culture/music/rockandpopfeatures/9212321/True-Adventures-Of-the-Rolling-Stones-author-Stanley-Booth-interview.html.
85. Bockris, *Keith Richards*, 248.
86. Richards, *Life*, 380.
87. Bockris, *Keith Richards*, 217.
88. Andersen, *Jagger Unauthorized*, 125.
89. "Why the Queen 'Refused to Hand Mick Jagger a Knighthood,'" *The Telegraph*, July 11, 2012, https://www.telegraph.co.uk/news/uknews/theroyalfamily/9391107/Why-the-Queen-refused-to-hand-Mick-Jagger-a-knighthood.html.

Chapter 17

1. Greil Marcus, *Lipstick Traces: A Secret History of the Twentieth Century* (Cambridge, MA: Belknap, 2009), 38–39.
2. Rorabaugh, *American Hippies*, 155, 178.
3. Rorabaugh, *American Hippies*, 179.
4. Rorabaugh, *American Hippies*, 179.
5. Rorabaugh, *American Hippies*, 167.
6. Rorabaugh, *American Hippies*, 196.
7. W.J. Rorabaugh, "How Hippies Created Today's American Culture," History News Network@myHNN, October 3, 2015.
8. https://www.cnbc.com/2017/08/10/silicon-valley-rediscovered-lsd.html.
9. Vincent Bugliosi and Curt Gentry, *Helter Skelter: The True Story of the Manson Murders* (New York: Norton, 2001), 136.
10. Bugliosi and Gentry, *Helter Skelter*, 137.
11. Bugliosi and Gentry, *Helter Skelter*, 140.
12. Bugliosi and Gentry, *Helter Skelter*, 137.
13. Jeff Guinn, *Manson: The Life and Times of Charles Manson* (New York: Simon & Schuster, 2014), 61–64 (pimping), 60–61 (Carnegie), 66–67 (Hubbard).
14. Bugliosi and Gentry, *Helter Skelter*, 140.
15. Bugliosi and Gentry, *Helter Skelter*, 137–46.
16. Rorabaugh, *American Hippies*, 88.
17. Bugliosi and Gentry, *Helter Skelter*, 140.
18. Guinn, *Manson*, 195.
19. Philip Norman, *Paul McCartney: The Life* (New York: Back Bay Books, 2017), 347.
20. "Bobby Beausoleil," Biography.com, accessed December 10, https://web.archive.org/web/20181020105326/https://www.biography.com/people/bobby-beausoleil-20902783.
21. Robert Ebert, "Interview with Kenneth Anger."
22. Guinn, *Manson*, 4.
23. Bugliosi and Gentry, *Helter Skelter*, 667.
24. Tim Ott, "Dennis Wilson and Charles Manson Had a Brief and Bizarre Friendship," Biography.com, accessed November 27, 2020, https://www.biography.com/news/charles-manson-dennis-wilson-friendship.
25. David Middlecamp, "Manson Family Murders Began after Cuesta Grade Arrest in SLO," *The Tribune*, November 17, 2017, https://www.sanluisobispo.com/news/local/news-columns-blogs/photos-from-the-vault/article185291003.html.
26. Middlecamp, "Manson Family Murders."
27. Rorabaugh, *American Hippies*, 87.
28. Linley Sanders, "Charles Manson Is Dead: What Was His 'Helter Skelter' Race War Plan?" *Newsweek*, November 20, 2017, https://www.newsweek.com/charles-manson-what-was-helter-skelter-race-war-plan-716625.
29. Ott, "Dennis Wilson and Charles Manson."
30. Scott A. Bonn, "Origin of the Term 'Serial Killer,'" *Psychology Today*, June 9, 2014, https://www.psychologytoday.com/us/blog/wicked-deeds/201406/origin-the-term-serial-killer.
31. Rorabaugh, *American Hippies*, 88.
32. Rorabaugh, *American Hippies*, 88.
33. "Charles Manson," *Encyclopaedia*

Britannica, accessed November 27, 2020, https://www.britannica.com/biography/Charles-Manson.

34. Kelly Dickerson, "Here's What David Bowie's Song 'Space Oddity' Is Really About," Business Insider, January 11, 2016, http://www.businessinsider.com/david-bowie-song-space-oddity-meaning-2016-1.

35. Paul Trynka, *David Bowie: Starman* (New York: Little, Brown, 2011), 105.

36. Bill DeMain, "The Story behind the Song: Space Oddity by David Bowie," Louder, June 20, 2021, http://teamrock.com/feature/2016-12-24/story-behind-the-song-space-oddity-david-bowie.

37. DeMain, "The Story behind the Song."

38. "Life on Mars," BBC, accessed November 27, 2020, http://www.bbc.co.uk/radio2/soldonsong/songlibrary/lifeonmars.shtml.

39. Nicholas Pegg, *The Complete David Bowie*, 6th ed. (London: Titan Books, 2011), 144.

40. George, *The Death of Rhythm & Blues*, xii.

41. George, *The Death of Rhythm & Blues*, 123.

Chapter 18

1. Hugh McLeod, *The Religious Crisis of the 1960s* (London: Oxford University Press, 2010), 130.
2. McLeod, *Religious Crisis*, 125.
3. McLeod, *Religious Crisis*, 125.
4. McLeod, *Religious Crisis*, 125.
5. Roger Kimball, *The Long March: How the Cultural Revolution of the 1960s Changed America* (New York: Encounter Books, 2001), 13.
6. Pattison, *Triumph of the Vulgarity*, 105.
7. Miles, *Paul McCartney*, 499.
8. Timothy Miller, "The Historical Communal Roots of Ultraconservative Groups," in *1*, ed. Jeffrey Kaplan (Lanham, MD: AltaMira Press, 2002).
9. Robert P. Sutton, *Modern American Communes: A Dictionary* (Westport, CT: Greenwood, 2005), 16.
10. *Commune* (Five Points Video, 2005).
11. *Commune*.
12. *Commune*.

13. Accessed November 27, 2020, https://www.history.com/this-day-in-history/dragnet-tv-show-debuts.

14. David H. Vowell, dir., "The Big Prophet," *Dragnet 1968*, season 2, episode 8, MCA TV, January 11, 1968.

15. David Mikkelson, "LSD Users Stare at the Sun, Snopes," Snopes, November 3, 1998, accessed November 27, 2020, http://www.snopes.com/horrors/drugs/lsdsun.asp.

16. David H. Vowell, dir., "The Big High," *Dragnet 1967*, season 2, episode 18, MCA TV, November 2, 1967.

17. Accessed November 27, 2020, https://www.psychologytoday.com/us/blog/ending-addiction-good/201404/studies-show-long-term-effects-cannabis-the-brain.

18. Vowell, "The Big High."

19. Allan Jones, "John Cale on the Velvet Underground & Nico: 'Everything Was Down-Tuned and Distorted,'" Uncut, August 26, 2018, http://www.uncut.co.uk/news/john-cale-on-the-velvet-underground-nico-30063.

20. Velvet Underground, "I'm Waiting for the Man," Genius, accessed December 11, 2019, https://genius.com/The-velvet-underground-im-waiting-for-the-man-lyrics.

21. Velvet Underground, "I'm Waiting for the Man."

22. Kimball, *The Long March* 148.

23. Rorabaugh, *American Hippies*, 68.

Chapter 19

1. "Stone Wall Riots," *Encyclopaedia Britannica*, accessed November 27, 2020, https://www.britannica.com/event/Stonewall-riots.
2. "Stone Wall Riots."
3. Echols, *Hot Stuff*.
4. "Stone Wall Riots."
5. "Stone Wall Riots."
6. "Full Moon over Stonewall," *Village Voice*, July 3, 1969, 1, 25, 29.
7. Echols, *Hot Stuff*.
8. "Anti–Vietnam War Demonstration Held," *New York Times*, November 15, 2011, https://learning.blogs.nytimes.com/2011/11/15/nov-15-1969-anti-vietnam-war-demonstration-held/.

9. Noah Adams, "Shots Still Reverberate for Survivors of Kent State," NPR, May 3, 2010, https://www.npr.org/templates/story/story.php?storyId=126423778.
10. Accessed November 27, 2020, http://chnm.gmu.edu/hardhats/weloveestablishment.html.
11. Woden Teachout, *Capture the Flag: A Political History of American Patriotism* (New York: Basic Books, 2009), 173–206; David Paul Kuhn, *The Hardhat Riot: Nixon, New York City, and the Dawn of the White Working-Class Revolution* (London: Oxford University Press, 2020).
12. Greg Prato, "Ohio by Crosby, Stills & Nash—Track Info," AllMusic, accessed February 12, 2023, https://www.allmusic.com/song/ohio-mt0035235318.
13. Dorian Lynskey, "Neil Young's Ohio—The Greatest Protest Record," *The Guardian*, May 6, 2010, https://www.theguardian.com/music/2010/may/06/ohio-neil-young-kent-state-shootings.
14. Ron Wynn. "That's the Way Love Is," *AllMusic*, accessed November 27, 2020, https://www.allmusic.com/album/thats-the-way-love-is-mw0000313058.
15. Dorian Lynskey, *33 Revolutions per Minute: A History of Protest Songs, from Billie Holiday to Green Day* (New York: HarperCollins, 2011), 156.
16. "Marvin Gaye," Biography.com, accessed February 12, 2023, https://www.biography.com/musicians/marvin-gaye.
17. "What's Going On," *Rolling Stone*, accessed November 27, 2020, https://www.rollingstone.com/music/music-lists/best-albums-of-all-time-1062063/marvin-gaye-whats-going-on-4-1063232.
18. Bob Gulla, *Icons of R&B and Soul: An Encyclopedia of the Artists Who Revolutionized Rhythm* (Santa Barbara: ABC-CLIO, 2008), 345.
19. John Bush, "What's Going On," AllMusic, accessed May 19, 2021, https://www.allmusic.com/album/whats-going-on-mw0000651085; Lynskcy, *33 Revolutions per Minute*.
20. "What's Going On," Genius, accessed May 19, 2021, https://genius.com/Marvin-gaye-whats-going-on-lyrics.
21. Accessed May 19, 2021, https://www.soundonsound.com/people/marvin-gaye-whats-going.
22. David Hepworth, *Never a Dull Moment: 1971—The Year that Rock Exploded* (New York: St. Martin's Griffin, 2017), 75.
23. "Marvin Gaye," *Billboard*, accessed January 25, 2023, https://www.billboard.com/artist/marvin-gaye.
24. John Bush, "Marvin Gaye—What's Going on Album Reviews, Songs & More," AllMusic, May 20, 1971, https://www.allmusic.com/album/whats-going-on-mw0000651085; William McKeen, *Rock & Roll Is Here to Stay: An Anthology* (New York: Norton, 2000), 529; David Katz, "Marvin Gaye What's Going On—40th Anniversary Edition Review," BBC, June 27, 2011, https://www.bbc.co.uk/music/reviews/pq9p/; Richie Unterberger, "Marvin Gaye," in *The Rough Guide to Rock*, ed. Peter Buckley (London: Rough Guides, 2003), 418.
25. Jordan Michael Smith, "Stop Imagining," American Conservative, November 13, 2019, https://www.theamericanconservative.com/stop-imagining/.
26. Will Lavin, "Yoko Ono Reacts to 'Imagine' Being Used in Olympics Opening Ceremony," NME, July 25, 2021, https://www.nme.com/news/music/yoko-ono-reacts-to-imagine-being-used-in-olympics-opening-ceremony-3001560.
27. William Ruhlmann, "Imagine," AllMusic, accessed March 25, 2021, https://www.allmusic.com/song/imagine-mt0011009899; "Can Russians Own Personal Property?" American Historical Association, accessed April 26, 2022, https://www.historians.org/about-aha-and-membership/aha-history-and-archives/gi-roundtable-series/pamphlets/em-46-our-russian-ally-(1945)/can-russians-own-personal-property.
28. Smith, "Stop Imagining."
29. Brad Schreiber, *Music Is Power: Popular Songs, Social Justice, and the Will to Change* (New Brunswick, NJ: Rutgers University Press, 2019), 124.
30. Luke 17:20–21.
31. David Shef, "*Playboy* Interview with John Lennon and Yoko Ono," *Playboy*, accessed October 19, 2020, https://www.namedat.com/1980-playboy-interview-with-john-lennon-and-yoko-ono/.
32. "Hinduism—Practice," *Encyclopædia Britannica*, accessed February 20, 2023, https://www.britannica.com/topic/Hinduism/Practice; "Buddhism,"

Encyclopædia Britannica, accessed February 20, 2023, https://www.britannica.com/topic/Buddhism; see, for example, R. Bauckham, "Universalism: A Historical Survey," Themelios, accessed February 20, 2023, https://www.theologicalstudies.org.uk/article_universalism_bauckham.html [universal salvation]; T.B. Talbott, *The Inescapable Love of God* (Eugene, OR: Cascade Books, 2014) [challenging translations and interpretations].

33. Ruhlmann, "Imagine."
34. Laurie Ulster, "The Legacy of John Lennon's Song 'Imagine,'" Biography.com, October 14, 2020, https://www.biography.com/musicians/john-lennon-imagine-song-facts.
35. Matthew 19:21–24 (KJV).
36. Joe Taysom, "The Misunderstood Meaning of Iconic John Lennon Song 'Imagine,'" Far Out Magazine, November 12, 2021, https://faroutmagazine.co.uk/john-lennon-imagine-real-meaning-communism/.
37. Sheff, "*Playboy* Interview with John Lennon and Yoko Ono."
38. "APA Dictionary of Psychology," American Psychological Association, accessed February 12, 2023, https://dictionary.apa.org/primal-therapy-https://dictionary.apa.org/primal-therapy.
39. "Dr. Janov's essential insight—that our earliest experiences strongly influence later well-being—is no longer in doubt.... His long-held belief that the brain, human development, and psychological well-being need to be studied in the context of evolution—from the brain stem up—now lies at the heart of the integration of neuroscience and psychotherapy."—Lou Cozolino, PsyD, professor of psychology, Pepperdine University, accessed January 26, 2023, https://www.prweb.com/releases/2011/12/prweb9039351.htm; Dr. Haley Peckham, "Epigenetics: The Dogma-Defying Discovery That Genes Learn from Experience," *Science of Psychotherapy*, July 17, 2013, accessed January 27, 2023, https://www.thescienceofpsychotherapy.com/epigenetics-the-dogma-defying-discovery-that-genes-learn-from-experience.
40. Bill Harry, *The John Lennon Encyclopedia* (London: Virgin Books, 2001), 408–10; Geoffrey Giuliano, *The Lost Lennon Interviews* (New York: Adams Media, 1996), 136–37. Original interview made in 1970.
41. Ulster, "The Legacy of John Lennon's Song 'Imagine.'"
42. https://genius.com/John-lennon-god-lyrics, accessed March 22, 2021.
43. 1 John 4:9.
44. "President Richard Nixon's 14 Addresses to the Nation on Vietnam," accessed November 27, 2020, https://www.nixonfoundation.org/2017/09/president-richard-nixons-14-addresses-nation-vietnam.
45. Meg Mathias, "Fred Hampton." *Encyclopædia Britannica*, accessed February 12, 2023, https://www.britannica.com/biography/Fred-Hampton.
46. Edward Jay Epstein, "The Black Panthers and the Police: A Pattern of Genocide?" *New Yorker*, February 13, 1971.
47. Epstein, "Black Panthers."
48. Marcelo Gleiser, "ExxonMobil vs. the World," NPR, November 30, 2016, https://www.npr.org/sections/13.7/2016/11/30/503825417/exxonmobil-vs-the-world.
49. Greene, *Life in America during the 1960s*, 73.
50. "Pentagon Papers," *Encyclopaedia Britannica*, accessed November 27, 2020, https://www.britannica.com/topic/Pentagon-Papers.
51. "Equal Rights Amendment Passed by Congress," History.com, accessed November 27, 2020, http://www.history.com/this-day-in-history/equal-rights-amendment-passed-by-congress.
52. "Paris Peace Accords Signed," History.com, accessed November 27, 2020, http://www.history.com/this-day-in-history/paris-peace-accords-signed.
53. Stephen Daggett, "Costs of Major U.S. Wars," Congressional Research Service, June 29, 2010, https://sgp.fas.org/crs/natsec/RS22926.pdf; "Vietnam War U.S. Military Fatal Casualty Statistics," National Archives, accessed November 27, 2020, https://www.archives.gov/research/military/vietnam-war/casualty-statistics#:~:text=April%2029%2C%202008.-,The%20Vietnam%20Conflict%20Extract%20Data%20File%20of%20the%20Defense%20Casualty,casualties%20of%20the%20Vietnam%20War.
54. "Welcome to the American Presidency Project: The American Presidency

Project," American Presidency Project, February 12, 2007, https://www.presidency.ucsb.edu/.
55. "Pentagon Papers."
56. "Watergate Scandal," *Encyclopaedia Britannica*, accessed November 27, 2020, https://www.britannica.com/event/Watergate-Scandal.
57. "Watergate Scandal."
58. C. Gribben, "Dominance of Evangelical Millennialism, 1970–2000," in *Evangelical Millennialism in the Trans-Atlantic World, 1500–2000* (London: Palgrave Macmillan, 2011).
59. "The New Right," U.S. History, accessed November 27, 2020, http://www.ushistory.org/us/58e.asp.
60. John Bear, *The #1 New York Times Best Seller: Intriguing Facts about the 484 Books that Have Been #1 New York Times Bestsellers since the First List, 50 Years Ago* (Berkeley: Ten Speed Press, 1992).
61. Cowan, *The Tribes of America*, 80.
62. Cowan, *The Tribes of America*, 7.
63. Cowan, *The Tribes of America*, 2.
64. Cowan, *The Tribes of America*, 80.
65. Cowan, *The Tribes of America*, 79.
66. Cowan, *The Tribes of America*, 90.
67. Cowan, *The Tribes of America*, 90.
68. Cowan, *The Tribes of America*, 14–15.
69. Cowan, *The Tribes of America*, 90.
70. Cowan, *The Tribes of America*, 3.

Chapter 20A

1. Stephen Thomas Erlewine, "The Rolling Stones," AllMusic, accessed January 2, 2021, https://www.allmusic.com/artist/the-rolling-stones-mn0000894465/biography.
2. Marion Leonard, *The Beat Goes On: Liverpool, Popular Music and the Changing City* (Liverpool: Liverpool University Press, 2010), 129; Wald, *How the Beatles Destroyed Rock 'n' Roll*.
3. Joe Layden and Noel Monk, *Runnin' with the Devil: A Backstage Pass to the Wild Times, Loud Rock, and the Down and Dirty Truth behind the Making of Van Halen* (New York: Dey Street Books, 2017), 191.
4. Bertrand, *Race Rock and Elvis*, 101.
5. Accessed November 27, 2020, https://www.newyorker.com/magazine/2018/09/24/the-unlikely-endurance-of-christian-rock.
6. Accessed November 27, 2020, https://www.newyorker.com/magazine/2018/09/24/the-unlikely-endurance-of-christian-rock.
7. Accessed November 27, 2020, https://www.nodepression.com/charlie-louvin-magic-songs-of-life/2/.
8. Accessed December 15, 2019, https://www.allmusic.com/album/toulouse-street-mw0000189834; accessed December 15, 2019, https://www.nytimes.com/2006/12/24/fashion/24norman.html.
9. Accessed November 27, 2020, http://www.washedred.com/content/?contentID=14.
10. Accessed December 15, 2019, http://www.washedred.com/content/?contentID=14.
11. Accessed November 27, 2020, https://www.allmusic.com/artist/barry-mcguire-mn0000787011/biography.
12. Accessed November 27, 2020, http://www.washedred.com/content/?contentID=14; accessed November 27, 2020, https://www.allmusic.com/artist/barry-mcguire-mn0000787011/biography.
13. Accessed November 27, 2020, https://www.allmusic.com/artist/barry-mcguire-mn0000787011/biography.
14. "Larry Norman," AllMusic, accessed November 27, 2020, https://www.allmusic.com/artist/larry-norman-mn0000132579/biography.
15. "Larry Norman"; David W. Stowe, *No Sympathy for the Devil: Christian Pop Music and the Transformation of American Evangelicalism* (Chapel Hill: University of North Carolina Press, 2013), 36–37.
16. Gregory Rumburg. "Rock for the Ages," *CCM Magazine*, October 1998, 55, 6.
17. Jason Ankeny, "Larry Norman," AllMusic, accessed November 27, 2020, https://www.allmusic.com/artist/larry-norman-mn0000132579/biography.
18. Ankeny, "Larry Norman."
19. Ankeny, "Larry Norman."
20. Ankeny, "Larry Norman."
21. Kelefa Sanneh, "The Unlikely Endurance of Christian Rock," *New Yorker*, September 17, 2018, https://www.newyorker.com/magazine/2018/09/24/the-unlikely-endurance-of-christian-rock.
22. "Kris Kristofferson," AllMusic, accessed November 27, 2020, https://www.

allmusic.com/artist/kris-kristofferson-mn0000774588; Gregory Alan Thornbury, "What Evangelicals Looked like before They Entered the Political Fray," *Washington Post*, March 20, 2018, https://www.washingtonpost.com/news/acts-of-faith/wp/2018/03/20/what-evangelicals-looked-like-before-they-entered-the-political-fray/?utm_term=.0d87c11b252d; Sanneh, "The Unlikely Endurance of Christian Rock."

23. "Born Again Christians," Encyclopedia.com, accessed January 21, 2023, https://www.encyclopedia.com/religion/legal-and-political-magazines/born-again-christians.

24. Sanneh, "The Unlikely Endurance of Christian Rock."

25. Sanneh, "The Unlikely Endurance of Christian Rock."

26. Accessed November 27, 2020, http://talesfromthelaboratory.typepad.com/tales_from_the_microbial_/2007/09/larry-normans-s.html.

27. Michael S. Hamilton, "The Dissatisfaction of Francis Schaeffer, Part 2," Christianity Today, March 3, 1997, https://www.christianitytoday.com/ct/1997/march3/7t322b.html.

28. Thornbury, "What Evangelicals Looked Like."

29. "Swaggart Plans to Step Down," *New York Times*, October 15, 1991, https://www.nytimes.com/1991/10/15/us/swaggart-plans-to-step-down.html.

30. Arsenio Orteza, "Larry Norman's Tragic Post-Mortem," *World Magazine*, July 12, 2008, https://web.archive.org/web/20080802001400/http://www.worldmag.com/articles/14180 [child]; "Larry Norman," AllMusic, accessed November 27, 2020, https://www.allmusic.com/artist/larry-norman-mn0000132579/biography [KGB].

31. Thornbury, "What Evangelicals Looked Like"; Jemayel Khawaja, "Mike Pence, Finding God, and the Shifting Agenda of Christian Music Festivals," BBC, March 21, 2017, https://www.theguardian.com/music/2017/mar/21/christian-music-festivals-mike-pence-politics-lifestyle-culture; Kurt Loder, "Bob Dylan, Recovering Christian," *Rolling Stone*, June 21, 1984, https://www.rollingstone.com/music/music-news/bob-dylan-recovering-christian-87237.

32. Dennis Hevesi, "Larry Norman, Singer of Christian Rock Music, Dies at 60," *New York Times*, March 4, 2008, https://www.nytimes.com/2008/03/04/arts/music/04norman.html Accessed 11/27/2020.

33. Hevesi, "Larry Norman."

Chapter 20B

1. Accessed November 27, 2020, http://www.museum.tv/eotv/bradybunch.htm.

2. Seth Margolis, "Comfy Old Shows Charm a New Audience," *New York Times*, July 12, 1998, InfoTrac Newsstand; accessed November 27, 2020, http://www.museum.tv/eotv/fatherknows.htm.

3. Accessed November 27, 2020, http://www.museum.tv/eotv/fatherknows.htm.

4. Joanna Weiss, "The Magic of 'The Brady Bunch' Was in Its Simplicity," Boston.com, July 17, 2011, http://archive.boston.com/bostonglobe/editorial_opinion/oped/articles/2011/07/17/magic_of_the_brady_bunch_was_in_its_simplicity/.

5. Accessed November 27, 2020, http://www.museum.tv/eotv/bradybunch.htm.

6. "The Brady Bunch Movie," IMDB.com, accessed December 27, 2020, https://www.imdb.com/title/tt0112572/; https://www.imdb.com/title/tt0118073/?ref_=tt_sims_tt.

7. *The Brady Bunch*, season 1, episode 19, "The Big Sprain."

8. *The Brady Bunch*, season 1, episode 1, accessed November 27, 2020, http://www.davidbrady.com/eb/bbtop10.html.

Chapter 21

1. Jon Savage and Johnny Marr, *England's Dreaming: Sex Pistols and Punk Rock* (London: Faber & Faber, 2016), 61.

2. Stephen Thomas Erlewine, "Led Zeppelin," AllMusic, accessed November 27, 2022, https://www.allmusic.com/artist/led-zeppelin-mn0000139026/biography.

3. Dave Thompson, *Robert Plant: The Voice that Sailed the Zeppelin* (Lanham, MD: Backbeat, 2014), 22.

4. Thompson, *Robert Plant*, 25–26.

5. Thompson, *Robert Plant*, 23.

6. Thompson, *Robert Plant*, 33.

7. Brad Tolinski, *Light and Shade:*

Notes—Chapter 21

Conversations with Jimmie Page (Toronto: McClelland & Stewart, 2013), 23.

8. Tolinski, *Light and Shade*, 23.
9. Tolinski, *Light and Shade*, 25.
10. Tolinski, *Light and Shade*, 29.
11. Tolinski, *Light and Shade*, 36.
12. "John Paul Jones," AllMusic, accessed November 27, 2020, https://www.allmusic.com/artist/john-paul-jones-mn0000231997/biography.
13. Tolinski, *Light and Shade*, 85.
14. "The 50 Greatest Drummers of All Time," *Modern Drummer*, accessed November 27, 2020, https://www.moderndrummer.com/article/march-2014-50-greatest-drummers-time.
15. Michael Hann, "Yes, Led Zeppelin Took from Other People's Records—but Then They Transformed Them," *The Guardian*, April 12, 2016, https://www.theguardian.com/music/musicblog/2016/apr/12/led-zeppelin-other-peoples-records-transformed-borrowed.
16. Tolinski, *Light and Shade*, 195.
17. John Mendelsohn, "Led Zeppelin," *Rolling Stone*, March 15, 1969.
18. Accessed November 27, 2020, https://genius.com/21157844.
19. Erlewine, "Led Zeppelin."
20. Gordon Fletcher, "Houses of the Holy," *Rolling Stone*, June 7, 1973, https://www.rollingstone.com/music/music-album-reviews/houses-of-the-holy-2-250354.
21. Travis Clark, "The 50 Best-Selling Albums of All Time," Business Insider, September 22, 2021, https://www.businessinsider.com/50-best-selling-albums-all-time-2016-9#6-pink-floyd-the-wall-45; Sarah Anderson, "The 50 Best-Selling Albums Ever," NME, November 12, 2010, https://www.nme.com/photos/the-50-best-selling-albums-ever-1419009.
22. Stephen Davis, *Hammer of the Gods* (New York: Berkley Books, 2002), 133.
23. Dave Lewis, *The Complete Guide to the Music of Led Zeppelin* (London: Omnibus Press, 2010).
24. Nigel Williamson, *The Rough Guide to Led Zeppelin* (London: Rough Guides, 2007), 230.
25. Katie Serena, "Aleister Crowley, the Occultist Who Horrified Early 1900s England," All That's Interesting, August 22, 2021, https://allthatsinteresting.com/aleister-crowley.
26. Landis, *Anger*, 183–84.
27. Landis, *Anger*, 183–84.
28. Fletcher, "Houses of the Holy."
29. Chris Salewicz, "Anger Rising: Jimmy Page and Kenneth's Lucifer," NME, 1977.
30. Accessed November 27, 2022, http://www.beausoleil.net/wizard/chronicles/fallen_angel_blues.htm.
31. John Feffer, "The Problem of Surplus White Men," accessed January 14, 2020, https://www.resilience.org/resilience-author/john-feffer, originally published by Foreign Policy in Focus, https://fpif.org/the-problemof-surplus-white-men.
32. "OPEC," *Encyclopaedia Britannica*, accessed January 14, 2020, https://www.britannica.com/topic/OPEC.
33. "The Sickened Economy," U.S. History, accessed January 15, 2020, https://www.ushistory.org/us/58b.asp.
34. "Classic Rock," accessed November 27, 2020, https://web.archive.org/web/20170604024643/http://www.robertchristgau.com/xg/music/60s-det.php.
35. Davis, *Hammer of the Gods*, 194.
36. Mark Beech, "Led Zeppelin Adds to 300 Million Sales with Live Album, 50th-Anniversary Surprises," *Forbes*, January 27, 2018, https://www.forbes.com/sites/markbeech/2018/01/27/led-zeppelin-adds-to-300-million-sales-with-live-album-50th-anniversary-surprises/#40ac2450ca59; accessed November 27, 2020, https://www.ledzeppelin.com/event/may-4-1973.
37. "Peter Grant Diets," accessed March 12, 2022, https://ultimateclassicrock.com/peter-grant-dies.
38. William Weir, "How the Marshall Amp Changed Rock," *The Atlantic*, April 11, 2012, https://www.theatlantic.com/entertainment/archive/2012/04/how-the-marshall-amp-changed-rock-and-the-meaning-of-loud/255705.
39. Lewis, *The Complete Guide to the Music of Led Zeppelin*.
40. Accessed November 27, 2020, https://www.msn.com/en-us/movies/gallery/15-things-you-never-knew-about-almost-famous/ss-AAe7aSf#image=13.
41. Accessed November 27, 2020, https://www.billboard.com/articles/columns/rock/6568422/led-zeppelin-starship-party-plane-mick-jagger-allman-brothers.
42. Joel McIver, "Zep-O-Philia," *Classic*

Rock Magazine: Classic Rock Presents Led Zeppelin, 2008, 126.

43. Ann Powers, *Good Booty: Love and Sex, Black and White, Body and Soul in American Music* (New York: Dey Street Books, 2017), 148, Aerosmith and Stephen Davis, *Walk This Way: The Autobiography of Aerosmith* (New York: HarperCollins, 2012), 225 (Steven Tyler).

44. Lori Mattix, "I Lost My Virginity to David Bowie," Thrillist, November 3, 2015, https://www.thrillist.com/entertainment/nation/i-lost-my-virginity-to-david-bowie.

45. Powers, *Good Booty*, 204.

46. Craig McLean, "Good Time Girl: Memories of Super Groupie Pamela Des Barres," *The Guardian*, May 6, 2018, https://www.theguardian.com/global/2018/may/06/good-time-girl-memories-of-a-super-groupie.

47. Powers, *Good Booty*, 209.

48. Powers, *Good Booty*, 209.

49. Powers, *Good Booty*, 208.

50. "Creedence Clearwater Revival, 'Fortunate Son,'" *Rolling Stone*, accessed November 27, 2020, https://www.rollingstone.com/music/music-lists/500-greatest-songs-of-all-time-151127/creedence-clearwater-revival-fortunate-son-40918/; Brandon Stosuy, "VH1's 100 Greatest Hard Rock Songs," Stereogum, January 5, 2009, https://www.stereogum.com/43591/vh1s_100_greatest_hard_rock_songs/franchises/list.

51. Led Zeppelin, "Whole Lotta Love," Genius, accessed November 27, 2020, https://genius.com/Led-zeppelin-whole-lotta-love-lyrics.

52. Bayles, *Hole in Our Soul*, 325.

53. Philip Auslander, *Performing Glam Rock Gender and Theatricality in Popular Music* (Ann Arbor: University of Michigan Press, 2006), 201.

54. Lisa Robinson, "Stairway to Excess," *Vanity Fair*, February 18, 2014, https://www.vanityfair.com/culture/2003/11/led-zeppelin-1970s-lisa-robinson.

55. Dave Lewis, *Led Zeppelin: Celebration II: The "Tight but Loose" Files* (London: Omnibus Press, 2003); Booth, *The True Adventures of the Rolling Stones*, 54.

56. Chris Salewicz, *Jimmy Page: The Definitive Biography* (New York: Da Capo, 2019), 447, 458.

57. Chris Welch, *Led Zeppelin* (London: Orion Books, 1994), 92–94.

58. Welch, *Led Zeppelin*, 92–94.

59. Bill Meredith, "Robert Plant," AllMusic, accessed November 27, 2020, https://www.allmusic.com/artist/robert-plant-mn0000830538/biography; Thom Jurek, "Raising Sand," AllMusic, November 27, 2020, https://www.allmusic.com/album/raising-sand-mw0000748589.

60. Accessed October 19, 2020, https://www.xxlmag.com/15-rap-songs-sample-led-zeppelin.

61. Ian Christe, *Sound of the Beast: The Complete Headbanging History of Heavy Metal* (New York: It Books, 2004), 4.

62. Christe, *Sound of the Beast*, 21.

63. Ozzy Osbourne and Chris Ayres, *I Am Ozzy* (Leicester, UK: W.F. Howes, 2010), 12.

64. Jessica Brain, "Peaky Blinders," Historic UK, accessed April 12, 2022, https://www.historic-uk.com/HistoryUK/HistoryofBritain/Peaky-Blinders.

65. Osbourne and Ayres, *I Am Ozzy*, 12; "The History of Council Housing," accessed November 27, 2020, https://fet.uwe.ac.uk/conweb/house_ages/council_housing/print.htm.

66. Osbourne and Ayres, *I Am Ozzy*, 17.

67. Osbourne and Ayres, *I Am Ozzy*, 31.

68. Steven Rosen, *The Story of Black Sabbath: Wheels of Confusion* (Chessington, UK: Castle Communications, 1996), 135; Osbourne and Ayres, *I Am Ozzy*, 31.

69. "Ozzy Osbourne—Mr. Crowley," Genius, retrieved February 15, 2023, https://genius.com/Ozzy-osbourne-mr-crowley-lyrics.

70. Tony Iommi, *Iron Man: My Journey through Heaven and Hell with Black Sabbath* (New York: Da Capo, 2011), 54 [horror], 81 [religion]; "Black Sabbath," accessed November 27, 2020, https://www.rockhall.com/inductees/black-sabbath.

71. Osbourne and Ayres, *I Am Ozzy*, 83.

72. "Black Sabbath," Genius, accessed November 27, 2020, https://genius.com/Black-sabbath-black-sabbath-lyrics.

73. Christe, *Sound of the Beast*, 9.

74. Christe, *Sound of the Beast*, 21.

75. "Black Sabbath," accessed November 27, 2020, https://www.rockhall.com/inductees/black-sabbath.

76. Christe, *Sound of the Beast*, 22.

77. "Snowblind," Genius, accessed No-

vember 27, 2020, https://genius.com/Blacksabbath-snowblind-lyrics.

78. Rosen, *The Story of Black Sabbath*.

79. "Black Sabbath," AllMusic, accessed November 27, 2020, https://www.allmusic.com/artist/black-sabbath-mn0000771438.

80. "Ted Nugent Biography," A&E, accessed October 19, 2010, https://www.youtube.com/watch?v=5XyUFvC6mDw. 0:33–0:40.

81. "Ted Nugent Biography."

82. Gay Rosenthal, "Behind the Music," Episode, Ted Nugent 1, no. 26, VH1, April 19, 1998.

83. Rosenthal, "Behind the Music."

84. Rosenthal, "Behind the Music."

85. Rosenthal, "Behind the Music."

86. "Ted Nugent Biography."

87. Rosenthal, "Behind the Music."

88. Rosenthal, "Behind the Music."

89. Accessed December 18, 2019, https://www.youtube.com/watch?v=M49j05LZ9WY.

90. As quoted by Michael Azerrad, *Our Band Could Be Your Life: Scenes from the American Indie Underground, 1981–1991* (New York: Little, Brown, 2001).

91. Azerrad, *Our Band Could Be Your Life*.

92. FanTC, "Ted Nugent Hibernation-Full," YouTube, December 16, 2011, https://www.youtube.com/watch?v=M49j05LZ9WY.

93. FanTC, "Ted Nugent Hibernation-Full."

94. FanTC, "Ted Nugent Hibernation-Full."

95. Ted Nugent, "Jailbait," Genius, accessed January 2, 2021, https://genius.com/Ted-nugent-jailbait-lyrics.

96. "50 Greatest Guitar Solos," Guitar World, accessed November 27, 2020, https://www.guitarworld.com/gw-archive/50-greatest-guitar-solos.

97. Jeb Wright, "Wildman Ted Nugent Boards the Midwest Rock 'n' Roll Express Tour," Classic Rock Revisited, accessed October 19, 2020, http://www.classicrockrevisited.com/show_interview.php?id=948.

98. Wright, "Wildman Ted Nugent."

99. "Ted Nugent," AllMusic, accessed November 27, 2020, https://www.allmusic.com/artist/ted-nugent-mn0000749970.

100. Michael Roberts, "Ted's World," Westword, July 27, 1994, http://www.westword.com/music/teds-world-5054209.

101. Timothy Johnson, "20 Inflammatory Comments from State of the Union Invitee Ted Nugent," MediaMatters, February 11, 2014, https://www.mediamatters.org/national-rifle-association/20-inflammatory-comments-state-union-invitee-ted-nugent; Nathan Smith, "The Five Most Repellent Things Ted Nugent Has Ever Done," Houston Press, August 14, 2014, http://www.houstonpress.com/music/the-five-most-repellent-things-ted-nugent-has-ever-done-6756533.

102. "Ted Nugent Dubs Next Tour 'Black Power 2013,'" *Rolling Stone*, February 22, 2013, https://www.rollingstone.com/music/music-news/ted-nugent-dubs-next-tour-black-power-2013-186780.

103. Timothy Johnson and Coleman Lowndes, "The 10 Worst Things NRA's Ted Nugent Said during His 'Black Power' Concert Tour," AlterNet, August 20, 2013, https://www.alternet.org/2013/08/10-worst-things-nras-ted-nugent-said-during-his-black-power-concert-tour/; "Ted Nugent's Response to New Haven Protesters & I Can't Quit You, Baby," YouTube, August 2, 2013, https://www.youtube.com/watch?v=y8XXAa4X2ng&feature=youtu.be&t=1m57s.

104. Johnson, "20 Inflammatory Comments"; "Ted Nugent Talks about MTV and Rap Music," YouTube, April 5, 2008, https://www.youtube.com/watch?v=q_tprD0_8LM.

105. Arlene Nisson Lassin, "Gene Simmons' Mom, the Holocaust, and Me," Huffington Post, April 17, 2015, https://www.huffingtonpost.com/arlene-lassin/gene-simmons-mom-the-hologene-simmons-mom-the-holocaust-and-me_b_7082854.html.

106. "Mending Kids International Honors Gene Simmons, Shannon Tweed-Simmons, Nick Simmons and Sophie Simmons at Annual Gala," November 11, 2013, https://www.prnewswire.com/news-releases/mending-kids-international-honors-gene-simmons-shannon-tweed-simmons-nick-simmons-and-sophie-simmons-at-annual-gala-231487311.html.

107. *Kiss: Beyond the Makeup* (VH1, 2000).

108. *Kiss: Beyond the Makeup*.

109. *Kiss: Beyond the Makeup*.

110. Accessed November 27, 2020,

https://web.archive.org/web/20150623120444/http://50.6.195.142/archives/70s_files/19761120.html.
111. Weezer, "Cheap Trick," accessed November 27, 2020, https://genius.com/Cheap-trick-surrender-lyrics; Weezer, "In the Garage," accessed November 27, 2020, https://genius.com/Weezer-in-the-garage-lyrics; Wilco, "Heavy Metal Drummer," Genius, accessed November 27, 2020, https://genius.com/3278166.
112. *Kiss: Beyond the Makeup.*
113. Fred Woodward, *Rolling Stone: The Illustrated Portraits* (New York: Chronicle Books, 2000), 214.
114. Steve Strauss, "Gene Simmons of Kiss Says This 1 Word Made Him a Millionaire," *Inc.*, accessed October 19, 2020, https://www.inc.com/steve-strauss/the-one-simple-word-that-gene-simmons-says-made-kiss-a-billion-dollar-business.html.
115. "Gene Simmons," *USA Today*, January 21, 2005, http://www.usatoday.com/community/chat/2002-02-01-gsimmons.htm; Laura Armstrong, "Kiss Goodbye," *The Sun*, May 19, 2016, https://www.thesun.co.uk/archives/uncategorized/1207321/rocker-gene-simmons-ive-slept-with-4800-groupies-but-my-wife-made-me-burn-all-the-polaroids.
116. Accessed November 27, 2020, http://www.ucdenver.edu/academics/colleges/CLAS/Programs/HumanitiesSocialSciences/Students/Documents/Gene%20Simmons%20and%20Terry%20Gross_Fresh%20Air.pdf.
117. Accessed November 27, 2020, http://www.ucdenver.edu/academics/colleges/CLAS/Programs/HumanitiesSocialSciences/Students/Documents/Gene%20Simmons%20and%20Terry%20Gross_Fresh%20Air.pdf.
118. "Kiss," Rock & Roll Hall of Fame, accessed November 27, 2020, https://www.rockhall.com/inductees/kiss.

Chapter 22

1. Michael Chabon in *McSweeney's, No. 33: The San Francisco Panorama Unbound* (San Francisco: McSweeney's, 2010).
2. Dave Marsh, *Before I Get Old*; Keith Altham, "Lily Isn't Pornographic, Say Who," NME, May 20, 1967; accessed January 20, 2020, http://magnetmagazine.com/2002/09/07/power-pop-the-70s-the-birth-of-uncool/.
3. Chabon.
4. Chabon.
5. Chabon.
6. "The Birth of Uncool," Magnet Magazine, September 7, 2002, http://magnetmagazine.com/2002/09/07/power-pop-the-70s-the-birth-of-uncool.
7. "The Birth of Uncool."
8. Chabon.
9. Rob Jovanovic, *Big Star: The Short Life, Painful Death, and Unexpected Resurrection of the Kings of Power Pop* (Chicago: Chicago Review Press, 2005), 295–96.
10. Jovanovic, *Big Star*, 30.
11. Holly George-Warren, *A Man Called Destruction: The Life and Music of Alex Chilton, from Box Tops to Big Star to Backdoor Man* (New York: Penguin, 2014), 10.
12. George-Warren, *A Man Called Destruction*, 15.
13. Jovanovic, *Big Star*, 28.
14. George-Warren, *A Man Called Destruction*, 72–73.
15. George-Warren, *A Man Called Destruction*, 84–85, 91–92, 95.
16. George-Warren, *A Man Called Destruction*, 56.
17. Jovanovic, *Big Star*, 51.
18. George-Warren, *A Man Called Destruction*, 103.
19. George-Warren, *A Man Called Destruction*, 103.
20. Jovanovic, *Big Star*, 94.
21. Jovanovic, *Big Star*, 92–93.
22. George-Warren, *A Man Called Destruction*, 110.
23. "Big Star—The Ballad of El Goodo," Genius, accessed February 12, 2023, https://genius.com/Big-star-the-ballad-of-el-goodo-lyrics.
24. Brad Elliot, "Pet Sounds Liner Notes," Pet Sounds (CD Liner), The Beach Boys (Capitol Records, 1999).
25. George-Warren, *A Man Called Destruction*, 64.
26. George-Warren, *A Man Called Destruction*, 107.
27. Jovanovich, *Big Star*, 113.
28. Jovanovich, *Big Star*, 187.
29. Jovanovic, *Big Star*, 210–11.
30. Rich Tupica, *There Was a Light: The Cosmic History of Chris Bell and the Rise*

of *Big Star* (New York: Permuted Press, 2022), 195–96, 332, 359.

31. Jovanovic, *Big Star*, 169.
32. Jovanovic, *Big Star*, 114–18.
33. Jovanovic, *Big Star*, 295–96 [concert list], 134–35 [Hummel quitting].
34. Jovanovic, *Big Star*, 140.
35. George-Warren, *A Man Called Destruction*, 187.
36. Jovanovic, *Big Star*, 43.
37. Jovanovic, *Big Star*, 137–38.
38. Jovanovic, *Big Star*, 147–53.
39. Jovanovic, *Big Star*, 147–53.
40. Jovanovic, *Big Star*, 151; Cub Koda, "Alex Chilton," AllMusic, accessed November 27, 2020, https://www.allmusic.com/artist/alex-chilton-mn0000620155/biography.
41. Gary Graff and Daniel Durchholz, *Musichound Rock: The Essential Album Guide* (Detroit: Visible Ink Press, 1999), 106.
42. Jovanovic, *Big Star*, 161.
43. Jovanovic, *Big Star*, 155.
44. George-Warren, *A Man Called Destruction*, 164.
45. George-Warren, *A Man Called Destruction*, 164.
46. Stewart Mason, "Jesus Christ," AllMusic, accessed November 27, 2020, https://www.allmusic.com/song/jesus-christ-mt0004043043.
47. Jovanovic, *Big Star*, 205.
48. George-Warren, *A Man Called Destruction*, 223.
49. Tupica, *There Was a Light*, 398–403.
50. Tupica, *There Was a Light*, 223.
51. Tupica, *There Was a Light*, 255.
52. Tupica, *There Was a Light*, 1.
53. Mark Deming, "Chris Bell," All Music, accessed January 10, 2021, https://www.allmusic.com/artist/chris-bell-mn0000105845/biography.
54. Deming, "Chris Bell."
55. George-Warren, *A Man Called Destruction*, 296, 308-309.

Chapter 23

1. Max Pearl, "Dancing on Our Own: Why White America Ditched Couple Dancing," TPM, March 9, 2015, https://talkingpointsmemo.com/theslice/why-white-america-started-dancing-alone.
2. https://talkingpointsmemo.com/theslice/why-white-america-started-dancing-alone [solo dancing]; Powers, *Good Booty*, 42 [hootchie-kootch and shimmy].
3. Lauren Vinopal, "Why White Men Can't Dance, according to Science," Fatherly, November 16, 2018, https://www.fatherly.com/health-science/science-explains-why-men-are-bad-at-dancing/ ["cooled down," lack of ballrooms and dancing]; Richard Powers, "Teen Dances of the 1950s," https://socialdance.stanford.edu/Syllabi/teen_dances.htm [reasons for decline in dancing].
4. Jason Ankeny, "Chubby Checker Biography, Songs, & Albums," AllMusic, accessed February 12, 2023, https://www.allmusic.com/artist/chubby-checker-mn0000116984/biography.
5. Elridge Cleaver, *Soul on Ice* (1999), 228.
6. Maxine Leeds Craig, *Sorry I Don't Dance: Why Men Refuse to Move* (New York: Oxford University Press, 2014), 116.
7. Wald, *How the Beatles Destroyed Rock 'n' Roll*, 241.
8. Echols, *Hot Stuff*, 250.
9. Pearl, "Dancing on Our Own."
10. Wald, *How the Beatles Destroyed Rock 'n' Roll*, 250.
11. Echols, *Hot Stuff*, 214.
12. Robert Townsend, dir., *Raw* (Paramount Pictures, 1987).
13. Chuck Klosterman, *Fargo Rock City: A Heavy Metal Odyssey in Rural North Dakota* (New York: Scribner, 2002), 65.
14. Craig, *Sorry I Don't Dance*, 190.
15. "Soul Train," *Encyclopaedia Britannica*, https://www.britannica.com/topic/Soul-Train.
16. Ta-Nehisi Coates, "Let's Do This like a Prison Break," *The Atlantic*, April 9, 2009, https://www.theatlantic.com/entertainment/archive/2009/04/lets-do-this-like-a-prison-break/9900.
17. Robert Palmer, "Stones Visit Memphis," *Rolling Stone*, August 14, 1975, https://www.rollingstone.com/music/music-news/stones-visit-memphis-193525.
18. Robert Christgau, "Classic Rock," accessed November 27, 2020, https://web.archive.org/web/20170604024643/http://www.robertchristgau.com/xg/music/60s-det.php.
19. David Zurawik, "On PBS, Six Hours of the 60s," *Baltimore Sun*, January 20, 1991, https://www.baltimoresun.com/

news/bs-xpm-1991-01-20-1991020182-story.html.

20. Neil McCormick, "We Gave Seventies Rock Stars a Licence to Behave Dadly," *The Telegraph*, February 7, 2015, https://www.telegraph.co.uk/culture/music/rockandpopfeatures/11395848/We-gave-Seventies-rock-stars-a-license-to-behave-badly.html.

21. Powers, *Good Booty*, 148 [Jimmy Page]; Davis, *Walk This Way*, 225 [Steven Tyler].

22. Annie Zaleski, "How a Rolling Stones Ad Spawned a Music Industry Revolution," UCR, April 23, 2016, http://ultimateclassicrock.com/rolling-stones-black-and-blue-ad/.

23. C.J. Chilvers, *The Van Halen Encyclopedia* (New York: Writers Club Press, 2001), 261, 269, 274.

24. Taylor Clark, "The 8½ Laws of Rumor Spread," *Psychology Today*, November 1, 2008, https://www.psychologytoday.com/us/articles/200811/the-8-laws-rumor-spread; Rod Stewart, *Rod: The Autobiography* (New York: Crown, 2013), 244–45.

25. Echols, *Hot Stuff*, 139.

26. Echols, *Hot Stuff*, 72, 75.

27. Echols, *Hot Stuff*, 72.

28. Echols, *Hot Stuff*, 72.

29. Powers, *Good Booty*, 210.

30. Tim Lawrence, "In Defence of Disco (Again)," *New Formations* 58 (Summer 2006): 128–46, http://www.timlawrence.info/articles2/2013/7/16/in-defence-of-disco-again-new-formations-58-summer-2006-128-46.

31. Eric Harvey, "Love Train: The Sound of Philadelphia," Black Grooves, December 12, 2008, https://blackgrooves.org/love-train-the-sound-of-philadelphia/ ["Love Train"]; Portia K. Maultsby, "History of Disco," Timeline of African American Music, accessed February 12, 2023, https://timeline.carnegiehall.org/genres/disco ["TSOP"].

32. Echols, *Hot Stuff*, 103.

33. Echols, *Hot Stuff*, 52.

34. Hadley Meares, "The Night When Straight White Males Tried to Kill Disco," Aeon, https://aeon.co/ideas/the-night-when-straight-white-males-tried-to-kill-disco; "Disco Music Genre Overview," AllMusic, accessed February 12, 2023, https://www.allmusic.com/style/disco-ma0000002552.

35. "The Birth of Disco," *Oxford Dictionaries Blog*, October 30, 2012, https://blog.oxforddictionaries.com/2012/10/30/the-birth-of-disco.

36. Meares, "The Night When Straight White Males Tried to Kill Disco"; David Nicholls, ed., *The Cambridge History of American Music* (Cambridge: Cambridge University Press, 1998), 372.

37. "Disco," AllMusic, https://www.allmusic.com/style/disco-ma0000002552/albums; Alexis Petridis, "The Legacy of David Mancuso: 'His Dancefloor Was a Kind of Egalitarian Utopia,'" *The Guardian*, November 15, 2016, https://www.theguardian.com/music/2016/nov/15/david-mancuso-the-loft-egalitarian-utopia.

38. "Disco," AllMusic; https://www.theguardian.com/music/2016/nov/15/david-mancuso-the-loft-egalitarian-utopia.

39. Echols, *Hot Stuff*, 57.

40. Andrew Kopkind, "Dialectic of Disco: Gay Music Goes Straight," *Village Voice*, February 12, 1979.

41. Echols, *Hot Stuff*, 58.

42. "Anti-Gay Organizing on the Right," PBS, https://www.pbs.org/outofthepast/past/p5/1977.html.

43. Echols, *Hot Stuff*, xxiii.

44. Echols, *Hot Stuff*, 28–29.

45. Echols, *Hot Stuff*, 28.

46. Echols, *Hot Stuff*, 64, 10.

47. Echols, *Hot Stuff*, 10.

48. Nadine Hubbs, "'I Will Survive': Musical Mapping of Queer Social Space in a Disco Anthem," *Popular Music* 26, no. 2: 236.

49. Lawrence, "In Defence of Disco (Again)."

50. Richard Dyer, "In Defence of Disco," History of Emotions, accessed February 12, 2023, https://www.history-of-emotions.mpg.de/en/texte/richard-dyer-in-defence-of-disco-1979#_ednref10.

51. Hubbs, "'I Will Survive,'" 236.

52. "Disco," AllMusic.

53. "Pop Singles of 1976," *Billboard*, December 25, 1976; "Pop Singles of 1977," *Billboard*, December 24, 1977, 64.

54. Bryan Wawzenek, "Top 10 Classic Rock Disco Songs," Ultimate Classic Rock, February 12, 2014, https://ultimateclassicrock.com/classic-rock-disco-songs/.

55. John Lynch, "The 15 Best-Selling Movie Soundtracks of All Time," Business

Insider, September 3, 2016, https://www.businessinsider.com/15-best-selling-movie-soundtracks-all-time-2016-9.
  56. Echols, *Hot Stuff*, 78, 177.
  57. Echols, *Hot Stuff*, 197–98.
  58. Lawrence, "In Defence of Disco (Again)."
  59. Meares, "The Night When Straight White Males Tried to Kill Disco."
  60. "Disco," AllMusic, https://www.allmusic.com/subgenre/disco-ma0000002552.
  61. Steve Johnson, "Shocked Jock," *Chicago Tribune*, November 6, 1994, https://www.chicagotribune.com/news/ct-xpm-1994-11-06-9411060017-story.html.
  62. Meares, "The Night When Straight White Males Tried to Kill Disco."
  63. Echols, *Hot Stuff*, 205.
  64. Meares, "The Night When Straight White Males Tried to Kill Disco."
  65. "1979 Chicago White Sox Schedule," https://www.baseball-reference.com/teams/CHW/1979-schedule-scores.shtml.
  66. Meares, "The Night When Straight White Males Tried to Kill Disco."
  67. Andy Greene, "Flashback: Watch 'Disco Demolition Night' Devolve into Fiery Riot," *Rolling Stone*, July 12, 2019, https://www.rollingstone.com/music/music-news/flashback-watch-disco-demolition-night-devolve-into-fiery-riot-206237/.
  68. Meares, "The Night When Straight White Males Tried to Kill Disco."
  69. Greene, "Flashback."
  70. Meares, "The Night When Straight White Males Tried to Kill Disco," quoting Steve Dahl and Dave Hoekstra, *Disco Demolition: The Night Disco Died* (Chicago: Curbside Splendor Publishing, 2016).
  71. "Classic Rock," accessed November 27, 2020, https://web.archive.org/web/20170604024643/http://www.robertchristgau.com/xg/music/60s-det.php.
  72. Meares, "The Night When Straight White Males Tried to Kill Disco."
  73. "Steve Dahl Recalls Disco Demolition in 1979," *ABC News*, July 16, 2016, http://abc7chicago.com/entertainment/steve-dahl-recalls-disco-demolition-in-1979/1422124/.
  74. Steve Dahl, "Disco Demolition Night Was Not Racist," Cuepoint, August 3, 2016, https://medium.com/cuepoint/disco-demolition-night-was-not-racist-not-anti-gay-3dfde114464.
  75. Dahl, "Disco Demolition Night Was Not Racist."

Conclusion

  1. "Peter Slap Obituary (2017)—Phoenix, Az—the Arizona Republic," Legacy.com, accessed February 12, 2023, https://www.legacy.com/us/obituaries/azcentral/name/peter-slap-obituary?id=15810423 ["turn down"]; Bob Barry, *Rock 'n' Roll Radio Milwaukee: Stories from the Fifth Beatle* (Charleston, SC: History Press, 2018), 29; Exodus 20:12 (KJV).
  2. White et al., "Using Death Certificates to Explore Changes in Alcohol-Related Mortality in the United States, 1999–2017."
  3. Noah Feldman, "Psychedelic Drugs Will Follow Pot's Path to Legalization," Bloomberg, May 15, 2021, https://www.bloomberg.com/opinion/articles/2021-05-15/psychedelic-drugs-will-follow-pot-s-path-to-legalization.
  4. Personal email on file with author.
  5. Randy Lewis, "Rock Hall of Fame Postscript," *LA Times*, April 20, 2015, https://www.latimes.com/entertainment/music/posts/la-et-ms-rock-hall-fame-induction-drugs-alcohol-sobriety-20150420-story.html.
  6. David Gates, "Dylan Revisited," *Newsweek*, October 5, 1997, https://www.newsweek.com/dylan-revisited-174056.
  7. "In Memoriam," accessed March 9, 2021, http://www.loureed.com/in memoriam.
  8. Guralnick, *Lost Highway*, 335.

Bibliography

Books

Aerosmith and Stephen Davis. *Walk This Way: The Autobiography of Aerosmith.* New York: HarperCollins, 2012.

Algren, Nelson. *A Walk on the Wild Side.* Ashland, OR: Blackstone Audio, 2010.

Altschuler, Glenn C. *All Shook Up: How Rock 'n' Roll Changed America.* Oxford: Oxford University Press, 2003.

Andersen, Christopher P. *Jagger Unauthorized.* New York: Dell, 1994.

Appleford, Steve. *Rolling Stones: It's Only Rock and Roll, Song by Song.* Collingdale, PA: Diane, 1997.

Appy, Christian G. *Working-Class War: American Combat Soldiers and Vietnam.* Salem: University of North Carolina Press, 1993.

Auslander, Philip. *Performing Glam Rock: Gender and Theatricality in Popular Music.* Ann Arbor: University of Michigan Press, 2006.

Azerrad, Michael. *Our Band Could Be Your Life: Scenes from the American Indie Underground, 1981–1991.* New York: Little, Brown, 2001.

Barry, Bob. *Rock 'n' Roll Radio Milwaukee: Stories from the Fifth Beatle.* Charleston, SC: History Press, 2018.

Bayles, Martha. *Hole in Our Soul: The Loss of Beauty and Meaning in American Popular Music.* Chicago: University of Chicago Press, 1996.

Bear, John. *The #1 New York Times Best Seller: Intriguing Facts about the 484 Books that Have Been #1 New York Times Bestsellers since the First List, 50 Years Ago.* Berkeley: Ten Speed Press, 1992.

The Beatles. *The Beatles Anthology.* New York: Chronicle Books, 2000.

Beaumont-Thomas, Ben. "David Bowie: Lou Reed's Masterpiece Is Metallica Collaboration Lulu." *The Guardian*, April 20, 2015. https://www.theguardian.com/music/2015/apr/20/david-bowie-lou-reed-masterpiece-metallica-lulu.

Bertrand, Michael T. *Race, Rock, and Elvis.* Urbana: University of Illinois Press, 2005.

Bockris, Victor. *Keith Richards: The Biography.* Boston: Da Capo, 2003.

Bockris, Victor. *The Life and Death of Andy Warhol.* New York: Bantam, 1989.

Bockris, Victor. *Transformer: The Lou Reed Story.* London: Harper, 2014.

Bockris, Victor, and Gerard Malanga. *Up-tight: The Velvet Underground Story.* London: Omnibus Press, 1996.

Booth, Stanley. *Keith: Standing in the Shadows.* New York: St. Martin's Griffin, 1996.

Booth, Stanley. *The True Adventures of the Rolling Stones.* Chicago: Chicago Review Press, 2000.

Bowman, Rob. *Soulsville, U.S.A.: The Story of Stax Records.* New York: Schirmer, 2010.

Bowman, Rob, Mick Jagger, Keith Richards, Charlie Watts, Ron Wood, Dora Loewenstein, Philip Dodd, and David Bailey. *According to the Rolling Stones.* London: Phoenix, 2013.

Bronson, Fred. *The Billboard Book of Number One Hits.* New York: Billboard Books, 2003.

Bugliosi, Vincent, and Curt Gentry. *Helter Skelter: The True Story of the Manson Murders.* New York: Norton, 2001.

Carter, John. *Sex and Rockets: The Occult World of Jack Parsons.* Port Townsend, WA: Feral House, 2005.

Cavendish, Richard. *The Black Arts: A Concise History of Witchcraft, Demonology, and Other Mystical Practices throughout the Ages.* Los Angeles: TarcherPerigee, 1968.

Chabon, Michael. In *McSweeney's, No. 33: The San Francisco Panorama Unbound.* San Francisco: McSweeney's, 2010.

Chilvers, C.J. *The Van Halen Encyclopedia.* New York: Writers Club Press, 2001.

Christe, Ian. *Sound of the Beast: The Complete Headbanging History of Heavy Metal.* New York: It Books, 2004.

Clauss, Kyle Scott. "49 Years Ago Today, James Brown Saved Boston." *Boston Magazine*, April 5, 2017. https://www.bostonmagazine.com/news/2017/04/05/james-brown-saved-boston-king/.

Cleave, Maureen. "How Does a Beatle Live? John Lennon Lives like This." *London Evening Standard,* March 4, 1966, 10.

Coates, Ta-Nehisi. "Let's Do This like a Prison Break." *The Atlantic*, April 9, 2009. https://www.theatlantic.com/entertainment/archive/2009/04/lets-do-this-like-a-prison-break/9900.

Cobb, James C. *The Most Southern Place on Earth: The Mississippi Delta and the Roots of Regional Identity.* Oxford: Oxford University Press, 1989.

Conniff, Brian P. "The Enduring Catholic Imagination of Bruce Springsteen." *America*, April 19, 2018. https://www.americamagazine.org/arts-culture/2018/04/18/enduring-catholic-imagination-bruce-springsteen.

Conrad, Peter, and Joseph W. Schneider. *Deviance and Medicalization: From Badness to Sickness.* St. Louis: Mosby, 1980.

Cosby, James A. *Devil's Music, Holy Rollers and Hillbillies: How America Gave Birth to Rock and Roll.* Jefferson, NC: McFarland, 2016.

Cotkin, George. *Feast of Excess: A Cultural History of the New Sensibility.* Oxford: Oxford University Press, 2015.

Craig, Maxine Leeds. *Sorry I Don't Dance: Why Men Refuse to Move.* New York: Oxford University Press, 2014.

Crowley, Aleister. *Confessions of Aleister Crowley.* London: Penguin, 1989.

Davis, Joshua Clark. "The Business of Getting High: Head Shops, Countercultural Capitalism, and the Marijuana Legalization Movement." *The Sixties: A Journal of Politics, Culture and Society* 8, no. 1 (2015): 27–49.

Davis, Stephen. *Hammer of the Gods.* New York: Berkley Books, 2002.

DeCurtis, Anthony. *Lou Reed: A Life.* New York: Little, Brown, 2017.

Delgado, Richard. *Critical White Studies: Looking behind the Mirror.* Philadelphia: Temple University Press, 1997.

DeRogatis, Jim. *Let It Blurt: The Life and Times of Lester Bangs, America's Greatest Rock Critic.* New York: Crown, 2000.

Didion, Joan. *Slouching toward Bethlehem.* New York: Farrar, Straus and Giroux, 1968.

Doss, Erika. *Elvis Culture: Fans, Faith, and Image.* Lawrence: University Press of Kansas, 1999.

Dunbar, Dirk. "The Evolution of Rock and Roll: Its Religious and Ecological Themes." *Journal of Religion and Popular Culture* 2, no. 1 (2002): 1–1.

Dunbar, Dirk. *Renewing the Balance.* Parker, CO: Outskirts Press, 2017.

Du Noyer, Paul. *Liverpool—Wondrous Place: From the Cavern to the Capital of Culture.* London: Virgin Publishing, 2012.

Dylan, Bob. *Chronicles, Vol. 1.* New York: Simon & Schuster, 2005.

Echols, Alice. *Scars of Sweet Paradise: The Life and Times of Janis Joplin.* New York: Picador, 2000.

Eisen, Jonathan. *The Age of Rock: Sounds of the American Cultural Revolution.* New York: Random House, 1969.

Elliot, Brad. Liner Notes for the Beach Boys, *Pet Sounds*. Capitol Records, 1999.

Faithfull, Marianne, and David Dalton. *Faithfull: An Autobiography.* New York: Cooper Square Press, 2000.

Feldman, Noah. "Psychedelic Drugs Will Follow Pot's Path to Legalization." Bloomberg, May 15, 2021. https://www.bloomberg.com/opinion/articles/2021-05-15/psychedelic-drugs-will-follow-pot-s-path-to-legalization.

Foster, B. Brian. *I Don't Like the Blues: Race, Place, and the Backbeat of Black Life.* Chapel Hill: University of North Carolina Press, 2020.

Frady, Marshall. *Martin Luther King, Jr: A Life.* New York: Penguin, 2005.

Freye, E. *Pharmacology and Abuse of Cocaine, Methamphetamines, Ecstasy and*

Related Designer Drugs: A Comprehensive Review on Their Mode of Action, Treatment of Abuse and Intoxication. Dordrecht: Springer, 2009.

Frontani, Michael R. The Beatles: Image and the Media. Jackson: University Press of Mississippi, 2007.

Gates, David. "Dylan Revisited." Newsweek, October 5, 1997. https://www.newsweek.com/dylan-revisited-174056.

George, Nelson. The Death of Rhythm & Blues. New York, Penguin, 2003.

George, Nelson, and Alan Leeds, eds. The James Brown Reader: Fifty Years of Writing about the Godfather of Soul. New York: Plume, 2008.

George-Warren, Holly. A Man Called Destruction: The Life and Music of Alex Chilton, from Box Tops to Big Star to Backdoor Man. New York: Viking, 2014.

Gillett, Charlie. The Sound of the City: The Rise of Rock and Roll. New York: Da Capo, 1996.

Gillon, Steven M. The Pact: Bill Clinton, Newt Gingrich, and the Rivalry that Defined a Generation. Oxford: Oxford University Press, 2008.

Gilmore, Mila. "Beatles' Acid Test: How LSD Opened the Door to 'Revolver.'" Rolling Stone, August 25, 2016. https://www.rollingstone.com/music/music-news/beatles-acid-test-how-lsd-opened-the-door-to-revolver-251417.

Giuliano, Geoffrey. Behind Blue Eyes: The Life of Pete Townshend. Lanham, MD: Cooper Square Press, 2002.

Giuliano, Geoffrey. The Lost Lennon Interviews. New York: Adams Media, 1996.

Goines, David Lance. The Free Speech Movement: Coming of Age in the 1960's. Berkeley: Ten Speed Press, 1993.

Goldberg, Danny. "All the Human Be-In Was Saying 50 Years Ago, Was Give Peace a Chance." The Nation, January 16, 2017. https://www.thenation.com/article/archive/all-the-human-be-in-was-saying-50-years-ago-was-give-peace-a-chance/.

Goldman, Eric Frederick. The Crucial Decade: America, 1945–1955. New York: Knopf, 1956.

Goldstein, Robert Justin. Political Repression in Modern America: From 1870 to 1976. Champaign: University of Illinois Press, 2001.

Gould, Jonathan. Can't Buy Me Love: The Beatles, Britain, and America. New York: Crown, 2008.

Graff, Gary, and Daniel Durchholz. Music hound Rock: The Essential Album Guide. Detroit: Visible Ink Press, 1999.

Greenberg, Jan, and Sandra Jordan. Andy Warhol, Prince of Pop. New York: Laurel Leaf, 2007.

Guinn, Jeff. Manson: The Life and Times of Charles Manson. New York: Simon & Schuster, 2014.

Gulla, Bob. Icons of R&B and Soul: An Encyclopedia of the Artists Who Revolutionized Rhythm. Santa Barbara: ABC-CLIO, 2008.

Guralnick, Peter. Careless Love: The Unmaking of Elvis Presley. New York: Back Bay Books, 2000.

Guralnick, Peter. Last Train to Memphis: The Rise of Elvis Presley. New York: Back Bay Books, 1995.

Guralnick, Peter. Lost Highway: Journeys and Arrivals of American Musicians. New York: Back Bay Books, 2012.

Hamilton, Michael S. "The Dissatisfaction of Francis Schaeffer, Part 2." Christianity Today, March 3, 1997. https://www.christianitytoday.com/ct/1997/march3/7t322b.html.

Handy, W.C. Father of the Blues: An Autobiography. New York: Da Capo, 1991.

Harrington, Joe S. Sonic Cool: The Life & Death of Rock 'n' Roll. Milwaukee: Hal Leonard, 2002.

Harry, Bill. The John Lennon Encyclopedia. London: Virgin Books, 2001.

Harvard, Joe. The Velvet Underground and Nico. New York: Continuum, 2004.

Harvard, Joe. "Velvet Underground and Nico." In 33 1/3 Greatest Hits, Volume 1, edited by David Barker. London: Bloomsbury, 2006.

Hepworth, David. Never a Dull Moment: 1971—The Year that Rock Exploded. New York: St. Martin's Griffin, 2017.

Herzhaft, Gerard. "Catfish Blues." In Encyclopedia of the Blues. Fayetteville: University of Arkansas Press, 1992.

Hoberman, J., and Jonathan Rosenbaum. Midnight Movies. New York: Harper & Row, 1993.

Hofmann, Albert. LSD: My Problem Child. Oxford: Oxford University Press, 2018.

Horn, David. Bloomsbury Encyclopedia of Popular Music of the World, Volume 11. London: Bloomsbury, 2017.

Horrocks, Roger. *Male Myths and Icons: Masculinity in Popular Culture*. New York: Palgrave Macmillan, 1995.

Hutchinson, Roger. *Aleister Crowley: The Beast Demystified*. Edinburgh: Mainstream Publishing, 2006.

Huxley, Martin. "Aerosmith: The Fall and the Rise of Rock's Greatest Band." In *Aerosmith: The Fall and the Rise of Rock's Greatest Band*. New York: St. Martin's, 1995.

Iommi, Tony. *Iron Man: My Journey through Heaven and Hell with Black Sabbath*. New York: Da Capo, 2011.

Jackson, Blair. *Garcia: An American Life*. New York: Penguin, 1999.

Jovanovic, Rob. *Big Star: The Short Life, Painful Death, and Unexpected Resurrection of the Kings of Power Pop*. Chicago: Chicago Review Press, 2005.

Kaczynski, Richard. *Perdurabo, Revised and Expanded Edition: The Life of Aleister Crowley*. Berkeley: North Atlantic Books, 2010.

Keyes, Ralph. *The Quote Verifier: Who Said What, Where, and When*. New York: St. Martin's, 2006.

Kimball, Roger. *The Long March: How the Cultural Revolution of the 1960s Changed America*. New York: Encounter Books, 2001.

King, B.B., and David Ritz. *Blues All around Me: The Autobiography of B.B. King*. New York: Avon Books, 1996.

King, Francis. *Modern Ritual Magic: The Rise of Western Occultism*. Stockholm: Prisma, 1989.

Klosterman, Chuck. *Fargo Rock City: A Heavy Metal Odyssey in Rural North Dakota*. New York: Scribner, 2002.

Kuhn, David Paul. *The Hardhat Riot: Nixon, New York City, and the Dawn of the White Working-Class Revolution*. London: Oxford University Press, 2020.

Kurlansky, Mark. *Ready for a Brand New Beat: How "Dancing in the Street" Became the Anthem for a Changing America*. New York: Riverhead Books, 2014.

Lachman, Gary. *Aleister Crowley: Magick, Rock and Roll, and the Wickedest Man in the World*. Los Angeles: TarcherPerigee, 2014.

Landis, Bill. *Anger: The Unauthorized Biography of Kenneth Anger*. New York: Harper, 1995.

Lavezzoli, Peter. *The Dawn of Indian Music in the West*. New York: Continuum, 2006.

Lawrence, Tim. "In Defence of Disco (Again)." *New Formations* 58 (Summer 2006): 128–46. http://www.timlawrence.info/articles2/2013/7/16/in-defence-of-disco-again-new-formations-58-summer-2006-128-46.

Layden, Joe, and Noel Monk. *Runnin' with the Devil: A Backstage Pass to the Wild Times, Loud Rock, and the Down and Dirty Truth behind the Making of Van Halen*. New York: Dey Street Books, 2017.

Leaf, David, dir. *The Night James Brown Saved Boston*. Shout Factory, 2008.

Lee, Matt, Craig Kallman, and Bill German. *Hot Stuff: The Ultimate Memorabilia Collection*. London: Wellback, 2021.

Leonard, Marion. *The Beat Goes On: Liverpool, Popular Music and the Changing City*. Liverpool: Liverpool University Press, 2010.

Lewis, Dave. *The Complete Guide to the Music of led Zeppelin*. London: Omnibus Press, 2010.

Lewis, Dave. *Led Zeppelin: Celebration II: The "Tight but Loose" Files*. London: Omnibus Press, 2003.

Lewisohn, Mark. *The Complete Beatles Chronicle*. Nevada City, CA: Harmony Books, 1992.

Lewisohn, Mark. *The Complete Beatles Recording Sessions: The Official Story of the Abbey Road Years 1962–1970*. London: Octopus Publishing, 2018.

Lewisohn, Mark. *Tune In. The Beatles: All These Years*. New York: Crown Archetype, 2013.

Lock, Graham. "The Fall Land on Their Feet." *New Music Express*, March 24, 1979.

Lomax, Alan. *The Land Where the Blues Began*. York, UK: Methuen, 1993.

Lynskey, Dorian. *33 Revolutions per Minute: A History of Protest Songs, from Billie Holiday to Green Day*. New York: HarperCollins, 2011.

Manning, Toby. *The Rough Guide to Pink Floyd*. London: Rough Guides, 2006.

Marcus, Greil. *Lipstick Traces: A Secret History of the Twentieth Century*. Cambridge, MA: Belknap, 2009.

Mattix, Lori. "I Lost My Virginity to David Bowie." *Thrillist*, November 3, 2015. https://www.thrillist.com/entertain

ment/nation/i-lost-my-virginity-to-david-bowie.

Maultsby, Portia K. "History of Disco." Timeline of African American Music. Accessed February 12, 2023. https://timeline.carnegiehall.org/genres/disco.

McKeen, William. *Rock & Roll Is Here to Stay: An Anthology*. New York: Norton, 2000.

McLean, Craig. "Good Time Girl: Memories of Super Groupie Pamela Des Barres." *The Guardian*, May 6, 2018. https://www.theguardian.com/global/2018/may/06/good-time-girl-memories-of-a-super-groupie.

McLeod, Hugh. *The Religious Crisis of the 1960s*. London: Oxford University Press, 2010.

McNally, Dennis. *A Long Strange Trip: The Inside History of the Grateful Dead*. New York: Crown/Archetype, 2007.

McNeil, Legs. *Please Kill Me: The Uncensored Oral History of Punk*. New York: Grove, 1996.

Miles, Barry. *Paul McCartney: Many Years from Now*. New York: Holt Paperbacks, 1998.

Miller, Timothy. "The Historical Communal Roots of Ultraconservative Groups." In *The Cultic Milieu*, edited by Jeffrey Kaplan. Lanham, MD: AltaMira Press, 2002.

Milner, Richard. "The Truth about the Christian Background of U2." Grunge, April 26, 2022. https://www.grunge.com/844162/the-truth-about-the-christian-background-of-u2/.

The Mojo Collection. 4th ed. Edinburgh: Canongate Books, 2007.

Murphy, J.J. *The Black Hole of the Camera: The Films of Andy Warhol*. Berkeley: University of California Press, 2012.

Neuhouser, Frederick. *Foundations of Hegel's Social Theory: Actualizing Freedom*. Cambridge, MA: Harvard University Press, 2003.

Newman, Kim. *Wild West Movies: Or How the West Was Found, Won, Lost, Lied about, Filmed and Forgotten*. New York: Bloomsbury, 1990.

Nicholls, David, ed. *The Cambridge History of American Music*. Cambridge: Cambridge University Press, 1998.

Norman, Philip. *John Lennon: The Life*. New York: Anchor, 2009.

Norman, Philip. *Mick Jagger*. Milan: Mondadori, 2013.

Norman, Philip. *Paul McCartney: The Life*. New York: Back Bay Books, 2017.

Nuwer, Rachel. "Andy Warhol Probably Never Said His Celebrated 'Fifteen Minutes of Fame' Line." *Smithsonian Magazine*, April 8, 2014. https://www.smithsonianmag.com/smart-news/andy-warhol-probably-never-said-his-celebrated-fame-line-180950456.

Osbourne, Ozzy, and Chris Ayres. *I Am Ozzy*. Leicester, UK: W.F. Howes, 2010.

Palmer, Robert. "Stones Visit Memphis." *Rolling Stone*, August 14, 1975. https://www.rollingstone.com/music/music-news/stones-visit-memphis-193525.

Pattison, Robert. *The Triumph of Vulgarity: Rock Music in the Mirror of Romanticism*. Oxford: Oxford University Press, 1997.

Pegg, Nicholas. *The Complete David Bowie*. 6th ed. London: Titan Books, 2011.

Perlstein, Rick. *Nixonland: The Rise of a President and the Fracturing of America*. New York: Scribner, 2009.

Perry, Charles. *The Haight-Ashbury: A History*. New York: Wenner Books, 2005.

Petridis, Alexis. "The Velvet Underground: *The Velvet Underground & Nico Super Deluxe*—Review." *The Guardian*, October 18, 2012. https://www.theguardian.com/music/2012/oct/18/velvet-underground-nico-super-deluxe-review.

Phull, Hardeep. *Story behind the Protest Song: A Reference Guide to the 50 Songs That Changed the 20th Century*. Santa Barbara: Greenwood, 2008.

Poirier, Richard. *The Performing Self: Compositions and Decompositions in the Languages of Contemporary Life*. New Brunswick, NJ: Rutgers University Press, 1992.

Powell, James Lawrence. *Dead Pool: Lake Powell, Global Warming, and the Future of Water in the West*. Oakland: University of California Press, 2008.

Powers, Ann. *Good Booty: Love and Sex, Black and White, Body and Soul in American Music*. New York: Dey Street Books, 2017.

Price, Lloyd. *sumdumhonky*. Beverly Hills: Cool Titles, 2015.

Prothero, Stephen. "On the Holy Road: The Beat Movement as Spiritual Protest."

Harvard Theological Review 84, no. 2 (April 1991): 205–22.

Raga, Suzanne. "13 Variations on 'Sex, Drugs, and Rock 'n' Roll' from around the World." Mental Floss, April 4, 2016. https://www.mentalfloss.com/article/77888/13-variations-sex-drugs-and-rock-n-roll-around-world.

Reich, Wilhelm. *The Sexual Revolution: Toward a Self-Regulating Character Structure*. New York: Farrar, Straus and Giroux, 1986.

Rhodes, Don. *Say It Loud! The Life of James Brown, Soul Brother No. 1*. Guilford, CT: Lyons Press, 2014.

Richards, Keith. *Life*. London: Weidenfeld & Nicolson, 2010.

Robinson, Lisa. "Stairway to Excess." *Vanity Fair*, February 18, 2014. https://www.vanityfair.com/culture/2003/11/led-zeppelin-1970s-lisa-robinson.

Rodriguez, Joseph. *City against Suburb: The Culture Wars in an American Metropolis*. Westport, CT: Praeger, 1999.

Rorabaugh, W.J. *American Hippies*. Cambridge: Cambridge University Press, 2015.

Rosen, Steven. *The Story of Black Sabbath: Wheels of Confusion*. Chessington, UK: Castle Communications, 1996.

Rumburg, Gregory. "Rock for the Ages." *CCM Magazine*, October 1998.

Salewicz, Chris. *Jimmy Page: The Definitive Biography*. New York: Da Capo, 2019.

Savage, Jon, and Johnny Marr. *England's Dreaming: Sex Pistols and Punk Rock*. London: Faber & Faber, 2016.

Scaduto, Anthony. *Mick Jagger: Everybody's Lucifer*. Philadelphia: David McKay, 1974.

Schaffner, Nicholas. *The Beatles Forever*. New York: McGraw-Hill, 1978.

Schonfeld, Zach. "How Creedence Clearwater Revival Became the Soundtrack to Every Vietnam Movie." Pitchfork, February 20, 2018. https://pitchfork.com/thepitch/how-creedence-clearwater-revival-became-the-soundtrack-to-every-vietnam-movie/.

Schreiber, Brad. *Music Is Power: Popular Songs, Social Justice, and the Will to Change*. New Brunswick, NJ: Rutgers University Press, 2019.

Sheff, David. *All We Are Saying: The Last Major Interview with John Lennon and Yoko Ono*. New York: St. Martin's Griffin, 2000.

Simmons, Matty. *Fat, Drunk, and Stupid: The Inside Story behind the Making of Animal House*. New York: St. Martin's Griffin, 2014.

Simonelli, David. *Working Class Heroes: Rock Music and British Society in the 1960s and 1970s*. Lanham, MD: Lexington Books, 2012.

Sounes, Howard. *Notes from the Velvet Underground: The Life of Lou Reed*. London: Transworld, 2018.

Spitz, Bob. *The Beatles: The Biography*. New York: Little, Brown, 2005.

Springsteen, Bruce. Liner notes for *Hammersmith Odeon, London '75*. Legacy Recordings, 2006.

Stewart, Rod. *Rod: The Autobiography*. New York: Crown, 2013.

Stowe, David W. *No Sympathy for the Devil: Christian Pop Music and the Transformation of American Evangelicalism*. Chapel Hill: University of North Carolina Press, 2013.

Strauss, William, and Neil Howe. "The New Generation Gap." *The Atlantic*, August 15, 2017. https://www.theatlantic.com/magazine/archive/1992/12/the-new-generation-gap/536934/.

Sutton, Robert P. *Modern American Communes: A Dictionary*. Westport, CT: Greenwood, 2005.

Talbott, T.B. *The Inescapable Love of God*. Eugene, OR: Cascade Books, 2014.

Teachout, Woden. *Capture the Flag: A Political History of American Patriotism*. New York: Basic Books, 2009.

Theoharis, Athan G., Richard H. Immerman, Kathryn Olmsted, and John Prados. *The Central Intelligence Agency: Security under Scrutiny*. Santa Barbara: Greenwood, 2005.

Thompson, Dave. *Robert Plant: The Voice that Sailed the Zeppelin*. Lanham, MD: Backbeat, 2014.

Tocqueville, Alexis de. *Democracy in America*. Edited by Harvey Claflin Mansfield. Chicago: University of Chicago Press, 2000.

Tolinski, Brad. *Light and Shade: Conversations with Jimmie Page*. Toronto: McClelland & Stewart, 2013.

Torgoff, Martin. *Can't Find My Way Home: America in the Great Stoned Age, 1945–2000*. New York: Simon & Schuster, 2004.

Trynka, Paul. *Brian Jones, the Making of the Rolling Stones*. New York: Viking, 2014.

Tupica, Rich. *There Was a Light: The Cosmic History of Chris Bell and the Rise of Big Star.* New York: Permuted Press, 2022.

Unterberger, Richie. "Marvin Gaye." In *The Rough Guide to Rock,* edited by Peter Buckley, London: Rough Guides, 2003.

Vogel, Joseph. "How Michael Jackson Made 'Bad.'" *The Atlantic,* September 10, 2012. https://www.theatlantic.com/entertainment/archive/2012/09/how-michael-jackson-made-bad/262162.

Wacker, Daniel, Sheng Wang, John D. McCorvy, Robin M. Betz, A.J. Venkatakrishnan, Anat Levit, Katherine Lansu, et al. "Crystal Structure of an LSD-Bound Human Serotonin Receptor." *Cell* 168, no. 3 (January 26, 2017): 377–89. https://www.cell.com/cell/fulltext/S0092-8674(16)31749-4.

Wald, Elijah. *How the Beatles Destroyed Rock 'n' Roll: An Alternative History of American Popular Music.* New York: Oxford University Press, 2011.

Warhol, Andy, and Pat Hackett. *Popism: The Warhol Sixties.* Boston: Mariner Books, 2006.

Watson, Steven. *Factory Made: Warhol and the Sixties.* New York: Pantheon, 2003.

Watts, Michael. "John Peel: 'If Something Has Me Confused, I Want to Play It on the Radio.'" *The Guardian,* September 30, 2015. https://www.theguardian.com/music/2015/sep/30/john-peel-1971-interview-melody-maker-michael-watts-rocks-backpages.

Wawzenek, Bryan. "Top 10 Classic Rock Disco Songs." Ultimate Classic Rock, February 12, 2014. https://ultimateclassicrock.com/classic-rock-disco-songs/.

Weiss, Robin. "The 'Rules' of Psychotherapy." *New York Times,* November 22, 2014. https://opinionator.blogs.nytimes.com/2014/11/22/the-rules-of-psychotherapy/.

Welch, Chris. *Led Zeppelin.* London: Orion Books, 1994.

Wellmann, Molly. *Handcrafted Cocktails the Mixologist's Guide to Classic Drinks for Morning, Noon & Night.* Cincinnati: F.W. Media, 2013.

White, A. M., I.-J. P. Castle, R. W. Hingson, and P. A. Powell. "Using Death Certificates to Explore Changes in Alcohol-Related Mortality in the United States, 1999–2017." *Alcoholism: Clinical and Experimental Research* 44, no. 1 (2020): 178–87.

Whitehead, John W. *Grasping for the Wind: The Search for Meaning in the 20th Century.* Grand Rapids: Zondervan, 2001.

Wiener, Jon. *Come Together: John Lennon in His Time.* Urbana: University of Illinois Press, 1991.

Williams, Paul. *Bob Dylan Performing Artist: The Early Years 1960–1973.* San Francisco: Underwood Miller, 1990.

Williamson, Nigel. *The Rough Guide to Led Zeppelin.* London: Rough Guides, 2007.

Wolcott, Victoria W. *Remaking Respectability: African American Women in Interwar Detroit.* Chapel Hill: University of North Carolina Press, 2001.

Womack, Kenneth. *The Beatles Encyclopedia: Everything Fab Four.* Santa Barbara: ABC-CLIO, 2014.

Woodward, Fred. *Rolling Stone: The Illustrated Portraits.* New York: Chronicle Books, 2000.

Wyman, Bill, and Richard Havers. *Rolling with the Stones.* New York: DK, 2002.

Yamin, Eli. *So You Want to Sing the Blues: A Guide for Performers.* Lanham, MD: Rowman & Littlefield, 2018.

Zirin, David. *People's History of Sports in the United States: 250 Years of Politics, Protest, People, and Play.* New York: New Press, 2009.

Websites

AllMusic, February 8, 2023. allmusic.com.

The American Conservative, February 11, 2023. http://www.theamericanconservative.com/.

American Psychological Association. Accessed February 12, 2023. https://dictionary.apa.org/.

Black Grooves, December 12, 2008. https://blackgrooves.org/love-train-the-sound-of-philadelphia/.

Brookings Institution, February 8, 2023. https://www.brookings.edu/.

Condé Nast. *New Yorker.* Accessed February 14, 2023. https://www.newyorker.com/.

History.com. A&E Television Networks. Accessed February 12, 2023. https://www.history.com/.

"The Journal of Roots Music." No Depression, February 8, 2023. https://www.nodepression.com/.

The Martin Luther King, Jr., Research and Education Institute. January 16, 2022. https://kinginstitute.stanford.edu/.

NameDat, January 16, 1970. https://www.namedat.com/.

Rolling Stone. Accessed February 12, 2023. https://www.rollingstone.com/.

"Washed Red." Washed Red—Christian Testimonies and Questions about God and Life. Accessed February 14, 2023. http://www.washedred.com/.

Videos

FanTC. "Ted Nugent Hibernation-Full." YouTube. YouTube, December 16, 2011. https://www.youtube.com/watch?v=M49j05LZ9WY.

PBS. "Drummer Bill Kreutzmann on Drugs, Money and the End of the Grateful Dead." PBS, July 6, 2015. Accessed June 4, 2021. https://www.youtube.com/watch?v=MEdhlX-hdNk.

Rosenthal, Gay. "Behind the Music." Episode. Ted Nugent 1, no. 26. VH1, April 19, 1998.

Index

abortion 108, 179–180; *Roe v. Wade* 179
acid rock (psych-rock, psychedelic rock) 65–75, 99–100; Grateful Dead's role 66–68
"The Age of Anxiety" (poem) 15
Ali, Muhammad 107
Altamont 155–156, 161
Altamont: The Rolling Stones, the Hells Angels, and the Inside Story of Rock's Darkest Day (book) 155
American Bandstand 24, 221
Anger, Kenneth 149–151, 160, 194
The Apartment (film) 27
Appalachia 3, 181
Arab Oil Embargo 179
arc of Western Civilization 1–4, 6, 33, 48, 110, 170, 232–235
Aristotle 46
Axton, Estelle 128–129

baby boomers 187
Baez, Joan 143, 175
Baldwin, James 23
Bay of Pigs 28
Beach Boys 103, 124, 140, 209–210, 214; Dennis Wilson's experience with Charles Manson 160, 213; *Pet Sounds* 72, 203
Beale Street 20, 22, 119
Beats (poets) 58–61, 68, 76; influence on hippies/psych rock 59–61
Beatles 33–46, **43**, 48, 51, 53, 58, 64–67, 71–74, 78, 83, 100–101, 102–105, 108, 114, 116, 126, 138, 145, 149, 153, 157–159, 182–183, 191–36–38; 192, 199, 205, 209–210, 212, 214, 220; *Abbey Road* 141–143; childhoods 36–38; connection with Aleister Crowley 149; *Ed Sullivan Show* 42; "Eleanor Rigby" 74; Epstein, Brian 34, 40, 83, 139; Hamburg and 39–41; *A Hard Day's Night* 44; Harrison **43**, 139; *Help!* 44, 46; influence in power pop 209–212; Lennon and McCartney chemistry 34, 38; *Let It Be* (album) 141; "Let It Be" (song) 37; Liverpool origins 33–36; *Magical Mystery Tour* (album) 65, 73, 78, 105, 139; *Magical Mystery Tour* (film) 65; Manson and 159; mythological status 98, 191; *Revolver* 72–73, 78, 98–99, 103, 139; Royal Command Variety Performance 41–42; *Rubber Soul* 44, 46; *Sgt. Pepper's Lonely Hearts Club Band* (album) 73, 78, 102–105; "She's Leaving Home" 105; Starr, Ringo 40, **43**; The White Album (*The Beatles*) 38, 73, 78, 140, 159; "Yellow Submarine" 74; *Yellow Submarine* (film) 74; yin-yang analysis and 8–11, 157; *see also* Dunbar's thematic stages; Lennon, John; McCartney, Paul
Beausoleil, Bobby 150, 160, 194
Beck, Jeff 116, 191–192, 200
Bee Gees 228, 231
Bell, Al 130–131, 135
Berry, Chuck 19, 23–24, 37, 50–52, 78, 124, 140, 194, 202, 205, 209, 230
Big Brother and the Holding Company 72, 102; *see also* Joplin, Janis
Big Star *see* power pop
Bill Haley and the Comets 19
Black Bear Ranch 165–166
Black gospel music 4, 7–8, 17–18, 20, 22–24, 37, 66, 115, 120–122, 124, 129, 156, 183–186, 212, 226, 232, 234
Black Panther Party 108–109
Black Power/Black Pride 102, 109, 123, 127, 134
Black Sabbath 9, 145, 199–202, **200**; *Black Sabbath* (album) 200; "Black Sabbath" (song) 200–201; Osbourne, Ozzie 5–6, 199–202
Blake, William 175

Index

Blues 3–5, 9, 11, 17–24, 41, 47, 50–51, 66–68, 72, 84, 101–102, 113–120, 124, 126, 140, 142, 152–154, 156, 191–193, 197, 199–200, 209, 222, 232
blues-rock 59, 85, 138, 142, 168, 194
Bob Wills and His Texas Playboys 18
Booker T and the MGs 102, 128–130
Boone, Pat 22, 25, 114
Bowie, David 59, 76, 89, 223, 230; *The Rise and Fall of Ziggy Stardust and the Spiders from Mars* 162; "Space Oddity" 161–163; use of "Space Oddity" by BBC 162
Box Tops 101, 213
The Brady Bunch 5, 187–190
Brando, Marlon 21
Brewster, the Rev. W. Herbert 20
British Invasion 4, 31, 44, 52, 58, 76, 99, 116, 124, 183, 206, 220–221, 234
Brown, James 5, 9, 10, 23, 52, 121–124, 126, 133–135, **135**, 205, 221, 230; Black business role 126, 134; Boston show, night of Martin Luther King, Jr. assassination 133–134; bringing mainstream to Black America 134; Brown "thread" 9–10; "Cold Sweat" 123; dance influence 221
Brown v. Board of Education 23, 30
Bruce, Lenny 27
Burroughs, William S. 59; *see also* Beats
Byrds 72, 74, 183, 212

Camus, Albert 61
capitalism 16, 25, 60, 123, 164
Carter, Jimmy 186
Carter family 18
Cassady, Neal 59, 65
Catholicism/pope 3, 11, 46, 77, 87, 96, 117, 145
Charlatans 65
Charles, Ray 23, 121, 124, 212
Cheap Trick 9, 206, 210–211, **211**, 214, 233
Chess Records 37, 50, 156, 192
Chilton, Alex *see* Big Star
Christianity 7–8, 24–25, 30, 53, 61, 89, 95, 98–99, 133, 146, 152, 180, 183–186, 217, 234; Christian rock 183–186; declines in church attendance 31, 96, 146; *see also* Jesus
CIA (Central Intelligence Agency) 62, 108; Bay of Pigs 28; LSD experiments 102
City of San Francisco Oracle (the *Oracle*) (periodical) 70, 91, 93, 95, 100
Clark, Dick 24–25
Classicism 3

Clayton, Merry 151–152
cocaine 62–63, 147, 154, 156, 197, 202, 222, 227
Cole, Nat King 121, 134
colonialism 61
Cooke, Sam 118, 121, 124, 129, 134
Cooper, Alice 8, 205
Count Basie Orchestra 51
Country Joe McDonald/Country Joe & the Fish 90, 136, 143, 174
country music/country-rock 3–4, 7, 11, 17–19, 21–24, 35, 40, 66, 101, 115, 116, 121, 127, 128, 155–157, 183, 212
Cowan, Paul 180–181
Coyote, Peter 165
Cronkite, Walter 132
Crosby, Bing 20
Crosby, David 11
Crosby, Stills, and Nash/Crosby, Stills, Nash & Young 68, 101, 171
Crowley, Aleister 5, 145–146, 194, 200; *The Book of the Law* 146–147; "Do What Thou Wilt" philosophy 145, 148
Crudup, Arthur 21
Cuban Missile Crisis 28–29
Czechoslovakian Revolution 11, 175

Dahl, Steve 229–231; *see also* Disco Demolition Night
Dalí, Salvador 79
Dartford (U.K.) 48–49
Darwin, Charles 146; *see also On the Origin of Species by Means of Natural Selection* (book)
Dean, James 21
Democratic Convention in Chicago, 1968 136
Demolition Night 229–231; gay nightclubs role in 225; influence of *Saturday Night Fever* and disco backlash 228, 230–231; peak popularity 227–229; reluctance of white people to dance 220–221; Studio 54 227–229
Detroit 4, 25, 43, 108, 109, 123, 126, 133, 158, 202; *see also* Motown
Devil's Music, Holy Rollers, and Hillbillies: How America Gave Birth to Rock and Roll 1, 17
Diddley, Bo 23, 50
Didion, Joan 91
Diggers 70, 92, 106
Disco (music and dance genre) 1, 4, 226, 231; black culture and dancing 221
Disco Demolition Night *see* Disco
Domino, Fats 18, 22, 36
"domino theory" 54, 56

Index

doo wop 23, 25
Doors 74–75, 101, 213, 222, 230
The Doors of Perception (book) 75
Dragnet (television show) 166–168
Dunbar, Dirk, Beatles thematic stages: One 41–44, Two 44–45, 71–72, Three 73–75, 102–16; Four 139–141; Five 141–143
Dylan, Bob 5, 8, 44–48, 59, 64, 67, 71–72, 76, 78–80, 84, 88, 143, 158, 186, 234; *Bringing It All Back Home* 47; childhood 45; Christianity/gospel music and 8, 46, 48, 186, 234; counterculture figurehead 5, 45, 48, 158; on high art 78; *Highway 61 Revisited* 47–48; impact on anti-war and civil rights movements 45–46; influence on Beatles 44, 46, 48, 72; *John Wesley Harding* 158; "Like a Rolling Stone" 4–5, 47–48; Warhol and 48, 76, 79

Eastern philosophies and religions 46
Einstein, Albert 16
Eisenhower, Dwight D. 15, 28–29, 45, 54, 56
The Electric Kool-Aid Acid Test (book) 65
Electric Kool-Aid Acid Tests (events) 66, 68–69, 71, 76
Emerick, Geoff 73, 103
Exploding Plastic Inevitable (EPI) 69, 76, 85

Faithfull, Marianne 150–151
FBI (Federal Bureau of Investigation) 101, 135, 177
femininity (feminism) 31, 94, 195, 224
5th Dimension 100, 126
Fillmore 69, 71–72
Flatt and Scruggs 19
Flying Burrito Brothers 155
folk music 31, 45, 60, 66–67, 71, 118, 136, 143, 171, 175, 182, 185; British 192–194
folk rock 44, 47, 70, 72, 172, 214, 220
Four Tops 127, 172
Frank Zappa & the Mothers of Invention 72
freaks 58, 61, 68, 72, 85, 86, 94, 108; *see also* hippies
Freed, Alan 20
Freud, Sigmund 4, 59
funk music 9, 116, 120, 123, 183, 194, 220–221, 224–225, 227
Funkadelic 224, 226–227

Gandhi, Mahatma 95, 149
Garcia, Jerry 59, 101; childhood 66; death 68; early career 66; *see also* Grateful Dead

Gaye, Marvin 52, 127, 230; family life 172; *What's Going On* 173; "What's Going On" 172–173
Gerry and the Pacemakers 124
Ginsberg, Allen 59, 63–64, 67, 100, 165; *see also* Beats (poets)
girl groups 25, 37, 127
Gladys Knight or Gladys Knight and the Pips 127, 222
glasnost 11
Gordy, Barry 37, 126–127, 172; *see also* Motown
Graceland 119
Graham, Bill (concert promoter) 71–72
Graham, Billy (preacher) 31
Grateful Dead 59, 64, 66–69, **68**, 72, 82, 101, 106, 143, 155, 158, 204, 227; contrasted with Velvet Underground 9, 76; "Deadheads" following 68; 74; "house band" of the Haight 67–69, 72; "Morning Dew," role of LSD 67–69; *see also* Garcia, Jerry
Great Depression 16, 77, 113, 122, 195
Great Migration 116–117, 125
Great Society 54, 134
Gurley Brown, Helen 31, 93
GWAR 6

Haight-Ashbury (the Haight) 58, 60, 61, 64, 66, 70, 72, 75–76, 90–91, 93–95, 99–102, 106, 137, 150, 158–159; *see also* San Francisco; Summer of Love
Hair (musical) 100, 184
Hall, Daryl (Hall & Oates) 124
Hamburg, Germany 39–41
Handy, W.C. 188, 120
Hard Hat Riot 171
Havens, Richie 143
Hayes, Isaac 130, 131, 135, 163, 224
Hell's Angels 68, 90–91, 155
Hendrix, Jimi 101–102, 142–143, 182
heroin 48, 59, 62–63, 76, 78, 80, 82, 84–85, 94, 106, 147–148, 151, 154, 156, 167, 168–169, 173, 191, 197; "Heroin," Velvet Underground song 85, 87; "Waiting for the Man," Velvet Underground song 168–169
"high" culture/art 78, 81
higher intelligence/higher power/God 25, 32, 53, 85, 89, 97, 109, 184–185, 235; Beatles' views after LSD experiences 73; Big Star reclaiming word of God in "Ballad of El Goodo" 214; Big Star references to 214–215; Black Sabbath's view of 201; countercultural view 63–64, 145, 167, 235; GWAR lacking any

higher intelligence 6; Keith Richards' view of 32; Lennon song "God" 176; Lennon song "Imagine" 174–177; Lloyd Price's experience of racists views of in South 113; Lou Reed's view 89, 234; political right view 109, 180; public opinion polls in '60s 96–97; U2 references to in "I Still Haven't Found What I'm Looking For 7–8
hippies 4, 8, 9, 58, 75, 78, 90, 99–102, 137, 158, 181, 184, 188, 195, 220; communes and communal living 92, 158; compared with East coast counterculture 86; origins of term 60–61; philosophy 68, 71, 90–91, 167; views on drugs 94–95; views on religion 95; views on sex 93–94, 222; Woodstock 143–144; see also freaks
Hitler, Adolf 22, 40, 149
Hoffman, Abbie 108–109, 136–137
Hofmann, Albert 62
Holly, Buddy 23, 25, 37, 39, 209
Holy Spirit 18, 22
homosexuality 9, 30, 77, 79, 81–83, 93, 150, 170–172, 190, 195, 223–226
Hoover, J. Edgar see FBI
Hot Buttered Soul (album) 135
Howl (book) 59
Howlin' Wolf 20, 52, 205
Hubbard, Al 63
Hubbard, L. Ron 148
Hunter, Robert 67
Huxley, Aldous 63, 145

Isley Brothers 42, 101,125, 215, 220

Jackie Brenston & His Delta Kings 18
Jackson, Mahalia 18, 121
Jackson, Michael 123
Jagger, Mick see Rolling Stones
James, Elmore 50
Janov, Dr. Arthur 2, 38, 176, 233
Jazz 3, 17–19, 23, 31, 39, 49, 51–2, 59–60, 66, 74, 114, 119, 121–123, 150, 193, 212–213, 219, 225, 230
Jefferson Airplane 72, 101, 106, 155
Jesus Christ 5, 30, 46, 89, 92, 95, 97–99, 113, 115, 121, 145, 150, 152, 169, 174–176, 182–186, 214, 217, 234; 150; hippies relating to 169, 175; "Jesus" (Velvet Underground song) 89; "Jesus Christ" (Big Star song) 217; Lennon, comment on "popularity" of Jesus 97–99, 183; see also Christianity
"Jesus freaks" (Jesus People movement) 5, 95, 182–186

Jesus People movement see "Jesus freaks"
Jim Crow/segregation, racial 17, 109, 113, 116–117, 120, 122
Jobs, Steve 159; see also Silicon Valley
John, Elton 223
Johnson, Lyndon, B. 54–55, 108, 107, 132, 136, 177–178
Johnson, Robert 18, 47, 51, 116, 152, 192
Joplin, Janis 59, 72, 101–102, 126
jump blues 18, 116
Jung, Carl 46, 63, 155
Junkie (book) 59

Kantner, Paul 143
Kennedy, John F. 28, 53–54, 178; assassination 42; Bay of Pigs 28; Cuban Missile Crisis 28–29
Kennedy, Robert 109, 136
Kennedy Onassis, Jacqueline 79
Kent State killings 171
Kerouac, Jack 58–59; see also Beats (poets); *On the Road* (book)
Kesey, Ken 63–67, 69, 94; see also Merry Pranksters
Khrushchev, Nikita 28
King, B.B. 18, 20, 72, 116–118
King, Dr. Martin Luther, Jr. 30–31, 57, 95, 107, 114, 133–134, 136, 177, 183
Kiss 205–208; Simmons, Gene, *Fresh Air* interview 207
Knack 211
Knight, Gladys 222
Korean War 29
Kupferberg, Tuli or Fugs 93, 136

The Lawrence Welk Show (television show) 178
Leary Timothy 734, 100, 104, 136
Led Zeppelin 9–10, 145, 191–199, 221, 230; Aleister Crowley and 194; excesses and "Whole Lotta Love" 196–198; social context 195–196; *The Song Remains the Same* (film), 94, 96; "Stairway to Heaven" 193–194
Left/right divide 9, 11, 57, 91, 109–110, 134, 136–137, 140, 165, 166–167, 169, 170–171, 174, 179, 180–181, 197, 201, 204, 214, 230
Lennon, John 5, 34–44, **43**, 46, 48, 51–52, 59, 71–74, 97–99, 103, 105–106, 137, 139–142; death 99; "Imagine" 172–177; Jesus comment 97–99, 183; *John Lennon/Plastic Ono Band* 158, 176; Ono and 34, 137, 142, 176; primal therapy work 38, 176; solo work 149, 158, 170–177, 183, 209, 211, 213, 234

Index

Lewis, Jerry Lee 8, 22–24, 26, 186
Little Richard 22, 24, 37, 50, 52, 67, 101, 122, 124, 129, 209, 223, 230
Little Rock High School 23
Liverpool (U.K.) 2, 25, 33–36, 38–40, 43, 74, 105
London 2, 25, 32, 34, 35, 39, 48, 50–51, 73, 97, 101–103, 108, 133, 146, 152; British Invasion as center 2, 52, 158, 183; contrasted with England's north 34–35; Crawdaddy Club 51; Ealing Club 50; Marquee (club) 51, 192; "Swinging London" 44, 52–53, 101
Lorraine Motel 130, 133
The Love-Ins (film) 100
LSD (lysergic acid diethylamide, "acid") 5, 61–62, 65, 69–70, 72–73, 76, 91, 94, 63–64; Barrett, Syd, use of 99–100; Beatles use of 73, 103–104; criminalization 70, 100, 106; early psych rock 72; effects 62–63, 65–66; Electric Kool-Aid Acid Tests 68–69; Haight-Ashbury, use in 64–67, 69, 82, 91; hazards of 70, 94, 99, 156, 167; Jobs, Steve, use of 159; legalization 94; MK-ULTRA 62; rock music, use in 66–67, 69
Lucifer Rising (film) 150, 194

Malanga, Gerard 83, 85
Mamas & the Papas 72, 90, 101
The Man in the Gray Flannel Suit (book) 16
Manifest Destiny 61
Manson, Charles 159–161, 194, 213
Mar-Keys 129
marijuana 6, 17, 54, 61, 220; Beats, use of 59; counterculture use as "casual drug" 63, 91, 94, 165, 232; criminalization 94; Dragnet, as depicted on 167; Dylan introducing to Beatles 46; effects 62–63; legalization 233; petition to legalize 108; Richards, Keith, criminal trial 153; "Sweet Leaf" 202
Martha and the Vandellas/Martha Reeves 127
Martin, George 40, 73–74, 103, 140
masculinity 5, 41, 60, 95, 223, 230
mass culture 78
McCarthy, Joseph (and McCarthyism) 28
McCartney, Paul 5, 34–44, 48–49, 51–52, 59, 73–74, 98, 102–105, 139–140, 142–143, 149, 160, 165, 209, 211, 213
McGuire, Barry 70, 184,
McKenzie, Scott 100
Melville, Herman 33
Memphis, TN 2, 19, 22, 47, 101, 118–119, 125, 131, 213, 217–218, assassination of Martin Luther King, Jr. 133; Beale Street 20, 22, 118; canceled Beatles show 98; Lorraine Hotel 130, 133; radio programming, early '50 20–21; sanitation strike 133; Stax Records, soul music hub, as 4, 25, 102, 120, 125, 127–131, 158, 212, 224; Sun Studio 5,18, 21, 212
Mercury, Freddie 223; *see also* Queen
Meredith, Hunter 155
Merry Pranksters 65
Methamphetamine 59, 76, 88, 94, 106, 155
miracles 126
Mitchell, Joni 143
MK-ULTRA 62
Moby Grape 72
Mod Squad (television show) 178
Modern Times (film) 16
Monroe, Marilyn 79–80
Monterrey Pop Festival 101–102, 130
Moore, Scottie *21*, 192
Morrisey, Paul 86
Motown Records/Motown (genre) 37, 116, 118, 120, 124, 127, 134, 162, 172–173, 182, 209; Origins 126; style of music 126–127; as subgenre of original rock and roll movement 116; *see also* Detroit; Gordy, Barry
Muscle Shoals, Alabama 125, 127
My Lai Massacre 132

National Lampoon's Animal House (film) 124–125
Nico 83–88, *86*; *Chelsea Girl* 88; discovered for Velvet Underground 83–84; *Velvet Underground & Nico* 85, 87–88; *see also* Velvet Underground
Nixon, Richard 108, 172, 176, 195; elected President 137; Pentagon Papers, role in 178; re-election 178; "silent majority" 177; Watergate 134, 179; work with Joseph McCarthy 28
Norman, Larry 184–185; *Only Visiting This Planet* 185
NOW (National Organization of Women) 108
nuclear arms 32; Cuban Missile Crisis 28–29; existential threat of 15–16, 28–29, 74, 145, 149, 176, 201
Nugent, Ted 202–205

On the Origin of Species by Means of Natural Selection (book) 146
On the Road (book) 59
Operation CHAOS 108

Index

Osbourne, Ozzie *see* Black Sabbath
Otis Day and the Knights 124

Pallenberg, Anita 151, 154
Parsons, Gram 157
Parton, Dolly 115
Pattison, Robert 25
Paul Butterfield Blues Band 47, 72
The Pentagon Papers 178
Pentecostalism 3, 18, 20, 22, 122, 129, 172, 180, 185, 232
Perkins, Carl 22–23, 209
Pet Sounds 72–73; influence on Beatles 103
Peter, Paul, and Mary 171, 220
peyote 59, 61
Philadelphia International Records (PIR) 224; *see also* Philly soul
Phillips, Dewey 20, 22, 228
Phillips, Sam 5, 18, 20, 22–23, 235
Philly soul 123–124, 226–228
Pink Floyd 99–100, 182; Syd Barrett's departure 99–100
Plimsouls 211
Pollock, Jackson 77
Pop art 69, 77–78, 185
Pope John Paul II 46
Porter, David 130–131
Posies 212, 218
post-punk 7, 210
power pop 209–218; Big Star 9, 210–218; Chabon, Michael 210, 212; Cheap Trick 9, 206, 210–*211*, 214, 234; Chilton, Alex 213–217; hopeless romanticism 210; *I Am the Cosmos* 218; *#1 Record* 214–215; *Radio City* 216; *Third/Sister Lovers* 217–218
Presley, Elvis 10, 19–24, *21*, 32, 43, 80, 114, 119, 192, 210; British Invasion acts and 36–37, 42, 50, 192; dance moves impact 219; *Ed Sullivan Show* 22; the "Elvis factor" 113–116; race legacy 9; *Triple Elvis (Ferus Type)* 78
Price, Lloyd 2, 114, 121
primal therapy 2, 5, 38, 176
Procol Harum 100, 182
prog rock 99, 182–183, 210
protest songs 5, 45, 170–172, 175
Protestantism 3, 96, 145, 184, 234
The Psychedelic Experience: A Manual Based on the Tibetan Book of the Dead 63, 73–74
Psycho (film) 27
Public Enemy 2, 4, 233–234; "Bring the Noise" 4
punk rock 5–6, 11, 76, 81, 83, 85, 142, 183, 203, 205, 210, 233

Queen (band) 223

R&B (rhythm and blues) 23, 35–36, 40–41, 44, 50–52, 82, 114, 116, 120–126, 128–129, 183, 192, 202, 212, 215, 202. 222, 224, 231
rap music (hip hop) 11, 118, 183, 205, 210
Reagan, Ronald 57; Berkeley Protests and 57, 137; comments on killing of Martin Luther King, Jr. 134; Vietnam War and 108
Redding, Otis 125, 129–131; "Try a Little Tenderness" 130
Reed, Lou 76, 84, 86–89, 168–169; childhood 81–82; electroshock therapy 81; *LuLu* 89; *Metal Machine Music* 89; religious/spiritual matters 89, 234; *Transformer* 88; *see also* Velvet Underground
Reich, Wilhelm 71
R.E.M. 7, 199, 212, 234
"Respect" 4
Richards, Keith *see* Rolling Stones
riots, urban 133–134, 136–137
Rodgers, Jimmie 18
Roe v. Wade 179
Rolling Stones 32, 44, 51–*53*, 60, 87–88, 101–102, 124, 126, 143, 145, 152, 182, 191, 214, 227; Altamont concert 155–156; *Black and Blue* 222; *Cocksucker Blues* (film) 156; excesses and aftermath 153–157; *Exile on Main Street* 156; "Gimme Shelter" 151–152; good and evil exploration 152–157, 192, 210, 222; "(I Can't Get No) Satisfaction" 9, 52, 102; *Invocation* (film) 151; Jagger, Mick 48–*53*, 79, 88, 123, 150–153, 223–224; Jones, Brian 50–*53*, 154, 157; Key, Bobby 157; knighting of Jagger 157; *Let It Bleed* (album) 151, 158; misogyny, claims against 221–222; musical style and influences 51–52; occult involvement 149–151; Oldham, Andrew Loog 52, 60, 157; Richards, Keith 24, 32, 48–*53*, 116, 150–157, 168, 191–192, Stewart, Ian 51; *Sticky Fingers* 87; "Sympathy for the Devil" 152, 155, 191; Taylor, Mick 154*Their Satanic Majesty's Request* 151; Watts, Charlie 51, 53; Wyman, Bill 51, *53*, 154; yin-yang analysis, as part 8–10
romanticism (the artistic and intellectual movement) 3
Romney, George 108
Ronettes 25, 37
Roth, David Lee 223–224; *see also* Van Halen

Sam & Dave 125, 130
San Francisco 9, 55, 58–61, 65, 68–72, 74–75, 85–86, 91–93, 100–101, 150, 185; *see also* Haight Ashbury; Summer of Love
"San Francisco (Be Sure to Wear Flowers in Your Hair)" 100
Santana, Carlos 143
Sartre, Jean-Paul 61
Satan/the Devil 147, 150, 153, 186, 201; "Sympathy for the Devil," as depicted in 152; "War Pigs" as depicted in 201; "Why Does the Devil Get All of the Good Music?" 185
Saturday Night Fever (film) 228
Saturday Night Fever (soundtrack) 228
Sedgwick, Edie 48, 80, 84
Seeger, Pete 171
Seltzer, Louis B. 15–16
Selvin, Joel 155
Shaft (film) 163
Shangri-Las 25
Shankar, Ravi 139, 143
Shirelles 25, 37
Silicon Valley 158–159; *see also* Jobs, Steve
Sinatra, Frank 20, 24
Skillet Lickers 18
Sleepy Hollow Hog Stompers 66
slave trade (U.K.) 34, 154
slavery (in the U.S.) 1, 3
Slick, Grace 101; *see also* Jefferson Airplane
Sly and the Family Stone 124, 158, 215, 224, 226, 230; *There's a Riot Goin' On* 58
Smith, Mark E. (The Fall) 4
Smokey Robinson 37, 126
Solanas, Valerie 80
Some Like It Hot (film) 27
Soul Train 221
Southern Christian Leadership Conference (SCLC) 30
Spinners 222
Springsteen, Bruce 7, 234
Stanley, Owsley "Bear" 64, 66, 101
Staples Singers 130
Stax Records 102, 120, 127–131, 135, 138, 162, 212; Big Star, distribution 125–127; Booker T & the MGs, house band 102, 128–130; King assassination, impact 135; Lorraine Hotel, hanging out 133; Monterey 102; racial mix 125
Stewart, Jim 127–130
Stewart, Rod 223, 227
Stonewall Uprising 170–171, 225
Summer, Donna **227**, 231
Summer of Love 9, 96, 99–100, 102, 106, 150, 193; *see also* San Francisco

Sun Records 37, 128, 212
Sun Studio 5, 18, 21–23, 119
Super Fly (film) 163
Supremes 127
Swaggart, Jimmy 186
Sweet Sweetback's Baadasssss Song (film) 163

Tallahatchie Correctional Facility **119–120**
T.A.M.I. Show (television show) 123–124
Teenage Fanclub 212, 234
Temptations 127
Tet Offensive 132
Tharpe, Sister Rosetta **19**
13th Floor Elevator 72
Thomas, Carla 128
Thomas, Rufus 128
Thompson, Hunter S. 94
Thornton, Big Mama 22
Tiananmen Square protest 11
Tibetan Book of the Dead (book) 63
Till, Emmett 23
Tocqueville, Alexis de 3, 234
Tolkien, J.R.R. 192–194
Tribes of America (book) 180–181
Truman, Harry 178
Turner, Ike 18, 119
Turtles 100
Tutwiler, MS 113, 118–120, **119**
"Twist and Shout," 42, 97, 220
2001: A Space Odyssey, 137, 161

U 2, 7–8, 186; "I Still Haven't Found What I'm Looking For" 7
USSR 11, 28, 32, 54–55, 140, 174; "Back in the U.S.S.R." 140

Van Halen 198, 223
Velvet Underground 9, 11, 69, **86**, 158; Cale, John 82, 85–89; commercial shortcomings 88; Exploding Plastic Inevitable 69, 76, 85; formation 82–83; "Heroin" 85, 97, 168; hippies, interaction with 86; influences on 59, legacy 76, 212; Morrison, Sterling 82–84, 86–88; musical style and influences 82–83; Tucker, Maureen 82–83, 88; *Velvet Underground & Nico* 84–85; "Waiting for the Man" 168–169; Warhol as manager 87, 89; yin-yang framework, place in 9; *see also* Reed, Lou; Nico
Vietnam War 53–56, 60, 90, 94, 107–108, 127, 151, 173, 177, 179, 213, 226; antiwar movement 90, 107, 133, 136, 138; background 54–55, the draft 55–56,

184, 214; misinformation regarding 108; Pentagon Papers 178; songs protesting 55–56, 74, 172, 214; television and 70
Virginia City, Nevada 65

A Walk on the Wild Side (book) 82
Warhol, Andy 2, 5, 9, 48, 69, 76–81, 83–89, 222, 227; *Campbell's Soup Can* exhibit 77; the Factory 69, 76–80, 83, 85, 89; *Triple Elvis (Ferus Type)* 78
Watergate 104, 179
Waters, Muddy 18, 47, 50–51, 116, 119, 197–198, 205
WDIA 20
Wenner, Jann 48
Who 44, 52–53, 65, 143, 160, 210, 221

Wild One (film) 21
Wilder, Billy 27
Williams, Hank 19, 48
Wilson, Brian 103, 214
Wilson, Dennis 160, 213
"woke"–MAGA divide 1
Woodstock 143–144, 155–157, 172, 185
World War I 32, 34, 49, 96, 116
World War II 29, 31, 39, 48–49, 54, 58, 199, 205

Yippies 109, 136
Young, Neil 101; *see also* Crosby Stills, Nash and Young
Young Rascals 100

www.ingramcontent.com/pod-product-compliance
Ingram Content Group UK Ltd.
Pitfield, Milton Keynes, MK11 3LW, UK
UKHW041927140426
5217IPUK00014B/355